Mormons & Cowboys, Moonshiners & Klansmen

Mormons & Cowboys, Moonshiners & Klansmen

Federal Law Enforcement in the South & West, 1870–1893

STEPHEN CRESSWELL

The University of Alabama Press
Tuscaloosa and London

∞
The paper on which this book is printed meets the minimum requirements of American National Standard for Information Science-Permanence of Paper for Printed Library materials, ANSI Z39.48-1984.

Library of Congress Cataloging-in-Publication Data

Cresswell, Stephen Edward.
Mormons and Cowboys, Moonshiners and Klansmen : federal law enforcement in the South and West, 1870–1893 / Stephen Cresswell.
p. cm.
Includes bibliographical references and index.
ISBN 0-8173-0530-0 (alk. paper)
1. Law enforcement—United States—History—19th century. 2. United States. Dept. of Justice—History—19th century. 3. Law enforcement—Southern States—History—19th century. 4. Law enforcement—West (U.S.)—History—19th century. I. Title.
HV8138.C675 1991 90-49013
363.2′0975′09034—dc20 CIP

British Library Cataloguing-in-Publication Data available.

Contents

Acknowledgments

Undoubtedly, the most enjoyable part of preparing this book has been the opportunity to visit the four chief court towns that I focus on—Oxford, Salt Lake City, Knoxville, and Tucson. I extend my sincere thanks to librarians and archivists in those cities, including the staffs of the University of Mississippi Library, Oxford; the U.S. District Court for Northern Mississippi, Oxford; the archives of the Mormon church at Salt Lake City; the McClung Collection at the Lawson McGhee Public Library in Knoxville; and the Arizona Historical Society at Tucson. Special thanks go to Becky Moreton in Oxford, Mississippi, who in 1982 helped me comb the courthouse attic and basement for records; the search turned up several useful issues of the old *Oxford Falcon*.

In other cities a number of people were very kind and helpful to me, including the staffs of the Federal Records Center at East Point, Georgia; the Arizona State University Library at Tempe; the Department of Archives and History in Jackson, Mississippi; the Hayes Historical Center in Fremont, Ohio; Alderman Library at the University of Virginia; the rare book room of the Brigham Young University Library at Provo; and the rare books, manuscripts, and law collections at the Library of Congress. Above all I thank the archivists of the Judicial, Fiscal, and Social Branch of the National Archives in Washington who helped me use the records of the Department of Justice and the U.S. Supreme Court.

This book grew out of a doctoral dissertation I wrote at the University of Virginia. I am especially grateful to a number of teachers and advisers at that school who were of great help to me—Charles W. McCurdy,

William B. Taylor, David A. Shannon, Daniel Meador, and Michael F. Holt. The library staff at West Virginia Wesleyan College has been very supportive, and I thank the college administration for helping me with the costs of interlibrary loan, photocopying, travel for research, and preparation of the manuscript.

I especially salute Professor Maxwell Bloomfield of Catholic University, who first made legal history come alive for me. Professor Bloomfield's enthusiasm and keen interest in the subject was contagious, and in the years since taking his courses I have continued to enjoy writing about, and teaching, legal history.

My father Ephraim Cresswell, who once served as an assistant attorney general in Mississippi, is responsible for my interest in government, the law, and Mississippi's history. He often served as a first reader and critic of the various chapters. My mother Catherine Cresswell has helped me in more ways than I can name. My wife Teresa Hamm has been the source of happiness that has kept me cheerfully at research and writing.

Stephen Cresswell
Buckhannon, West Virginia

Mormons & Cowboys, Moonshiners & Klansmen

1

The Department of Justice and Federal Law Enforcement

I

The Civil War was the greatest project the U.S. government had yet undertaken. Successful mobilization of great armies, factories, farms, and railroads was a signal achievement. In the years after the war the nation grew quickly and in a number of ways. It does not really matter which economic indicators are examined—the growth was stunning. It took only about twenty years after 1870 for railroad mileage, lumber production, and the value of manufactures to triple. In the same twenty-year period the acreage of corn, wheat, oats, cotton, and tobacco doubled, as did the number of cattle being raised on U.S. farms and ranches. The output of the nation's coal mines doubled in these two decades, and the yield of precious metals more than quadrupled. Population did not quite keep up with the economic growth, but the increase nevertheless was healthy. From less than 40 million people reported in the 1870 census, the population grew to more than 62 million by 1890.[1]

The federal government was also growing rapidly in this period. New congressional committees, cabinet departments, courts of appeals, and independent commissions, such as the Civil Service Commission, abounded. Recent studies portray the president as growing weaker in the last decades of the nineteenth century, while the executive departments grew increasingly independent of the president and developed closer ties with Congress. And as in the antebellum United States, both courts and political parties played a dominant role in the nation's life.[2]

Historians Everette Swinney and Robert J. Kaczorowski have pointed to the changes in the nature of national citizenship.[3] In the early 1870s federal courts across the nation prepared to assume their new role as the final protector of citizens' basic rights, under a number of laws such as the Civil Rights Act of 1866. But along with new rights came new responsibilities. Among the new demands made on the nation's citizens was the necessity of obeying the federal criminal code, which was not only becoming more voluminous but was also moving into completely new areas. In addition, citizens were called on to serve as witnesses and jurors in ever-increasing numbers of criminal cases.

Prior to the Civil War the federal criminal statutes were few in number.[4] Among the federal crimes recognized in the antebellum United States were counterfeiting, mail robbery, smuggling, embezzling federal funds, and resisting or impersonating a federal officer. But during and after the war, with the national government growing in power, the list of federal crimes rapidly grew longer. Federal attorneys in all parts of the nation were soon prosecuting violators of new criminal laws. Federal prosecutors tried members of the Ku Klux Klan for "going in disguise upon the public highway," Appalachian mountaineers for moonshining, Mormon settlers of Utah for their practice of polygamy, and New York machine politicians for fraudulently registering ineligible voters. Residents of Minnesota were tried for illegally trading with Indians, while in Dakota Territory prosecutions were initiated against settlers who fenced public lands.

This book is designed to probe the realities of federal law enforcement in the late nineteenth century. The method used is the case study, so that each of four central chapters looks at a different judicial district: two in the West and two in the South. Examining these four districts will tell us a good deal about the nation's criminal law enforcement, relations between the federal government and states and local communities, and the workings of the national government itself. These four case studies will also inform us about the relation of the South and West to the rest of the country.

For our purposes the United States has been divided into three regions—North, South, and West. The southern region is defined as the sixteen states where slavery existed in 1863 (and therefore includes the border states of Missouri, Kentucky, West Virginia, Maryland, and Delaware). The western region includes Dakota Territory, Nebraska, Kansas, and states and territories to their west. The western region also includes the judicial district of western Arkansas, in which Indian Territory cases were tried—and Indian Territory cases far outnumbered cases for the western counties of Arkansas. The northern region includes Minnesota, Iowa, and all states to the east that are north of the border states named above.

Historians have long recognized that the South and West lagged far behind the North in economic development.[5] The value of northern manufacturing in this period was more than five times that of the South and West combined. More surprisingly, the North also dominated the production of raw materials. As in manufacturing so in the production of nonprecious metals did the North produce five times the output of the two other regions combined, and the North accounted for well over half of the nation's agricultural production. The only major area in which the South or West outproduced the North was the mining of precious metals; the West produced over 99 percent of these important products.[6]

Given the North's overwhelming economic dominance, it is clear that the relationship of the three regions was not a simple reciprocal one: South and West producing raw materials while the North produced finished goods. The North led the field in both raw and finished products. While northern industrialists did need the raw materials produced in the other two regions, they also looked south and west for markets and for potential fields of investment.

The subordinate status of South and West was reinforced by the fact that they had relatively little political power in Washington. Because of their smaller populations, both regions were easily outvoted in the House of Representatives. The North had 185 members in 1880, while the South had 121. The West had only nineteen voting members and a number of voteless territorial delegates. In the Senate the situation was better: The North and South each had thirty-two members, while the West had twelve. In several other measures of power the South and West did not do very well at all. Among the speakers of the House of Representatives and presidents of the Senate during the period 1870–1892, eleven were from the North, two from the South, and none from the West. The Supreme Court justices, who played such an important role in federal law enforcement, included sixteen from the North and three each from the South and West. No chief justice and no president of the United States was from the West or South in this era. And of the members of the president's cabinet, fifty-seven were from the dominant North, while only fifteen were from the South and two from the West.[7]

What all this means, of course, is that throughout the late nineteenth century the government in Washington churned out criminal statutes, Supreme Court opinions, and executive orders and decisions that were inimical to the South and West. Only when leaders of the two regions worked together did their situation improve. In 1890, for example, southern and western senators worked together to support western silver and defeat the "Force Bill" dealing with southern elections. But such conscious collaboration was uncommon. One of the chief unstated goals of many congressmen in this period was to crush unwanted heterogeneity in states and territories. Criminal laws aimed at such "deviants" as Chinese immigrants, Mormon polygamists, Ku Klux Klansmen, and isolated mountaineer distillers were common. To federal law enforcement officers fell the task of working for a uniform, homogenized nation.[8]

An examination of the statistics of federal criminal cases in the late nineteenth century shows that the South and West differed significantly in several respects from the North. When we look at numbers of cases per 10,000 persons over the period 1871–1890, the differences are striking:

- NORTH: Fourteen cases per 10,000 persons
- SOUTH: Fifty-four cases per 10,000 persons
- WEST: Seventy-two cases per 10,000 persons[9]

The higher number of cases per capita in the South and West is in part related to the fact that Congress passed certain laws that were aimed at these regions, while few criminal laws specifically targeted the North. There was little doubt that the Ku Klux Act of 1871 was aimed at the South, or that the antipolygamy laws were aimed at practices in the western territories, especially Utah and Idaho.

What is amazing is that even region-neutral crimes such as postal fraud, embezzlement, and smuggling were at least three times as common in the South and West. Certain elements in southern and western society made the violation of federal laws more common than in the North. Widespread dislike of the federal government flourished in the South in the wake of the Civil War and Reconstruction, along with a belief that criminal law was a state and not a federal matter. Endemic poverty also made remunerative crimes more attractive. In the West crimes were often easier to commit because isolation meant that eyewitnesses could be avoided, and lack of adequate facilities for travel and communication made investigation and apprehension of criminals difficult. The "get rich" mentality of many who went west meant that if one could not find a lode of gold or silver, land fraud or mail robbery could be a viable alternative. In both regions firearms were everywhere, and violence was more acceptable than in the staid North.[10]

But if in one sense the South and West seem to have tenaciously resisted the enforcement of federal laws, in another sense these two regions were just like the North. Conviction rates for federal cases in the three regions are virtually identical—the rates vary by less than a percentage point. In North, South, and West the conviction rate was about 53 percent for the ten years after 1876. Even if most people in a southern or western community were opposed to the enforcement of a federal law, the prosecutor was able to empanel a jury that was willing to convict. Certain congressional enactments helped federal attorneys obtain juries that would vote for conviction, while many southern and western federal judges encouraged reluctant jurors to convict by handing down an abundance of suspended or very lenient sentences.[11]

Federal attorneys across the nation faced a number of serious obstacles in their attempts to enforce the criminal laws. The courts ran out of money with alarming regularity, resulting in cases that were delayed or dismissed altogether. The Justice Department, which theoretically directed federal attorneys and other court officers, was exceedingly loath to instruct its subordinates and left them to guess at national policy matters. In the South and West in particular, other problems arose. In many judicial districts in these two regions, federal officers met the overwhelming resistance of a majority of the population. Attorneys and marshals were snubbed, harassed, refused food and lodging; were arrested, sued, threatened, beaten, shot, even poisoned. In many districts the army was called upon to help enforce the laws. When U.S. attorneys or marshals found they had insufficient weapons to fight resistance to the laws, they prodded the attorney general, lobbied Congress, and visited the president. If public opinion was not with them, they published pamphlets, made speeches, sent letters to newspapers, even wrote books.

I have here portrayed a partnership in enforcing the federal laws; the chief actors are the Justice Department's local field officers such as U.S. attorneys and marshals, and national officials such as the attorney general and solicitor general. Federal judges will occasionally play a role but will not be emphasized because legal historians have long overemphasized the judges' role at the expense of that of prosecutors and marshals. In the remainder of this chapter we will focus on the attorneys general and the functioning of the Washington office of the Justice Department; later our focus will shift from Washington to the federal court towns of the South and West, and the U.S. attorneys and marshals will then receive their due.

II

Members of the First Congress provided for "a meet person learned in the law" to serve as the new nation's lawyer, an officer who would furnish legal advice for the executive branch and protect the interests of the United States before the Supreme Court. The Congress studiously avoided creating a department of law, and for nearly one hundred years this "person learned in the law," the United States' attorney general, paid for his fuel, quarters, and clerk out of his own pocket. The same statute that established the office of attorney general also created the posts of U.S. attorney and marshal. In each federal judicial district, a U.S. attorney would appear on behalf of the United States before the district courts, while a marshal would serve as the courts' executive officer, summoning jurors and witnesses and making arrests. The U.S. attorneys and marshals did not answer to the attorney general, and in fact they had no superior but the president. The various cabinet secretaries would send these field officers advice and requests from time to time but did not have the power to make positive instructions.[12]

The first attorney general, Edmund Randolph, was quick to see the folly of having a chief attorney in the capital city and a lesser attorney in each judicial seat, with no relation between the two. At Randolph's request, President George Washington asked Congress for a law that would give the attorney general power to instruct the U.S. attorneys, but Congress failed to act. Other proposals to strengthen the attorney general's office appeared before Congress in 1819, 1822, 1829, 1845, 1854, 1855, 1866, and 1869. But the attorney general remained a minister without portfolio.[13]

As a lone individual, the attorney general could not provide all the legal services the executive departments required. Although he did provide advice on important legal questions, he could not handle the crush of routine business—drawing up contracts, for instance, or examining land titles. Accordingly, by the time of the Civil War most departments had hired their own attorneys. Congress created "solicitor" positions in the Departments of State, War, Navy, Post Office, Treasury, and in the Bureau of Internal Revenue.[14]

Finally, two statutes of the 1860s gave administrative integrity to the nation's legal officers. An 1861 law placed the U.S. attorneys and marshals under the direction of the attorney general, and in 1869 Congressman Thomas A. Jenckes introduced a bill to create a Department of Justice. Jenckes noted that the hiring of government lawyers in Washington had grown reckless, and that legal expenses were mushrooming. The cost-saving nature of the bill can be seen by the fact that it was referred to the House Committee on Retrenchment, a committee set up to scale back government spending after the Civil War. Jenckes also defended his bill by noting that, since each department was hiring its own lawyers, different cabinet officers were getting different legal advice on similar questions. Furthermore, a lawyer who was hired by a cabinet secretary might well give the legal opinion he thought his superior wanted to receive.[15]

Only about twenty-five congressmen disapproved of Jenckes's plan; they believed that creating a new department was likely to increase, not decrease, government expenses. The bill passed on a voice vote in the House of Representatives in April 1870 and cleared the Senate two months later, also on a voice vote. President Ulysses S. Grant was quick to sign the bill, and the Department of Justice came into being on July 1, 1870.[16]

Nine men occupied the position of attorney general during 1870–1893; the first of these was Amos T. Akerman. Akerman was forty-nine years old when he took office; although born in New Hampshire, he had lived in Georgia for twenty-eight years at the time of his appointment. Akerman had served reluctantly in a Confederate "home guard" unit late in the Civil War; he was a firm Unionist before the war and an undeviating Republican afterward. Georgia had not yet been readmitted to Congress when Akerman's nomination was made public, and wags were fond of saying that they hoped when Akerman got into office "he may have enough influence to get his state into the Union." Akerman had garnered valuable experience as a U.S. attorney in northern Georgia; he was the only individual in the nation's history to be promoted directly from U.S. attorney to attorney general. As the federal prosecutor in north Georgia, Akerman had worked for black political rights; as attorney general, too, much of his energy was directed toward protecting black civil rights in the South under the newly passed Enforcement Acts. Akerman was eased out of office after only eighteen months' service—some felt that he was too much of a crusader for the civil rights of freedmen, while others took offense at his attempts to stymie railroads' hunger for public lands.[17]

Akerman's successor was a former U.S. senator from Oregon, George H. Williams. In contrast to Akerman, Williams was willing to recommend pardons for most violators of the Enforcement Acts and was a firm friend of railroads. He darkened the reputation of the Justice Department by his lavish expenditures from the "contingent fund"; he and his wife were often seen at social occasions in the extraordinarily expensive carriage he had purchased with departmental funds, and he was fond of giving gold pens to departmental employees. Such practices were in poor taste during the panic of 1873, and in fact, it developed that during the panic Williams had borrowed Justice Department funds to meet household expenses. As Williams's reputation sank lower, Grant exercised extremely poor judgment—nominating his attorney general to be chief justice of the United States. While the nomination was pending, Williams obliged one of the senators whose vote he needed for confirmation by agreeing to drop certain Enforcement Act cases in the senator's state. As news of this "deal" became known, even the Republican newspapers begged Grant to reconsider, and the president finally withdrew the nomination. Williams resigned from the attorney generalship in 1875.[18]

Two other attorneys general served very briefly under Grant. Edwards Pierrepont, a prominent New York attorney, served long enough to effect a thorough reorganization of the Department of Justice. Pierrepont set up Bureaus of Legal Investigations, Official Correspondence, Criminal Law, the Supreme Court, the Court of Claims, and Chief Clerk. When Grant appointed Pierrepont minister to England, he named Alphonso Taft (father of the future president) attorney general. Taft was a former Whig, a conservative Republican and an Ohio judge at the time of his appointment. A graduate of Yale Law School, Taft was the first attorney general to hold a law degree. He was head of the Justice Department less than eleven months.[19]

Charles Devens served a full four-year term as attorney general under President Rutherford B. Hayes. Devens was a quiet, studious man, always motivated by his perception of what was "honorable," or what was his "duty." He tried to follow in Akerman's footsteps and enforce the Enforcement Acts, but black voting and Republican participation in the South proved elusive goals. A Democratic Congress provided the Justice Department with limited funds, and, for much of his tenure, Devens was forced to curtail the department's activities and limit the prosecution of all kinds of cases. He seemed relieved when in 1881 he was able to return to his home state of Massachusetts, where he soon received an appointment to the state supreme court.[20]

James A. Garfield's chief legal officer was Isaac Wayne MacVeagh, who earlier had served in a variety of posts including that of minister to Turkey. To MacVeagh fell the task of prosecuting the Star Route cases, cases of gross fraud on the part of many of the nation's contractual mail carriers. MacVeagh sensed that the prosecutions would be difficult and was quick to use the excuse of Garfield's death to tender his resignation. The new president, Chester A. Arthur, wanted to show the country that he was moving to punish the perpetrators of Star Route frauds and begged MacVeagh to stay on, but to no avail.[21]

Arthur's logical second choice was Benjamin Harris Brewster, who was already serving as chief of the department's Star Route prosecutors. Brewster spent three years and a great deal of money overseeing these cases, but the results were disappointing. The defendants had both powerful friends and expensive lawyers, and, by delay and by tampering with jurors and witnesses, most were able to avoid conviction. Brewster was an idealist and used the post of attorney general to lobby Congress for important reforms of the U.S. legal system. He suggested that the old English common law forms for indictments be dropped and that indictments be written in plain English. He suggested dispensing with the reading of bulky indictments at arraignments, instead having the judge or other court officer briefly explain the charges to the defendant. Brewster also suggested that judges allow prosecutors to amend indictments for minor errors rather than throwing them out. But Congress was not ready for Brewster's visionary ideas.[22]

With Grover Cleveland's administration came the only Democratic attorney general in the years 1870 to 1893, Augustus Hill Garland. Garland was ill during much of his tenure and gave uneven attention to the attorney generalship. It is not surprising that Garland—a southern Democrat—did not pursue cases under the Enforcement and Civil Rights acts; in fact he seemed to spend more energy complaining to Congress because black and white prisoners were sometimes held together in federal prisons. Although Cleveland was elected on a platform of a nonpartisan civil service, Garland presided over the gradual replacement of Republican U.S. attorneys and marshals with Democrats. In theory, the removals were "with cause," being made on the basis of complaints that the attorneys or marshals were "obnoxious partisans." By the time Garland left office no Republican attorneys or marshals remained in service. Like Williams, Garland managed to besmirch the reputation of the department. Although the department was handling a case testing the validity of Alexander Graham Bell's telephone patent, Garland held stock in a rival to the Bell Company and stood to gain if Bell lost the suit. When asked about newspaper articles that condemned him, he always replied, "I haven't read them." Finally, he grudgingly admitted that there was "something worthy of thought" in the suggestion that he should have disposed of the stock. But though there is evidence that Cleveland longed for Garland's resignation, Garland served a full four years.[23]

The final attorney general to be considered was William Henry Harrison Miller, who received his curious name because he had been born during the "log cabin and hard cider" campaign, and his father, a farmer, had passionately supported Harrison. By coincidence, Miller met the elder Harrison's grandson in Indianapolis, and they became law partners. President Benjamin Harrison chose as his attorney general his most trusted adviser, his former partner. Like Devens, Miller took his responsibilities very seriously and was preoccupied with ideas of "honor" and "duty." He kept a close watch on his subordinates and expected them not only to achieve victories in the district courts but to show courtesy and compassion for the defendants being prosecuted. Miller was the last of the attorneys general who worked vigorously for black civil rights in the nineteenth century. Like Devens and Garland, he served a full four years in office and retired only when his chief left office. Miller's retirement in 1893 provides a convenient ending point for the chronological period we will study. After 1893 the landscape of federal law enforcement changed markedly. The creation of new tiers of federal courts, new law enforcement bureaucracies, and whole new classes of federal criminal statutes ushered in a new era of national law enforcement. Also by the early 1890s the faces of both the South and the West were changing. The superintendent of the census announced that there was no longer a frontier line in the West; and in the South new state constitutions would soon disfranchise the remaining black voters in that region.[24]

The attorney general in the late nineteenth-century United States had many and diverse duties: He was to supervise the spending of the regular appropriation for the expenses of U.S. courts; to provide opinions on points of law for the president and department heads. He represented the United States before the Supreme Court, either in person or through his assistant, the solicitor general. He examined land titles for the department heads, considered requests for presidential pardons, and advised presidents on the constitutionality of bills sent by Congress for executive approval. But the most important duty of the attorney general, and the one emphasized in this book, was his supervision of the U.S. attorneys and marshals. By this supervision he had a hand in all that was done in the federal courts.[25]

The Washington office of the Justice Department was a kind of command center where a handful of lawyers and clerks attempted to direct the nation's legal business. But "command center" is too modern a term, for, as C. Vann Woodward has written of this period, "Washington was still in the handicraft era of office methods and administrative technique." For Woodward, the perfect symbol of Washington was "the ink-stained government copy clerk scribbling away at his ledgers."[26]

In the Washington office about twenty clerks were responsible for reading the eight thousand letters received each year and routing them to the proper attorney or to the chief clerk. The clerks made two copies of each outgoing letter, the original and a letterbook copy. They also copied tens of thousands of opinions, briefs, contracts, and titles. The office hours nominally were from 9:00 A.M. to 4:00 P.M., but employees did not go home until the work was completed. The doors of the department's offices closed at 2:00 P.M., so that during the last few hours of the day clerks and lawyers were able to work without interruption from office seekers and other visitors. Excepting Sundays, the office was closed only six days per year.[27]

Although it was the clerks and their incessant copying that kept the department running smoothly, the attorneys general did not always give the clerks the respect that was due them. Attorney General Akerman discouraged a young Georgian who sought a clerkship: "If you mean to amount to something in life, a service in a clerkship here is a very poor preparation. In most cases a young man who begins as a clerk never gets very far beyond that place. He becomes timid, dronish, unelastic, and unfit to paddle his own canoe. Study law, . . . mix with the people, read industriously, and in ten years you will rejoice that you never subsided into a clerkship."[28]

That not all the clerks were mindless scribblers can be deduced from the fact that one clerk third-class wrote poetry while he was off duty—the poet Walt Whitman, who had earlier been dismissed as a Navy Department clerk because of his "immoral" writing. Other clerks, such as the chief clerk, the law clerk, and the pardon clerk, wrote letters and legal memoranda on their own. The clerks who went to work for the Justice Department gave up much of the independence enjoyed by the other male members of their families (who were largely self-employed businessmen), but, like other federal employees, they were participating in the building of a new, respectable middle class of federal bureaucrats.[29]

Of course, both the volume of business and the nature of the work force changed over the course of the twenty-four years considered here. The number of criminal cases handled by the department rose from 6,713 cases in 1873 to 21,935 in 1891. The number of civil cases rose in a like manner. Similarly, the number of U.S. attorneys supervised from Washington rose from forty-two in 1871 to seventy-three in 1893, and the number of marshals rose proportionally. To meet this rising flood of business, some additions and improvements were made in the Washington office. The number of Washington employees rose from fifty-two in 1871 to ninety-eight in 1891, but sixteen of the employees in the latter year had been added only because the department now owned its own building: These sixteen included charwomen, firemen, watchmen, and two "conductors of the elevator." Considering the staggering increase in volume of cases, the rise from fifty-two to eighty-two lawyers and clerks was not adequate, and, indeed, throughout the period attorneys general begged Congress for authorization for a larger Washington staff. Such authorization was only rarely and reluctantly given.[30]

Office methods changed somewhat as the years wore on. The first female employees were hired in 1874 when the department hired five women copyists; Justice lagged well behind several other departments in the hiring of women. Typewriters first came into use in the Justice Department about 1880; in 1883 Attorney General Brewster reported to Congress that the department employed nine "operatives upon the type-writer," and he sought authorization for three more. "An expert operative performs more than twice as much work as has been done by the pen," Brewster concluded, "and the work produced by the type-writer is always neat and legible." The department hired its own telegrapher early in the 1880s so that it could communicate with attorneys and marshals with a minimum of delay in important cases.

But the modest increase in the office staff and the addition of a few modern methods proved insufficient for handling the burgeoning work load of the Justice Department.[31] Letter writing was the very heart of Departmental operations, and even in the first year of the department's existence correspondence was overwhelming. Attorney General Akerman wrote to a friend, "I am on the rack from morning till night, and frequently far into the night, and yet, with all that, I can hardly keep down the pile of business."[32]

Akerman was firm about the rules of departmental correspondence. He chastised a U.S. attorney: "Your letter relates to several subjects. For convenience of reference and for other reasons, it is desirable that each official letter should relate only to one." A U.S. attorney in Mississippi understood the conventions: He began his letters with the standard "I have the honor to report," even if it meant saying "I have the honor to report that the 'Ku Klux' have commenced their outrages in my district again."[33]

Particularly difficult were letters from powerful senators and congressmen who sought to influence the department's policy. A letter from Alabama's Senator John Morgan was typical. In 1877 he asked Attorney General Devens to drop all pending Enforcement Act cases in his state. Devens answered that the attorney general was bound to see all the laws faithfully executed; "he cannot exercise the pardoning power." But usually, if a congressman complained of a U.S. attorney's actions, the attorney general ordered an investigation, if only to placate the legislator.[34]

Citizens from all over the country asked for the legal opinion of the nation's highest legal officer; usually, a form letter was sent in reply stating that the laws prohibited the attorney general from giving opinions to anyone save the president or cabinet officers. In other instances, citizens would report a violation of federal law. During the period of Ku Klux Klan operations in the South hundreds of freedmen reported brutal attacks and violations of their civil rights. In such cases the attorney general could only ask the U.S. attorney to investigate and to prosecute if possible. Some of the citizens' letters related to matters that clearly were not in the jurisdiction of the Justice Department. One man sent thirty names and addresses, then stated, "The persons mentioned herein have been engaged in a scheme to murder me, by producing emissions from me, which has prevented me from doing my professional duty. Now the question is, must I slay these persons? Or will the Department do it?"[35]

At times the pressure of correspondence grew so strong that attorneys general made serious oversights. In a routine letter to Akerman, an Arizona U.S. attorney happened to mention that it was difficult to conduct business without a federal marshal. A chagrined attorney general replied, "I am surprised to find that no person is acting as Marshal. I. Q. Dickason was nominated and confirmed by the Senate last April. . . . Will you give me any information in your power as to whether he intends to accept?"[36]

But even when the attorneys general were able to keep up with correspondence, they were hampered in directing vigorous enforcement of the laws by a recurring lack of funds. Congress, and particularly the usually Democratic House of Representatives, was not generous with appropriations for the department or for the federal courts, and the attorney general frequently was forced to ask his subordinates in the field to curtail their activities. Devens in 1877 instructed U.S. attorneys to limit the number of witnesses called and to "urge upon the grand juries short sessions."[37]

When possible, Devens tried to salvage the prosecution of cases by reducing expenses elsewhere. He reported to Congress in 1877 that, whenever a courtroom lease had expired in the states and territories, he had leased smaller courtrooms and smaller offices for judges, attorneys, and marshals. But in that same year he reported that he had been forced to dismiss twenty-nine assistant U.S. attorneys—and these dismissals would result directly in postponements and dismissals of cases. Devens begged Congress for an adequate appropriation, noting that U.S. attorneys and marshals had been serving without pay, and that many of them had "advanced from their own means the expenses which have been necessary to the operation of the courts."[38]

Attorney General Garland was forced to send a circular to all his U.S. marshals in April 1885, announcing euphemistically that the appropriation was "in a reduced condition." The Department of Justice was nearly out of money. Garland asked the marshals to send him suggestions for the reduction of expenses. Also he told the marshals that juries should continue to meet, but "their payment will be delayed until the next Congress meets, and possibly till March or July of the year 1886." Short grand jury sessions, unpaid petit jurors, fewer witnesses, smaller offices, laid-off attorneys—this was not the stuff of a vigorous enforcement program.[39]

Federal prosecutors often responded to this situation with complaints and even resignations. U.S. Attorney Walter Van Dyke's action was not unusual; he sent his resignation to the attorney general, saying, "The office don't pay for the abuse and annoyances." Both attorneys and marshals were paid by fees in the late nineteenth century, and this fact had some unfortunate consequences. U.S. attorneyships in quieter districts paid very poorly, and only young and inexperienced attorneys would accept them. Sometimes an attorney would resort to "drumming up" all sorts of trivial cases merely to increase his fees. And nearly all federal attorneys had a private practice, small or large, on the side. In the western states, attorneys complained that the fee structure did not take into account the West's inflated prices, including the typically high legal fees. From California, U.S. Attorney L. D. Latimer pointed out that in trying an important case he would receive a fee of $10 or $20 in greenbacks (scorned in the mining regions), while the opposing lawyers received $2,000 to $5,000 in gold.[40]

Even had there been sufficient money to pay lawyers, marshals, jurors, and witnesses, efforts to enforce federal laws would have been hampered by the lack of a detective force. Two departments of the government had their own detectives: The Treasury Department had its Secret Service; the Post Office Department, its team of postal inspectors. But the Department of Justice had no "Bureau of Investigation" in this period. As the attorneys general pointed out, violations of federal law were discovered only by citizens' complaint, or perhaps when a marshal read of an apparent violation in the local newspaper. Occasionally, the department would agree to hire a detective in a given district, if the U.S. attorney asked for one and promised that success was likely, but these detectives would work for only a limited time, and on only one case or group of cases. Another method of obtaining information was to offer rewards. Again, it was the U.S. attorney who requested the offer of a reward, and the reward was usually for the arrest of a person, already indicted, who was in hiding.[41]

The greatest impediment to the efforts of attorneys and marshals to enforce the nation's laws was local resistance. In district after district, bands of citizens opposed the enforcement of federal laws. Sometimes the resistance was organized, as in the case of Georgia moonshiners who formed a group called the Distillers' Union to harass federal officers and intimidate witnesses. In other cases in the South and West, rural neighbors informally watched the marshal and his posse and kept lawbreakers informed of their movements. Commonly, federal judges sympathized with their neighbors who had broken the law, and jurors, too, repeatedly sided with the defendant and against the "government lawyer." Nor was resistance to federal officers limited to courtrooms. Defendants and their allies socially ostracized U.S. attorneys and marshals, engaged in threats and character assassination, and in many cases waylaid and physically attacked them.[42]

Not only private citizens, but local and state officers as well, fought the Justice Department. Questions of federalism plagued U.S. attorneys as congressional legislation continued to move into areas traditionally reserved to the states. When federal officers prosecuted Klansmen, local district attorneys complained that the Klansmen's real crime—murder or assault—was a state offense and that the national government had no right to get involved. When marshals shot and killed moonshiners in the southern mountains, local officers initiated murder prosecutions, then grew infuriated as the cases were removed to federal courts. In Utah the Mormon legislature passed laws punishing adultery and cohabitation, then were shocked to see federal officers prosecuting devout Mormons under these very laws, to further the national antipolygamy policy. Over and over, state and local officials retaliated by arresting and jailing federal officers for alleged crimes committed in the line of duty, or by arresting them on frivolous charges for the purpose of harassment and delay. These kinds of state-federal conflicts were often bitter and could severely handicap the work of Justice Department officers.

This study of federal law enforcement in the South and West will bring forward many of the elements consistent across the whole panorama of southern history, and the whole of western history. C. Vann Woodward, in *The Burden of Southern History,* listed a number of threads common to southern history. One was the widespread feeling that the South should be "a white man's country," with blacks playing no leadership roles. Another was southerners' experience as a "People of Poverty" in a nation of plenty. Further, the South, unlike the nation as a whole, experienced defeat: not only military defeat, but "long decades of defeat in the provinces of economic, social, and political life." All of these threads will show up clearly in our studies of southern law enforcement.[43]

For western history, historian Patricia Nelson Limerick consciously emulated the synthesis that Woodward provided for southern history. In *The Legacy of Conquest,* Limerick identified a number of important trends that are evident throughout the story of the West. Like the South, the West has been a region of conflict between groups. But rather than a struggle between two races, western history featured conflicts between Anglos, Hispanos, Chinese, Japanese, Catholics, Protestants, Mormons, European immigrants, and dozens of major Indian groups. Conflict between groups ranged from gunfights to lynchings to riots to lawsuits. Like the South, the West experienced many years of economic deprivation, although the West knew cycles of boom and bust rather than long stagnation. As in the South, a favorite scapegoat for regional problems has been the federal government. If Indians were violent, or if land or timber was unavailable, or if robberies were widespread, Westerners ultimately put the blame squarely on the shoulders of the U.S. government. The trends of western history that Limerick enumerates also played a central role in the history of federal law enforcement in the West.[44]

Our focus is on four particular judicial districts and on how attorneys and marshals, working with the attorney general, attempted to enforce federal criminal laws in each district. Individual case studies will examine in turn criminal cases in the districts of northern Mississippi, Utah, eastern Tennessee, and Arizona. In the first two chapters the focus is narrow: voting rights cases in Mississippi; and polygamy prosecutions in Utah Territory. The third and fourth case studies look at groups of cases. In Tennessee our focus is on crimes against the federal Treasury—counterfeiting, moonshining, and fraudulent pension claims. In the Arizona chapter the emphasis is on federal efforts to prepare a territory that was seen as "lawless" for its eventual admission to the Union as a state.

The stress in each of the case studies is on midlevel federal bureaucrats working in the isolated court towns of the several states and territories. Although they did not enjoy the elevated prestige and high salaries earned by presidents, congressmen, and Supreme Court justices, federal attorneys and marshals decided with great autonomy what kinds of cases would be tried and how vigorously they would be tried. In appeals, they decided what kinds of arguments should be laid before the court; the reported court opinions often contained passages taken almost verbatim from the U.S. attorney's brief. Attorneys and marshals worked for increased support from Congress in the shape of larger appropriations, a restructuring of the judiciary, and more tightly drafted criminal legislation. They even sought to mold national public opinion. Against massive opposition of the local community, they often achieved a remarkably successful enforcement of the federal laws.

Each of the kinds of laws treated in the case studies was certain to incite resistance in the states and territories where it was enforced. Resistance is to be expected when a government adopts powers that it never before has exercised, and in each district the federal government dared to tamper with long-established folkways of a large number of citizens. Dominant whites in Mississippi knew that the state government had always controlled elections, and so they objected to the Enforcement Acts; they also objected to outside interference in the system of race relations that had been developing there for over a century. In the case of Utah, although the practice of "plural marriages" was only a few decades old in 1870, the Mormons' firm and genuine religious beliefs meant that their resistance would be strong and long lasting. To them it was unthinkable that they should disobey God merely to conform to a new law passed by Congress. Congress was wrong, they reasoned, and later and wiser legislators would correct the error.

Impoverished distillers in Tennessee were engaged in a practice dating "back to the time of Noah," and they were not going to change their folkways merely to conform to this novel idea of a permanent federal tax on liquors. The Arizona officers of the Justice Department worked to limit the economic opportunity of go-getter settlers, incurring their enmity along the way by protecting the rights of Indians and by preventing citizens from plundering public lands. In the following chapters, then, we will explore and assess the story of some very difficult chapters in the enforcement of federal authority.

2

Enforcing the Enforcement Acts in Northern Mississippi

I

Ten years after Appomattox the Civil War was still being fought in Mississippi. In public debate, in editorials in the party press, even in violent campaigns, Mississippians dealt with the same divisive issues that had led them to secession and a catastrophic war. The war had disrupted two-party politics in Mississippi, but soon after military rule ended in 1870 the Democratic and Republican parties were active there. The Democrats fought for the legacy of the Confederacy—for states' rights, white supremacy, and home rule. The Republicans, on the other hand, sought a unified nation, a strong central government, and the abolition of blacks' subjugation. About 57 percent of Mississippi's population was black, and, with the support of many former Whigs, the freedmen, and Union soldiers who settled in the state, the Republican party won firm control in the early 1870s.[1]

Democrats found much to loathe in Republican rule. The system of public schools was an expensive novelty, all the more upsetting because it sought to educate black children at public expense. The state's finances went through repeated crises, which the Democrats credited to Republican misrule and extravagance. And Democrats were aghast to see former slaves serving as legislators, sheriffs, even members of Congress. Mississippi had never lost its frontier heritage of violence, and it is not surprising that angry and frustrated Democrats turned to force in an attempt to curb the perceived excesses of Republican rule. Violence against blacks in particular was deeply ingrained in many Mississippians, and by the early 1870s the Ku Klux Klan was riding there, as elsewhere across the South.[2]

The motivations of Republican congressmen in enfranchising blacks and encouraging their political participation clearly were mixed. Certainly, these congressmen expected that blacks would give the Republican party their overwhelming support—and in this they were not disappointed. But also they saw political participation as a tool, or weapon, with which blacks could defend themselves and maintain civil, if not social, equality. The use of the U.S. Army to support and protect freedmen was unpopular in the North, and it was expensive; hence the desire of Republican leaders to encourage blacks to protect their own interests. The more radical of the Republican congressmen saw black civil and political equality as the culmination of the long struggle to end slavery in the United States, and to make a reality the declaration that all men are created equal and endowed with inalienable rights. Finally, two-party politics and the orderly transfer of power were the national norm; regions that did not conform were soon the targets of remedial legislation by Congress.[3]

Faced with violent opposition to the political participation of blacks in the South, Congress passed a number of laws designed to enforce the right to vote and specifically to break up the Ku Klux threat. The first of these Enforcement Acts was enacted on May 31, 1870. It was a long and complex statute, but, most importantly, it defined a number of misdemeanors and felonies and provided punishments for these offenses. Among the newly defined crimes were the failure of any official at any election to do his duty—to register voters, receive lawful votes, and prepare accurate returns. Also penalized were private citizens who "by force, bribery, threats, intimidation, or other unlawful means, shall hinder, delay, prevent, or obstruct" any citizen from voting or registering to vote. These crimes were defined by the First Enforcement Act as misdemeanors, with punishment to consist of a fine of not less than $500, or imprisonment from one to twelve months, or both. The act also made it a felony for persons "to band or conspire together, or go in disguise upon the public highway, or upon the premises of another, with intent to . . . injure, oppress, threaten, or intimidate any citizen" from the enjoyment of any right secured by the Constitution. Penalties for this felony were to be a fine of up to $5,000 and imprisonment not to exceed ten years. A final, important section authorized the president to use the military to enforce the statute.[4]

Congress passed a second Enforcement Act on February 28, 1871. This statute sought to insure free and honest congressional elections in cities, northern and southern, that had a population of at least twenty thousand. The fairness of elections in those cities was to be insured by special deputy marshals and by supervisors of election appointed by federal judges. A later modification of the act stated that federal judges might appoint election supervisors for smaller cities as well, although in smaller cities these officers must serve without pay.[5]

The Ku Klux Act of April 20, 1871, like the earlier Enforcement Act of 1870, defined a series of crimes and provided punishments. Among these crimes were hindering or intimidating federal officials, tampering with witnesses or jurors in U.S. courts, and preventing a qualified citizen from voting. The Ku Klux Act also repeated the language from the First Enforcement Act dealing with going in disguise upon the premises of a citizen with the purpose of depriving him of equal protection of the laws. For these crimes the fines were to be between $500 and $5,000, at the discretion of the court, or imprisonment from six months to six years, or both. The act empowered the president to use the military to enforce the statute, and it also authorized him to suspend the writ of habeas corpus if necessary, although this latter authorization would expire in June 1872. No person was to serve as a grand or petit juror in a U.S. court who, in the opinion of the judge, was in complicity with "a combination or conspiracy" against the laws (for example, the Klan); every prospective juror was required to swear that he had never advised or aided such conspiracies.[6]

These three laws, then, were the laws with which U.S. attorneys throughout the South tried to assure fair, honest, two-party elections. But of course, the meaning of the laws was clarified, if not modified, by decisions of the U.S. Supreme Court. After enthusiastic federal prosecutors had tried over a thousand Enforcement and Ku Klux cases, the Supreme Court impeded the prosecutions by two decisions handed down in 1876. In *United States v. Reese* the Court held that Congress derived the power to regulate voting at state elections only from the Fifteenth Amendment. The Court therefore invalidated two sections of the First Enforcement Act because they defined crimes of hindering voters without stating that such hindering must be based on "race, color, or previous condition of servitude."[7]

In *United States v. Cruikshank* the Court agreed that Congress had the power to protect U.S. citizens in all rights secured to them by the Constitution. On the other hand, noted the Court, the list of rights secured by the Constitution was quite small. For instance, the right to peaceable assembly (often used by federal attorneys in prosecuting Klansmen who broke up Republican meetings), although mentioned in the First Amendment, was not really based on, or secured by, that amendment. "The right of the people peaceably to assemble for lawful purposes existed long before the adoption of the Constitution," read the opinion in *Cruikshank*. This right had always belonged to citizens under any just government and so was not a right granted by the Constitution. Only a few kinds of "peaceable assembly" were guaranteed by the Constitution; among these was the right to assemble to petition Congress. Similarly, the right to bear arms long antedated the Constitution; thus the Second Amendment was included in the Constitution not to grant a right to citizens, but only to prevent Congress from tampering with this traditional right. And finally, as in the *Reese* case, so in *Cruikshank,* the court overturned Enforcement Act convictions because the indictments did not specifically allege that the crimes were perpetrated because of the victims' race.[8]

In light of the Supreme Court's dim view of many kinds of black rights in the late nineteenth century (social rights, for example, and jury rights), it is perhaps surprising that these two decisions are the only major blows to federal enforcement of voting rights. The two sections of the First Enforcement Act nullified by *Reese* were quickly reworded and reenacted by Congress, while federal prosecutors began to take care to allege in indictments that the primary cause of the crime was the victim's race. In one case, handed down in 1884, the Supreme Court approved of federal efforts to enforce voting rights. In this case of *Ex Parte Yarbrough* the defendants argued that, under Article I, Section 4 of the Constitution, state legislatures were responsible for running congressional elections, and therefore the Enforcement Acts were an invasion of the states' reserved powers. The Court admitted that the Constitution allowed state legislatures to make many decisions regarding the holding of congressional elections and the qualifications of voters, but it declared that such elections were nevertheless national, and that Congress had the clear right to regulate national elections. All in all, the U.S. Supreme Court provided no insurmountable obstacles to federal enforcement of the right to vote in the 1870s and 1880s.[9]

Two federal judicial districts saw impressive numbers of federal election cases in the late nineteenth century—South Carolina and northern Mississippi. Together, these two districts accounted for 48 percent of federal election cases tried in the United States between 1871 and 1884. Prosecutors in South Carolina handled 1,504 cases in this period, while the number in northern Mississippi was 1,072. The cases in South Carolina have been rather widely studied; here and only here did the president use his power to suspend the writ of habeas corpus, and here soldiers and marshals made some five hundred arrests within the space of a few weeks. At one point in 1872 more than twelve hundred cases were pending, while nearly a hundred had just been concluded. But there were two serious shortcomings of federal efforts under the Enforcement Acts in South Carolina. One was that the overwhelming majority of cases were handled in the brief period between 1871 and 1874—1,317 of the 1,504 cases were concluded in this period. And second, the conviction rate in South Carolina was abysmal: Only 168 of 1,504 cases resulted in conviction. To be sure, most of South Carolina's cases were not acquittals but were "nolle prossed" (that is, prosecution was dropped), and in this respect South Carolina was not unlike the rest of the United States. Across the country, the Enforcement Acts were among the most nolle prossed laws in the nation's history.[10]

Northern Mississippi offers some interesting contrasts to the record in South Carolina. The writ of habeas corpus was not suspended, nor did the military ever make arrests. And although there was in northern Mississippi a heavy crush of cases in the early 1870s, there was also a significant number of cases in most years thereafter, through 1884. And, most interesting of all, 55 percent of the election cases in northern Mississippi resulted in convictions. The comparable rate in South Carolina was 11 percent, and 28 percent across the United States. A comparison of the disposition of cases in northern Mississippi, South Carolina, and the nation as a whole is shown in Table 2.1.

II

Northern Mississippi was a judicial district comprising somewhat less than half the state's land area, and somewhat more than half its population. The district was not a homogeneous region, of course; it stretched

Table 2.1. Enforcement Act Cases, 1871–1884

	Northern Mississippi	South Carolina	United States
Convictions	585	168	1529
Acquittals	142	61	502
Nolle prosequi	345	1275	3355
Total	1072	1504	5386
		Percentages	
Convictions	55	11	28
Nolle prosequi	32	85	62

Note: Statistics are from Table B for each year of the *Annual Report of the Attorney General* (Washington, 1871–1892).

from the rich delta cotton fields in the west to the dirt farms in the rolling hills of the northeast. Racially, the district ranged from 86 percent black in the delta county of Bolivar, to 87 percent white in the hill county of Tishomingo. Taken as a whole, the district's population was about 56 percent black. All of the state's cities (Natchez, Vicksburg, and Jackson) were in the southern district, while only a few moderate-sized towns, such as Columbus and Corinth, graced northern Mississippi. The court town in the northern district was Oxford, a small university town with some fifteen hundred inhabitants. The judge for northern Mississippi, after 1866, was Robert A. Hill, the moderate appointee of President Andrew Johnson. Hill served as district judge for both the northern and southern districts of the state, so though he made his home at Oxford, he also traveled regularly to Jackson to hold court there. But, as would be expected, each judicial district in Mississippi had its own U.S. attorney and marshal.[11]

In 1871 the newly appointed U.S. attorney for northern Mississippi was G. Wiley Wells, a thirty-one-year-old lawyer who originally hailed from upstate New York. Wells had served in the Union army under General Philip H. Sheridan; he was proud of having fought in thirty-seven battles. After the war, he took a law degree at Columbian College in Washington, D.C., then returned to the South to make his career, settling at Holly Springs in north Mississippi in 1869. It is not clear what political

Judicial District of Northern Mississippi, 1880

connections led to Wells's selection for the post of U.S. attorney for northern Mississippi in July 1870, but he wasted no time in seeking indictments of Klansmen under the newly enacted First Enforcement Act. In June 1871 the eyes of the nation turned to the hot, dusty town of Oxford, where the country's first enforcement case was about to be heard.[12]

Wells had secured the indictment of twenty-eight residents of Monroe County who, in disguise, had visited the home of a freedman named Aleck Page, tied him up, dragged him from the house, hanged him, and buried him. Among those indicted were several blacks whom the defendants had recruited to hold the horses and dig the shallow grave. Although it was generally admitted that Page had been killed because of his role as a political leader of his community, the indictment simply alleged that the defendants had gone in disguise upon the premises of Page, having conspired to deprive him of his constitutional right of life and liberty, and the right to be free from unreasonable search and seizure. The indictment was well drawn, clearly stating that the defendants had conspired against Page because of his race.[13]

The six attorneys who represented the defendants sought to have their clients released on a writ of habeas corpus, arguing that, when all the verbiage was stripped away, the defendants were simply charged with murder, which was a state and not a federal offense. The hearing on the motion for a writ of habeas corpus, held early in July 1871, quickly turned into a rehearsal of the evidence on the merits of the case. Wells and his several assistants proved the facts of Page's murder, while the defendants' attorneys attempted to prove that their clients were free from guilt. The sordid facts of the murder captured national attention, as Page's wife described how the men had taken her husband from her in their small cabin "and led him forth to die." One of Page's friends described finding the body, barely covered with earth and with the noose still around its neck. The defendants did not deny that disguised men had killed Page, but each singly denied being involved. A parade of wives and sisters occupied the witness stand, swearing that each defendant was gravely ill and in bed on the night of Page's murder, or else sitting up with a sick family member.[14]

Belatedly, after almost all the evidence was in, Wells asked the court to strike out the testimony on alibis, as it was not pertinent to the question of the legality of the indictment. Judge Hill refused to admit the validity of Wells's point, but the taking of testimony abruptly ended. Each side then offered its closing arguments. Colonel R. O. Reynolds, speaking for the defendants, argued that a U.S. court could not try a case of murder "committed by one citizen of a state against another"; he also argued that this case could not properly be brought under the Enforcement Act because Page's constitutional rights had not been violated: Protection of life was not guaranteed by the Constitution.[15]

U.S. Attorney Wells gave a brief and simple summation. In the wake of the Civil War, he argued, the powers of the national government had increased. Freedmen were in effect wards of the government, and Congress had the duty to frame legislation that would secure to them the rights of U.S. citizenship. Among these, explicitly stated in the Fifth Amendment, was the right to avoid being deprived of life, liberty, or property without due process of law. Wells did not deny that the twenty-eight defendants had committed the state offense of murder, but he asserted that they had also committed a violation of the Enforcement Act, which was securely based on the Fourteenth and Fifteenth amendments. Judge Hill agreed with Wells, saying that "life and liberty are among the rights and immunities intended to be secured to every citizen of the United States under the Constitution." Like Wells, Hill admitted that prior to the Civil War this would have been a state murder case and could not have been anything else. But the Fourteenth Amendment had been added to the Constitution, and the Enforcement Act was a piece of legislation necessary to enforce the amendment.[16]

Hill required ten defendants to post bail of $5,000, while others were freed on their own recognizance. The actual trial of the twenty-eight defendants in March 1872 was something of an anticlimax. Wells feared that because all but one of the prosecution's witnesses were black, while the defendants' witnesses were "some of the best people in the community," he might not be able to get twelve jurors who would vote to convict. With the attorney general's blessing, therefore, Wells engaged in plea bargaining and dropped all charges except "conspiring to temporarily deprive Aleck Page, Jack Dupree, and Abram Waruble, of their personal liberty." The defendants accordingly pled guilty, and Hill postponed sentencing. He later fined the Klansmen $25 each plus costs and required that each post a $1,000 peace bond, which would be forfeited if during a two-year period the defendant again conspired to deprive a citizen of his rights.[17]

Meanwhile, Wells was working at a furious pace preparing other cases. Late in 1871 he reported to the attorney general that he had pending five hundred indictments under the Enforcement Acts, with a grand jury in session preparing more. "My days are spent in the grand jury room, while my nights are spent drawing indictments," wrote Wells. The situation "gives me little or no time to prepare my cases for trial." But despite the caseload, Wells vowed to persevere because the only alternative was to "turn away men who have appealed to me for protection from outrage & death." Indeed, black Mississippians quickly learned that Wells was a man who could and would help them. Time after time, after a brutal beating at the hands of night-riding Klansmen, grossly injured victims would appear on Wells's doorstep at all hours, seeking aid and the timely arrest of the perpetrators. Wells nourished his image as a swashbuckler and would often mount up with Marshal James H. Pierce and his deputies, and ride off to infested counties to make arrests.[18]

U.S. Attorney Wells was relieved to note that by 1873 the Klan was all but dead, blacks were voting in large numbers, and whites were often willing to testify, if not enthusiastically, in Enforcement Act trials. But this period proved to be the calm before the storm. Until 1873 the Republican tide in Mississippi had been strong. This was not surprising in a state with a black majority, but the number of whites in Mississippi's Republican party was not insignificant either. Among these were former Whigs, as well as former Democrats who favored the national Republican ideology—a high tariff, hard money, and civil service reform. A number of settlers from the North, Wells included, involved themselves in Republican politics. The Democratic party was demoralized, sometimes reaching out for black support, sometimes not; it was a party without a strategy and virtually devoid of zeal.[19]

Then, in the 1873 campaign, Mississippi's two feuding U.S. senators, both Republicans, left Washington and came home to do battle for the governorship. James Lusk Alcorn made a strong bid for mass white support; toward blacks, his attitude was placid and a bit paternalistic. Opposing Alcorn was General Adelbert Ames, a former military governor of Mississippi and son-in-law of the infamous (in white Mississippi) Benjamin Butler of Massachusetts. Ames was a radical Republican and never seemed uncomfortable with the label. His support of blacks was vocal and undeviating. The campaign split the Mississippi Republican party into two wings. Conservatives and moderates, and especially native white southerners, supported Alcorn, while radical Republicans, including most blacks and former Union soliders, supported Ames. Although Ames won a solid victory, many disaffected whites left the Republican party. Gradually, a strategy began to present itself to Democrats. If, by a propaganda campaign, it was made to seem the duty of every white "loyal Mississippian" to vote Democratic, and if 10 or 15 percent of blacks could be prevented from voting, the Democrats would be able to win statewide elections. Thus was unveiled, in the congressional campaign of 1875, "the Mississippi Plan" soon widely copied throughout the South.[20]

Democratic campaign rhetoric denounced the Republican party as a party of greedy northerners and insolent blacks. At Clinton, a small town near the state capital, Democrats disrupted a Republican meeting, and a fierce race riot followed. Similarly, a Republican meeting in Yazoo County was disrupted by Democratic violence; the ensuing fighting lasted several days. Finally, a paramilitary group of whites seized from the Republicans the control of Yazoo County's government. Violence against black Republicans was widespread, and threats of harm were legion. Governor Ames, seeing white Republicans flee the party and black Republicans stay home in fear, appealed to President Grant for military aid to suppress the violence and insure a free election. Ames was careful to use in his telegram the very words prescribed by the Constitution: "Domestic violence prevails in various parts of the state beyond the power of the state authorities to suppress. The legislature cannot be convened in time to meet the emergency." Ames's application for military aid was dated September 9, 1875.[21]

Grant asked his attorney general, Edwards Pierrepont, to monitor the situation and advise him as to whether he should provide troops. Pierrepont alerted the army and prepared a proclamation for Grant to issue, calling upon violent persons to disperse. But Pierrepont grew increasingly dubious about the propriety of using the army in Mississippi. He could not understand why Ames did not raise forces from within the state to quell the disturbances. Writing to Grant, he mused that the Constitution and laws treating federal military intervention in a state were not intended "for a case where the state authorities were supported by a very large majority of the people and where the State Government was not found inadequate to the emergency after some effort." But Ames argued that the state was already on the verge of a race war, and use of a militia made up largely of blacks could only aggravate the situation.[22]

Two other factors troubled Grant and Pierrepont. One had to do with national Republican politics. Many northern voters were not attracted by the image of a party that used the army to support "Negro domination" in the South. A gubernatorial election in Ohio particularly interested Grant, and Republicans there begged him to refrain from further military operations in the South. Writing of the violence in Mississippi, Grant used words that were soon widely quoted by bitter Republicans in the South: "The whole public are tired out with these annual, autumnal outbreaks in the South."[23]

Meanwhile, a number of moderate Republicans of the Alcorn mold were attempting to salvage the white wing of the Republican party by deemphasizing black rights and seeking to avoid a show of force by the national administration. Ironically, one of these men was G. Wiley Wells, the zealous prosecutor of the Ku Klux Klan. Wells bolted from the Republican congressional nominating convention in his district and, in a second "Republican" convention, secured the nomination for himself. Democrats were pleased at the split and chose not to nominate a candidate of their own. Most Democrats supported Wells, hoping to see the regular Republican nominee defeated. Wells and a number of other Alcorn Republicans (including Alcorn himself) journeyed to Washington to urge the administration to refuse the use of troops in the pending canvass. Receiving conflicting reports from Mississippi Republicans, Attorney General Pierrepont took the unusual step of sending an agent to Mississippi to weigh the situation and calm the feuding parties and factions. This agent, George K. Chase of New York City, was specially employed by the Justice Department for this assignment, and he took with him several detectives. Although he made his headquarters at Jackson, Chase planted detectives in the northern district as well, most notably in Bolivar and Lowndes counties.[24]

Chase quickly befriended Governor Ames, then sought a meeting with two leaders of the Democratic party, Ethelbert Barksdale and James Z. George. Chase told the Democrats that he had the power to recommend use of federal troops in Mississippi, but that he would prefer to see a "truce." Ames accordingly agreed to disband the largely black state militia, the Democrats promised to provide a campaign free of violence and intimidation, and Chase promised to advise against the use of troops. Ames and Chase kept their sides of the bargain. The militia was disbanded and Grant decided against the use of troops. But violence against blacks who were involved in politics continued unabated, and in the last days of the campaign Chase informed Pierrepont and the president that the use of troops would be advisable after all. Grant therefore ordered the local commander to "prevent bloodshed in case of disorders," but by then the damage had been done. The Republicans had all but abandoned their campaign.[25]

The use of a confidential Justice Department agent to weigh the situation in a southern state was unparalleled in departmental history; after careful evaluation, the conclusion is inescapable that agent Chase was a dupe. At a congressional hearing on affairs in Mississippi, held in 1876, congressmen questioned Chase and Barksdale closely. Barksdale recalled that at his first meeting with Chase, Chase had spilled the beans. The agent had told Barksdale and George that the country was tired of the use of troops, and that the attorney general did not think they were needed. Later, when outrages against black Republicans resumed, Chase would invariably demand of Barksdale an explanation but, just as invariably, was satisfied with the explanation provided. Chase enjoyed his stay in the Magnolia State, becoming a good friend of Ames and finally moving into the Executive Mansion. Chase and Ames enjoyed a pleasure trip to New Orleans and often played croquet on the mansion's lawn.[26]

Testifying before the congressional committee, Chase repeatedly talked about the "niggers" in Mississippi and reported that the chief goal of Mississippi Democrats was to assure that "the nigger did not rule the Anglo-Saxon." When questioned about his political views, Chase answered, "I never voted but twice in my life, and then I think I voted the Democratic ticket." Incredulous congressmen asked Chase how he had been selected for his delicate mission. He answered that the attorney general "knew that I was a businessman and that I had some capacity for managing men and things."[27]

Republicans were routed in the 1875 Mississippi election. Only one regular Republican was elected to Congress—the incumbent black congressman from the "worm district" of the Mississippi delta, John R. Lynch. Four Democratic congressmen were elected, while the Republican bolter G. Wiley Wells achieved an impressive victory with much Democratic support. Wells resigned his attorneyship several days after the election; he served most of his term as congressman but, despairing of being reelected, accepted President Hayes's offer of a diplomatic post at Shanghai in June 1877. After a brief service there, Wells settled in Los Angeles, building a lucrative corporate practice. He never returned to Mississippi.[28]

After the Chase fiasco, Grant's new attorney general, Alphonso Taft, hoped to rebuild the department's reputation in Mississippi. To replace Wells, Taft selected a state prosecuting attorney named Henry B. Whitfield. Whitfield had made some heroic efforts to prosecute Klansmen under state law, and he had been a regular correspondent of Wells and of the various attorneys general, giving advice and urging greater support for Republican voters. Unfortunately, Whitfield's nomination gave the department a second black eye.[29]

Whitfield was an adherent of the Wells-Alcorn wing of the party, and he had incurred the undying wrath of Ames Republicans. His enemies concocted a plan to achieve his ouster from office: They accused him of forgery and of taking advantage of gullible blacks in cashing drafts for them. The charges were never proved, but as the investigations dragged on it became apparent to the attorney general that Whitfield's reputation had been destroyed. And, as is often the case with accusations made against public officials, the deep and searching investigations showed that Whitfield was probably guilty of "questionable," although not illegal, financial dealings. Finally, after three months in office Whitfield was removed "for the good of the Department." The search for a U.S. attorney for northern Mississippi was reopened.[30]

The man finally selected was Thomas Walton, a native of Georgia but a longtime resident of Mississippi. Walton, forty years of age, had earned both a liberal arts and a law degree from the University of Mississippi. He had served as a state prosecuting attorney, a chancery judge, and a professor of law at Ole Miss. In July 1876 a grand jury assembled at Oxford, and Walton had no shortage of potential Enforcement Act cases for offenses committed during the 1875 campaign to bring to the panel's attention.[31]

Some of the witnesses whom Walton summoned before the grand jury testified that at a polling place at McLeod's Store the managers never even opened the polls—and 640 voters, nearly all of them black, were registered to vote there. Others testified that Democrats in Noxubee County grabbed black voters' ballots and altered them or replaced them with Democratic ballots. Typical was the case of a freedman named J. Monroe Edwards, a Republican leader who received a note from a Mr. John Harlan stating that if Edwards were seen in the county after January 1, 1876, Harlan "would get Joe Jack Hunter down on him." Edwards's offense was that he "would not consent to vote with the whites"; he fled his home for several weeks but finally returned and was living in fear. At Shuqualak in Noxubee County young white men armed with pistols and sticks crowded the polling place, demanding that black voters show their ballots. Democratic "spotters" took down the names of freedmen who voted Republican; these would then be denied employment or otherwise harassed. Many blacks did some spotting of their own; one such spotter, named Elisha Bryson, supplied the grand jury with a list of thirty-two whites who had intimidated voters at the polling place.[32]

Walton and most other Mississippi Republicans were deeply disappointed at the grand jury's actions in the face of this kind of testimony. The jury refused to find any indictments in these election cases but instead wrote a report, which was made public. "The fraud, intimidation, and violence perpetrated at the late election is without a parallel in the annals of history," the report began. Although the evidence heard was sufficient to frame thousands of indictments, the grand jurors' report ended by simply recommending to the people of Mississippi "that they make an earnest appeal to the strong arm of the U.S. government to give them the protection that is guaranteed to every American citizen" or else "exclaim farewell to liberty, farewell to the freedom of the ballot box."[33]

The grand jurors evidently hoped for protection by the military "strong arm" of the government; Walton was disappointed that they refused to try to use the judicial "strong arm." He had a half-dozen possible explanations for the jurors' recalcitrance, but the most convincing explanation is that they were afraid, and also that they knew the witnesses would be afraid to testify or would be killed before they could do so. Walton was deeply disturbed by his first brush with Enforcement Act cases and was never again eager to tackle them. He became instead a great prosecutor of moonshiners and achieved hundreds of convictions. He also became a candidate for Congress. Like Wells, he sought white support, but many Republicans felt that he was no better than a Democrat. He answered such accusations in a testy letter to the attorney general, stating that he was campaigning not only for himself, but also for Hayes, and that he was one of the few Republican officeholders in the state who was working earnestly to secure another Republican presidential administration.[34]

One other such officeholder was James H. Pierce, who had been serving as northern Mississippi's federal marshal for six years. Pierce issued a call for one hundred "reliable men" to serve as deputy marshals to observe voter registration in counties where registrars were not likely to agree to enrol blacks. Writing to the attorney general, Pierce reported that in Monroe, Lowndes, and Noxubee "there seems to be a perfect reign of terror, and unless quick and positive action is taken to suppress it, there will be no election held" in those counties. Pierce did not grasp the realities of the situation, for he asked Attorney General Taft to furnish one company of troops for each county, or at the very least ten companies for the whole of the northern district. With these troops and his one hundred deputies, Pierce wrote, "I can assure a quiet and fair election," but otherwise Republicans would continue to fear for their lives and would refuse to go to the polls.[35]

But of course, the troops were not sent, the campaign was violent, and a large mass of Republican voters stayed away from the polls. Testifying before yet another congressional investigation of Mississippi elections, Assistant U.S. Attorney Harvey R. Ware reported that intimidation of black voters in 1876 was so severe that hundreds of blacks "were afraid to, and did not, sleep in their cabins, but in the woods." A new voter registration law, passed by the Democratic legislature, had provided a new tool for black disfranchisement. This law required each voter to state, "under oath, in what election district of the county he resides . . . and in what portion of said district." Under this statute the registrars required black voters to identify not only their election district, but also the township, range, and section in which they lived. The number of Republican votes cast in north Mississippi in 1876 was ludicrous. In Lowndes County, for example, the party had polled 2,785 votes in 1873; in 1876 only two hardy Republican voters made the trip to the polls.[36]

In a formerly Republican congressional district U.S. Attorney Walton counted himself fortunate to receive 37 percent of the vote. Although several of Walton's campaign appearances had been broken up by violence, and a number of his supporters had been shot, he continued to show reluctance to initiate Enforcement Act cases. Writing to Attorney General Charles Devens, Walton asked permission to drop most of the pending election cases. In the wake of the recently announced *Reese* and *Cruikshank* decisions, he argued, "bringing the facts within the letter of the statute" would be difficult or impossible. Devens, on the other hand, saw that the recent Supreme Court decisions did not block all Enforcement Act cases, and he urged perseverance. Walton's tenure in office came to an abrupt close, however, when he died in the catastrophic yellow fever epidemic of 1878. Walton died a hero's death; as the newspapers pointed out, he refused to leave the pestilent area but stayed behind "doing all in his power to relieve those stricken with the scourge." Attorney General Devens, firmly committed to free and fair political participation in the South, realized that under Whitfield and Walton the Enforcement Act program had faltered. He looked for a man of vision and energy to resume vigorous prosecutions. He found his man in Greene C. Chandler, a former state judge from the Gulf Coast.[37]

Chandler was a native of Alabama but had moved to Mississippi at an early age. As a young man, he had taught school, read and practiced law, served in the legislature, and edited a newspaper. He had served as a colonel in the Confederate army and was an early convert to Mississippi's Republican party. In 1870 he had been appointed a state judge and had served a full six-year term. At the time of his appointment as northern Mississippi's federal attorney in December 1878, Chandler was forty-nine years old. In his first report to Attorney General Devens, Chandler stated that his investigation of the recent congressional election "shows a more shameless corrupting of the ballot box than was ever witnessed in this country." Typical of the many cases of election fraud was an incident at a preponderantly black precinct where white men "pretending to be drunk created a disorder at the polls; the inspectors took the box away from the disturbance and secretly stuffed it with Democratic ballots."[38]

Chandler was confident he would be able to achieve a large number of indictments and convictions. One reason for his confidence was a new political party opposing the Democrats in north Mississippi, as elsewhere: the Greenback party, which hoped to solve the problem of a depressed economy by increasing the supply of money. Unlike the Republican party, which was able to win few new recruits among the dominant white element of Mississippi society, the Greenback party grew quickly and could claim to be a second "white man's party." The Greenback party, the new U.S. attorney informed Devens, "is strong, and has many desperate men in it," men who demanded a free ballot and a fair count. In the pending Enforcement Act cases, Chandler reported, the prosecution witnesses would be white men who had voted Democratic most of their lives, and this fact should help insure convictions. Although he was able to bring to trial only nine cases arising from the 1878 election, Chandler did much better with 1880 election cases. In these cases he secured seventy-two indictments, which resulted in forty-five convictions and only seven acquittals (with twenty cases dismissed). For fiscal year 1881, in fact, Chandler's record for achieving both indictments and convictions in Enforcement Act cases was unsurpassed in the United States.[39]

United States v. George Askew et al. was typical. Five men who had served as election clerks or supervisors in Oktibbeha County in the 1880 election were indicted for neglect of duty, specifically for refusing to receive all lawful votes offered. A second count charged that the men "wilfully, fraudulently, and improperly [did] destroy the ballots given at said election by David Tobb, Grant Hamilton, and a large number of other" qualified voters. The five men pled guilty, and Judge Hill levied a fine of $50 on each, plus costs. Chandler also tried cases of intimidating voters, failing to hold an election, making a false poll book, stuffing ballot boxes, refusing to register eligible voters, obstructing a federal election supervisor, and erasing names improperly from a poll book.[40]

Greene C. Chandler exuded confidence in 1881, reporting to outgoing Attorney General Devens that neither grand nor petit juries had shown any disposition "to screen any guilty person, and I accept this fact as a good omen for the future." Although a petit jury would occasionally refuse to convict, even on solid evidence, Chandler was generally pleased that the grand and petit jurors "showed a laudable disposition to indict and bring to punishment all violators of the [election] laws." This "laudable disposition" to indict and convict was especially gratifying to Chandler because the juries were a motley aggregation of men "of all colors, and all shades of political opinion."[41]

The incoming Arthur administration was quick to develop a distinctive southern policy. Showing less and less confidence in the moribund southern Republican party, President Arthur began to display an interest in non-Republicans who were willing to battle the Democrats and thus breathe new life into two-party politics in the southern states. The first group to capture Arthur's imagination was the "Readjuster" party in Virginia, which hoped to "readjust" the debt of the Old Dominion so as to ease the taxpayers' burden. The Readjusters had won impressive electoral victories, and they seemed to be interested in cooperating with the Republicans on the national level.[42]

Arthur next turned his gaze to north Mississippi, where a popular Democratic politician named James R. Chalmers had broken relations with his fellow partisans and announced his candidacy for Congress on the "Independent" ticket, with Greenback party support. Arthur regarded Chalmers's candidacy as an important experiment and urged Republicans in Chalmers's district to offer their encouragement. The national Republican party provided monetary contributions, and Arthur's attorney general, Benjamin Harris Brewster, urged Justice Department officials in northern Mississippi to make it clear that any unfair election practices would be severely punished. The attorney general wrote to Marshal Joseph L. Morphis, noting that, although Morphis could not appoint the "special election deputies" mentioned in the Second Enforcement Act (because these deputies could be used only in cities of more than twenty thousand inhabitants), he should appoint as many regular deputies as were necessary to keep "the peace of the United States."[43]

Chalmers won a substantial victory at the polls but was fraudulently counted out by Democratic election officers. In Tate County, a Greenback party stronghold where Chalmers had won by a large margin, a clerical error attributed 1,472 votes to "J. R. Chambless" instead of J. R. Chalmers. The Democratic candidate was thus declared elected and given the certificate of election. After a long credentials fight in the House of Representatives, Chalmers was seated, but with only a few months remaining in his term. President Arthur's experiment in fostering non-Republican opposition to Democratic rule in Mississippi was far from being an unqualified success.[44]

Meanwhile, Greene C. Chandler's four-year term as U.S. attorney had expired, and Arthur sent his renomination to the Senate. Writing to Judiciary Committee Chairman George F. Edmunds, Attorney General Brewster noted that Chandler was an officer "of more than average ability. . . . The records show that Mr. Chandler has prosecuted more violators of election laws (successfully) than any U.S. Attorney now in service; and from this I have assumed that he is a competent officer, unbiased in any manner, even in cases of this character, for convictions are not usually secured in political cases by attorneys who excite the antagonism of their opponents."[45] Chandler's reappointment was approved by the Senate, but he was not able to maintain his successful program of convictions under the Enforcement Acts. The Democratic party, concerned by the threat of Greenbackers and Independents, was again billing itself as the only protector of white men's rights, and white jurors accordingly grew unwilling to punish Democrats who practiced election fraud or intimidation.

Although in fiscal year 1882 Chandler secured eleven Enforcement Act convictions, more than in any other district in the nation, he also saw eleven of his cases result in acquittals, and five more were dismissed. In 1883 he was able to achieve seven convictions, but four cases resulted in acquittals and twenty-seven were dismissed. In 1884 Chandler did a little better, again convicting more Enforcement Act violators (eleven) than any other federal attorney in the United States. This time there were seven acquittals and six dismissals.[46]

Because grand juries often refused to find indictments, Chandler turned to the device of "informations." An information is equivalent to an indictment but is drawn up by a public official instead of a grand jury. For many years U.S. attorneys in northern Mississippi had been prosecuting cases of illegal distilling by information; now Chandler began framing informations for violations of the Enforcement Acts. But Judge Hill was not pleased with the prosecutor's actions. In the first trial to arise under an information, the judge quashed the information on a technicality. This was the case of *United States v. E. M. Watson et al.*, which involved election officials issuing false returns. Chandler asked permission to amend the information "so as to conform to the views of the court." But Hill noted that a grand jury was then in session and told Chandler that he must take the case before the grand jury.[47] Chandler "rose in apparently some excitement, and declared that he could not be dictated to by the Court as to the course he would pursue in these election cases." Hill responded blandly that it was unjust to proceed in important criminal cases without action by the grand jury. Chandler, really angry now, remarked that if the perpetrators of these gross violations of the purity of elections, these crimes that "shocked every civilized man on the continent," were to be saved even from a trial, then he would continue all cases and seek instructions from the attorney general. But Attorney General Brewster had no solutions. He was sympathetic but could only urge Chandler to try to obtain a grand jury that would indict.[48]

Meanwhile, Chandler followed in the footsteps of Wells and Walton and announced his candidacy for Congress. Like his predecessors, he sought black votes but avoided speaking out on racial issues. Chandler campaigned on a platform of protectionism, education of the masses, civil service reform, and the supervision of corporations "so as to restrain the greed of monopolists." He conducted a vigorous campaign at first, and the Democrats saw that he was no figurehead candidate but actually intended to be elected. In a number of joint appearances with his Democratic opponent, the crowds seemed to appreciate Chandler's economic ideas. But Democratic roughnecks were soon breaking up every joint appearance, and Chandler was forced to cancel all further joint meetings in order to protect his supporters from violence. Although he continued to speak at Republican rallies, attendance was sparse, and in the general election the U.S. attorney received only 18 percent of the vote.[49]

In this same 1884 election the Democratic administration of Grover Cleveland came to power. Cleveland had been elected on a platform of civil service reform and an end to the spoils system, and he initially retained in office both U.S. Attorney Chandler and Marshal Morphis. Soon, however, letters were flooding into the Justice Department, complaining of the partisan zeal of both men. The editor of the weekly *Oxford Falcon* wrote to the new attorney general, Augustus Hill Garland of Arkansas, complaining that Marshal Morphis was "universally regarded as the head and front of opposition to the Democratic party." Morphis called meetings of Republicans and Independents, the editor reported, but because the meetings were secret it was not known what went on there. The Democrat who defeated Chandler for Congress complained of "bitter speeches" that his opponent had made in the campaign and quoted Chandler as saying, "We Republicans know our strength in this district—we know how many votes we ought to have and if they are suppressed. . . . I expect to see that the guilty parties are indicted and convicted."[50] The complaining congressman also claimed that Chandler had abused candidate Cleveland "in language that I would not like to repeat in this letter (I will give it if desired)." In the wake of complaints such as these, both Chandler and Morphis were removed.[51]

During the four years of the national Democratic administration, the Republican party in Mississippi lost strength even more rapidly than before. In September 1885 the Republican Executive Committee declined to run a slate of candidates for state office. Speaking for the committee, John R. Lynch noted, "It is a fact well known to all that we no longer enjoy the privilege of having popular elections in this state. Officers are appointed by Democratic Committees and Conventions, and their election, so called, is nothing more than a matter of form. So far as this state is concerned, we do not live under a republican form of government." With a Democratic administration and a southern Democrat as attorney general, it is perhaps not surprising that the Enforcement Acts were not enforced during the four years after 1884.[52]

The new U.S. attorney for northern Mississippi was Charles B. Howry, forty years old and a native of Oxford. Howry had been a captain in the Confederate service, then had earned his law degree at Ole Miss, studying under Professor L.Q.C. Lamar. In 1871 G. Wiley Wells had approached Howry and asked him to serve as assistant prosecutor in the Ku Klux cases of that year. As Howry's son later recalled, however, Howry realized that the Klan "in the main served a great and useful purpose in protecting the native white population from intolerable oppression and degradation. . . . My father realizing this promptly declined [the] offer."[53]

Howry served as U.S. attorney until the end of the Cleveland administration. When he left office a routine examination was made by a roving auditor of the Justice Department; this agent reported that Howry seemed to be guilty of "working the office for all it was worth," bringing a large number of cases and enriching himself by the fees. By refusing to consolidate related cases, and by convincing defendants to ask for a jury trial instead of pleading guilty, Howry was able to maximize his fees. But if Howry was really guilty of "working the office for all it was worth," there is one unusual aspect of his record. In his four years in office Howry received no fees for Enforcement Act cases, for no such cases were brought during his tenure.[54]

By the time the Republicans regained control of the White House in 1889, Mississippi's Republican party was all but dead. The Harrison administration promised support for southern Republicans, and in August 1889 Mississippi Republicans met at Jackson and optimistically decided to field a slate of candidates for state offices. J. R. Chalmers, now a loyal Republican, was nominated for governor. *The New York Times* called the nominating convention a "windy" affair: "The delegates were doing all the speaking of the campaign in the convention, as they realized it was about the only opportunity they would have." Chalmers told blacks attending the convention "to go quietly to their work, but to keep the Republican prayer book in their pocket and stand by the faith." Before ten days had passed Chalmers and the other Republicans had all withdrawn their candidacies—moderate Democrats had begged them not to have public meetings "or the killing of Negroes would commence again." With the Republican party so incredibly weak in the state, it was useless to hope for vigorous action by grand juries, and the new U.S. attorney, Henry Clay Niles, was able to achieve no indictments under the Enforcement Acts.[55]

Niles was a forty-year-old native of Mississippi who had served as a special assistant U.S. attorney in election cases in 1880 and 1881. Niles had also done incredibly well in running for the state legislature in 1877 and again in 1886. In Attala County, which had forty-eight hundred voters with a white majority of a thousand, Niles had won election (as a Republican) both times. In his letter of application for the U.S. attorneyship, Niles noted that he could provide letters of recommendation from Mississippi's congressmen but would prefer not being selected "to asking such men to endorse me—men who hold their present position by reason of fraud and all manner of violence. . . . Mississippi is as much a Republican state as Massachusetts."[56]

Although he brought no new election cases into court, Niles did display a concern for blacks in Mississippi. In one strange incident at Aberdeen, whites—angry at the decision of the secretary of war and other officers of the Harrison administration not to call for the half-masting of the U.S. flag on the death of Jefferson Davis—had hanged the secretary of war in effigy from the corner of a building that was under construction. A hapless black construction worker attempted to move the effigy, which was in the way of his work, and the effigy fell to the street. In the presence of an angry crowd of three to five hundred of Aberdeen's "best citizens," the worker, Henry Fans, was driven up and down the streets by a bricklayer wielding a whalebone whip and was given about two hundred lashes. He was then taken to the railroad station and put on a northbound train.[57] Niles made diligent efforts to investigate the case, but few citizens of Aberdeen would discuss the matter. Meanwhile, Marshal John S. Burton conducted a laborious search for Fans but was unable to find him. A number of Aberdeen residents were also looking for Fans, Burton reported, "to kill him or bribe him into silence or cooperation." But Fans could not be located.[58]

Niles was more successful in investigating the case of F. G. Blevins, a black clerk in a railway post office. President Harrison had infuriated whites all over the South by appointing a large number of blacks to well-paid positions as mail clerks. Blevins was fired upon by angry whites as his train passed near McCool, Mississippi. Niles immediately proceeded to McCool, where he found whites muttering that "the d--n nigger must go"; nearly all whites seemed to approve of the shooting, and no whites would talk to the attorney. With only a few, reluctant, black witnesses, Niles, "finally succeeded" in getting the grand jury to return a bill of indictment against four young men for assaulting a federal officer. By the time the case came to trial Niles had only two witnesses; a black woman who had seen the shooting had been either "bribed or terrorized" into silence. Fortunately, one of the defendants confessed, and then two others were convicted. Two defendants were sentenced to three years in a federal penitentiary, while a "young and sickly" accomplice was sentenced to six months' imprisonment and a $500 fine.[59]

But Niles was discouraged to see a curtain of intractable racism fall across north Mississippi. Writing to Attorney General William H. H. Miller, he reported, "The truth cannot be concealed—this section is growing more lawless each year—and the fruitful cause of most of it, proceeds from a corrupt ballot." Oaths were disregarded, Niles continued, while "our best citizens" would not censure a ballot thief but "boldly teach the doctrine that the end justifies the means." A man named F.M.B. Cook had recently been killed for daring to oppose the Democrats, but Niles had heard only one white man condemn the murder. "The same spirit that produced the Civil War is still rampant," reported Niles, in spite of all the talk of the "New South." The federal government, he concluded, "has few friends in court, in this section."[60]

Attorney General Miller responded that it was "deplorable that such a state of things exists, and that there seems to be no complete remedy therefor." Miller encouraged Niles to persevere in his efforts to enforce federal criminal law in the district. Miller added that the indictment and conviction "of the young men who fired into the train is a bright spot, and is very creditable to your administration of your office." But the fact remains that Niles's administration of his office resulted in no Enforcement Act indictments or convictions (see Table 2.2). Certain events in the early 1890s, which will be considered later, made it a certainty that the enforcement program begun under the Grant administration would remain dormant for many decades to come.[61]

No one knew, when Greene C. Chandler left office in 1885, that northern Mississippi's last Enforcement Act cases of the nineteenth century had been tried. Changes came to the northern district—a new courthouse at Oxford, dedicated in 1885, a second meeting place for the

Table 2.2. Election Cases Disposed of in Northern Mississippi

Fiscal Year	Cases	Prosecutor(s)
1871	0	Wells
1872	325	Wells
1873	268	Wells
1874	120	Wells
1875	187	Wells
1876	152	Wells, Whitfield, Walton
1877	2	Walton
1878	0	Walton
1879	9	Walton, Chandler
1880	0	Chandler
1881	72	Chandler
1882	27	Chandler
1883	38	Chandler
1884	24	Chandler
1885	0	Chandler
1886	0	Chandler, Howry
1887	0	Howry
1888	0	Howry
1889	0	Howry
1890	0	Howry, Niles
1891	0	Niles

Note: Statistics are from Table B for each year of the *Annual Report of the Attorney General* (Washington, 1871–1891). For information on the service dates of Justice Department employees, see *Register of the Department of Justice* (Washington, 1871–1891; issued irregularly).

federal court provided (at Aberdeen) about the same time, and the promotion of the Republican Henry C. Niles to the position of district judge in 1891. But the Republican party was virtually lifeless, and white public opinion forbad the punishment of the "loyal election workers" of the Democratic party. Along with South Carolina, Mississippi was left with the weakest two-party system in the nation, and the lowest rate of voter participation. The Justice Department's efforts to bring Mississippi into the mainstream of the nation's political life had failed.

III

The history of Enforcement Act prosecutions in northern Mississippi suggests several important questions. First, why were so many cases tried there, and why was the conviction rate higher by far than in any other judicial district in the nation? And why, in the long run, was the enforcement program there a failure? Why did north Mississippi fail to develop a free, two-party electoral system? Why did the Fifteenth Amendment promise of black enfranchisement come to naught? Answers to these questions will be suggested in the asking of several others. What aid did the U.S. attorneys and marshals receive in the performance of their duties, and what obstacles hindered them? What motivated these officials, and how did they view their role as federal officers in northern Mississippi?

The U.S. Army gave its aid to Justice Department officials in northern Mississippi, but the aid was uneven over time, and the removal of troops from Mississippi and the rapid decline in numbers of Enforcement Act cases there occurred simultaneously. One hundred ninety-eight soldiers were stationed in Mississippi in 1870; the number reached 559 by 1872, then declined to forty-six by 1874. Although 529 soldiers were in the state in 1875, most of these had fled the yellow fever epidemic in New Orleans and were sojourning in north Mississippi's health resort, Holly Springs. In 1877 and the years thereafter, there were no soldiers stationed in Mississippi.[62]

Whereas in South Carolina the U.S. Army had been employed in making arrests in the anti-Klan crusade and had thus supplemented the efforts of the marshal and his deputies, in north Mississippi all arrests were made by Justice Department officers. Nevertheless, these officers often requested an army escort, and the secretary of war usually granted their request. Some career army officers were uncomfortable with the employment of federal troops as a posse, as can be seen by the annual report for 1870 of General Henry W. Halleck, commander of the Division of the South. Halleck recommended that marshals be required to secure, before troops could be used, a court order stating that a civilian posse could not be obtained. This would save the army money "and would relieve army officers from much of the responsibility they are now obliged to incur in the performance of disagreeable duties, which can hardly be said to legitimately belong to the military service." But the next year General Alfred H. Terry, in his annual report as commander of the Department of the South, simply noted that in no instance had soldiers aiding U.S. marshals failed to perform "this difficult and delicate service in a perfectly satisfactory manner." By 1872 Mississippi had been placed in the Department of the Gulf, and in that year its commander reported that there was no doubt but that the use of troops had allowed marshals to serve process in many instances where they could not otherwise have succeeded. This commander, Colonel William H. Emory, hastened to add that the troops had not been used "for the attainment of any partisan object whatever."[63]

In their correspondence with the attorney general in the early 1870s, the federal attorneys and marshals constantly pushed for continued military support. In an early Ku Klux case in May 1871, Marshal James H. Pierce wrote to the attorney general that he had warrants for twenty Klansmen who lived in an isolated town "thirty-five miles from any railroad." Pierce worried that he would not be able to effect the arrests since the suspects "live in a community of Ku Klux," and he requested a military escort. Attorney General Akerman passed Pierce's request on to the secretary of war, who granted it. Akerman assured Pierce that troops would always be supplied in sufficient force "to aid and protect you in the execution of your duty." And indeed, troops were regularly supplied to the marshal throughout the early 1870s.[64]

Although Marshal Pierce and his deputies were grateful for the army's help, they had one common complaint: The army almost invariably supplied escorts of infantry, while cavalry was so much more useful. As early as June 1871, a deputy involved in arresting members of the Ku Klux Klan wrote bluntly to Akerman, "We wish to crush this thing right here and we need cavalry to accomplish it." The infantry, reported the deputy, was willing but not fast enough. The inadequacy of infantry was explained by a young lieutenant stationed in Mississippi: "Infantry could not move two miles before the cry of 'Yankees are coming' would be spread over a circuit of six miles, giving, of course, ample time for the wicked to flee." Sometimes cavalry was available for use in north

Mississippi, but intensifying conflicts with western Indians drained mounted soldiers away from the state. Several Justice Department officials suggested renting horses for the infantry, but the army did not like this plan—cavalry was meant to be mounted, and infantry was not.[65]

Like the local Justice Department officials, army field officers sometimes found it difficult to get explicit instructions from Washington. Army officers in Mississippi were especially nervous during political campaigns, not knowing whether to exert a tremendous effort to insure fair elections or to sacrifice all in order to preserve the honor of the army as a nonpartisan service. Official army correspondence often sounded a lot like official Justice Department correspondence. "What shall I do?" asked the field officer. "Use your own judgment," came the reply from Washington. In the 1875 Mississippi election, when the Grant administration wavered between protecting Republican voters and avoiding a show of force, Secretary of War William Worth Belknap ordered General Christopher C. Augur to have troops ready to suppress disorder in the upcoming election, "on receiving a proper call for such assistance." Augur knew that Governor Ames and officials of the Grant administration did not see eye to eye on the need for troops, and he asked Belknap by telegraph whose call for aid was to be deemed "proper." Belknap conferred with the attorney general and with the president, then told Augur, "I am directed to say that further instructions are not deemed necessary. You are expected to be vigilant and to do your duty discreetly."[66]

The pressure to reduce expenses was always strong upon the secretary of war, and Marshal Pierce and U.S. Attorney Wells received at least a dozen letters in 1872 and 1873 asking them for their opinion of the advisability of removing troops from north Mississippi. To one such letter from Attorney General George H. Williams, written in April 1872, Wells replied that Klan violence was ubiquitous in his district and that only the presence of the army kept the Klan from overrunning north Mississippi completely. The government should do whatever was necessary, Wells lectured sternly, to protect "parties whose only crime is that they are loyal to the Government." Several months later, after yet another inquiry as to the propriety of removing troops, Wells replied simply, "The removal of these troops from the state would be the most disastrous thing that could be done." Although the Klan appeared to be broken, Wells assured Williams that it was only dormant, and that the removal of troops would be perceived by Klansmen as a sign of weakness. It was impossible for the marshal to make arrests without the aid of federal soldiers, Wells added.[67]

In July 1872, at the height of the Ku Klux prosecutions in the district, Marshal James H. Pierce found that he had no place to keep his prisoners. Federal prisoners were usually kept at the Lafayette County jail at Oxford, but this facility was not nearly large enough to hold the hundreds of persons now under arrest. With the permission of the attorney general, Pierce set up a jail at the army camp at Holly Springs. "The military officer has fed them," reported Pierce, "and looked after their wants." Pierce continued to keep federal prisoners at the Holly Springs post until their number once again grew manageable. At the request of the commanding officer, however, Pierce did appoint a civilian "warden" and paid him with departmental funds.[68]

Although there were no soldiers stationed in Mississippi after 1876, it is conceivable that troops from a nearby state could have been used to aid the northern district's federal marshal. Yet such a request was never made, probably because after the Klan was suppressed violent resistance to arrest was generally not offered. In 1879 the Democratic Congress passed a bill prohibiting the use of federal troops as a posse. Attorney General Devens almost immediately issued an opinion stating that, while the new law was certainly constitutional, it did not affect the president's power to use the military to combat resistance to federal laws. But after 1874 the U.S. Army and the Justice Department ceased to work together in enforcing the Enforcement Acts in the northern judicial district of Mississippi.[69]

In the enforcement program in northern Mississippi, the U.S. attorney and marshal benefited from aid offered by the Justice Department itself; specifically, authorization for the hire of detectives, special deputies, and assistant attorneys. The zealous Marshal James H. Pierce, who served from 1870 until 1877, early saw the need for the employment of detectives in northern Mississippi, especially in ferreting out the details of Klan murders and "outrages." When Akerman refused to authorize the hire of a detective because of insufficient funds, Pierce hired one anyway, at his own expense. The detective succeeded in gathering much information that was useful in the trial of Aleck Page's murderers and also uncovered information that prevented a jailbreak. After Pierce received the detective's bill for $200, he approached Akerman again, describing the detective's success and adding that he would have to pay the bill if the department would not. Akerman finally agreed to authorize payment of the bill but warned that in the future Pierce must spend only money "authorized by law."[70]

One month later Akerman wrote to Wells and Pierce that Congress had made a small appropriation for "the more effective enforcement of the laws in the Southern states." The attorney general added that it was clear that Congress had in mind the punishment of Enforcement Act violations. One thousand dollars was available for northern Mississippi, Akerman said, if Wells and Pierce thought they could use it "to employ skilful detectives who will bring to light the crimes in question." Wells was quick to accept the offer. The money would supply the aid needed, he reported, to suppress the Ku Klux and break up "this nefarious gang of ruffians."[71]

Wells had other ways of buying information. In the spring of 1872 he wrote eagerly to the department, asking permission to hire local attorney William F. Dowd as special assistant. Dowd had been approached by a number of Klansmen who sought to retain him as counsel; after listening to their stories, he was "disgusted" at these "lawless desperadoes" and refused to represent them. Now he was willing to give the government information about them, provided he was granted a $5,000 retainer! Neither Wells nor Attorney General George H. Williams worried much about the propriety of the deal, and Dowd was quickly hired. Wells assured his superior that it was the best use of $5,000 the government could make. And Dowd did provide invaluable aid to the overworked Wells.[72]

Whenever Enforcement Act cases piled up on the dockets, the U.S. attorney would request the hire of a special assistant U.S. attorney, and almost invariably his request would be granted. Occasionally, as in the case of assistants Harvey R. Ware and James R. Chalmers, the appointee was required to handle Enforcement Act cases in both the northern and southern districts. Sometimes, as in the case of Dowd, Democratic lawyers were hired as assistants. But Akerman's opinion usually prevailed. Akerman told the U.S. attorneys that, although many people believed that Democratic prosecutors would be more successful with southern juries, he opposed their hire. Writing to a U.S. attorney for southern Mississippi, Akerman put it this way: "If the juries are going to find their verdicts according to their liking or disliking the politics of the prosecuting lawyer. . . . the sooner such depravity is made manifest to the country the better."[73] He concluded, "A man who is friendly to a law, is apt to be more efficient in prosecuting for its violation."[74]

The U.S. attorneys general were not reliable advisers for their subordinates, the attorneys and marshals. When they wished to give advice, they did so. If approached for advice on a specific case, however, they would usually answer that the U.S. attorneys' cases "cannot be tried in the office of the Attorney General." Attorney General Akerman, the first head of the new Department of Justice, had strong feelings about the Ku Klux Klan. It was, he wrote, "the most atrocious organization that the civilized part of the world has ever known." He went to South Carolina to supervise the federal attorney's actions there, while he sent Solicitor General Benjamin H. Bristow to Oxford. Bristow became the department's expert on northern Mississippi; the U.S. attorney's letters to Washington were often routed to Bristow for comment before reply. Because Akerman was a southern Republican, it is not surprising that he supported a vigorous enforcement program in the northern district of Mississippi.[75]

His successor in office, former U.S. Senator George H. Williams of Oregon, was less interested in supplying patient support to Justice Department officers in the Magnolia State. Williams's attitude can be seen in examining his actions in the matter of J. E. Gillenwater. Gillenwater was indicted for violation of the Enforcement Act; he was arrested but escaped. He then assaulted a witness in the case, tried to arrange for the murder of Pierce and Wells, and shot a horse out from under Pierce. Gillenwater next surrounded himself with heavily armed lieutenants and hid in the swamps. Wells asked Williams for military aid—not an unreasonable request, especially since troops had been stationed nearby to help enforce the laws. But Williams replied, "I can render no aid in re-arresting Gillenwater. You must rely upon the marshal and his deputies." When Gillenwater or an associate killed a deputy marshal, Wells suggested that the department offer a reward for the arrest of the murderer. But Williams declined to authorize a reward because he believed it was simply a state case of murder, and because it could set an unfortunate precedent—soon no such cases could be solved without the offer of a reward. "I have no special instructions," Williams concluded. The marshal should be able to "succeed in killing or capturing the men."[76]

Williams even refused to authorize payment of $25 to the owner of the horse that Gillenwater had shot while Pierce was in pursuit of the fugitive. The owner, decided Williams, should have known the risks of loaning the horse to a U.S. marshal pursuing a desperate criminal. Finally, after serious intimidation of black voters in Lowndes County in 1874, Wells began to prepare for a vigorous assault on "this second outbreak" of the Klan. In a letter to Williams, Wells demanded, "I desire to know whether I will be sustained by the Department in taking vigorous active measures" in Enforcement Act cases. Williams bristled at Wells's letter and declared that Wells was not justified in inquiring whether he would be sustained. "You are expected by this Department to prosecute all violations of the laws of the United States."[77]

President Hayes's attorney general, Charles Devens, insisted on a vigorous enforcement program. When he found that, in northern Mississippi, U.S. Attorney Walton was reluctant to try Enforcement Act cases, he prodded. When Walton suggested discontinuing a case because the facts could not be proved to the satisfaction of the court, Devens replied, "I am not convinced that this would be sufficient ground for refraining from the prosecution"—after all, the grand jury had been convinced. Similarly, after Chandler was installed as prosecutor, Devens's solicitor general advised, "If you feel that you have done your utmost, and that it is utterly impossible to hope for convictions," then continue the cases. Do not dismiss them, the solicitor general added, "as something may occur to enable us to hope for better juries." Later, on the verge of leaving office, Devens wrote a circular letter to all U.S. attorneys in the South, asking for "vigorous prosecutions" of election cases but warning that "a few cases that will really result in punishment" would do more to achieve a respect for the law than "a vast number of cases where no convictions can be had."[78]

In 1874 an unsigned article ran in *The Nation* under the title "The Inflation of the Attorney General." The author reported that the attorney general's office had become "a kind of political bureau, to which competitors for the government of sovereign states carry their petitions and proofs. . . . Political parties send in to him statements of their grievances, and ask him for redress against the tyranny of the local rulers."[79] And indeed, as chief prosecutor of the Enforcement Acts, the attorney general was in an awkward position. Although he was expected to enforce all the laws of the United States without respect to party, he was also a member of a presidential administration (always Republican, through 1885) that hoped to foster its own political success. In north Mississippi as elsewhere in the South, it was almost always the Republican voters who were intimidated and assaulted, almost always Democrats who stuffed ballot boxes. It was always a Democratic defendant who was escorted to jail by federal troops requested by the Republican attorney general. The attorneys general enforced the laws properly, but the stark, partisan dividing line between defendants and prosecutors meant that the appearance of evil was always present.

And "the inflation of the attorney general's office" was present as well. By directing prosecutions of the men who violated the election laws, by requesting that troops be on duty during campaigns and elections, and by prodding the marshals to do what they could to insure fair elections, the attorney general's office became an important political institution. Every two years, before the congressional elections, the attorney general sent a circular letter to the marshals, and sometimes to the U.S. attorneys, describing their election-related duties. In an 1875 circular Attorney General Alphonso Taft emphasized that the Enforcement Act applied to campaigns—public meetings, speeches, and parades—as well as to the election itself. In 1882 Benjamin Harris Brewster sent a hundred copies of abstracts of the Enforcement Acts to Marshal J. L. Morphis so that each of his "election deputies" might have a copy. In a separate letter to Morphis, Brewster warned of reports received in Washington that convicted election law violators were being appointed state election officers, and he urged Morphis to watch these men closely. In a circular telegram to all U.S. attorneys after the 1880 elections, Devens directed them to "see that all alleged election frauds in your district are vigorously prosecuted. Send report promptly as possible, even if only preliminary."[80]

An important tool of the attorneys general in seeking a successful enforcement program in the South were the annual reports, in which recommendations for congressional action were made: for better laws or for larger appropriations. In his report for 1876 Alphonso Taft made no specific recommendation but discussed the justness of the whole Enforcement Act program in the South. Taft acknowledged that the Fifteenth Amendment was highly unpopular among white southerners but said that it had been "forced upon the people of the Union" when it became clear that the rights of the freedmen could not otherwise be preserved. Although Taft acknowledged the fact that it was "inconvenient" to have a large mass of "unintelligent voters," he said that blacks had "a clear title to the ballot, of which I know no fair or even practicable way to deprive them." He ended by calling for more energetic efforts at mass education.[81]

Charles Devens reported at great length details of the Enforcement Act prosecutions in his annual reports between 1877 and 1880. In 1878 he complained that the lack of an investigative branch of the department was a great hindrance. Two years later he told Congress that the recent 1880 elections in the South had been more quiet and peaceful than those of years past, but this was because people had stayed home from the polls in resigned fear, and "these [election] crimes have thus done their work." Devens continued, "Those who have sought to defeat honest elections have found that they may do so more readily by allowing voters to deposit their ballots, and then defrauding them in the count." Finally, Devens attempted to prod Congress into action: "I respectfully submit to the consideration of Congress whether the time has not now arrived when an election law should be passed which shall take into the control of United States officials all elections for members of Congress." Devens added, "The only objection that can be made to such a law is that it will be attended by additional expense; but when we consider that . . . fraud in any section of the Union is not only the greatest wrong against the people of that section, but equally against the people of all other sections, to whose interests an honestly elected Congress is vital, the limited expense is a matter of trifling consideration."[82]

Attorney General Miller, writing angrily in his first annual report, informed Congress that in the 1888 election, by various means, "the popular will was stifled and falsified, and returns obtained wholly at variance with what would have been the result of a free and fair vote honestly counted." But the enforcement program in the South had expired, and even the vigorous Attorney General William Henry Harrison Miller was not able to revive it.[83]

All in all, the attorneys general acquitted themselves well in their role in overseeing the Enforcement Act program in the South. They showed a greater disposition to provide U.S. attorneys and marshals with advice and direction than they did in other kinds of cases. Although the long series of Enforcement Act prosecutions appeared to many to be a partisan crusade, this appearance could not be helped. Republicans rarely intimidated, rarely engaged in ballot box stuffing—if only because they

Attorney General Charles Devens, who noted in 1880 that, although southern elections were now more tranquil, the peace resulted from many voters staying home from the polls in fear. Election crimes "have thus done their work," Devens concluded. Courtesy of Hayes Presidential Center.

were the weak party in the South during most of the period. The Republican attorneys general oversaw the prosecution of those who violated election laws, and those violators were Democrats. On the other hand, it would be naive to deny that the attorneys general did not hope for Republican victories in north Mississippi and elsewhere, or to deny that they hoped that the Enforcement Act program would help the Grand Old Party to achieve such victories.[84]

The U.S. attorneys were also active and loyal Republicans, with the exception, of course, of Cleveland's appointee Charles B. Howry. And, like the attorneys general, the U.S. attorneys typically acted fairly and properly in the delicate business of prosecuting Democratic political activists. A part of their success in conducting election cases may be attributed to the fact that they were excellent attorneys. Of the men who served as U.S. attorneys in this period, only Chandler and Niles did not have a law degree; Walton had been a professor of law. And while Chandler and Niles had no law degree, each served with distinction as a judge. The question then arises: Why would promising young attorneys, native southerners such as Walton, Chandler, and Niles, have sacrificed their very reputations by transforming themselves into that terrible ogre, the southern Republican?[85]

G. Wiley Wells, a northerner and veteran of the Union army, fell into the Republican party almost naturally. But what of Thomas Walton, a Confederate veteran and former Democrat? L.Q.C. Lamar hypothesized that Walton joined the Republicans because he believed that only they could restore the state to order and prosperity. Walton also approved of the party's platform on such matters as economic policy and civil service reform. Walton's downplaying of racial issues in his 1876 congressional campaign irritated a number of Republicans. He declared from the podium at New Albany that the South was the region of his family, "and of my forefathers all of whom have been here, every separate branch of which has been here without admixture of foreign or northern blood." Today the Democratic party was the party of violence, the candidate asserted, and that alone merited his disapprobation. While it was true that many northern Republicans spouted hatred of the South, "a political party does not rest on the basis of affection." And Walton then launched into a discussion of the Republican platform.[86]

Thomas Walton was infuriated late in 1877 when Attorney General Devens sought to appoint Orlando Davis, a prominent Democratic lawyer, to be assistant attorney under Walton. "For me and a Democrat to live in the same office would be simply an impossibility—I had as well try to go to bed with a viper. I like these fellows well enough in their place, but their place is not in my office." When Devens made the appointment over Walton's objections, Walton refused to give Davis any duties. After two months of drawing a paycheck, Davis resigned in disgust, and Walton had to do without an assistant. But for him, no assistant at all was better than a Democratic assistant.[87]

Walton's successor, Greene C. Chandler, was a former Confederate colonel and had served as a state legislator in Confederate Mississippi. In a letter of application for the U.S. attorneyship, Chandler wrote, "From boyhood I was a firm believer in good money and protection, and among my earliest recollections was my father's support of Harrison and Clay on these questions." When the Civil War ended and Mississippi's parties were reorganized Chandler "naturally and logically" allied himself with the Republican party.[88]

Although as a congressional candidate, Chandler, like Walton, stressed national economic issues, he was deeply interested in race relations in Mississippi. Delivering the keynote speech at the 1876 Republican Convention in the state, he noted that the Democrats were accusing their opponents of "taking the Negroes by the hand and proposing to give them the rights enjoyed by [whites.]" Chandler went on to say that he did not deny what the Democrats alleged; after all, this was a republic, and equality of rights was at the heart of republican ideology. Chandler concluded, "Republicanism ends where privileged classes begin." Although the former slaves still had a long way to go, Chandler called their progress in the first decade of freedom "impressive."[89]

Racial violence disturbed Chandler profoundly, and this undoubtedly led him to prosecute Enforcement Act cases with vigor. Even after leaving the post of U.S. attorney, Chandler was constantly thinking about race relations. Finally, in 1888 he had printed and "distributed widely" a tract titled "The Negro in Politics. The Paramount Political Question of the Day." Chandler began by observing that the bitter struggle over black political participation was really no one's fault. Since the Fourteenth and Fifteenth amendments had been imposed from outside the state, it was only natural that whites should resent them. Nor was it surprising that blacks should demand political equality. But the lengthy fight over blacks' suffrage in the state had achieved nothing, and if it went on it would continue to achieve nothing. And because of widespread intimidation and fraud, practiced now by Democrats upon themselves in factional struggles, all political life in Mississippi was without meaning.[90]

Chandler's surprising solution was that the federal government should organize western territories for blacks and provide for homesteads there. Blacks could run their own territorial governments, and soon the "Negro Territories" would be admitted as states, with full congressional representation. If, to the modern eye, Chandler's plan seems extraordinarily defeatist, it was nevertheless a logical result of ten years of frustrated efforts to salvage black participation and a bipartisan political life in north Mississippi. The outlook in 1888 was bleak, and Chandler's plan reflects this.[91]

The last U.S. attorney considered here, Henry Clay Niles, was the son of a Whig congressman. The younger Niles was active in Mississippi's Republican party from its inception. Niles's beliefs were from the more radical end of the Republican spectrum. He was proud of having voted, as a delegate to the 1880 national convention, "thirty-five times for Mr. Blaine and once for General Garfield." Niles must have led a lonely existence in Mississippi, because he did not enjoy dealing with Democrats, socially or professionally. He just did not like them. A few other Justice Department officials have left to posterity their reasons for joining the Republican party. Marshal James H. Pierce joined in order to work for a United States wherein "even the most humble citizen of the land may feel that his life and property are safe, and that he can express his loyalty and give his support to the government without fear of being deprived of his life." And Harvey R. Ware, who served as an assistant U.S. attorney, testified at a congressional hearing that he had been a Democrat until 1874, but he objected to the violence and had therefore joined the Republicans.[92]

Analyzing the enforcement program in Mississippi's northern district, one is struck by the fact that U.S. attorneys and marshals did not confine themselves to the formal requirements of their offices. Attorneys did not merely seek indictments and convictions, nor did marshals confine themselves to serving judicial process and keeping prisoners. The case of the swashbuckling attorney G. Wiley Wells was mentioned above; he enjoyed riding with Marshal Pierce and assisting in the making of arrests. In an 1871 letter to Solicitor General Bristow, Wells remarked that he and Pierce had just returned from an expedition to Tishomingo

Miſſiſſippi-Kuklux in ihrer Vermummung.

Men wearing Ku Klux Klan disguises, from Tishomingo County. U.S. Attorney Wells had a photograph taken, from which this engraving was made and published a number of times—here in a German-language publication. Wells's purpose was to give the world tangible proof of the Klan's existence. Courtesy of Mississippi Department of Archives and History.

County—"We captured five KK with disguises." Even more important, Wells had a photograph taken of men wearing the Ku Klux disguises. He presented one copy to the congressional committee investigating the Klan, and a second copy was sent to *Harper's Weekly*, where it was published twice within one year and seen by hundreds of thousands of citizens. The congressional committee, too, published the photograph, which excited great interest across the nation because the Klan was a new and little-understood organization; many southerners claimed that the Ku Klux was a figment of the northern imagination. By capturing the disguises and distributing the photograph, Wells showed the world tangible proof of the existence of the Invisible Empire and attempted to gain national support for the anti-Klan crusade.[93]

Early in 1872, Wells again tried to bring to the attention of the nation evidence of the Klan's terrible actions in north Mississippi. He asked the attorney general for permission to hire a stenographer at departmental expense. As the confessions were taken down and made public, Wells explained, more and more Klansmen would come forward and admit guilt. The evidence would also form a permanent record of federal prosecutors' actions "and will forever estop any person from asserting that the prosecutions under the Enforcement and Ku Klux Acts were for any other purpose than that of protecting the lives and property of citizens."[94] The attorney general at this time was the reluctant George H. Williams, who told Wells that stenographers had already been employed in the Carolinas, and that the public record of Klan doings was full enough. Six years later Greene C. Chandler also sought permission to hire a stenographer, and for similar reasons: If the evidence "could go to the country it might serve to change the views of some politicians who affect to believe in the fairness of Mississippi elections." Unfortunately, Devens's reply to his subordinate's request is no longer extant.[95]

Marshal James H. Pierce was an active lobbyist for support from Washington for Mississippi's enforcement program. In 1876 he wrote to Attorney General Alphonso Taft, asking how many special deputies he might appoint for the upcoming election. He reported that at the last election the polls had been crowded by Democratic election officials who engaged in acts of intimidation of black Republicans. These black Republicans would not vote, Pierce warned, "if they have to be pulled around by a lot of fierce young Democrats." Pierce appointed 239 special deputies for the election, but afterward he reported that "the authority of my deputies to enforce election laws was utterly ignored by local officials." The campaign of 1876 was the worst he had ever seen in Mississippi, Pierce reported: "Almost the entire white population of Mississippi is one vast mob." The terrorism "paralyzed justice, and made human rights a mockery." The intimidation was unparalleled, the marshal concluded, and "I intend the American people shall know of it." This letter was written from Memphis.[96]

At the same time there appeared in *The New York Times* a letter to the editor, written from Memphis and signed by an initial, as was customary: "P., of Oxford, Mississippi." The letter stated that in Mississippi there was "a more defiant spirit manifesting itself than I ever knew during the war. . . . Could the people who saved the Union but know the actual facts, they would never permit Tilden to become President" by the votes of Mississippi and other southern states. The letter concluded: "By no means should the electoral vote of Mississippi be counted, for I tell you there is no doubt, if Republicans had been allowed to vote as they wished, without being threatened in all manner of ways, beaten and killed, Mississippi would have voted for Hayes by a 20,000 majority."[97] But of course, Mississippi's vote was counted for Tilden, since the state returning board was Democratic. Only in three southern states that had Republican returning boards was Hayes given the certificate of electoral votes; such was the effect of the massive campaign of voter intimidation.

This frank letter to *The New York Times*, which was widely assumed to be by Pierce's hand, made Pierce the most despised man in north Mississippi, and the new attorney general, Charles Devens, soon wrote to him, "I think it will be advisable . . . for you to resign." Devens did not articulate the reasons, although he said that some were reasons "we have heretofore spoken of." That the Hayes administration was not angry at Pierce for some wrong committed is seen by the fact that after asking for the resignation, Devens in the next sentence offered to place Pierce in a position in the Treasury Department in Washington. Pierce meekly resigned, thanking Devens for helping him get a new position.[98]

It was not uncommon for U.S. attorneys to give unsolicited reports or advice to the Justice Department or even to the president. G. Wiley Wells and two other prominent Republicans journeyed to Washington in 1875 and met with Bristow and then with Grant. They warned that Governor Ames's radicalism was making race the single political issue in the state and warned of the "color line politics" that would likely result. Unfortunately, their advice led to the visit of agent G. K. Chase to the state. Greene C. Chandler in 1882 mailed a memo to Attorney General Brewster, suggesting changes in federal election laws. Chandler echoed Devens's earlier call for complete federal control of congressional elections; but, barring that, he urged that marshals be empowered to appoint one deputy for every polling place, if needed, with broad powers to guard the ballot box, witness the count, and compel the assistance of bystanders in the event of a disturbance. By the end of the memo Chandler was losing touch with reality—suggesting the usefulness of two deputy marshals at each polling place, "one outside to protect the voters, and one inside to protect the votes." Congress never came close to enacting stringent election procedures of the kind Chandler sought.[99]

Sometimes U.S. attorneys journeyed to Washington to testify before congressional investigating committees. Such committees investigated Mississippi's elections of 1871, 1875, 1876, 1878, 1880, 1882, and 1883. Among those who testified were Wells, Walton, and Assistant U.S. Attorney Ware. Walton's testimony before the so-called Boutwell Committee of 1876 was particularly rich and detailed. Walton began by informing the committee that politics in Mississippi now almost invariably followed racial lines. Nearly all whites were Democrats, and Republicans were all either blacks or white federal officials. Within the Republican party, Walton added, whites and blacks often did not have good relations. Although he was an undeviating Republican, the attorney continued, "my personal influence with the Negroes is not a bit greater than that of any Democrat in my county, not a particle."[100]

When asked the reasons for the violent political troubles of the State of Mississippi, Walton first pointed to the fact that "nearly everyone down there has some kind of arms. . . . Almost every man, black or white, who has money enough to buy firearms, has them. It is the greatest place on the face of the earth for pistols." When a congressman asked why white Mississippians felt so strongly that blacks must not control politics, even though blacks were in the majority, Walton answered:

> One reason is that negroes are negroes, and another is because the negroes are ignorant and the white people are more intelligent. [Whites] look upon the negroes with a kind of horror, as supporting a body of men whom the whites say are going to rob them. . . . One party

> is regarded as guilty of the outlawry of bloodshed, and the other of the outlawry of thieving; and I believe the white people down there are generally inclined to think that stealing is a baser crime than killing, and that breaking a man's head is not half so mean and contemptible as cutting his purse.[101]

If the Justice Department officers in northern Mississippi were activists, they were opposed by an equally activist, and numerically much larger, group of white Democrats. With only a few exceptions, all of the newspapers in the State of Mississippi were Democratic journals, and when these papers reported the proceedings in Enforcement Act cases their language was bitter. An 1874 letter to the editor, discussing northern Mississippi, was typical: "Many a farm is uncultivated, many a wretched wife is in rags, and many a helpless child has suffered intolerable pangs of hunger because those remorseless villains and adventurers sent down by Grant to ravage and destroy, would secure rewards for convictions, to be effected by negro perjury."[102]

The *Jackson Weekly Clarion* wrote eloquently, if not accurately, about some 1871 Enforcement Act cases. "Men have been dragged from their homes without knowledge of the cause of their arrest, at the suggestion of malicious and procured perjurers." A few weeks later the *Clarion* described the impending trial of several Ku Klux Klansmen: "All is now in readiness. The prisoners are now at hand. The grand jury has been packed with such material as will be likely to bring in indictments." And Judge Hill "sits, in all the mock majesty of civil law in harmony with the bayonet." And, making a perhaps logical connection, the paper asked its readers, "Do you oppose the arbitrary arrest of citizens? . . . If so, register and vote for men committed against these wrongs which are perpetrated by the Republican administration at Washington."[103]

The U.S. attorneys often complained that the entire white community was arrayed against the enforcement of the Enforcement Acts. G. Wiley Wells reported that James H. Pierce was unable to get near the murderer of a deputy marshal because "spotters" in the community kept the suspects informed of the marshal's movements. In another instance, shortly before the appointment of Henry B. Whitfield to be U.S. attorney, Whitfield warned Wells that the entire white community of Lowndes County was sympathetic to those who were practicing violent intimidation, and that as jurors they would not convict in cases of whites' assaults upon blacks. At the end of his letter, Whitfield asked Wells to reply by mail, and not by telegraph—the telegraph was operated by Democratic partisans, while the mails were federal and thus safe. Wells sent a copy of Whitfield's letter to the attorney general, adding that the latter might make any use of it "except its publication, as in that event it might cause the death of its author."[104]

The most galling aspect of the Democrats' resistance to the Enforcement Acts was the fact that violators of the law inevitably became heroes. When Aleck Page's murderers returned home to Monroe County after their habeas corpus hearing, the *Jackson Weekly Clarion* reported their arrival: "The platforms about the depot were crowded with people, in fact the whole city [of Aberdeen] seemed to have assembled for the purpose of welcoming back to old Monroe the victims of villainous subornation . . . who had been kidnapped from their quiet homes, leaving their crops to the mercy of the grass, and their wives and little ones unprotected."[105] When their train pulled into the station, the Klansmen heard "the shouts of hundreds of warm-hearted people," and cannons were fired in celebration.

Similarly, when in 1882 three young men who had been convicted of ballot box stuffing returned home to Clay County, they were met by a large crowd of their neighbors; a local matron delivered a poem in their honor, which began:

> Our welcome gallant trio,
> Clay County's free-born sons!
> Convicted of true manhood
> Thrice welcome honored ones.[106]

The community decided to raise money to pay the young men's fines; the women held a concert as a fund-raiser, while the men organized a "glass ball shoot." Reporting these events to Attorney General Brewster, a disgusted Marshal J. L. Morphis concluded that the purpose of the fund-raising effort was to "hold these young men and others steady for the work at the next election." This kind of hero making was still going on as late as 1890. When Marshal Burton investigated the case of Henry Fans, who had been given two hundred lashes for accidentally dropping the effigy of the secretary of war, he found that the people of Aberdeen had raised money and reimbursed the bricklayer who administered the lashes for the cost of the whalebone whip.[107]

Attorneys, marshals, witnesses, and jurors suffered abuse and assault, were ostracized from the white community, and some were even murdered for their role in Enforcement Act cases. When he testified before the 1871 congressional investigation of the Klan, Wells was asked why he had dismissed certain cases. He replied that the key witnesses "were run off or somehow disappeared. . . . I have done everything I could to obtain information in regard to them, but it is impossible to find out where they are." Two months after giving this testimony, Wells telegraphed Attorney General Williams that four witnesses who had just testified before the grand jury had been cruelly murdered. Wells, angry at Williams's apparent reluctance to seek military support for his subordinates, added a final question to his telegram: "Can loyal men have protection? . . . I cannot get witnesses, as all feel it is sure death to testify before a grand jury." In 1873 Wells again had to report to Washington the murders of numerous witnesses who had just testified before the grand jury.[108]

U.S. attorneys often felt like aliens in a distant land, even though all but Wells were native southerners and longtime residents of Mississippi. Even Wells, testifying before the 1871 congressional investigation, recalled that before he instituted the Enforcement Act cases he had been warmly received by the people of the northern distict, but after the prosecutions were instituted "the most violent and slanderous attacks upon me were begun." During the height of the Ku Klux prosecutions Wells received a letter warning him that he was about to be killed and advising him to remain armed and alert. Wells dutifully sent the letter to Washington, so that "if any accident should befall there will be a permanent record on file and data from which facts might be developed." Assistant U.S. Attorney Dowd, who handled hundreds of Enforcement Act cases, later recalled that "I was threatened and I was repeatedly informed I was in constant danger." Henry B. Whitfield was sure that behind the attacks on his character were men who had recently committed election outrages, men "who know that I have the evidence necessary for their prosecution and conviction. They want, above all things, to destroy me if possible."[109]

In the early days of the Ku Klux prosecutions a deputy marshal reported to Attorney General Akerman that U.S. Attorney Wells, who had incurred the wrath of the Klan, "on Saturday last received such a dose of poison that we despaired of saving his life on Sunday and Monday." Shortly thereafter both Wells and Pierce felt obliged temporarily to move

After the murder of four witnesses before the federal grand jury, U.S. Attorney G. Wiley Wells fired off an angry letter to the attorney general: "Can loyal men have protection? . . . I cannot get witnesses, as all feel it is sure death to testify before a grand jury." From *Illustrated History of Los Angeles County, California* (Chicago, 1889).

their offices to Holly Springs, "owing to the unpleasant attitude which has ever characterized the citizens of Oxford towards U.S. officials."[110]

Undoubtedly, it was the marshal and his deputies who suffered the most from snubs, threats, and assaults. In his regular reports to the attorney general, Marshal Pierce gave details of wholehearted resistance to his efforts to make arrests and summon witnesses. Citizens refused to serve on posses, and, in fact, whole communities sympathized with those who had committed violent violations of the Enforcement Acts. The marshal reported that when he made arrests in Starkville in 1871, "Threats were freely made that the prisoners would be released, and that they should not be allowed to leave town." On this same trip Pierce found that witnesses were as difficult to summon as the prisoners were: "The witnesses were all colored, and I had to hunt them up and take them as it were by force with me, their fears of personal harm deterring them from coming at will."[111]

Friends of the defendants finally developed the ingenious plan of using local and state law enforcement to delay action by U.S. officers. Accordingly, state officers arrested U.S. deputy marshals on frivolous and imaginative charges. In July 1871 Wells reported to Akerman that three deputy marshals had been arrested; two months later he wrote, "Every person who has acted as a U.S. Deputy Marshal & aided in the arrest of Ku Klux [has] been either imprisoned or are under indictment."

In one particularly outrageous incident, a deputy marshal was told to arrest James J. Bell for violation of the Enforcement Act. Fifteen soldiers of the U.S. cavalry accompanied the deputy. The men surrounded Bell's home and then searched it; several women were home, but Bell could not be located. As they were leaving the area a "special Deputy U.S. Marshal" with dubious credentials approached them, armed with a genuine order from a U.S. commissioner for their arrest. (U.S. commissioners are the federal equivalents of justices of the peace or magistrates.) The warrant charged the sixteen men with a violation of the Enforcement Acts: The men "had conspired to intimidate, molest, and make afraid the ladies of the household of said James J. Bell." The heavily armed party refused to surrender; Attorney General Akerman later ordered Wells to ask Judge Hill to remove the U.S. commissioner. The commissioner, it turned out, was upset because his own son had been indicted under the Enforcement Acts and was due to be arrested by the marshal.[112]

During the habeas corpus proceedings in the case of Aleck Page's murderers the mood in north Mississippi was tense, and the streets of Oxford were watched by a detachment of U.S. soldiers. L.Q.C. Lamar, a local attorney, quarreled with one of the deputy marshals involved in the Enforcement Act cases; later, in open court Lamar rebuked the deputy for being abusive to the citizens of Oxford. When Judge Hill failed to censure the deputy, Lamar lost his temper and denounced the court. As Marshal Pierce rose to restore order Lamar advanced, wielding a chair, then dropped the chair and struck Pierce in the face, "breaking a small bone at the cap of the eye." In later testimony before an 1871 congressional investigation of the Klan, a different deputy marshal reported that after Pierce was struck the prisoners jumped over the bar.

Q. How many prisoners were there?
A. Twenty-eight.
Q. And they jumped over the bar and rolled up their sleeves?
A. As if going in to have a good time.
Q. Did they try to escape?
A. No, sir; they were going in to help Lamar.[113]

Finally U.S. soldiers entered the courtroom and, after the crowd heard the click of their rifles, order was restored.[114]

The deputy marshal with whom Lamar had quarreled, one Charles H. Wissler, was indeed an unpopular character, fond of drink and sometimes argumentative. His involvement with the Justice Department stemmed from the fact that his in-laws were notorious leaders of the Ku Klux Klan in north Mississippi, and he was willing to supply detailed evidence against them. He did testify, and his testimony was instrumental in securing convictions. But shortly after Wissler testified, he was shot and killed, the bullet entering through the window of his house to strike him as he stood among his wife and children.[115]

J. E. Gillenwater, already mentioned, was guilty of multiple violations of the Enforcement Acts; after being arrested, he managed to escape, killed a deputy marshal, and put a contract on the lives of Pierce and Wells—an action for which he was later indicted. While Pierce was attempting to capture him, Gillenwater shot at Pierce and hit his horse. Meanwhile, a black porter at the hotel in Corinth was taken by armed men and severely beaten; it was alleged that he had informed the marshal of Gillenwater's movements. Marshal Pierce sent Deputy R. T. Dunn to Corinth to investigate the beating of the porter. But while asleep in his hotel room Dunn received a shotgun blast to the head and was killed instantly.[116]

A month later, while summoning witnesses in an Enforcement Act case, another deputy marshal was "kicked, cuffed, & knocked about generally"; he was then forced onto a southbound train, "although his duties carried him north." The records further show that a deputy marshal named Reed was shot and wounded while serving process in Ku Klux cases, but the details in his case unfortunately have not been preserved. And Marshal Pierce, soon after the appearance of the letter to *The New York Times*, reported to the attorney general from Memphis, "I am just now the object of no little abuse, at the hands of the mob. I am in receipt of intelligence from home that I am to be assassinated on my return." Pierce added that he was not frightened but would appreciate an escort of soldiers.[117]

Even burglary was practiced to prevent marshals from exercising their duty in enforcing the Enforcement Acts. In October 1884 someone broke into the marshal's office in Oxford and stole "every letter, telegram, and printed circular pertaining to elections" that was on file. Marshal Morphis hurriedly wrote the attorney general for replacement copies of instructions for the deputies who would be working at the upcoming election.[118]

Other hindrances to Justice Department officers in the northern district of Mississippi were lack of funds and the difficulty of getting Congress to pass timely deficiency appropriations. It was not unusual for the clerk of the court to enter in the minute book, "It appearing to the Court that the Marshal has no funds with which to pay jurors and witnesses and cannot procure them until an appropriation for the purpose is passed by Congress, all causes to which the United States is a party are postponed."[119] Marshal Pierce met some of the court expenses with credit, then found that Congress was slow to provide him with money to pay off these obligations. Pierce complained to Washington, "[Being] a poor man . . . the delay embarrasses me in meeting payments which I promised." In 1874 Pierce spent a great deal of money escorting prisoners; "I used my own money and money which I borrowed." Pierce and Wells managed to reduce expenses and ended up with a surplus of funds; Pierce begged Attorney General Williams for permission to use the surplus to pay Wells, instead of sending the funds to the Treasury. Otherwise, Wells would have to wait for the annual deficiency appropriation, and this would be a hardship since he had not been paid in over a year. But the attorney general could not give the needed permission.[120]

The jury system is a logical starting point in the search for the reasons for the failures of northern Mississippi's enforcement program. When indictments were not returned and when verdicts of not guilty were found, the grand and petit juries must bear a part of the responsibility. The U.S. attorneys recognized this, and when Enforcement Act cases were going well, they praised the juries in reports to Washington; if cases failed, the juries were usually assigned the blame. In 1880 Greene C. Chandler reported a number of successful prosecutions of men who had expelled voters from the polling place by force of arms; he attributed this success to the jurors, who were "from the interior of the district, remote from the most corrupt political centers." In December 1882, after a hung jury in a certain election case, Chandler acknowledged the failure but told the attorney general brightly, "The Judge has promised me a new jury after the holidays."[121]

The refusal of the grand jury of the December term of 1876 to find any indictments, despite overwhelming evidence of election violations, became somewhat of a cause célèbre after most northern newspapers published the grand jury's report. Attorney General Taft asked Walton for an explanation for the jurors' inaction; Walton reported that one juror was upset because his own son was implicated by the evidence, a few others refused to indict because they were afraid of "exciting odium at home." Still others hoped to win favors from the Democrats by earning the reputation "of having obstructed and paralyzed these prosecutions." Some jurors simply recognized that the witnesses were so afraid that they would not testify freely in a public trial.[122]

The Democratic press in Mississippi always described the federal grand and petit juries as "packed," packed with Republicans and also packed with blacks. Typical was the statement of the *Aberdeen Weekly*, which reported that the U.S. court at Oxford had become an "engine for the apparent venting of political spleen," and that jury panels were "made up almost solely from one political party, full of soreness and revenge." The report concluded, "Are innocent men to be dragged from their homes, rudely separated from their wives and children, to be incarcerated in loathsome prisons without redress? Law, O Law! How many crimes have been committed in thy name?"[123]

This kind of article deeply troubled Marshal James H. Pierce, and he told Akerman about them, adding, "While I asked no man how he voted when I summoned him as a juror, I knew the fact that he was not a Ku Klux, and that he would be no obstruction to the enforcement of the laws." Wells had written a letter to the editor answering the charges of jury packing, but Pierce did not think that was the proper course. Akerman replied that Pierce placed too much weight upon "the censures of a party press." It would be idle, Akerman continued, "to attempt to enforce the laws through the agency of jurors who are unfriendly to the laws of the government," and Pierce did well to avoid that kind of juror.[124]

It is a difficult task for the historian to assess the validity of these newspaper complaints. Were northern Mississippi's juries in fact "packed" with Republicans or illiterate blacks? While the jurors' names are included in the court's minute books, it would be a herculean task to attempt to trace the party affiliation and race of a large sample of these jurors. Fortunately, one historian has completed such a project: Drew L. Kershen has made an exhaustive study of federal grand jurors in a Louisiana district, using census reports and other data. Of all the federal grand jurors who served in this district in the 1870s, Kershen found that about 31 percent were black. Only eight out of more than two hundred grand jurors were illiterate, while only thirty were active partisans. Of course, Louisiana and Mississippi might have had different sorts of grand jurors, and some scattered data, happily, has been preserved regarding the composition of grand and petit jurors in Mississippi. There is no hint in this data that northern Mississippi was much different from Louisiana.[125]

One particularly nice document that has been preserved was printed in the *Oxford Eagle* of January 16, 1879. Marshal Morphis, angered at persistent reports that his juries were packed with Republicans, had the sitting grand and petit juries draw up affidavits, each juror swearing as to how he had voted in recent elections. Of the twenty-three grand jurors, two were absent when the affidavit was drawn up; sixteen had voted for Samuel J. Tilden in 1876; three for Hayes; and two had not voted. In the 1878 congressional contest—a two-party race that pitted

Greenbackers against Democrats—ten jurors had voted Greenback, six Democratic, and five had not voted. The petit jurors gave information only as to the congressional race. Of the twenty-four members of two sitting petit juries, thirteen had voted Democratic, five for the Greenback party, and six had not voted.[126]

Information about two other juries has survived. The recalcitrant grand jury of December 1876 was made up of seven blacks and eleven whites. The foreman testified before a congressional hearing that, of the eighteen jurors, two were outspoken Democrats, two or three were "rather independent," and the rest were Republican. The 1882 petit jury that convicted the three young men of Clay County (heroes of the poem quoted above) consisted of ten whites and two blacks; party composition was not recorded. All things considered, the growing difficulty of achieving indictments and convictions should be attributed to the lack of any real opposition to the Democratic party in the state. By 1885 the vast majority of citizens were either Democrats or not politically involved, and as jurors such citizens were not likely to show much zeal in bringing in indictments and convictions in election cases. An 1879 federal statute took the power of drawing up jury lists away from the U.S. marshal and put it in the hands of a bipartisan "jury commission." Although juries in northern Mississippi had never been without Democratic members, now half the names on the jury lists were Democratic. As one U.S. attorney complained, "I [do] not have challenges enough to keep the ballot thieves out of the jury box."[127]

While jurors may be blamed for failures to indict and convict, northern Mississippi stands out from other judicial districts because there were so many indictments and convictions. The obvious question then is: If there were so many convictions in northern Mississippi, why did free and fair political participation disappear in the region? Why was the district's enforcement program at once a great success (statistically), and a great failure (de facto)? An important answer is found in the person of Judge Robert Andrews Hill, who presided over the federal court in Oxford in the years 1866–1892.[128]

Hill was born in Tennessee in 1811 and had served as a schoolteacher, a constable, and a justice of the peace. His legal training, notes one biographical sketch, "was acquired as a justice of the peace." He moved to Mississippi's Tishomingo County in 1855 and soon began serving as a probate judge, continuing in that position until 1865. He took no active part in the Civil War. Hill had been a Whig in antebellum politics; after the war he was never politically active. As a former Whig, a former Tennessean, and a Unionist, he caught the attention of President Andrew Johnson, and in 1866 Johnson appointed him district judge for both districts of Mississippi.[129]

When U.S. Attorney Wells began bringing hundreds of Enforcement Act cases before his court in 1872, Hill gave a great deal of thought to sentencing and decided to give the same sentence in almost all cases. This sentence consisted of a $25 fine and the posting of a $1,000 peace bond, which would be forfeited if the defendant again violated any citizen's constitutional rights. Anxious to show the nation that the citizens of northern Mississippi wanted to enforce the laws, Hill encouraged defendants to opt for a jury trial. By making it clear that citizen-jurors in his court were willing to convict, he hoped to avoid the South Carolina experience of military arrests and the suspension of the writ of habeas corpus.[130]

The standard Hill sentence of $25 plus a peace bond was not invariable. An examination of the records in one hundred of the 446 cases that ended in conviction in 1872 and 1873 reveals that Hill gave a prison sentence only once. In this case of savage Klan assault, Hill sentenced the defendant to five years in prison. In a very few cases a monetary fine of more or less than the usual $25 was assessed—the amount varying from $10 to $1,000 in these early Klan cases. But in the vast majority of the Enforcement Act cases of 1872 to 1874 the pattern was a plea of not guilty; a jury trial resulting in conviction; a $25 fine and $1,000 peace bond. After the early mass of cases, Hill began to give more individual consideration to sentencing. In election cases tried by Greene C. Chandler, for instance, fines of $5, $10, $25, $35, and $50 were all common. In these cases the device of the peace bond was dropped, and no prison sentences were handed down.[131]

In a typical case of 1874 a grand jury returned an indictment, in January, against Willis and Davis Younger for crimes committed at a state election in 1872. The indictment charged that the Youngers (and others unknown) "with force and arms did among themselves wickedly and corruptly combine, confederate, and band together with intent to injure and oppress" one Monroe Holmes, because Holmes had exercised the right of suffrage secured to him by the Fifteenth Amendment. A second count charged that the defendants did with a certain pistol "feloniously, wilfully, and of malice aforethought seek to kill and murder & commit other wrongs to him the said Monroe Holmes." Unfortunately, the extent of Holmes's injuries was not recorded. The two Youngers pled not guilty; in June a petit jury found them guilty, and Judge Hill fined them each $10 and required them to post a $1,000 peace bond.[132]

In a typical case of the Chandler years, W. E. Weaver and eight others, all of them state election officials, were indicted in December 1880. The defendants were charged with preventing three named persons from speaking in advocacy of their candidate in the 1880 congressional campaign, "by force, intimidation, and threats." The nine men pled guilty, and in January 1881 Judge Hill fined each $35.[133]

Throughout the 1870s and early 1880s Justice Department officers were unhappy with Hill's lenient sentencing. In the early 1870s a deputy marshal sent the attorney general a list of "necessities" for northern Mississippi; the deputy cited the need for more cavalry, suspension of the writ of habeas corpus, and said also, "We need a judge but that I suppose we cannot have." Attorney General Akerman was quick to become dissatisfied with Hill; responding to the complaint of the U.S. attorney, he wrote, "Yours is not the only district where the judiciary succumbs to the pressure of a local sentiment. There is no remedy but the harsh and difficult one of impeachment." Concluding his assessment of Hill, Akerman added: "It is my opinion that nothing is more idle than to attempt to conciliate by kindness that portion of the Southern people who are still malcontent. They take all kindness on the part of the Government as timidity, and hence are emboldened to lawlessness by it. . . . It is the business of a judge to terrify evil-doers, not to coax them."[134]

Wells sent Attorney General Williams a glowing account of his many convictions of Klansmen, then added, "If our kind hearted judge can only be kept from destroying the effect produced by the convictions of these midnight assassins, I can within six months rid this entire district of Ku Klux." When Chandler sent a similar glowing account of his many Enforcement Act convictions, Devens relayed his congratulations. "I desire, however," said the attorney general, "that you will respectfully urge to the court the propriety of imposing the sentence of imprisonment attached by the statute to [these offenses] rather than to inflict merely the punishment of a fine." If only fines are levied, Devens continued, "I fear the same crimes will be repeated." Chandler answered that he agreed wholeheartedly with Devens, and he had asked Hill to impose a prison sentence, but the judge believed "the certainty of punishment was more important than its severity." Devens wrote back yet again, saying that Hill's ideas were nonsense, and he urged Chandler to continue to seek prison sentences. But Hill imposed no prison sentences in election cases after 1874.[135]

After the next term of court Chandler reported to Devens that though he had secured a number of Enforcement Act convictions, Hill had not imposed a fine of more than $10, and in one case fined three men $1 each. Chandler argued with the judge in open court, and his zeal made some of the waiting defendants so nervous that they changed their pleas to guilty. Chandler told the attorney general that if every man convicted of election violations could be sent to the penitentiary for two or three years there would be an end to "these great crimes that now disgrace our state." The judge was too close to the white citizens of the community, Chandler concluded, and he would consider requesting that Judge Hill "exchange work with some other judge" in the trial of Enforcement Act cases. A disgusted attorney general agreed with Chandler that Hill's imposition of fines of $1 or even $10 amounted to "a deliberate trifling with the execution of the laws of the United States." Two years later Chandler noted hopefully that in election cases "the judge has promised to punish the next I convict." But either Hill did not keep his promise, or his idea of punishment was quite different from that of Chandler.[136]

Like Wells, Pierce, and Morphis, Hill sometimes used the local newspapers to speak to the people of the district. But his words often sound like the words of a Sunday school teacher urging the golden rule upon his charges. In one such published letter Hill urged the voters of north Mississippi to act fairly and peacefully on election day 1875, and "you will thus have shown to the world that, though composed of different races and entertaining different opinions, we are capable of self-government, and can all live together in peace." Hill also carried on extensive private correspondence with presidents and attorneys general. Soon after the first Enforcement Act cases were heard in his court, Hill wrote proudly to Akerman, noting the many convictions that were returned. Akerman answered with some advice to Hill. After noting the great disaffection felt by most southern whites toward the national government, Akerman noted, "This disaffection is not a thing to be won by wooing. Enough of that has already been done in vain. Six years of lenity have not melted it. It will only disappear before an energetic . . . exercise of power."[137]

After failing to get Akerman's sympathy, Hill began corresponding with

Solicitor General Bristow, who had visited the district in 1871. To Bristow, Hill bragged that the court's actions had "restored peace and quiet to north Mississippi." Regarding sentencing in the Ku Klux cases, Hill noted that many were clamoring for stiff sentences and were "mad with all who will not carry out their feeling of enmity, and with whom none but a *Jeffries* of a judge would be satisfactory." Turning to the political situation, Hill ended his letter by warning Bristow that white Republicans in the state were guilty of "stirring up the Negroes."[138]

In an 1881 letter to Garfield's attorney general, Wayne MacVeagh, Judge Hill noted that of all cases he found Enforcement Act cases to be the most difficult. Again giving his favorite aphorism, Hill told MacVeagh, "I have found that it is certainty more than severity in punishment that prevents crime. Acting on that I have adopted as a general rule the milder punishment." MacVeagh wrote back that he was glad to hear that Hill's court was indeed upholding the Enforcement Acts. But "I only hope that your people will soon learn to recognize the political rights of their fellow colored citizens freely and fully. Until they do we will certainly do all in our power to compel them to do so."[139]

In 1889 Judge Hill advised the new president, Benjamin Harrison, regarding southern appointments. Many were urging Harrison to appoint blacks to office, noted Hill, but really "the true interest of the colored race is not to seek or obtain office, and thereby avoid the antagonism which is sure to arise if they are constantly seeking office." A few months later Attorney General Miller asked all federal judges for suggestions for an improved judicial system and for their general observations on the workings of the federal judiciary. Hill was happy to send such a general observation: "My experience is that it is not the severity, but the certainty of punishment that prevents crime."[140]

Certainly, no one, not even Democratic zealots, ever accused Judge Robert A. Hill of severity. And in the person of Judge Hill, we have the answer to the puzzle of northern Mississippi's high conviction rate in Enforcement Act cases: Jurors knew that the penalties would be light, and they therefore did not hesitate to bring back convictions. And as for the question of why, despite the high conviction record, fair elections became a lost cause and black voting almost unknown, the answer is that the leniency of the judge meant that fear of prosecution was not a substantial deterrent to crime. But of course, it would not be fair to make the district judge shoulder the entire blame. If Hill had imposed

Attorney General I. Wayne MacVeagh wrote to Mississippi's federal judge in 1881: "I only hope that your people will soon learn to recognize the political rights of their fellow colored citizens freely and fully. Until they do we will certainly do all in our power to compel them to do so." Courtesy of Hayes Presidential Center.

severe penalties, jurors would certainly have been less willing to convict their neighbors. Historian Kermit Hall has suggested that one of the beauties of federalism is the fact that U.S. judges are local men who are attuned to their districts. Judge Robert A. Hill was very much attuned to the beliefs of the local white power structure. Unfortunately, this had an adverse effect on prosecutors' efforts to bring free elections back to the State of Mississippi. At any rate, the only thing that makes the northern district of Mississippi fundamentally different from other districts is the fact that a combination of aggressive Democrats, energetic prosecutors, and a mild judge led to large numbers of Enforcement Act convictions.[141]

As to the question of why Mississippi failed to develop a free and honest political system after the war, the answer is the same as the answer for the other southern states. The successful use by the Democrats of "color line politics" meant that the Republican party faded in power, and very few whites were willing to support it. Blacks had the strength of numbers but were weak in virtually every other way, and they were returned to the subordinate position they had previously occupied in Mississippi. Failure of support for the enforcement program on the national level also played a part; the crucial time here was 1875, when, because of the lack of support by the Grant administration, the first wholesale disfranchisement of Republicans took place. The delirious Democrats then regained their confidence. The lack of vigorous support for Mississippi's Republican party by the national administration was founded upon a failure of northern voters to support aggressive defense of black rights. As Grant put it, "the whole public" grew tired of "these annual autumnal outbreaks." And the Grand Old Party found that it was able to wield great power even without the votes of Mississippi's Republicans.[142]

The fate of black voting in Mississippi was sealed in 1890, when a convention of delegates met in Jackson to consider revising the state's constitution. Addressing the issue of voter qualifications, one delegate told the convention, "It is no secret that there has not been a free ballot and a fair count in Mississippi since 1875, that we have been preserving the ascendancy of the white people by revolutionary methods. In other words, we have been stuffing ballot boxes, committing perjury, and here and there in the state carrying the elections by fraud and violence."[143] In a similar vein, a citizen wrote to the *Jackson Clarion-Ledger*, "The old men of the present generation can't afford to die and leave their children with shotguns in their hands and perjury on their souls, in order to defeat the Negroes. The Constitution can be made so that this will not be necessary."[144]

Accordingly, the Mississippi Constitution of 1890 provided that all voters must pay a poll tax well in advance of the election and must either be literate or able to explain a section of the constitution when read to him. Of course, the adequacy of the would-be voter's explanation was determined by the white, Democratic voting registrar. Only a very few blacks, most of them in the delta, were allowed to register under the new constitution.[145]

On the national level, President Harrison urged Congress (both houses controlled by his party) to enact a new Enforcement Act, the so-called Force Bill. But though the bill passed the House, it was defeated in the Senate in a bargain struck between Democrats and Silver Republicans. A furious Harrison railed at Congress. To the Democrats who spoke against the Force Bill on the grounds that the states should deal with voting rights themselves, Harrison argued, "We have a right to ask whether they are at work upon it. Do they suggest any solution? When and under what conditions is the black man to have a free ballot? When in fact is he to have those full civil rights which have so long been his in law?"[146] Harrison concluded by telling Congress to do something now and not leave these civil rights questions as a "heritage of woe" to the next generation.[147]

Harrison was optimistic in thinking the next generation would tackle the civil rights questions. The "heritage of woe" was passed from generation to generation into the twentieth century. Although Mississippi's federal attorneys and marshals were successful in their late nineteenth-century Enforcement Act cases, Mississippi ultimately was left outside the mainstream of the U.S. political system. Even compared with other southern states, Mississippi was remarkable for the weakness of its opposition parties and for its incredibly low voter participation. Nor was black disfranchisement the only cause of this low level. Even among white voters participation was extraordinarily sparse. After 1890 Mississippi deviated greatly from the norm of U.S. politics. Given the limited electorate and the one-party system, John R. Lynch was close to the truth when he asserted, "So far as this state is concerned, we do not live under a republican form of government."[148]

It is fitting that an important act of the civil rights drama of the 1960s was acted out in Oxford, Mississippi, with federal marshals playing a central role. In the attempt to desegregate the University of Mississippi, 166 U.S. marshals were injured in a twenty-four-hour period, but their work was completed, and James Meredith was admitted to the university. Voting rights victories soon followed. In the five years after 1960 black voter registration increased by 700 percent in the state. In 1986 Mississippi sent a black congressman to Washington for the first time in one hundred years. Change has come slowly to north Mississippi, but the progress has been substantial. With northern public opinion firmly behind the civil rights movement of the 1960s, with sympathetic presidents, judges, and congressmen, and a courageous group of local activists, great civil rights progress was made. In the 1880s these elements were lacking, and the effort to secure black civil rights in north Mississippi failed and failed miserably.[149]

3

One Man, One Wife
Combating Polygamy in Utah Territory

I

On the Western Slopes of the Rocky Mountains, members of the Church of Jesus Christ of Latter-day Saints sought to build the kingdom of God on earth. Violence at the hands of their neighbors had forced the Mormons to abandon earlier settlements in Ohio, Missouri, and Illinois; finally, they found a secluded home near the southern edge of the Great Salt Lake. Congress organized Utah as a U.S. territory in 1850, and President Zachary Taylor appointed the Mormons' leader, Brigham Young, to be the first territorial governor. For the Mormons, there was no clear distinction between the administration of the church and the administration of the territory. As Brigham Young put it, "We cannot talk about spiritual things without connecting them with temporal things, neither can we talk about temporal things without connecting spiritual things with them. They are inseparably connected."[1]

Church leaders, including Young, knew that if the violent persecutions of the past were to be avoided, Mormons would have to dominate the new territory completely. In part this domination would be economic: Mormons soon would be encouraged to buy only Mormon goods and only from Mormon merchants. Cooperative church-sponsored businesses would be encouraged. Domination would also be maintained through control of the territorial government. But though Young was to be governor, judges and other officials were sent into the territory from "back east," and they soon reported that Mormon citizens refused to recognize any leaders except church leaders. In an early assertion of federal power, President James Buchanan dispatched a small army to Utah in 1857; although pitched battles with the Mormons initially seemed likely, peace was soon obtained. The church and the U.S. government began an uneasy truce that would last for several years.

The non-Mormons (termed *Gentiles* by the Mormons), although present in Utah only in small numbers, by 1870 began to denounce angrily the church's economic and political domination of the territory. They pointed out a number of ways in which Mormon society deviated from the usual U.S. pattern. Utah was devoid of public nonsectarian schools; Utah had a wholly Mormon militia, intimately connected with the church; and the economic life of the territory was collectivist, directed by Mormon authorities. Elections were controlled rather thoroughly by the church hierarchy, and in short, Utah seemed to be an un-American theocracy. But the most potentially explosive "deviation" by Utah Territory from the U.S. norm was the Mormon practice of polygamy.

Mormon theology held that there existed countless numbers of souls waiting to enter earthly life. After a soul was united with a body at birth, and after growth and maturity, families could be formed, and in the resulting births more souls were given bodies. If a man lived a good and clean life, he would spend eternity with his family on one of the millions of existing worlds. Procreation was, then, a high priority for Mormon believers—so that souls might be granted bodies, and so a man's family would be a large and happy one throughout all eternity. Polygamy, or the system of "plural marriages," was the logical result of this theology. The doctrine was first embraced by the church in 1843; by 1870 there was a growing number of growing plural families in Utah.[2]

The isolation so cherished by Brigham Young and the other pioneers was short-lived. With the completion of the transcontinental railroad in 1869, increasing numbers of Gentiles came to Utah, including, most notably, miners, merchants, and litigious lawyers. Soon a vocal and economically powerful 10 percent of Utah's population was Gentile. Dissatisfaction with Utah's theocratic, polygamous society grew quickly in the ranks of non-Mormons, and some of the earliest and most insistent calls for federal action came from the territory's Gentile residents. The newcomers complained to Washington both because they found polygamy to be sinful and un-American, and because the Mormons seemed intent on keeping Gentiles outside the economic system of the territory.

A Mormon family at Farmington, Utah, 1888. The husband sits in the doorway, surrounded by his six wives and a number of children. Courtesy of Western History Collections, University of Oklahoma Libraries.

In 1870 the Department of Justice was represented in Utah by U.S. Attorney Charles H. Hempstead and Marshal M. T. Patrick. There were in the territory three district courts, presided over by judges appointed by the president to four-year terms and approved by the Senate. The judges of the district courts, sitting *en bloc*, constituted the Utah Supreme Court. The district courts in Utah Territory had a dual function. First, they heard criminal cases involving violations of federal statutes and civil cases to which the United States was a party; and second, they heard cases involving violations of territorial laws and civil suits between private parties. In 1852 the territorial legislature had passed a law emphasizing the dual nature of the courts.[3] This law provided for a territorial attorney general and marshal; these officers would handle all cases before the district courts that did not involve the United States. This territorial statute further provided that juries for all cases should be drawn from lists prepared by local probate courts.

Congress had long been interested in moving against the Latter-day Saints' practice of plural marriage; in 1862 the Morrill Act had made such "bigamy" in the territories a federal offense.[4] Enforcement of the act was postponed in the heat of the Civil War, but by 1866 the question was being asked: Why have there been no convictions under the Morrill Act? In response, the newly appointed U.S. attorney, Hempstead, formerly a captain at Utah's Camp Douglas, reported that, because of local control of juries, it was absurd to think of seeking indictments for bigamy—Mormon juries presumably would refuse to indict or convict "celestially married" persons for bigamy.[5] In 1870 President Grant sent Edward B. McKean to the territory to serve as district judge and chief justice of the supreme court. McKean acted quickly, striking down the 1852 territorial statute that had established the offices of territorial attorney general and marshal and ruling that the U.S. attorney and marshal were the only competent officers for his court in any type of case. McKean also held that, in all cases, jury lists provided by the Mormon-dominated probate courts would no longer be used, and that juries were to be summoned by the U.S. marshal by an open venire. (Under an open venire the marshal is called upon to select jurors in any way he sees fit and is not supplied with a list of names).[6]

Hempstead was quick to complain to the attorney general. McKean's rulings had doubled his work load with no increase in salary. Hempstead's fees, he reported, "are a mere bagatelle. . . . Any respectable attorney at the bar, would receive a fee on the defense [of a single case] exceeding the amount of my salary for four years." The unhappy U.S. attorney accordingly resigned his position, but, at the urging of Grant and Attorney General Amos T. Akerman, he agreed to stay on, "at least until you can find some suitable person, with sufficient patriotism to perform onerous duties in Zion without adequate proper compensation."[7] Seven months later, in August 1871, Hempstead insisted that his resignation be accepted, and President Grant and the attorney general began the search for a suitable replacement.

Meanwhile, Chief Justice McKean appointed Robert N. Baskin, a Salt Lake City attorney, to serve as U.S. attorney *ad interim*.[8] In the words of the staunchly Mormon historian Orson F. Whitney, Baskin "brought to the discharge of his new duties, not only talent and experience, but an intense hostility to the Mormon church."[9] Indeed, Baskin moved quickly and decisively against a number of the church's most powerful leaders. But at first he encountered a significant obstacle: There were no funds with which to proceed in territorial cases. For years the first comptroller of the U.S. Treasury had paid the expenses of federal cases before the Utah district courts, but in all other cases the expenses had been paid by the territorial legislature. The legislature had indeed appropriated its share of the expenses of the district courts but had stipulated that these funds could be dispersed only to the territorial marshal—an officer no longer recognized by the district courts. Pleas went out from Baskin and the other federal officials, asking that the Justice Department provide the money needed to run Utah's courts, but the attorney general answered sadly that the only remedy lay with Congress. Finally, U.S. Marshal Patrick agreed to advance the funds from his own pocket, and in September 1871 the Third District Court convened at Salt Lake City, with Judge McKean presiding.[10]

The U.S. marshal summoned prospective grand jurors by an open venire; among those summoned was George Q. Cannon, a church leader and editor of the *Deseret News*. Acting U.S. Attorney Baskin questioned Cannon as follows:

Q. Are you a member of the Church of Jesus Christ of Latter-day Saints?
A. I am.
Q. Is not polygamy one of the fundamental doctrines of that church?
A. Plurality of wives is a doctrine of the Church.
Q. Do you believe the revelation which teaches this doctrine to the Church to be from God and binding upon his people?
A. I do.[11]

Baskin then asked that Cannon be excused, as it was expected that the grand jury would investigate several cases of adultery arising from plural marriages. Cannon and the other Mormons on the panel were all excused, and a grand jury made up entirely of Gentiles was selected. This grand jury, after presentations by Baskin, indicted Brigham Young, George Q. Cannon, Salt Lake Mayor Daniel H. Wells, and an apostate Mormon named Henry Lawrence for "lewd and lascivious cohabitation," an offense under territorial statute.[12]

Baskin chose to proceed under the territorial statute because of flaws in the Morrill Act, which had stipulated that polygamists should be tried as bigamists since they entered into additional marriages while the first spouse was still living. To secure a conviction under the Morrill Act, it was necessary to prove both the first and subsequent marriages, but, because plural marriages were performed secretly, it was very difficult to prove them. Baskin decided that it would be easier to prove cohabitation than bigamy. He was much criticized in the Mormon press, however, for ignoring the intent of the legislature, as he prosecuted Mormon leaders under a statute designed to prohibit sexual sins, not the divine institution of plural marriage.

Baskin also secured the indictments of another aggregation of church officials, this time for murder. Brigham Young, Mayor Wells, Hosea Stout, and Heber Kimball were indicted for "directing" a murder in 1857. The primary witness in these cases was Bill Hickman, who had confessed to a number of murders, many of which he claimed were committed at the direction of church authorities.

Meanwhile, the search for a new U.S. attorney continued. Two likely candidates refused to be considered because the office did not pay well—these were J. H. Wickizer, special agent of the Post Office Department, and George R. Maxwell, register of the United States Land Office. Finally, a sixty-seven-year-old Chicago lawyer wrote to Solicitor General Benjamin H. Bristow, who was an old acquaintance. This lawyer, George Caesar Bates, sent the solicitor general a report of the recent great Chicago fire. "Now in that grand fire," he told Bristow, "I lost everything I had on the earth, save the clothes on my person. . . . I come now to solicit alms." If appointed federal attorney for Utah, Bates wrote, "I will go there to reside permanently, and poor as I am will take with me a better law library than there is today west of Illinois. I have no family to look after, never drink, nor smoke, nor gamble."[13]

At length, Bates, who had served as U.S. attorney for Michigan during the administrations of William Henry Harrison and Zachary Taylor, was selected for the post in Utah. Again writing to Bristow, Bates confided, "Do not think me an old and foolish man when I tell you that I actually wept tears of joy" on receiving the appointment. Shortly before leaving for the territory, Bates assured the president that he would never regret "the noble charity to a poor conflagrated lawyer. My entire worth is one old satchel, three old shirts, and three pairs of stockings. But I have pluck, integrity, and sense, and will succeed by God's blessing."[14] On his arrival in Utah Territory, he dramatically telegraphed the attorney general, "Here. Will do equal and exact justice though the heavens fall."[15]

Of course, the first cases to occupy Bates's attention were the cases of Brigham Young and the other church leaders charged with murder and lewd and lascivious cohabitation. Bates found that, despite the indictment, Brigham Young had absented himself from the Third District and was in fact vacationing near Utah's southern border. While the Mormons pointed out that Young always traveled south in the winter, the Gentiles were of the opinion that he had fled in fear or to show his contempt of the court. Young's lawyers assured Bates that the prophet would return if he were allowed to post bail. Bates eagerly telegraphed this information to Attorney General Akerman, adding, "Do you approve?" Akerman responded sternly, "Make no agreement as to bail while Young absconds."[16] Judge McKean ruled that Young must appear before his court in early January.

Not a few Utah citizens were surprised when the aged Brigham Young made the rugged four hundred-mile trip in the dead of winter to appear in court on January 2, 1872. Bates angered many Gentiles by recommending that Young be allowed to post bail. "The return of the defendant, the condition of his health, etc. [are] proper considerations to be weighed in favor of bail"; even Aaron Burr and Jefferson Davis, Bates noted, had been allowed to post bail.[17] It is instructive that the U.S. attorney compared Young's case to that of the alleged traitors Burr and Davis. For federal prosecutors, Young and his church were not only guilty of violent and lascivious crimes but, most importantly, were guilty of conspiring against the federal government.

Ignoring Bates's recommendations, McKean declined to admit Young to bail, instead placing him in the custody of Marshal Patrick. Because of the ill health of the defendant, however, McKean hinted that the marshal and the prophet might consider an agreement whereby Young would be kept in custody in his own house. This agreement was in fact reached. Young described his "confinement" in a letter to his son Willard, who was a West Point cadet: "As you will naturally feel anxious to know to what extent I am deprived of my liberty, I assure you anyone would find it difficult to know there is any guard here at all. The marshal sits in my office or goes outside to walk, or to ride, or go to the theater, or elsewhere, but never follows me, nor asks any questions, nor knows where I go. . . . From this you will readily perceive the whole thing is a farce, and we have many a good joke about it."[18]

In preparing the cases against Brigham Young and the others, Bates asked permission to hire a number of lawyers as special counsel for the government. But Attorney General Akerman believed "the government ought not to show any unseemly zeal to convict Brigham Young" and pointed out that a large staff of prosecuting lawyers might have that appearance. However, since Robert Baskin had already been involved in these cases on behalf of the government, Bates might hire him as special counsel.[19] Bates was also distressed by the lack of funds to conduct these important cases. As he wrote to the attorney general, Marshal Patrick had already advanced $13,000 from his own funds and was unable to continue this support. Bates went on to argue, "Brigham Young is rich, but the U.S. authorities are penniless. . . . Cannot some means be devised to put in funds to meet Brigham Young in court with the necessary weapons?"[20]

Meanwhile, the Gentiles were growing less and less pleased with the new U.S. attorney. His placid, oft-repeated promise of "equal and exact justice" was not what many impatient Gentiles wanted to hear, and many of them suspected that Bates was developing increasingly cozy relations with the Mormon church. Baskin, working as special counsel in the cases against the church leaders, later recalled that "it was evident to me that for some unaccountable reason he had changed his former intention of trying the cases, and did not intend to do so." Baskin therefore resigned his position and fired off an angry report to the attorney general. McKean and Bates quarreled on a number of issues, and in February 1872 both men went to Washington to make suggestions to Congress and the president as to what measures were needed to prosecute polygamists successfully. McKean evidently asked that Bates be removed, and the attorney general wrote to Bates, a mere three months after Bates had assumed office, "I am directed by the President to inform you that your resignation as Attorney of the United States for Utah Territory will be accepted by him." Bates ignored the hint, claiming that the people of Utah supported him and pointing out that no charges had been made. As Congress was not in session, Grant delayed in naming a successor. But Governor George I. Woods wrote to the president warning that Bates "has been in constant, confidential communication with your enemies—writing and telegraphing of the 'situation' to Brigham Young's attorneys with as much zeal as though he were counsel for the defendant."[21]

Indeed, Bates's highest priority seemed to be the rebuilding of his own finances. He was particularly interested in seeking out mining speculators as clients and was otherwise seeking to expand his private practice. When Bates heard that his friend the solicitor general was considering resigning, he wrote to him: "If you are going to resign, come here with me. We can make a fortune out of mining litigation in two years. These criminal causes out of the way I think we could easily earn $50,000 per annum by the law. That is better than office, which brings nothing but 'Honor.' Can honor set a leg? No. Can honor clothe your wife? No. Nor feed your child."[22]

In the spring of 1872 the U.S. Supreme Court shocked the judges and attorneys of Utah by ruling that McKean had erred in ousting the territorial attorney general and marshal and in ignoring the territory's jury selection laws. Writing the court's unanimous decision in the case of *Clinton et al. v. Englebrecht*, Chief Justice Salmon P. Chase concluded that the territorial policy of the federal government "has ever been that of leaving to the inhabitants all the powers of self-government consistent with the supremacy and supervision of National authority."[23]

The immediate effect of the Supreme Court's decision was to quash over one hundred indictments that had been found by improper grand juries; Marshal M. T. Patrick freed forty prisoners from his custody and turned over to the territorial authorities twenty others. Among those released were Brigham Young and the other church leaders charged with murder and lewd and lascivious cohabitation. The long-range result of the decision in *Clinton* was the paralysis of Utah's district courts. Chase's opinion had declared that the territorial marshal was indeed the proper officer to summon juries, but the Utah Supreme and district courts had formally ousted the incumbent marshal, J.D.T. McAllister, on the grounds that he did not hold an appointment from the federally appointed governor, as was required for officers of the territory. Without a territorial marshal, the Utah courts could summon no legal grand or petit juries. The lack of funds for conducting territorial prosecutions remained a problem. The utter paralysis of the Utah district courts can be seen by referring to Table 3.1, which is based on the annual reports of judicial business in Utah, mailed each year to Washington by the U.S. attorney. The table includes both federal and territorial criminal cases.

Utah Territory was not, however, totally devoid of courts during this long interlude. As in many other territories, so in Utah the legislature had expanded the jurisdiction of county probate courts to include many kinds of lawsuits and criminal prosecutions. For years U.S. officials in Utah had been appalled to see the probate courts, with their Mormon judges, trying an increasing number of important criminal cases. After *Clinton* the probate courts and the Mormon ecclesiastical courts were the only courts functioning in the territory.[24]

By 1873 President Grant, Attorney General George H. Williams, and

Table 3.1. Criminal Cases in Utah's District Courts

	1870	1871	1872	1873	1874
Assault	5	11			
Rape		2			
Manslaughter	14	25			
Accessory to murder		1			
Riot	9				
The crime against nature		1			
Lewd Cohabitation		5			
Dueling		1			
Larceny, burglary	12	15			
Receiving stolen goods	1	3			
Stealing cattle		2			
Embezzlement, forgery		4			
Horse stealing		5			
Perjury		1			
Highway robbery		1			
Arson		1			
Illegal militia cases		8			
Robbing U.S. mail	5	1			
Internal Revenue crimes	8				
Resisting a U.S. Marshal		1			
Counterfeiting		2			
TOTAL	54	90	0	0	0

Sources: The table is based on the following correspondence: Governor Vaughn to Attorney General Akerman, January 20, 1871 (Source-Chronological File for Utah Territory, Records of the Department of Justice, Record Group 60, National Archives); (SCF/UT); M. T. Patrick to Attorney General Williams, March 16, 1872, SCF/UT; George Caesar Bates to Williams, November 27, 1872, SCF/UT; William Carey to Williams, October 18, 1873, SCF/UT; Carey to Williams, August 31, 1874, SCF/UT. See also the *Annual Reports of the Attorney General* for 1871–1875 (Washington, D.C.: GPO, 1871–1875).

the Congress were being flooded with letters and visitors demanding that action be taken to remedy the judicial problems of Utah. Grant himself had always mistrusted the Mormons, and, with the advice of staunch anti-Mormons such as Senate Chaplain John P. Newman, he began to take action. In 1873 Grant sent two new judges to the territory and reappointed McKean; George R. Maxwell was appointed U.S. marshal, and Bates was finally replaced by William Carey of Illinois. Carey's attitude quickly won the approval of the president and the attorney general. Carey wrote, "The sooner it is understood in this territory that in merely speculative theology and in all matters pertaining to communion and intercourse with the Deity all are perfectly free to entertain such views as seem to them good, but when they become citizens . . . the Constitution and laws of the country are for them as well as for others, the Supreme Law of the land, . . . the better it will be for all concerned."[25]

On February 14, 1873, Grant sent to Congress a special message advising legislation designed to overrule the Supreme Court's decision in *Clinton et al. v. Englebrecht* and to correct the problems of the judiciary in Utah Territory. "The general judicature of the Territory," Grant told Congress, ought to be "under the direct supervision of the National Government." That special legislation was imperative was made clear, Grant continued, "by several years of unhappy experience." The president concluded by demonstrating his perception of the seriousness of the situation in Utah: "Apprehensions are entertained that if Congress adjourns without any action upon this subject, turbulence and disorder will follow, rendering military interference necessary—a result I should greatly deprecate."[26]

Congress acted on the president's message by passing the Poland Act, introduced by Luke Potter Poland, a congressman from Vermont. The Poland Act, announced Senator Matthew H. Carpenter smugly, was "an act to correct an error of the Supreme Court of the United States." Section 7 of the act expressly disapproved the 1852 Utah territorial statute that had set up the offices of territorial attorney general and marshal. Sections 1 and 2 declared that the U.S. attorney and marshal were the sole prosecuting and executive officers of the Utah district courts. The act also made it clear that the Mormon-dominated probate courts had "no civil, chancery, or criminal jurisdiction whatever" but were limited to the settlement of estates and questions of guardianship. Jury lists in the district courts were to be drawn up jointly by the clerk of the district court and the probate judge of the county in which the court was held. Congressman Poland expected that this procedure would result in jury lists half Mormon, half Gentile. Poland defended his bill by declaring that, although he felt "no special hostility" toward the Mormons, "the fact is undeniable that these people are as directly hostile to the Government of the United States as was ever any portion of the country when it was in the darkest hour of rebellion."[27]

When the long-awaited news of the passage of the Poland Act reached Utah in June 1874, the Gentile *Salt Lake Tribune* announced in its headline, albeit prematurely, "The Last Relic of Barbarism Extirpated from the Earth." In the words of a Utah district judge, the Poland Act "set the courts to running." Of course, problems remained; the marshal complained that Mormon citizens would not agree to serve on posses, and that the Mormon legislature was continuing to refuse to provide his office with the funds needed to try territorial cases. Assistant U.S. Attorney D. P. Wheedon had other complaints: "Mormons will swear on being empaneled that they have no prejudice and will find a verdict according to the evidence" but then refuse to convict. Wheedon recalled a recent trial wherein he had proved adultery by overwhelming evidence, and the court had given a charge favorable to conviction. But though "the defendants offered no evidence . . . the jury were a majority Mormon & they acquitted in two hours."[28]

Former prosecutor George Caesar Bates complained to the attorney general that U.S. Attorney Carey was working to bar Mormons from service on grand juries. Carey responded that he objected to Mormons as grand jurors only if they had "conscientious scruples against finding indictments for violations of the law of Congress prohibiting polygamy," just as persons were barred from grand jury duty who had "conscientious scruples" about capital punishment.[29] To the first grand jury assembled in Salt Lake City after passage of the Poland Act, Carey explained that certain questions had "divided the people and caused bitter animosities for many years: that the sooner these questions were settled the better." Carey told the grand jury, which was composed of both Mormons and Gentiles, that he proposed to try several test cases and let the U.S. Supreme Court settle these divisive legal issues.[30]

In the most important of these test cases Brigham Young's personal secretary was indicted for violation of the Morrill Act. Church leaders had long hoped to bring the question of the constitutionality of the Morrill Act before the U.S. Supreme Court, and in *United States v. Reynolds* Carey benefited from the complete cooperation of the defendant. Although Carey easily achieved a conviction, the Utah Supreme Court overturned the lower court decision on the grounds that the jury had not had the proper number of jurors. As Carey prepared for a second trial, George Reynolds and his family grew uneasy at the prospect of a prison term, and in the second trial Carey received no assistance from the defendant.[31]

The second trial began on December 9, 1875, in Salt Lake City. Carey carefully questioned each prospective juror as to whether he believed that the plural marriage system was of God, and whether he would be capable of finding a verdict of guilty if the facts warranted it. An angry defense attorney countered by asking Gentile jurors if they "had not a strong bias or prejudice against the practice of polygamy," thus seeking their exclusion, but the judge overruled such questioning. When finally empaneled, the jury consisted of nine Gentiles and three Mormons who swore that they were capable of rendering a guilty verdict. Reynold's marriage to Mary Ann Tuddenham was proved by the testimony of her parents, who saw the ceremony performed at the Endowment House in 1865. Reynold's second wife, Amelia Jane Schofield, had testified freely at the former trial but could not now be located. Carey introduced evidence to show that Reynolds was purposely keeping the witness away, and he then called to the witness stand the court reporter, who read Schofield's testimony from the earlier trial. The defense attorneys, grasping at straws now, objected that the record as read did not show that the "Reynolds" mentioned therein was the same Reynolds who was now on trial. This objection was overruled.[32]

The defense then called Orson Pratt and Daniel H. Wells, church leaders who testified that the duty of polygamy was enjoined by the Bible and other holy books, and that the penalty for male church members who failed to practice polygamy, circumstances permitting, was "damnation in the life to come." The presiding judge, echoing Carey's arguments and anticipating the words of the U.S. Supreme Court decision, charged the jury that "in matters of opinion, and especially in matters of religious belief, all men are free. But parallel with and dominating over this is the obligation which every member of society owes to that society; that is, obedience to the law."[33] The jury deliberated two hours and returned a verdict of guilty; thus Carey achieved what no other U.S.

attorney had ever achieved, a conviction under the 1862 Morrill Act. But of course, Carey's "victory" came only with the assistance of the Mormon church, assistance that would not likely be granted in other polygamy cases.

In the appeal of the *Reynolds* case to the territorial supreme court, Carey felt that it was obvious that the First Amendment did not protect violators of criminal law. His brief centered on justifying the reading of testimony of a former trial—which he argued was permitted in cases where a witness is kept away by the connivance of the defendant. Carey sent a copy of his brief to the attorney general for use in the appeal to the U.S. Supreme Court. Attorney General Charles Devens also ignored the issues of religious freedom in his brief and discussed only technical aspects of the trial.[34] Given the briefs prepared by Carey and Devens, it is surprising that Chief Justice Morrison Waite's opinion is a terribly important discussion of First Amendment religious rights—in fact, the opinion in *Reynolds v. United States* is the Court's first major statement on the Constitution's protection of religion. Waite's decision, which has been ably discussed by a number of legal historians,[35] declared that though the Constitution protected every man's religious beliefs it did not protect every action that might be undertaken in the name of religion. A person's religious beliefs could not justify an overtly criminal act.[36]

Although Carey was an able and fair-minded U.S. attorney, he was removed from office in 1876. The Gentile *Salt Lake Tribune* could not understand why he was not achieving large numbers of convictions for polygamy, and it led the successful campaign to have Grant send a new attorney. The new prosecutor, Sumner Howard of Michigan, won few friends during his service from 1876 to 1878. He sought no new indictments for polygamy, probably because he was waiting for the Supreme Court decision in *Reynolds*, which was not handed down until 1879. Howard moved with the greatest vigor against those who were cutting timber on government land. He sought and achieved monetary settlements on behalf of the government, but he pointed out to the attorney general that it was essential that a timber sales agent be appointed for Utah Territory—the timber on government land was needed for the development of the mining industry and railroads.[37]

In one other class of cases Howard moved strongly. These cases, which he called the "church murders," involved the murder of apostates or Gentiles by Mormons, possibly directed by church officials. These cases have been studied elsewhere and will not be treated at length here because they were out of the mainstream of federal efforts to end polygamy and assert supremacy over Utah.[38] Many of these cases were decades old by the time Howard brought them to trial; they had not been successfully pursued earlier because of a feeling that Mormon jurors would protect Mormon defendants.

The most important murder case Sumner Howard prosecuted was the trial of former Mormon bishop John D. Lee for his part in the celebrated Mountain Meadows massacre of 1857. Utah, in that year, had been in a state of near-hysteria, in the midst of a great revival of religion and at the same time receiving news that the U.S. Army was en route to Utah to "subdue the Mormons." In the ensuing period of mistrust of non-Mormons, a party of westering settlers passed through Utah on their way to California. John D. Lee, along with several other Mormons and a group of Indians, planned and executed an attack on the travelers, killing all the adults and some children—at least 120 persons were murdered. The church's response to the massacre was to place most of the blame upon the Indians and to point out that Brigham Young had at one point humanely instructed Mormons to sell food to settler parties to prevent starvation. Mormons also reported that some of the victims of the massacre had been particularly unruly and obnoxious to the residents of southern Utah and to the Indians.

U.S. Attorney Carey had resurrected the Mountain Meadows case and had tried Lee for the first time in 1874; Carey had attempted to implicate a number of church authorities but was unable to achieve a conviction. Sumner Howard adopted a more pragmatic strategy in Lee's second trial, held in 1876. By giving up the effort to implicate high authorities of the church, Howard gained their cooperation, and even Brigham Young supplied an affidavit that helped secure Lee's conviction.[39] But Utah's non-Mormons were angry at Howard's failure to bring polygamy cases to trial, and, early in 1878, he resigned and was replaced by Philip T. Van Zile, a thirty-four-year-old former judge from Michigan.

Van Zile was interested in moving quickly against the institution of plural marriages. In one of his first letters to the attorney general he reported, "I am going to indict some much married individuals and shall try to make this coming year tell on that institution peculiar to this people, 'polygamy'." During his more than five years of service, Van Zile was able to achieve only one conviction of a "much married individual," but, like Carey, he was able to guide an important test case to the U.S. Supreme Court. The case of *Reynolds v. United States* had determined that the federal government could indeed prosecute persons who practiced polygamy in the name of religion, but *Reynolds* had not really cleared the way for polygamy prosecutions. Because it was a test case, Mormon jurors had been willing to convict one man of polygamy in order that the U.S. Supreme Court might rule on the constitutionality of the Morrill Act, but it was unlikely that future Mormon jurors would be so cooperative. By guiding the test case of *Miles v. United States* to the Supreme Court, Van Zile sought to test the constitutionality of exclusion of Mormons from juries in polygamy cases.[40]

John H. Miles was accused of marrying three women at the Endowment House in Salt Lake City on the same day but in separate ceremonies. Van Zile successfully objected to all prospective jurors who stated that they believed polygamy was commanded by God, and that God's law was higher than Congress's law. The second of Miles's three alleged wives, Carrie Owen Miles, had grown dissatisfied with her marriage, and she testified as to her own marriage to Miles. Several other witnesses testified to the marriage of Miles to Emily Spencer, and the jury brought back a conviction in a matter of minutes. Miles was sentenced to five years in a federal penitentiary; his attorneys took his case to the Utah Supreme Court, where the appeal failed, and then to the U.S. Supreme Court. The defense attorneys argued that the lower court had erred in allowing Carrie Owen Miles to testify: Although in fact she was the second and thus extralegal wife, Miles admitted being married to her but denied being married to anyone else. Thus Miles's attorneys argued that until proved otherwise, Carrie Owen Miles was the legal wife and had no right to testify against her husband. The defense lawyers also argued against the legality of exclusion of Mormons from the petit jury.[41]

Van Zile was extremely interested in the *Miles* case, and he carefully prepared a brief that was sent to the Justice Department for use in the U.S. Supreme Court hearing. "If this case wins," Van Zile told the attorney general solemnly, "Good-bye polygamy." Van Zile pressed for an early hearing before the supreme bench, and in April 1881 the Court announced its decision: The United States had lost its case. But *Miles* was actually a victory for Van Zile, because, although the decision stated that the lower court should not have allowed the apparently legal wife to testify, it went on to agree that those who believed in polygamy and seemed incapable of rendering a guilty verdict should be excused from juries in cases arising under the Morrill Act.[42]

Van Zile devised one plan of action in which he was ten years ahead of his time. The Morrill Act had declared that no religious institution in the territories could hold property in excess of $50,000. Although most observers were sure the Mormon church held property valued well in excess of this sum, no action had ever been taken—in part because much of the property was held in Brigham Young's and not in the church's name. Young died in 1877, and in his death Van Zile saw an opportunity. Young's heirs and the church trustees engaged in a civil suit to determine which of Young's property was his own, and which held in the name of the church. One can almost see the gleam in the federal prosecutor's eyes as he wrote to the attorney general: "The trial of the suit commenced by the heirs will I think develop the facts and bring to light plenty of property. What do you think of this plan: Wait till this suit of the heirs has concluded or nearly so and when facts enough are gathered commence a case to get this property for the U.S.!"[43] The attorney general was not prepared to institute a suit to deprive a church of its property, provisions of the Morrill Act notwithstanding, and Van Zile's plan was not approved. Only after ten more years of frustrated efforts against the Mormon church and the institution of polygamy would Congress and the Department of Justice again consider plans to seize church property.

But even as early as 1882 it was clear that federal officers were making scant progress toward the elimination of polygamy. Twenty years after the passage of the Morrill Act U.S. attorneys had achieved only two convictions under this federal law. U.S. Attorney Van Zile, federal judges in Utah, Attorney General Brewster, and President Chester Arthur all began to push Congress for further weapons in the war on polygamy. These lobbying efforts resulted in the passage of the Edmunds Act in 1882. Introduced by Senator George F. Edmunds of Vermont, the Edmunds Act made polygamy in the territories a federal offense punishable by a fine of not more than $500, and imprisonment for a term of not more than five years. A man committed polygamy who, having a living wife, subsequently married another, or who simultaneously entered into marriage with more than one woman. The Edmunds Act also defined the lesser offense of unlawful cohabitation, in which a man lived with more than one woman. The penalty for unlawful cohabitation in the territories was a fine of not more than $300, or a term of imprisonment not to exceed six months, or both. In trials arising under either offense, jurors could be challenged for living in polygamy, or for believing in the rightness of polygamy, or for refusing to answer any question that might tend to criminate them. Polygamists were barred from voting or holding office, and all offices having to do with elections and voter registration were declared vacant. A Utah Commission was created, to consist of five men who would oversee voter registration and elections. Section 6 of the Edmunds Act gave the president the power to grant amnesty to those who had engaged in polygamy prior to the passage of the act but had abandoned the practice.[44]

Philip Van Zile was one of Utah's more politically active U.S. attorneys. Running for congressional delegate in the tumultuous 1882 election, in which many polygamists were hurriedly disfranchised, Van Zile won an unprecedented 20 percent of the vote in his race against the candidate of the Mormon People's party. In this election many of his supporters who were former Mormons and former polygamists were disfranchised; he later wrote to Attorney General Benjamin H. Brewster and suggested that the president consider granting amnesty to those former polygamists who were now "loyal citizens." Van Zile urged prompt action, "on account of the local elections being near at hand." He suggested a test oath for potential recipients of amnesty, which read in part: "I am not a member of the Church of Jesus Christ of Latter-day Saints nor do I believe in its covenants of polygamy. . . . I will do all I can to resist the said church in its efforts to oppose the laws and obstruct the due course of justice." A notation made in the Department of Justice stated that the oath seemed "sufficiently stringent."[45]

After further consideration, however, the attorney general grew uneasy with the wording of Van Zile's proposed oath; he worried that it violated the "religious test" clause of the Constitution. Brewster discussed the matter with the president, then circulated Van Zile's text to other Justice Department officers. Solicitor General Samuel F. Phillips recommended replacing mention of the Mormon church with more general wording. Phillips also recommended that the president issue a blanket pardon to all persons who would go before a district court and swear to the oath. After all, noted Phillips, "the (generally) ignorant class" who would be applying for amnesty would be as impressed by an oath in open court as they had been by an oath in the Endowment House. The department's pardon clerk, James Staunton, was also uneasy with the specific mention of the Mormon church, and the oath was accordingly revised. In 1884 President Arthur began to issue the proclamations of amnesty to former polygamists.[46]

After five years of service, Van Zile resigned his position early in 1884. For the first time since Buchanan's administration, a Utah man was chosen for the post of U.S. attorney—although the appointee, William H. Dickson, had lived in Utah for only two years. Dickson was thirty-six years old, and a Canadian by birth. For eight years he had practiced law at Virginia City, Nevada, and had come to Utah in 1882. Just as Van Zile resigned in 1884 an emergency arose in Utah that required the immediate attention of a U.S. attorney—thus was the Utah resident Dickson chosen.[47]

The emergency arose from the fact that a number of Mormon citizens had filed suit against members of the Utah Commission, charging that the commissioners had illegally deprived them of the right to vote. Commissioner Ambrose B. Carlton was greatly upset by these suits: As he wrote to the attorney general, if the Mormon citizens should win their cases, the commissioners "will be personally liable for costs and damages—unless Congress shall, after infinite delay, reluctantly pass an act of indemnity." As an afterthought, Carlton added that the cases were also important in the general struggle for federal supremacy in Utah. Van Zile was absent from the territory and on the verge of resigning when the suits were called, and Dickson was appointed to handle the cases, first as special counsel, then as U.S. attorney.[48]

The persons suing the commissioners argued that they had never been convicted of polygamy; several of them were in fact immune from prosecution because of the statute of limitations. Voting registrars appointed by the commissioners and acting under their direction had refused to register the complainants because they could not swear that they were not now living in polygamy. One of the complainants had been denied the right to register only because she was a woman, although the legislature had indeed enfranchised women in 1870. Dickson's brief was carefully constructed, and, as was becoming customary in important cases, he sent a copy to the attorney general for use in appeals before the U.S. Supreme Court. Dickson argued that the commissioners were protected because, as officers with a judicial function, they were not liable to lawsuits; the proper course for the complainants, he argued, would have been to seek writs of mandamus compelling the registrars to register the voters. While the complainants' attorneys argued that their clients had not been convicted of polygamy, Dickson pointed out that Section 8 of the Edmunds Act was designed not to punish polygamists but to protect the ballot box from "persons, who by their hostility to the National authority and refusal to yield obedience to the laws of Congress, have shown themselves to be unsafe custodians of political power."[49]

Dickson did not make the pretense of keeping the Mormon church out of his brief. "It is well known," he wrote, "that in Utah there was a sect, or church, which, at the time of the passage of the Edmunds Bill was . . . teaching and encouraging disobedience to the laws of the United States"; these facts were of such notoriety that the courts must take cognizance of them. Regarding the plaintiff who had been denied the right to vote because she was a woman, Dickson argued that, although the Utah Organic Act of 1850 did give the legislature the right to prescribe voter qualifications, maleness was clearly a tacit requirement. In all the world, he explained, "wherever the right of suffrage existed, by universal consent its exercise was restricted to the male sex, for social and physiological reasons unnecessary here to recount." Dickson neglected to mention that most non-Mormons saw women's suffrage as an obstacle to secularization of the territory: Mormon women would presumably vote as their husbands did, thus increasing the power of Mormon voters, while Gentile men were much more likely to be single.[50]

In the Utah Supreme and district courts, the commissioners prevailed, and the complainants carried an appeal to the U.S. Supreme Court. Attorney General Brewster used most of the arguments made by Dickson, with one exception: Regarding the question of women's suffrage, he declined to make any argument but submitted the matter to the judgment of the high court. On March 23, 1885, the Supreme Court rendered its decision. The Court held that the members of the Utah Commission had overstepped their authority by devising rules and oaths to be used by the election officials—the Edmunds Act had not given them this authority, and it was up to the local registration officials (appointed by the commissioners) to weigh each potential voter by the standards of the Edmunds Act and the laws of the territory. The Court agreed that persons living in polygamy should be excluded from the voter rolls even if they had never been convicted, but on the issue of women's suffrage the lower courts were overruled—the territorial legislature was competent to prescribe voter qualifications, subject only to possible modification by Congress.[51]

Many historians have spoken of "the crusade" by federal officials against Mormondom, a crusade that is said to have been inaugurated by the appointments of Dickson as U.S. attorney and Charles S. Zane as Utah's chief justice.[52] Indeed, the convictions achieved for polygamy and unlawful cohabitation rose markedly after these two men took office in 1884, as can be seen by referring to Table 3.2.

But the sharply rising number of convictions was not so much a result of the supposed crusading spirit of these men, as of the fact that in 1884, by the case of *United States v. Clawson*, a final major barrier to wholesale convictions under the Edmunds Act was removed. Past federal attorneys had also been zealous and desirous of moving against the plural marriage system—Baskin, Carey, and Van Zile come to mind—but each of them faced a number of almost insurmountable obstacles. Among these were Mormon control of territorial cases, lack of funds, and the unwillingness of Mormon jurors to convict polygamists.

The *Clawson* controversy arose because of a shortage of jurors in the Third District Court. Under the Poland Act of 1874, jury lists in Utah were made up jointly by the clerk of the district court and the judge of the probate court for the county in which the district court sat. Each of these men contributed one hundred names to the jury list, and, in practice, the clerk submitted only the names of Gentiles, while the probate judge contributed only the names of Mormons. Under the Edmunds Act, however, most of the names on the Mormon side of the list became worthless, at least in cases involving polygamy or unlawful cohabitation. Mormons sat on juries in these cases only if they believed that polygamy was wrong or that the law of Congress must be obeyed and violators punished. The problem, then, was that the jury lists in each district contained only two hundred names, almost half of which were useless in polygamy cases, and from these lists must be formed grand and petit juries for the four terms of court held each year.[53]

In September 1884, at the impaneling of a federal grand jury in Salt Lake City, the list of names was exhausted before the jury was complete. After seeking the advice of Assistant U.S. Attorney Charles Stetson Varian, Judge Zane ordered the marshal to summon jurors on an open

Table 3.2. Conviction for Polygamy and Unlawful Cohabitation in Utah Territory

Fiscal Year	Bigamy and Polygamy	Unlawful Cohabitation	U.S. Attorney(s)
1875	1		Carey
1876			Carey, Howard
1877			Howard
1878			Howard, Van Zile
1879			Van Zile
1880			Van Zile
1881	1		Van Zile
1882			Van Zile
1883			Van Zile
1884	2	1	Van Zile
1885	1	38	Dickson
1886	5	107	Dickson
1887	2	212	Dickson, Peters
1888	4	326	Peters
1889	6	294	Peters
1890	10	114	Peters, Varian
Total	32	1092	

Sources: U.S. Congress, House, "Convictions for Polygamy in Utah and Idaho," House Executive Document 447, 50th Cong., 1st sess. (1888). "Report of the Utah Commission," with "Annual Report of the Secretary of the Interior," reports for 1888, 1889, 1890, House Executive Document 1, 50th Congress, 2d Sess., 51st Congress, 1st sess., 51st Congress, 2d sess., respectively.

Note: Because of changes in the period of reporting, and other minor discrepancies in reports received from court clerks in Utah, the totals given may be slightly high. But undoubtedly, there were at least 1,050 convictions for these crimes in Utah Territory. For attorneys and their terms, see *Register of the Department of Justice* (Washington, D.C.: GPO, 1871–1891). The *Register* was issued annually but was not published in 1875, 1877–1882, 1885, or 1887–1890. Charles H. Hempstead also held one earlier appointment. Robert N. Baskin is not listed here because he never received a presidential appointment. Appointed by Judge McKean to serve as U.S. attorney ad interim, he had many important duties in 1871.

venire. Zane believed that his action, although not specifically approved by statute, was legal under common law. Petit juries were also summoned by open venire at this term of court, and one of these petit juries convicted Bishop Rudger Clawson of polygamy and unlawful cohabitation. He was sentenced to pay a fine of $800 and to serve four years in the penitentiary. Clawson's attorneys took an appeal to the Utah Supreme Court on the grounds that persons who believed in polygamy had been excluded from the grand jury, while the Edmunds Act seemed to allow such exclusions only for petit juries. The attorneys also objected to the summoning of a petit jury by open venire, because the Poland Act gave explicit instructions for the summoning of juries but did not mention the use of an open venire.[54]

The brief for the United States in this appeal was prepared by Dickson's assistant, Charles S. Varian. Varian argued that, in cases involving the United States, territorial district courts were governed by the common law if there was no statute to the contrary. The use of an open venire when jury lists were exhausted was clearly permitted under common law. Varian also analyzed Congress's intent in passing the Poland Act: The sole purpose of the act was to provide juries where there had been none. To suppose that Congress intended the jury lists to be restricted to two hundred names, even as the territory was rapidly growing, was "to convict Congress of a wicked and stupid design" to deprive Utah's citizens of the right to a trial by jury. The passage of the Edmunds Act had put an additional strain on Utah's courts, Varian noted; did Congress intend that even still the jury lists must be limited to two hundred names? "Were great Senators and distinguished representatives, in the ostensible effort to crush out polygamy in the territories, endeavoring to find a way not to do it?" No, reasoned Varian, Congress knew that the common law, "the great mother of our jurisprudence," provided a way for the courts to "aid themselves." The Utah Supreme Court sustained Varian's position, and Clawson's attorneys carried the case to the U.S. Supreme Court on a writ of error. Again, the U.S. attorney gave a copy of his brief to the attorney general, and in January 1885 he urged that the *Clawson* case be pushed forward with great dispatch because jury lists were again exhausted, and an open venire seemed the only remedy.[55]

Announced early in 1885, the decision in *Clawson v. United States* cleared the way for numerous, vigorous prosecutions of polygamists. The U.S. Supreme Court upheld both the exclusion of Mormons from the grand jury and the summoning of a petit jury by open venire. The effect of the *Clawson* decision can be seen by the fact that prior to the decision U.S. attorneys had obtained only five convictions for polygamy and unlawful cohabitation; then, in 1885 alone, in the wake of the Supreme Court decision, Dickson and his assistants obtained thirty-eight convictions.[56]

Late in 1885 both Dickson and his assistant Varian offered their resignations, stating that the compensation was "utterly inadequate" for jobs requiring such labor and responsibility. Quickly, Senator Edmunds wrote to Attorney General Augustus Hill Garland, urging that Dickson and Varian be asked to withdraw their resignations and promising that Congress would provide more adequate compensation. It would be unfortunate, moaned Edmunds, to lose two officers "so capable, so faithful, so successful." The attorney general did as Edmunds suggested and asked Dickson and Varian to stay on. They agreed, then admitted that, in addition to dissatisfaction with the salary, they had wished to give the Democratic president, Grover Cleveland, an opportunity to replace them with men of his own party. Early in 1887 Dickson did leave office, although Varian stayed on, and Cleveland appointed George Peters, a forty-year-old Ohio lawyer and former mayor of Columbus, to the position of U.S. attorney. Senator Allen Thurman assured Cleveland that Peters was "a sound and reliable Democrat."[57]

Also early in 1887 Congress considered further legislation to assert federal supremacy over Utah Territory. The majority report of the House Judiciary Committee pointed out that it was injurious to all the people of the United States for Utah to be so firmly in the control of the Mormons. Particularly injured were those who might want to go to Utah but were prevented by Mormon control of the economic and political life of the territory. The parallel with arguments over slavery in Kansas is striking: Potential citizens of a territory must have the same economic and political rights as they enjoyed in their home states. Pushing for a more homogenized United States, Congress in February 1887 passed the Edmunds-Tucker Act. In its most important provisions, this law called on the attorney general, through his representatives, to institute suits to forfeit and escheat to the federal government all property held by the Mormon church in excess of the $50,000 limit imposed by the Morrill Act. Places of worship, parsonages, and cemeteries were exempted from forfeiture. The church was disincorporated, and the attorney general was to take the steps necessary to wind up its financial affairs. Women's suffrage was abolished, "illegitimate" children of polygamous marriages were disinherited, the Mormon militia was abolished, and federal judges in Utah were given the power to appoint the commissioner of schools. Prospective voters were required to swear that they would obey the polygamy laws and not teach or advise disobedience thereto.[58]

To new U.S. Attorney George Peters, then, fell the task of instituting proceedings to forfeit and escheat to the government the affected property of the Mormon church. One gets the feeling that Peters, who had practiced law for fourteen years in Columbus, Ohio, either lacked self-confidence or was incompetent. A letter to President Cleveland had warned at the time of Peters's appointment that everyone in Columbus knew "that he is as innocent of legal knowledge as an unborn babe." The files of the Department of Justice are full of requests by Peters for help; he asked that either the department send an attorney to aid him, or that the attorney general send him a brief for use in the church property cases. "If left alone," Peters added, "of course I will do the best I can." Writing to Peters, the attorney general seemed unusually worried and urged him to "prepare carefully," to be fully familiar with pertinent points of law. "Do not leave anything legitimate undone to insure success," wrote Solicitor General George A. Jenks, adding that the department would send an attorney to aid Peters if this became absolutely necessary. Finally, Attorney General Garland wrote to Colorado's U.S. attorney, Henry W. Hobson, "Go to Salt Lake City as soon as possible to assist. . . . Do not fail."[59]

When Hobson arrived, he found that Peters had asked that a receiver be appointed to gather together the church property affected by the Edmunds-Tucker Act, on the grounds that the Mormon church had been taking action to scatter and hide this property. Unfortunately, Hobson reported to the department, Peters had been able to gather little evidence of the church's actions, because "the Mormons had run off all the witnesses." After consulting with Peters, "he and I adopted the policy of making a great noise about the testimony we were going to put in, and we got the other side a little scared for fear we would open up things a good deal more than they wished. Really we could not have done so, but they did not know how much testimony we had."[60] As a result, the church attorneys agreed to a statement of facts admitting that, in Hobson's words, "the church has been making away with its property."[61]

The court agreed to the appointment of a receiver and named U.S. Marshal Frank H. Dyer. Instituting suits to recover church property, Dyer hired, as his counsel, Attorney George Peters. The Justice Department was never comfortable with two of its employees involved in this way, but it stopped short of requiring them to drop their roles as receiver and counsel, respectively. Later, when Dyer sought compensation of $25,000 as receiver, and Peters $10,000 as special counsel, great disgust was voiced by the attorney general and many congressmen. Not only did these sums seem especially high, but the attorney general pointed out that, as Justice Department employees, Dyer and Peters should have been working to keep the church property intact; in seeking to attach $35,000 of the property, they were working against the government's interests. Hobson was again sent to Salt Lake City, where he spoke out against the exorbitant compensation; he urged the court to delay the granting of any compensation, since it was possible that the U.S. Supreme Court would nullify all the proceedings and return the property to the church. Hobson added, "No man is more earnest than I in desiring to break up this church so far as it is in opposition to the laws of this country, but we should proceed with due regard for the law." The court took Hobson's advice and postponed the matter of compensation; eventually, Dyer received $10,000 for his services, while Peters was allowed $4,000.[62]

Soon after Dyer had assumed the position of receiver, Wilford Woodruff, the heir apparent to the leadership of the Mormon church, wrote in a letter to a friend: "Well[,] lightning has just struck; Dyer the marshal came and turned us all out. . . . They demand our Money, our Bank Notes, but miss much—as they are on the warpath they must find those if they can. I don't know where the End is but it must come to an end sometime—there is no road without a turne [sic]."[63]

In due time, Dyer was able to gather together over $1 million in real and personal property of the church. The Edmunds-Tucker Act had earmarked the escheated property for the use of Utah's public schools—presumably, this would help "Americanize" the disloyal territory—but before Utah's admission as a state the property was returned to the church, less the sums already expended.[64]

By the end of 1888 attorneys for the United States and those for the church had settled the many and complex suits and other proceedings, in order that the validity of the Edmunds-Tucker Act might be tested before the U.S. Supreme Court. Peters and Hobson sent their notes and briefs to Solicitor General Jenks. Hobson emphasized that, although the church attorneys would argue "vested rights" and cite the *Dartmouth College* case, the Utah legislature had had, in reality, no right to charter the Mormon church—the legislature had violated the constitutional provision respecting "the establishment of religion."[65] Peters, in his brief, pointed out that, although the Edmunds-Tucker Act might seem harsh, Congress has almost unlimited power to govern the territories. Peters added that the Utah law incorporating the Mormon church was subject to congressional disapproval, as was any other territorial law.[66]

The brief that Attorney General Garland and Solicitor General Jenks prepared for use in *The Late Corporation of the Church of Jesus Christ of Latter-day Saints v. United States* made these same points but went on to argue that Congress had the right to dissolve the charter of a corporation that flagrantly misused its powers: "Bigamy is a crime, and has been since 1862, in the Territories of the United States. Being a crime it affects the public well-being and morals. . . . This corporation maintained and spread the practice of polygamy, which is immoral and criminal. It therefore became a fit subject for the application of the police powers as applied by Congress in the passage of the acts of 1862 and 1887."[67] This final point especially impressed the high court, which sustained the validity of the Edmunds-Tucker Act and the actions taken by federal officials thereunder. Since church funds had been used to attempt "to oppose, thwart, and subvert the legislation of Congress and the will of the government of the United States," Congress had been justified in moving against this property. The high court handed down this decision in May 1890.[68]

The Republican Benjamin Harrison was elected president in 1888, temporarily displacing the Democrat Cleveland. Peters was removed, and in January 1890 Charles Stetson Varian was named to take his place. Varian has already been mentioned as an assistant U.S. attorney under W. H. Dickson; a native of Ohio, Varian was forty-three years old at the time of his appointment. He had lived in Nevada for fifteen years, holding a number of offices including speaker of the state House of Representatives and U.S. attorney, before coming to Utah with his law partner W. H. Dickson in 1882. Varian had served as assistant U.S. attorney from 1884 to 1887.[69]

In 1890 the situation of the Mormon church in Utah was this: For many decades, its members had been contracting plural marriages they believed to be sanctioned by God, and by their marriages they had developed family ties that were doubtless as strong or stronger than those developed by non-Mormons. The Mormon church had been actively involved in the economic and political life of the territory because its leaders conceived of a church that was central in all aspects of its members' lives. But now, the church had been disincorporated, its property forfeited; many of its members were disfranchised, barred from juries, and disqualified for public office. Children of plural marriages had been declared by congressional enactment to be bastards and were thus disinherited. More than a thousand Mormon men had been convicted of polygamy or unlawful cohabitation, while many others were resisting arrest on the "underground." No end to arrests and convictions was in sight. Gentiles were beginning to win local elections, and Congress seemed to be giving favorable consideration to a law that would disfranchise citizens for mere membership in the Mormon church, a law that the Supreme Court had hinted would be valid.[70]

At last, President Woodruff came to the "turn in the road" he had earlier foreseen, and he issued his famous manifesto, dated September 27, 1890. The manifesto stated that he, Woodruff, planned to obey all the laws of Congress and advised members of the church to do likewise. The General Conference of the church accepted the manifesto as "authoritative and binding." That the manifesto was of God was demonstrated by George Q. Cannon, who read from the sacred Book of Doctrines and Covenants: "Verily, verily I say unto you, that when I give a commandment to any of the sons of men, to do a work unto my name, . . . and their enemies come upon them and hinder them from performing that work; behold, it behoveth me to require that work no more at the hands of those sons of men."[71]

Shortly after the issuance of the manifesto, Attorney General William H. H. Miller wrote to Varian suggesting the propriety of moving "somewhat slowly" against those who had violated the Edmunds Act in the past. "It is true," he admitted, "I do not feel entirely clear that this manifesto will be acted upon in all cases in good faith," and Varian should not dismiss pending cases but continue them. "We ought not to discourage, but encourage parties who may be disposed to act under [the manifesto] in good faith." What had been wanted all along, Miller reasoned, was the suppression of polygamy, and not mere punishment;

"if the practices cease we may well afford to be magnanimous as to past offenses."[72]

Varian, however, disagreed in part. While he did feel that "much consideration should be given to this misguided people," he doubted the wisdom of continuing pending cases. Varian pointed out that those who promised future obedience to the laws were given nominal sentences. What the U.S. attorney found particularly troubling was the fact that the manifesto seemed to touch only the formation of new marriages—what of the existing ones? Speaking more reassuringly, he told the attorney general that "you may rest assured that no harshness, or even imprudence . . . shall prevail in the administration of the laws at this critical period." What Varian proposed was a test of the church's sincerity. Many Gentiles in Utah suspected that Woodruff had issued the manifesto in hopes of achieving Utah's speedy admission as a state. After that, with Utah much less subject to the control of Congress, the practice of plural marriage might be resumed. Varian informed Miller that a number of polygamy cases were about to be tried at Ogden. Rather than continue the cases, as Miller suggested, Varian recommended proceeding, then asking those convicted to promise to obey the Edmunds Act. In the past, the U.S. attorney asserted, those who promised obedience had been publicly denounced by the church press; it would be enlightening to see if the church or its press acted differently now.[73]

U.S. Attorney Varian also had the opportunity to question President Woodruff directly as to the meaning of the manifesto. In proceedings to decide the disposition of the property escheated to the United States, the church leaders were anxious to prove that the church was no longer in opposition to any law of the United States—the church hoped to recover some or all of the property, for use in building and maintaining places of worship, and for other charitable purposes. Wilford Woodruff was sworn and questioned by Varian. Varian read what seemed to be ambiguous passages from the manifesto, then questioned Woodruff closely as to their meaning. Woodruff made it explicit that the manifesto was intended to call on Mormons to dissolve all existing polygamous relationships. Gradually, federal judges and attorneys began to show less zeal in seeking the conviction of longtime polygamists; in the words of one historian, "Gentiles became willing to wink at long-established polygamous relationships." Prosecution under the Edmunds Act continued at a lesser rate for a few years, drawing to a close by 1894. The Mormon

Attorney General William H. H. Miller instructed the federal attorney in Utah to move slowly against polygamists in the wake of the Woodruff Manifesto: "We ought not to discourage, but encourage parties who may be disposed to act under it in good faith." Courtesy of U.S. Library of Congress.

church published a report early in the twentieth century, giving the number of polygamous families in 1890 as 2,451, in 1899 as 1,543, and in 1903 as 897. From time to time even today, newspapers report instances of "fundamentalist Mormons" who have returned to the practice of plural marriage, but it is sometimes difficult to arouse the interest of federal or local prosecutors.[74]

II

The preceding section was designed to answer the question: Who were the Justice Department officials in Utah and what did they do? There remain questions as to the caliber of the attorneys and marshals, their motivations and ideologies, the obstacles they encountered in performing their duties, and the aid they received.

Perhaps no aid received was more important than that supplied by the U.S. Army. The strongest symbols of federal power in Utah were the courts and the army. These two institutions had a reciprocal relationship, each offering aid to, and requiring aid of, the other. Early in the 1870s, when there was a lack of funds for judicial business in the territory, Marshal M. T. Patrick found himself unable to afford guards or food for his prisoners. With the permission of the commanding officer at Camp Douglas, Lieutenant Colonel Henry A. Morrow, Patrick kept prisoners at the base, where they were fed, quartered, and guarded by the army. Such actions were common throughout the 1870s, until Congress began making special appropriations for Utah's judicial expenses.[75]

There was never large-scale armed conflict between the Mormons and the army during this period, but minor confrontations were not uncommon. Many non-Mormons were of the opinion that, in the words of the *Salt Lake Tribune*, "the presence of an American soldier on the streets of Salt Lake City has about the same effect upon the temper of a Latter-day priest as the waving of a scarlet banner before the eyes of a taurine quadruped. A solitary blue coat, with army buttons, has frequently been the signal for our city police to fall upon the wearer like wolves thirsting for a lamb's blood."[76] The *Tribune*, a Gentile paper, neglected to mention that the "lambs" thus fallen upon were often drunk and disorderly.

Typical of these unhappy incidents was the case of Private Thomas Hackett. Hackett, allegedly intoxicated on the streets of Salt Lake City, pushed one Solomon P. McCurdy, an elderly retired judge, into a muddy ditch. Hackett was arrested and jailed by city officials. Colonel Morrow, acting under standing orders to "liberate and return to your command, by force if necessary," soldiers detained in this way, sent a detachment to ask for the release of Hackett. When city officials refused to surrender the hapless prisoner, soldiers of the Second Cavalry battered the door of the jail with a telegraph pole, and Hackett, thinking himself a hero, leapt to freedom—and was collared by an officer and carried to the guardhouse at Camp Douglas. As a result of this incident, the city authorities sued Morrow for $3,000 in damages, and U.S. Attorney Carey successfully defended him. Within two months, to prevent further friction, the army erected a guardhouse in Salt Lake City for the detention of disorderly soldiers.[77]

U.S. attorneys sometimes overstepped the bounds of decency in making requests of the army. After the second trial of John D. Lee for his role in the Mountain Meadows massacre, Lee was held at Camp Cameron pending execution. Meanwhile, U.S. Attorney Sumner Howard requested a body of soldiers to guard Lee on the day of his execution and to "shoot him under the sentence of the court and the direction of the marshal." Attorney General Alphonso Taft replied somewhat curtly that troops were not to be used in matters of civil justice, although if a military guard were essential to prevent Lee's release, it would be provided.[78]

In other "church murder cases" Sumner Howard counted on the military to prevent the outbreak of violence during the arrest of Mormon suspects, then complained to Attorney General Devens that, just as arrests were about to be made, the force at Fort Douglas was being reduced. Devens answered that the troops unfortunately were needed for the Indian wars, but he warned that the marshal should not make arrests "until the military is ready to sustain." If there were not enough troops in Utah to back up the marshal, Devens would attempt to have President Hayes send more.[79]

In 1886, when President George Q. Cannon was finally located and arrested for unlawful cohabitation, troops were used to escort the marshal and his prisoner to Salt Lake City, the deputy marshal having reported "intense excitement" there over Cannon's arrest. The incidents here recounted are intended as examples only, as there were dozens of cases in which military escorts were provided to the U.S. marshal, or federal prisoners were kept at military bases because of a lack of funds or for additional security. It should also be added that the army and Justice Department officials aided each other in many matters that had nothing to do with the Mormons—for instance, U.S. Attorney Varian obtained an injunction to stop the Salt Lake Rock Company from polluting the water supply of Fort Douglas.[80]

Another form of aid that benefited U.S. attorneys and marshals in the performance of their duties came from the Justice Department itself, in the form of authorization for special detectives and the offer of rewards. As late as December 1878 Attorney General Devens complained to Congress that his office was "not provided with the means of any general system of investigation of infractions of the laws." Only six months later U.S. Attorney Van Zile wrote to Devens, suggesting that he be authorized to hire detectives who would gather evidence of polygamous marriages. With proper evidence, Van Zile reported, "I could make Mormonism shake in her boots before next January." Devens answered, "I desire to assist you all in my power," and he sent the paltry sum of $200. Van Zile, obviously taken aback, acknowledged receipt of the money and promised, "I shall undertake to use this carefully and make it accomplish as much as possible."[81]

Several years later Van Zile's successor W. H. Dickson also wrote to the Justice Department, suggesting a "secret detective service" to uncover violations of the Edmunds Act. Dickson pointed out that most Mormons who could afford it maintained separate residences for their wives and claimed to be living with only one. But, doubtless, "the husband visits and cohabits with all of them in turn. These visits are made under the cover of darkness and with all possible secrecy." Without a detective service, Dickson concluded, some convictions of the "masses" might be possible, but no more, and he felt it was important that the church leaders be made to "realize the efficacy of the law and feel its might." Attorney General Brewster approved of Dickson's plan and sent $600. Samuel H. Gilson was the first detective hired, and he quickly obtained evidence that resulted directly in the indictment of ten important Mormon leaders, including the editor of the *Deseret News*, the president of the Salt Lake stake, and one of the twelve apostles of the Mormon church.[82]

Shortly after this, U.S. Marshal Elwin A. Ireland also requested special funds from the department, this time for the hire of additional deputies for use in serving process. Although it was possible to serve warrants and subpoenas in the cities, Ireland reported that in rural areas he encountered many obstacles, and the citizens resisted "by every means short of violence." Sheriffs, deputies, town police, and even telegraphers and railroad men were used to watch the marshal and his deputies "and to aid criminals and witnesses in escaping." When he asked to buy food in isolated areas he was told that "his kind is not wanted here" and was refused. The only hope was to strike at an unusual hour and round up the witnesses "like a lot of wild cattle," but this would require many deputies, which would require special funds. This time, Attorney General Brewster wrote back that no special fund for use of the marshal was necessary but that, if Ireland would seek the department's permission for special deputies in each case, the hire of such deputies would usually be approved. In 1886 Congress provided an appropriation of $5,000 for "more effective prosecution of crimes in Utah," and much of this money was used for the hire of additional deputies when needed.[83]

In addition to funds supplied for detectives and deputy marshals, the Justice Department also supplied funds for rewards from time to time. U.S. Commissioner William McKay first recommended that a reward be offered for the arrest of President John Taylor, who was charged with unlawful cohabitation; McKay was of the opinion that "nothing but money will bring him from under his dung hill." U.S. Attorney Dickson, although more refined in his choice of words, also had a low opinion of Taylor, and he told Attorney General Garland, "It is evident that he lacks the courage to meet the consequences of his transgressions, and this gives reason to hope that if he were placed under arrest and compelled to answer for his crime, he would, rather than suffer imprisonment himself, counsel his followers to yield obedience to the laws."[84]

Taylor was never arrested; he died "on the underground" in 1887. The department's offer of a $500 reward for President George Q. Cannon had the desired result, however. Cannon, who, like Taylor, was charged with unlawful cohabitation, was betrayed and captured in 1886.

Although U.S. attorneys and marshals enjoyed the support of the Justice Department in the matter of detectives and the offer of rewards, the attorney general and his assistants were in other ways utterly useless to the officials in Utah. When asked for advice or instructions, the attorneys general almost invariably had none to give. The majority of U.S. attorneys wrote to Washington shortly after their appointment, asking the attorney general for general instructions. Sumner Howard wrote, "I most respectfully ask you to send me such general and special instructions as you may have to give." His request was ignored. Philip Van Zile asked the attorney general for a statement of the policy of the Department of Justice. Attorney General Devens's answer was framed in the usual way: "You speak of your desire to consult with me as to a settled policy to be pursued. I do not think this is necessary. It is our settled policy to enforce the laws of the United States firmly and resolutely, but judiciously. . . . In regard to any further indications of a settled policy I cannot make them."[85]

Nor were the attorneys general more helpful when specific problems were submitted. U.S. Attorney George Caesar Bates complained to the department that there were no funds to try Brigham Young—"What are we to do? That's the question." Bates's request for help or advice was ignored, and he wrote again, chastising the attorney general for failing to respond, "and I am left to grope on." Bates finally began issuing orders to the attorney general, telegraphing, "Instruct me to postpone causes until March and report to Congress in person." When Van Zile wished to come to Washington to discuss several important cases with Attorney General Devens, Devens discouraged him, saying that "it would be impossible either for myself or any of my assistants to go over with you the detail of the various cases in Utah." U.S. attorneys were expected to make the important decisions, Devens concluded. In this instance, as in so many others in the late nineteenth century, the attorney general clung to the old notion of the law as a solitary and independent profession, while his subordinates in the field discerned the value of a true bureaucracy, with clear statements of policy and a regular exchange of ideas between the department head and his officers.[86]

The refusal of attorneys general to give general or specific advice, although common, was not invariable. It has already been mentioned that Solicitor General Jenks sent a good deal of advice to lawyer George Peters in the church property cases, and in other instances, too, specific advice was given. General advice was occasionally sent from Washington, as when Attorney General Garland mused in 1885, "Perhaps the practice of polygamy may be more successfully met by the conviction of large offenders than by the conviction of every offender in the community."[87]

If the Justice Department often left the U.S. attorneys to "grope on," it was not always averse to sending advice or veiled instructions to the

In a rare policy statement by a U.S. attorney general, Augustus Hill Garland told his subordinates in Utah in 1885, "Perhaps the practice of polygamy may be more successfully met by the conviction of large offenders than by the conviction of every offender in the community." Courtesy of U.S. Library of Congress.

judges of the district courts. The true status of Utah's federal judges was never clear. The U.S. Supreme Court made it explicit in *Clinton et al. v. Englebrecht* that the judges were not analogous to U.S. judges in the various states (for instance, they did not enjoy lifetime tenure), but, clearly, the judges were not intended to be mere functionaries of the executive branch that appointed them. When, in 1875, Judge Jacob Boreman moved to force Brigham Young to pay alimony during the course of a divorce suit brought by a plural wife, Attorney General Edwards Pierrepont wrote to U.S. Attorney Carey that it was clear the alimony was improper, adding: "This is a matter of much importance and requires immediate attention. Consult with Judge Boreman at once. Show him this letter and suggest that he give careful consideration to the subject, and act discreetly and wisely in the matter. Report to this Department after your interview with the Judge, and give the results of that interview."[88] Pierrepont was clearly threatening to recommend Boreman's removal; the judge stiffly retorted, again through the intermediary Carey; "I have no answer to make, further than to say that the attorney general upon reflection will see that such a suggestion to a judicial officer is not proper." But Boreman did then go on to explain that, in ordering Brigham Young to pay alimony, he was only enforcing the earlier order of an earlier judge, and he had not been called on to reopen the case on its merits.[89]

Fifteen years later Attorney General William H. H. Miller wrote to U.S. Attorney Varian, suggesting leniency in the wake of the Woodruff Manifesto. The last sentence of Miller's letter reads, "Show this to the judges." Varian did as he was told. In at least one instance a Justice Department employee in Utah asked the attorney general to intercede with the district judges: Henry W. Hobson wrote to the attorney general in 1889, concerning the compensation of the receiver and his attorney in the church property cases. Hobson asked that Attorney General Garland write to the judges, urging delay in awarding the compensation: "A letter from you to that effect would have much more weight with the Court than any suggestion of mine."[90]

Clearly, the Justice Department had some power over the district judges of Utah. As the legal adviser to the president, the attorney general had a great deal to say about who would be appointed and who removed. By statute, the attorney general was given the responsibility of reviewing the judges' frequent requests for leaves of absence. But in spite of this, the attorney general, as a representative of the United States (often a party before the district courts), could not properly give advice or instructions to the judges. Nevertheless, he sometimes did so.

Evaluating the caliber of the men who served as U.S. attorneys and marshals is a difficult task. One reason for this is that most of them are truly forgotten men in U.S. history, men about whom very little can be known. Some U.S. attorneys are relatively well-known in Utah history (Baskin, Dickson, and Varian), while for others not even the skeleton of a biography can be constructed (Carey and Bates). Still others fall somewhere in between. The task of assessing most U.S. attorneys is, then, made difficult by the fact that we do not know where they were educated or what they did before they were U.S. attorneys, nor do we often know what they did after they left office. Judging their actual performance in office is also difficult. In writing to the Department of Justice, of course, they never declared themselves to be failures, while if someone else declared one to be a success or a failure, we have to wonder about the motivation of the person making the report. Utah in the 1870s and 1880s was a politically charged place, and Gentiles screamed for the removal of such slow-moving attorneys as Bates, while Mormons cried out for relief from aggressive prosecutors such as Dickson. In some instances—Sumner Howard, for example—both Gentiles and Mormons insisted on the removal of a U.S. attorney. Howard was neither corrupt nor unsuccessful as a prosecutor, and all we can assume is that he was personally repugnant to the people of Utah, or at least was politically unsuccessful in a place that was highly political.

That the caliber of the U.S. attorneys in Utah was high can be seen by the fact that they were greatly sought after as private attorneys after leaving office—most notably by the Mormon church. Charles Hempstead resigned from the U.S. attorneyship in 1871 because the compensation was too small; several months later he appeared in the district court as attorney for Brigham Young and defended him from the prosecutions of the new U.S. attorney, George Caesar Bates. Bates was removed from office in 1872, and he quickly surfaced as a church attorney. Even W. H. Dickson, that vigorous prosecutor of polygamists, defended the Mormon church after he left office, in the case of *The Late Corporation of the Church of Jesus Christ of Latter-day Saints v. United States*. The biggest catch by the Mormon church in its hiring of counsel was in the suits against the Utah commissioners: The church was able to hire the former U.S. attorney general, Wayne MacVeagh. Other U.S. attorneys went on to distinguished careers after leaving Utah; Sumner Howard served as a U.S. judge in Arizona, while Philip Van Zile became an author of legal textbooks published by West and other respected houses.[91]

If it is difficult to assess the caliber of the U.S. attorneys, it is doubly so with the marshals. For nearly every marshal, there is a large collection of letters in the Justice Department files alleging fraud and corruption, alongside other letters stoutly defending the marshal. The marshals excited controversy because they controlled a great deal of money, and because they were in charge of spending it—hiring deputies, renting court rooms, buying rations for prisoners, and contracting to enlarge the penitentiary. Those whom the marshal did not patronize with the government's funds often nursed grudges, and those who were upwardly mobile politically often sought the marshal's place. Those who were arrested and imprisoned by the marshal often developed a personal dislike of the man. Studies of other western territories show that charges against federal officers were more often based on emotionally charged politics than on actual misconduct. But in a few instances in Utah, marshals were dismissed with cause.[92]

Marshal George R. Maxwell was dismissed because his books were in total disarray—whether fraudulently or not was never conclusively settled. Marshal William Nelson was dismissed with cause early in 1878; one of the complaints against him was that he treated his prisoners harshly, hoping to induce them to inform on others. Marshal Frank H. Dyer, as mentioned above, sparked criticism for his role as receiver in the church property cases and for seeking compensation of $25,000 as receiver. Dyer was removed from office soon after the Republicans resumed control of the executive branch in 1889. But even under Democratic Attorney General Garland, Dyer had been investigated and found wanting. The Justice Department examiner reported that Dyer charged the government for seed potatoes, used federal prisoners to raise the potatoes, then sold the potatoes to the government for prison rations. Dyer charged the government for feed for his cows, used prisoners to tend the cows, and sold the milk to the government. In the face of this report, Garland calmly asked Dyer to consider mending his ways![93]

As with U.S. attorneys so with the marshals, biographical data is scarce. One common element in their biographies is service as a Union soldier. Marshal Maxwell suffered two broken legs and a broken collarbone early in the war; later, he lost three fingers and his left leg was amputated. The other marshals also served with valor in the Union army, although admittedly they bore fewer scars. Only Cleveland's appointee Frank H. Dyer was not a Union veteran; Dyer had supported the Confederacy.[94]

The work of the Justice Department in Utah was hindered by a number of obstacles. One of these was the low salary paid to U.S. attorneys: $250 per annum plus fees (this remuneration was uniform throughout the nation). One of the constant complaints of the attorney general was that he was unable to hold good men in U.S. attorney positions—private practice was so much more lucrative. So, in Utah, we have U.S. Attorney Hempstead resigning in 1871 because his fees were "a mere bagatelle"; we have George Caesar Bates telling the solicitor general that if he could only get his "official" cases out of the way, he hoped to "make a fortune out of mining litigation" on the side. Sumner Howard sent in his resignation in 1877, explaining that he had served as long as possible, suffering much pecuniary loss. In 1885 W. H. Dickson and his assistant submitted their resignations, their major motivation in so doing being the "utterly inadequate compensation." It is certain that these U.S. attorneys were not simply dropping hints, hoping to have their salaries raised; they knew that the attorney general did not have the power to raise their salaries, and their dissatisfaction with their remuneration was usually unvoiced until the time of their resignation.[95]

Another financial problem of U.S. attorneys and marshals was the lack of funds to carry on their official business. Each year, the attorney general complained to Congress that the Mormon-dominated legislature refused to pay its share of court expenses, and, after much delay, Congress usually provided the needed funds. In 1871 Charles Hempstead reported, "The courts are without a dollar with which to carry on their business." His letter was also signed by the three district judges, the marshal, the clerk of the Utah Supreme Court, and the acting governor. In this situation, Marshal M. T. Patrick eventually advanced the needed funds, taking out a loan in his own name and using his army pension, while Deputy Marshal B. L. "Pony" Duncan mortgaged some property to raise money. For lack of cash, jurors and witnesses were paid with "certificates of attendance," which were to be negotiable at some future date.[96]

Similar financial crises occurred almost yearly in this period. In 1886 Marshal Ireland telegraphed the Justice Department, "Courts in first second & third districts in session . . . Not a dollar for Jurors & Witnesses." In a follow-up letter, Ireland warned of the danger of postponing cases. The Mormon leaders, he wrote, "should not have an opportunity to delude and encourage their people in the belief that the government is relaxing in the slightest degree its efforts to enforce obedience to the laws." The attorney general, apprised of the crisis, began the slow process of seeking relief from Congress.[97]

Attorneys who came to Utah to serve the Justice Department found that, on the frontier, law offices were managed differently than those back east. Philip Van Zile reported to Attorney General Devens that, when he came to Utah, "I found the office in a perfect hurly-burly. No files of cases and papers all thrown in a heap." Similarly, George R. Maxwell recalled that, when he was first appointed marshal, he found "no court houses for the occupation & use of the U.S. Courts; no jails for the incarceration of U.S. prisoners; no records—no nothing, & all of which had to be provided at once; and no funds."[98]

Marshal Maxwell exaggerated when he said that there were no courthouses, for the courts always had places to meet, such as they were. When Judge Edward B. McKean issued his order ousting the territorial marshal, he found himself ousted from his courtroom by the Mormon landlords of the building. For one and a half years thereafter his court met in a hayloft over a livery stable. Different courtrooms were rented from time to time; for many years the federal courtrooms at Salt Lake were so positioned as to be offended by the stench from nearby privies—and were located below a brothel. In 1884 Attorney General Brewster, noting that the rooms above the courtroom "have a character that brings reproach upon the U.S. officers to some extent," ordered the marshal to take steps to rent the upper rooms as well, so as to remove "the objectionable parties."[99]

Perhaps the greatest hindrance to the U.S. attorneys and marshals in the performance of their duties was the fact that they were in effect in an "alien land," far from their friends and families and wholly ostracized from the close-knit Mormon majority. Marshal Maxwell entered into his duties with the announced intention of showing "malice toward none & charity towards all," but he felt that, because of the Mormons' failure "to obtain a convert & instrument in me," he became socially ostracized and the target "for their most malevolent & deadly shafts." Elwin A. Ireland, looking back on his service as marshal, recalled that "character, reputation, family, all were assailed by the Mormon people, and even attempts at assassination and bribery were not wanting." Assessing the position of a U.S. attorney in Utah, W. H. Dickson wrote in 1887 that no incumbent could honorably do his duty "and escape the bitter enmity of the vast majority of the people here—an enmity that is not always scrupulous in its methods."[100]

U.S. Attorney Varian, writing a brief account of his years in office, seemed particularly disturbed by the memory of an event that had occurred when he and W. H. Dickson had been invited to the Tabernacle to hear the Mormons' "declaration of grievances and protests." After the meeting, Varian recalled, he and Dickson had risen to go and had been booed and hissed by the vast crowd, composed largely of women. He attributed the crowd's actions to the continual verbal attacks made on U.S. authorities by church leaders; certainly, the federal attorney's role in prosecuting these women's husbands also played a part.[101]

A number of other incidents of greater and lesser severity serve to demonstrate the friction between Mormon citizens and Justice Department officials. One night in September 1884, unknown persons attacked the homes of Dickson, Varian, and U.S. Commissioner McKay, hurling glass jars full of human excrement through the windows, jars that broke on the interior walls and carpets.[102]

Also during the tenure of Dickson and Varian, members of the Salt Lake City police force and others initiated an undercover operation, hoping to induce federal officials to commit crimes of lust. A brothel was opened in the city, with secret compartments for observation provided, and prostitutes were imported. Off-duty police officers took turns watching at the peepholes, while the madam sent enticing notes to federal officeholders. The most important of the men thus ensnared was Assistant U.S. Attorney S. H. Lewis. Lewis was tried for "lewd and lascivious conduct" before a justice of the peace, and three men testified that they had watched the act of copulation through a peephole. Lewis was found guilty, and he took an appeal to the federal district court.[103]

The motive of the Mormons in the case is clear. The national press was full of talk about Mormon lust and licentiousness; the plan here was to show that the very men who were prosecuting polygamists were guilty of their own kind of lasciviousness. But before the federal court, Charles S. Varian defended his colleague and attacked the Mormon witnesses: "I do not believe any American jury would believe such infamous

Looking back on his service as Utah's federal marshal, Elwin A. Ireland recalled that "character, reputation, family, all were assailed by the Mormon people, and even attempts at assassination and bribery were not wanting." Courtesy of Utah State Historical Society.

scoundrels, who have crawled to the threshold of the house of the harlot." The judge agreed with Varian, pointing out that the police and their accomplices had committed a crime to induce others to commit crime, while the purpose of the law was to prevent crime. One of the policemen was later tried and convicted for his part in the "conspiracy to open a house of ill fame."[104]

In other cases armed conflict between U.S. officials and the Mormons was either threatened or consummated. On one occasion, during a trial in the "hayloft court," U.S. Attorney Carey was startled as the door opened with a violent slam, "and in rushed twenty or thirty stalwart men wearing pistols." These men were believed to be members of the "Danites," a militant group of Mormons. Carey and the judge ignored the "menacing group," and nothing further came of this attempt to intimidate the district court. In another instance in 1877 Sumner Howard brought Robert T. Burton before a U.S. commissioner, charging him with having committed murder in the Morrisite schism of 1862. Again the Danites, or men believed by Howard to be Danites, rushed in, and the commander of the Mormon militia entered and argued furiously. Howard and the commissioner were sufficiently intimidated to release Burton on bond. Howard reported, "It is very significant that Gen. Wells, their military leader, should be the first man to show a disposition to 'bulldoze' the courts." Howard promised to endeavor to "keep cool," but he sought and received assurances that the U.S. Army was ready to sustain him.[105]

In several instances friction between Justice Department officials and Mormons led to actual assault or gunplay. In November 1885 Deputy Marshal Henry F. Collin was waylaid and attacked in a dark alley by one or more men and was beaten; he managed to shoot one of his assailants and then fled. The injured man turned out to be Joseph W. McMurrin, a Mormon by faith and a watchman by trade. An investigation cleared Deputy Collin of any wrongdoing; McMurrin was too badly injured to come into court, and he finally fled to Europe. McMurrin had announced that his grudge again Collin was personal, but Charles S. Varian was of the opinion that "there is no doubt that Collin was attacked because of his zeal and efficiency as a deputy marshal." Only two weeks before the McMurrin assault, Deputy Collin had been attacked by Andrew D. Burt, sheriff of Salt Lake County. Burt believed that Collin was responsible for reports in the *Tribune* that Burt was a "spotter," a man who trailed the marshal and his deputies in order to keep the Mormons informed. Burt's only weapons were his fists, and Collin was not seriously injured. On another occasion the sons of George Q. Cannon, furious over their father's being brought to trial, assaulted prosecutor W. H. Dickson at the Continental Hotel.[106]

One final incident will be recounted here: the case of Deputy Marshal William Thompson, who, while attempting to arrest one Edward M. Dalton for unlawful cohabitation, shot and killed the fleeing suspect. Many were of the opinion that, because Dalton's crime was a mere misdemeanor, the deputy's actions were unwarranted. Deputy Thompson was charged with the territorial offense of manslaughter, and, as in all territorial criminal cases, the U.S. attorney (actually, his assistant Varian) was responsible for prosecuting. "It was the duty of the U.S. attorney to state the law governing the case to the court and jury," Varian wrote later, and he took the controversial step of announcing that, because of the wording of the territorial manslaughter statute and because of federal statutes dealing with marshals, Thompson was clearly not guilty. The Mormon community was furious at Varian's way of "prosecuting" Thompson, but the judge agreed with Varian and so charged the jury, which brought back an acquittal. Mormon leaders took their complaints directly to the Department of Justice but received no satisfaction; the *Deseret News* denounced Thompson and Varian as murderers and was quickly met with a libel suit that it settled out of court.[107]

The remaining question, and a very important one, is the question of the ideology and motivation of the U.S. attorneys: How did they see their role in Utah? How did they personally feel about the Mormon church and the institution of polygamy? In the absence of a "settled policy," did the U.S. attorneys serve without any direction from Washington?

One ideological tie bound together the U.S. attorneys in the period covered here: With one exception, all were Republicans. The one exception was Cleveland's appointee, George Peters. As has already been made clear, none of the U.S. attorneys was a Mormon. Another trait that binds together the U.S. attorneys is their invariable tendency to underestimate the tenacity of the Mormon church and the loyalty of polygamous Mormons to their plural families. Several hours after his arrival in Utah Territory in 1871, George Caesar Bates wrote to Attorney General Akerman: "I can see clearly . . . that Judge McKean and I can within six months Enforce the Law, End Polygamy, and Give Peace to this beautiful Territory." In 1879 Philip Van Zile reported to the attorney general, "A few convictions of the 'big fellows' would settle the matter of polygamy"; and in February 1885 W. H. Dickson assured his superiors in Washington that "within one year if the present pressure on the guilty is continued . . . the church will command submission to the laws."[108]

Although federal efforts against polygamy, especially in the 1880s, have often been portrayed as a crusade by Protestant Christians against the Mormon church, the U.S. attorneys do not fit into this model. After extensive research, it has been possible to link only one of the nine federal attorneys examined here with Protestant religion; if the others were church members, they were not very vocal about it. Of the two great leaders of the alleged crusade, it is enlightening to note that Chief Justice Zane was an agnostic, and prosecutor C. S. Varian was a Unitarian. What disturbed Justice Department officials in Utah about the Mormon church was not the religious side of the issues, but the social and political side. Polygamy was wrong because Congress had passed a law prohibiting it, also because the monogamous family was considered a cornerstone of U.S. civilization. The Mormon church was wrong because it sought to maintain a strong political and economic role, and this was un-American. Despite the fact that a number of Mormon beliefs were repugnant to Protestant Christianity, only the illegal and socially wrong institution of plural marriage was noticed by U.S. attorneys.[109]

What was important to the U.S. attorneys can be most convincingly seen by looking at their own writings. Over and over, W. H. Dickson reported to the attorney general that "the Mormon masses are today arrayed against the enforcement of the laws of the United States." In 1914, looking back at his service as U.S. attorney, Charles S. Varian recalled, "Practically an entire people were in open hostility and rebellion against the government of the United States." Confronted with this perceived rebellion, the U.S. attorneys were not content merely to prosecute cases under the laws. They became lobbyists, orators, movers, activists.[110]

Perusing the Justice Department files, one is struck by the vast numbers of requests for leaves of absence by Utah's federal attorneys—did these men really vacation so extensively? Then one notices the reasons given for the requested leave: "to come to Washington at my own expense." In Washington the attorneys (and marshals, too) lobbied Congress, nagged the attorney general, assisted in arguments before the Supreme Court, even met with the president. As early as 1870 U.S. Attorney ad interim Robert N. Baskin was in Washington lobbying for the

After he had left federal service, former U.S. Attorney Charles S. Varian declared of the Mormons that "practically an entire people were in open hostility and rebellion against the government of the United States." Courtesy of Utah State Historical Society.

Cullom bill, which, although introduced by Congressman Shelby Cullom of Illinois, was, in the words of Brigham Young, "concocted in Salt Lake City by a pettifogger named Baskin." The Cullom bill passed the House but stalled in the Senate. The Poland Act later supplied the relief Baskin had worked for, and he was involved in lobbying for that piece of legislation as well. Marshal Maxwell, too, was active in lobbying for the Poland Act. Facing complete paralysis of Utah's federal courts, Maxwell spent eight months in Washington at his own expense, meeting with congressmen.[111]

Only months after the passage of the Edmunds Act U.S. Attorney Van Zile was in Washington pushing for further legislation; Van Zile reported that the Edmunds Act would work "in the course of time, but it would be a hundred years." The U.S. attorneys also lobbied when a judgeship was vacant or about to be vacated—for instance, William Carey led the fight to save the zealous Edward B. McKean from removal, but to no avail.[112]

As mentioned earlier, only one of the U.S. attorneys can be linked to organized Protestant religion—Philip Van Zile—and in fact he seems to be linked by written records to the Congregational church on only one occasion. But he chose an excellent occasion on which to speak out against polygamy: He prepared an address, not for a single church, but for the annual conference of all Congregational churches in his home state of Michigan. The address, titled "The Twin Relic," was prepared in written form and sent to Michigan, where it was read before the conference. The address is in fact the most outspoken condemnation of polygamy by any Justice Department official. Van Zile began by pointing out that polygamy undermined the family, which was a cornerstone of U.S. civilization. The Mormon wife, instead of being a properly loving wife and mother, "is reduced to a mere animal or machine. She no longer lives, she simply exists, to be used by, and to serve the foul purposes of a licentious beastly man." Van Zile's lurid words were tailored to a church audience, which would certainly have been less interested in a detailed legal treatment of "the Utah question." It is certain that Van Zile's moral polemic furnished the fodder for many an antipolygamy sermon in the churches of Michigan, and hence his address reached and influenced a great many people.[113]

Van Zile also reached out to the East in other ways. In December 1880 the editor of the Chicago *Inter-Ocean*, an important Republican organ, wrote to Van Zile: "The *Inter-Ocean* has some pronounced views on the Mormon question, and we are quite impatient because nothing is done.

We do not wish to accuse yourself and your colleagues of a lack of zeal, but we know of no reason why we should not do so."[114] The editor, William E. Curtis, concluded by asking Van Zile to supply the name of someone in Utah who might keep the *Inter-Ocean* apprised of the situation there. Van Zile volunteered his own services. No longer addressing a church audience, the attorney used reasoned political arguments in writing for the Republican paper. "The true Americans in Utah are the Gentiles and Apostates," began one Van Zile editorial. All that the Gentiles wanted, he added, was "to see the 'Mormons' obey the law and respect the government of the United States." Again intimating that the Edmunds Act would not be sufficient to end polygamy and the political domination of the Mormon church, Van Zile urged, "Turn over the Territory of Utah into the hands of loyal, true Americans, no matter if it falls into the hands of but ten men." Van Zile continued, "The North was right when it said men who were disloyal should be disfranchised, and the government of the Southern states turned over to those who obey the law and love their country, and her institutions. And was that principle any more right then than now?"[115]

Van Zile even attempted to stimulate the interest of the president in the Mormon question. In September 1879 he sent Rutherford B. Hayes a copy of a lurid, anonymous pamphlet titled "The Mormon Endowment House! Graphic Exposure of the Treasonable Institution Where Polygamous Marriages are Solemnized."[116]

W. H. Dickson, too, in the mid-1880s sought to serve as a molder of national opinion. Dickson had his opportunity when members of the Grand Army of the Republic, a powerful veterans' organization, stopped in Salt Lake on their way to a huge "encampment" in San Francisco. At the "campfire" held in Salt Lake City, the veterans were greeted by a banner that read pointedly, "Our Loyal People Welcome the Country's Veterans." Dickson was asked to address the meeting and, like Van Zile, tailored his argument to fit his audience. "The Mormon church is steeped in disloyalty," Dickson began. "The people who are adherents of this church are steeped in disloyalty." Church leaders regularly preached "that the government was the enemy of the Mormon church." Dickson specifically asked the Union veterans to support him in his call for disfranchisement of the Mormons: "Why should the government hesitate to wrest from these disloyal citizens the ballot? The people here do not really exercise the franchise. They do as they are told."[117]

Dickson included at the beginning, middle, and end of his speech a very direct request that the veterans attempt to stir up national public opinion. He said at one point, "I say to each one of you, when you go back to your homes in the East, do not forget us; talk these things over with your neighbors, until the popular sentiment becomes aroused." One of the Grand Army leaders, General James Beaver of Pennsylvania (himself a lawyer and Republican politician) responded to Dickson's speech by saying that this was a great opportunity "for the government to show its power." The Mormon *Deseret News* noted sourly that Dickson's speech "made the heart of every man who had worn the blue beat as it had not done for twenty years." In one final effort to make his words count, Dickson had his speech printed in pamphlet form for broad distribution.[118]

The U.S. attorneys, then, played a major role as lobbyists, movers, and molders of opinions. But what was their relationship to the national political scene? To what extent were these attorneys playing out a role assigned them by the federal bureaucracy in Washington? To what extent were the U.S. attorneys molded by Congress, the president, and the attorney general? It is easiest to dismiss first of all the attorneys general. In questions relating to polygamy and the Mormon church, the nation's chief legal officer was surprisingly passive. Each December the attorneys general made their annual report to Congress, the most important part of which contained suggestions for legislation. The attorneys general sought, year after year, the necessary weapons to enforce the existing acts of Congress. But not one ever suggested stronger measures against polygamy or ever suggested action against the Mormon church. Most commonly, the attorney general asked for funds for his subordinates in Utah who were left poor by the Utah legislature's failure to deliver the needed funds. And in 1877 the attorney general reported that the Poland Act was deficient in one respect: The jury panels therein provided were too small, so the marshal was often left with insufficient jurors. The attorneys general viewed themselves as counsel for the president and department heads, as counsel for the United States before the Supreme Court (along with the solicitor general), and as general supervisor to U.S. attorneys and marshals. Legislative leadership seemed to play little role in their self-perception, hence they were not lobbyists for stringent anti-Mormon legislation and were not outspoken against the evils of polygamy or the danger of theocracy.[119]

U.S. presidents, on the other hand, showed real leadership and strength of purpose on the Utah question. Although recent historians of U.S. bureaucracy speak disparagingly of the power of the president in the late nineteenth century, presidents did exercise a major leadership role on the question of polygamy. Speaking of the Mormons, Grant told Congress in a special message in 1873 that "no class of persons anywhere should be allowed to treat the laws of the United States with open defiance and contempt." Hayes had other worries: that polygamy threatened "the sanctity of marriage and the family relation," which was "the cornerstone of our society and civilization." Hayes also worried that Utah was not open to general immigration from the states, because of "intolerant and immoral institutions." Any Mormons who were listening to the inaugural address of James A. Garfield must have been given hope as he lamented the fact that "the Constitutional guarantee of freedom of religion is not upheld in Utah," but Garfield quickly made it clear that he was not speaking out against congressional abridgment of the rights of the Mormon people; his concern was that there was an "established religion" in the territory. Chester Arthur asked Congress to attack the law-defying Mormons with "the stoutest weapons which Constitutional legislation can fashion"; his pet plan was to dissolve every existing part of Utah's government and to replace it with a "governing commission." Even the Democrat Grover Cleveland, reputed to be friendly to the Mormons, reported that after the disfranchisement of twelve thousand Mormons, elected officials in Utah were still men who upheld polygamy. "Thus is the strange spectacle presented of a community . . . sustaining by their suffrage a principle and a belief which set at naught that obligation of absolute obedience to the law of the land." With the support of the president, a majority of congressmen were usually willing to pass legislation attacking "polygamy and theocracy."[120]

Several recent studies of federal legal action in Utah in the late nineteenth century have been unsympathetic to the national government. One of the chief complaints raised is the fact that, although Congress claimed to be moving against the sexual sin of polygamy, the courts construed the Edmunds Act crime of "unlawful cohabitation" so loosely that prosecutors did not need to prove sexual intercourse or even the sharing of a bedroom.[121] Of course, this kind of complaint is flawed on its face. Federal officials never claimed that their efforts against the Mormons were simply aimed at sexual sins; these efforts were aimed at crushing unwanted, un-American diversity and what was seen as "theocracy" in Utah Territory. Lurid stories of polygamy were useful in marshaling public opinion, but plural marriage was clearly only one target of federal action. Still, complaints might be made about the courts' handling of cases such as *United States v. Cannon*.[122]

A grand jury indicted Angus M. Cannon in February 1885, charging him with unlawful cohabitation with two plural wives. When the case came to trial Cannon offered to prove that he had entered into a pact of nonintercourse with his second, extralegal wife. He pointed out that, although his two wives still lived under his roof, he slept with only one. The two wives had separate living quarters and separate kitchens; Cannon ate meals with each in turn. The U.S. attorney argued that questions of sexual intercourse and shared bedrooms were immaterial in proving cohabitation. The judge agreed and charged the jury: "It is not necessary that the evidence should show that the defendant and these women, or either of them, occupied the same bed or slept in the same room," nor was it necessary that the prosecution prove that the defendant "had sexual intercourse with either of them." Cannon was convicted and sentenced to six months in jail, with a $300 fine. The U.S. Supreme Court upheld his conviction.[123]

The prosecutor and trial judge believed that Cannon was a proper target for federal prosecution because, by living with both his wife and former plural wife under the same roof, "he held them out to the world . . . as his wives."[124] Some recent historians have argued that under rulings such as *Cannon* a defendant would be convicted not because of his actions but because local public opinion believed that he was still the husband of a plural wife.[125] But it certainly could be argued that living under the same roof with a plural wife was an "action" in violation of federal law. Other cases proved more complex.

Orson P. Arnold, for example, was indicted for cohabitation in 1885; he pled guilty and promised to withdraw from his second wife, Fanny. But one year later Arnold was indicted again for cohabitation with two women—with his legal wife and with his plural wife Fanny. In this case, prosecutors admitted that Fanny was now living in a separate house. The crucial testimony was over the continued social relations of Arnold with Fanny. Some of these relations could be explained on humanitarian grounds—the defendant's visits to Fanny's sickbed, for example, and an all-night visit when their infant daughter was ill. But prosecutors argued that there was no "explanation" for an overnight trip to Ogden (Arnold and Fanny had separate hotel rooms with a connecting door); neighbors testified that Arnold escorted Fanny and her sister home from the theater on a number of occasions; and Fanny testified that she had invited Arnold to take dinner with her and the children several times, and he had accepted.[126]

Arnold was found guilty despite the lack of a shared residence. Again, the test for the court was whether Arnold by his public actions "indicated to the world that he was visiting and associating with his wife as her husband."[127] A case such as Arnold's brings up another thorny question, and that is the matter of support of former plural wives and their children. Several historians have argued that federal policy was heartless, since it called on Mormon men to abandon their former plural wives and children, leaving them without food or shelter.[128]

Actually, the courts seemed to take the attitude that husbands might support their former plural wives and children if done very quietly and impersonally (so as not to "hold out" the woman to the world as a wife).[129] But this continued to be a muddled legal question and was not cleared up during the six-year period of vigorous prosecution. The federal government constructed an institution for women who were abandoned in Utah or who wanted to leave their plural husbands, but few women sought shelter there.[130] Certainly, the Mormon church, which was largely responsible for the flood of plural marriages performed after 1862 in defiance of federal law, could have provided food and shelter for any families that were abandoned. Admittedly, the church's power to do this would have waned by 1888, as the federal government began to seize its property. But the reality seems to be that homeless and hungry wives and children were more a potential evil cited by the Mormons' lawyers than an existing problem.[131]

Justice Department officials in Utah during the 1870s and 1880s are without a doubt controversial figures. Mormons complained that attorneys and marshals worked to break up families, to disfranchise citizens, even to disincorporate a church and seize its property. Certainly, this chapter in U.S. history provides the greatest example of the federal government's moving against an organized religion.

But the federal officials who moved against polygamy and church control in Utah were sure that almost everything that was American was threatened there—never mind that the Mormons often professed patriotism. The monogamous family was threatened in Utah; the separation of church and state was threatened there; the tradition of nonsectarian public schools was threatened. The Republican and Democratic parties failed to take root in Utah. Trends toward private enterprise, so strong in the East, were not followed in Utah, where collectivism overseen by the church was the pattern. In the wake of the Civil War, with a newly strong federal government, great pride was taken in the fact that the United States was no longer a mere collection of states and territories but was a single, increasingly unified and homogeneous nation. Utah threatened this and was thus targeted for action first by the president and Congress, and then by the lawyers, marshals, and clerks of the Justice Department bureaucracy.

Utah emerged from the great struggle a more conventionally American place, with a strong Gentile community living peacefully alongside the Mormon majority, a working system of public schools, and legitimate two-party politics. On January 4, 1896, a great celebration in Salt Lake City marked the achievement of statehood. Sharing the glory that day were Mormons and Methodists, Republicans and Democrats, U.S. troops and the local Utah National Guard. The national government by its actions had made certain that unwanted diversity would be kept out of the Union. By 1896 Utah was, for better or worse, a place similar in most important respects to the nation of states that it joined.

4

Guarding the Treasury in the Southern Highlands
Federal Law Enforcement in Eastern Tennessee

I

In the twenty-five years following the Civil War some of the fiercest resistance to federal laws occurred in the mountainous counties of east Tennessee. But though Tennessee had been a member of the Confederacy, east Tennessee was overwhelmingly Unionist, and in the years following the war it was also firmly Republican. Indeed, when Attorney General Charles Devens sent a telegram to eastern Tennessee's U.S. attorney (and to all other federal attorneys in the southern states), urging that frauds in the recent 1880 election be vigorously prosecuted, the attorney was surprised. There were no frauds in the recent elections, replied Xenophon Wheeler. "Indeed I have never heard of election frauds being committed in east Tennessee, at any election."[1]

Why would a Unionist and Republican region offer violent resistance to the enforcement of federal laws? The answer lies in the severe poverty of east Tennessee. Coal mining was conducted only on a very limited scale in this period, and there were no important industries in the region. The mountainous topography made profitable farming an impossibility, and east Tennessee remained outside the mainstream of U.S. commercial agriculture. The majority of east Tennessee residents struggled to eke out a living by planting corn, growing apples and peaches, and raising chickens. Under conditions of intense poverty, many of the citizens of east Tennessee succumbed to the temptation to improve their finances by defrauding the U.S. government. These frauds included counterfeiting, pension frauds, and moonshining.[2]

Counterfeiting was surprisingly common in east Tennessee, and it took many forms. Spurious coins sometimes were put into circulation, while in other cases false greenbacks or banknotes were printed; or banknotes might be surreptitiously "raised" to a higher denomination. Although the number of counterfeiting cases never equaled the number of pension or moonshine cases, there were at least a few at nearly every term of court throughout the late nineteenth century, and eastern Tennessee was one of the worst districts in the nation for counterfeiting. It should be added, moreover, that most of the persons convicted of counterfeiting were not the actual "artisans" who did the printing, minting, or alteration, but individuals who had purchased spurious money and intentionally circulated it. In eastern Tennessee bogus $20 banknotes were readily available at a purchase price of $2.50.[3]

A somewhat more common type of fraud in the late nineteenth century was the filing of false claims against the government. During the Civil War, Congress had provided for payment of bounties to men who would volunteer for the army, and pensions for those who were disabled in military service. Pensions were also provided for the widows and minor children of soldiers who had died in service. By 1890 more than a third of the federal budget went for payment of veterans' pensions. In the three years immediately following Appomattox the U.S. Pension Office was overwhelmed with applications for pensions and bounties, while the War Department received a vast number of applications for reimbursement for food and forage provided to the Union army. The number of applications peaked in 1867 and then began to decline.[4]

But in the early 1870s private "pension agents" began actively to solicit business, and many of the more unscrupulous agents would lie readily in order to secure to their clients a pension. These agents would prepare affidavits swearing that men who had never been in uniform had served, or that widows who had no children had several. In Unionist Tennessee the pension agents were highly successful, and the Pension Office noticed that the number of applications was again on the rise. U.S. attorneys began to initiate prosecutions under statutes designed to punish persons for "making or presenting false claims to the Government." Tennessee was a hotbed of fraudulent pension activity. This former Confederate state submitted from two to four times as many pension applications as were submitted from such northern states as New Jersey, Connecticut, or Minnesota.[5]

But the most important frauds against the government, especially in the late 1870s and thereafter, were cases of "illicit distilling." Congress had provided for a tax on liquors in 1862 in order to help finance the war effort. Many citizens were surprised when Congress failed to rescind the tax after the war, but the tax had proved too profitable to discard. In the period 1870–1893 the government raised more than a third of its revenues by the tax on liquors; the tariff provided most of the remainder.[6]

The mountaineers of east Tennessee resented the liquor tax, in part because they had been making liquor all their lives without government interference, and the tax seemed an unjust intrusion: It sought to stifle their folkways. But also, most of the illicit distillers simply were too poor to pay the tax cheerfully. The crops most commonly grown in east Tennessee (corn, apples, and peaches) were bulky and difficult to get to market, and fruit was difficult to store during periods of a glut on the market. Both fruit and corn could be readily converted into a compact and imperishable product by the distiller's art. A farmer who raised corn could take twenty bushels to market in his wagon, losing much of it over rough roads. The same wagon could hold forty bushels of corn once made into moonshine, and the price received for moonshine was much better. The wagon load of corn would net $10, while the wagon load of moonshine (made from twice as much corn) would net at least $150—and, as an assistant U.S. attorney noted, for whiskey, unlike corn, "There is always a market." But in order to protect government receipts, U.S. attorneys initiated criminal prosecutions against the moonshiners, some eight thousand such prosecutions in eastern Tennessee during 1870–1893. About 80 percent of these cases were for retailing liquor without a license, which was much easier to prove than the more serious charge of illicit distilling. Virtually all illicit distillers were also illicit retailers.[7]

II

In the late nineteenth century the State of Tennessee was divided into three judicial districts; the eastern district was made up of thirty-four mountainous counties. The district court met twice yearly at Knoxville, and in 1880 Congress designated Chattanooga a second court town. The district judge in 1870 was Connally F. Trigg, a Unionist Tennessean ap-

Converting crops to whiskey spelled economic survival for many mountain families, such as this one at a typical illegal distillery in the southern Appalachians. Courtesy of Southern Historical Collection, Wilson Library, University of North Carolina at Chapel Hill.

pointed by President Abraham Lincoln in 1862. The positions of marshal and U.S. attorney were filled by S. P. Evans and Eldad Cicero Camp, respectively. Grant had appointed both men within a month of his first inauguration. Eldad Cicero Camp, the U.S. attorney, was forty years old in 1870; a native of Ohio, he had remained in the South at the conclusion of his service as a Union soldier. Although he was a carpetbagger, carpetbaggers were not badly treated in east Tennessee, and he was quickly accepted into local society. Camp died in 1913, having lived in Knoxville for forty-eight years.[8]

During Camp's tenure in office, moonshine cases were relatively few in number: He handled sixty-three such cases in 1870, while his successors would handle as many as six hundred in a single year. Most of Camp's efforts as U.S. attorney were directed toward punishing those who were filing false pension and bounty claims with the government. But in the midst of these numerous and complex prosecutions, he received an abrupt letter from the acting attorney general, Benjamin H. Bristow: "I

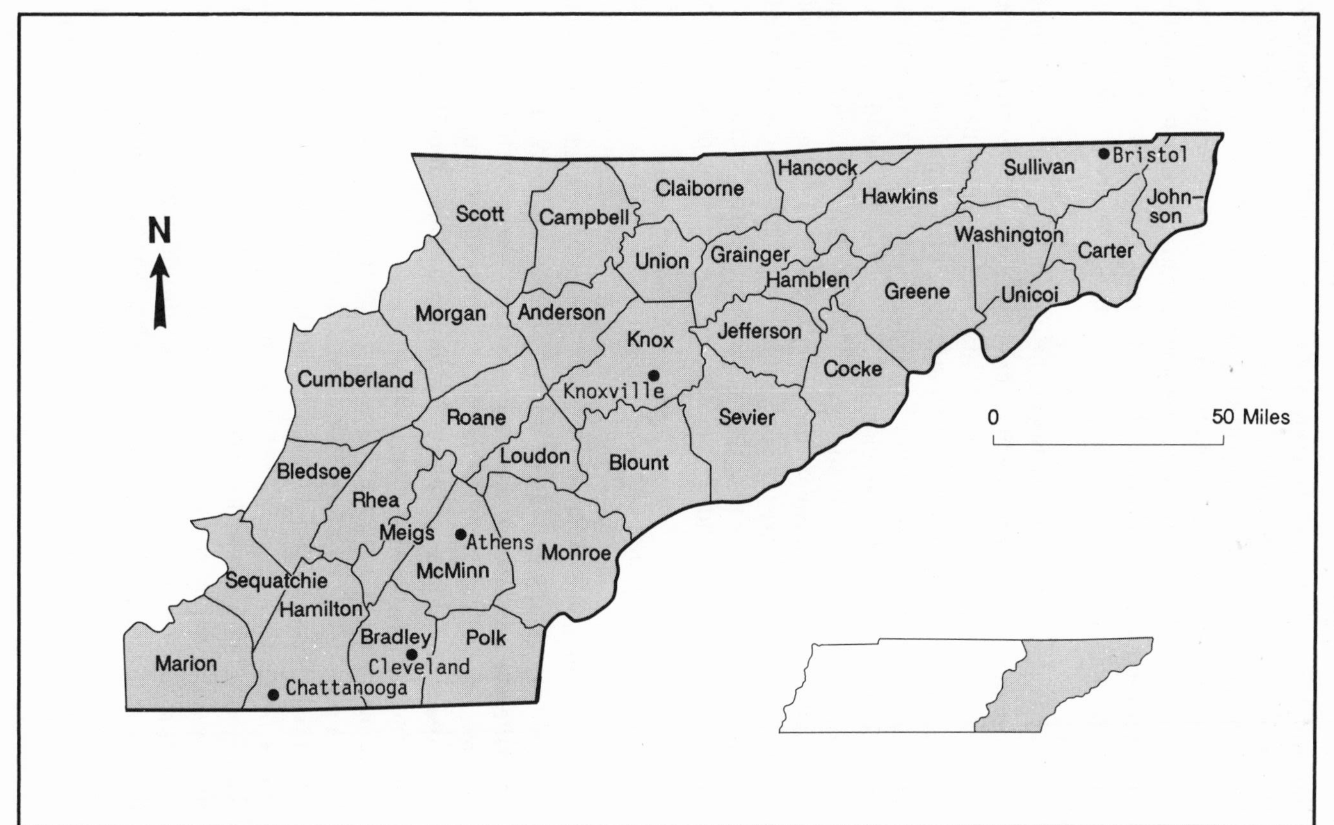

Judicial District of Eastern Tennessee, 1875

transmit, herewith, to you the copy of an order, issued by the President of the United States, suspending you from the office of Attorney of the United States for the eastern District of Tennessee."[9]

On inquiring, Camp found that three Republican members of Congress from Tennessee had asked for his removal because he was bringing too many prosecutions of various kinds. To the public, complained the congressmen, it appeared that Camp was seeking to enrich himself by fees.[10]

Camp was quick to write the president, complaining of the unjustness of his removal. "I want an investigation by the Attorney General," wrote Camp, "if any charges are preferred." Camp was sure that the three congressmen hoped to appear to be "protectors of their constituents" from his own "zealous and successful prosecutions of criminal offenders." The U.S. attorney asked to be reinstated, after which he would resign for the good of the party if that was what Grant wanted. Grant accordingly did reinstate Camp, and twenty days later Camp sent in his resignation. But the congressmen were not successful in shielding their constituents from prosecution, for the man they recommended as Camp's successor, and the man Grant did indeed appoint, was not lax in his determination to prosecute.[11]

The new U.S. attorney, George Andrews, was a native of Vermont but had lived in Knoxville since 1855. His biographer stated that "he had no gifts as an advocate or jury lawyer," generally making sound, well-reasoned arguments that often "utterly failed to register with the jury." Nevertheless, he achieved an excellent record for convictions of counterfeiters, moonshiners, and perpetrators of fraudulent claims during the eight years he held the post of U.S. attorney. Andrews took the oath of office on the first day of January 1872.[12]

Among the most important cases Andrews tried was *United States v. Boyd*, a case of bounty and pension fraud. J. S. Boyd was a popular and influential citizen of east Tennessee who had gone into business as a claims agent. He had also directed the actions of a number of subordinate agents, but Andrews focused first on Boyd because Boyd was "the most wealthy, the most intelligent, the most guilty of the conspirators." Andrews easily secured more than two dozen indictments charging Boyd with presenting false claims to the Pension Office, and the accused was arrested and allowed to post a $35,000 bond. But on September 11, 1872, U.S. Attorney Andrews reported to the attorney general that Boyd's charred body had been located on a lonely mountainside; friends of the deceased reported that they had been with Boyd when several armed masked men accosted Boyd and ordered the friends to flee.[13]

Colonel L. B. Whitney, an operative of the Treasury Department's Secret Service, was in east Tennessee at the time, and he began to investigate Boyd's untimely demise. Whitney found that a young black servant of Boyd had died of typhoid a few days before, and that Boyd and friends had exhumed the body and burned it. Boyd himself had skipped bond. His bondsmen were not a part of the scheming, and, faced with the loss of their $35,000, they took steps to find the accused. They finally located him in Canada; he had made the fatal error of sending to a friend, asking for Knoxville newspapers that reported his escape.[14]

Boyd was tried in January 1873. District Judge Trigg and Circuit Judge H. H. Emmons ruled that Andrews must proceed on one indictment at a time, and Andrews chose the case of the pension of Martha J. Upton, a black woman whose husband had been killed in the Union army. Boyd had prepared the pension application stating that the woman had six children, although in reality she had only four. The woman testified that the application had never been read to her.[15]

Andrews engaged in some sharp arguments with defense counsel over the crucial question of whether evidence could be submitted showing that Boyd habitually presented false claims to the government. Defense counsel argued that Boyd was now on trial only for the Martha Upton claim; evidence of other claims was not pertinent. But the judge agreed with Andrews, who quickly began to submit dozens of examples of Boyd's frauds. For instance, he introduced as evidence pension applications submitted by Boyd on behalf of the supposed widows of Samuel Eliot and George Rose, then called Eliot and Rose to the stand, who, in the words of a local paper, "testified in *propria personae* to their present existence on this mundane sphere." Neither of the witnesses knew anything of Boyd's claims, and neither had received any money from him. The Treasury Department provided witnesses who testified that the claims in question were indeed presented and paid, and Andrews brought in bank tellers who testified that the applications were in Boyd's handwriting. Boyd was found guilty on January 31, and he then pled guilty in several other cases. He was sentenced to five years' imprisonment and a $5,000 fine in the Martha Upton case, and a fine of $1,000 in each of the other cases.[16]

Andrews also handled dozens of counterfeiting cases while in office. Generally, such cases came to his attention when a local citizen wished to earn some money by informing or by serving as a government investigator. A typical case began when a Knoxville lawyer named James N. Ray was sitting in his office with a friend. As the friend later recalled, Ray "mentioned that times were very dull, and that in consequence thereof he had been thinking of investigating the counterfeiting business which he thought was carried on through the country pretty extensively." Ray told his friend that he would have to give up lawyering soon if he could not win a government reward. Ray and his friend were successful in their investigations of several counterfeiters, and Treasury agents soon stepped in and made arrests (with the help of twenty-five deputy marshals); Andrews worked for convictions.[17]

Would-be informants and investigators sometimes approached Andrews directly. One Samuel N. Newton offered to sell information sufficient to indict ten men who were passing counterfeit quarters and bogus notes of the Traders Bank of Chicago. Andrews sent Newton's proposal to Attorney General Pierrepont, urging that it be accepted, as "this section of the country is deluged with counterfeit money." Andrews reported that, although he had sent a number of important operators to the penitentiary a year earlier, "the evil does not seem to be much lessened."[18]

In 1876 Grant appointed Green B. Raum to be his commissioner of internal revenue, and Raum quickly initiated a major attack on the nation's moonshiners. The offensive thus initiated was actually a joint effort of internal revenue collectors and Justice's field officers. The "raiding parties" that visited stills consisted of the collector, the marshal, and their deputies; the revenue agents destroyed stills, the marshals made arrests and seized the illicit liquor. The collectors also worked to develop the evidence, while the U.S. attorneys drew indictments and tried cases. Between 1878 and 1881 "Raum's War," as it was sometimes called, cost the government $285,000 but resulted in increased tax receipts of $2,583,000 in the same four-year period. In east Tennessee, in the three years after July 1876, 159 stills were seized or destroyed, 663 persons were arrested by raiding parties, and four members of the raiding parties were killed and two seriously wounded. In 1878, the peak year of Raum's War, George Andrews tried 512 revenue cases, of which 371 resulted in convictions, with only nine acquittals (the remaining cases were nolle prossed).[19]

Attorney George Andrews resigned his office early in 1879, and President Hayes named as his replacement the Chattanooga attorney Xenophon Wheeler. Like his two predecessors, Wheeler was a northerner by birth; he was a Union soldier who settled in Chattanooga at war's end. Wheeler is something of an enigma because he did not like to correspond with the Justice Department. U.S. attorneys in this period were required to make only one wholly statistical report each year, and any additional reports, complaints, and suggestions were voluntary. Xenophon Wheeler did not choose to make voluntary reports. From his annual statistical report, we know that he continued to prosecute a large number of moonshiners—between 341 and 491 cases per year during his four years in office. As had been the case with George Andrews, only about ten of his moonshine cases each year resulted in acquittal. Wheeler also handled a large number of fraudulent claim cases. Typical among these was the case of Eli May, who falsely claimed to have provided pasture and forage for the Union army, and the case of Ewing W. Carbrook, who was guilty of embezzling the pension of his wards, the minor children of a slain soldier.[20]

Wheeler resigned from the U.S. attorneyship in February 1883 and was replaced by James M. Meek. Meek was a native Tennessean; he had been a Unionist member of the state legislature in the war years. He was sixty-two years old at the time of his appointment. During Cleveland's administration, examiners from the Justice Department complained that Meek took little interest in his position as U.S. attorney and that most of the work was accomplished by his assistant, John P. Smith. Under Meek and Smith, the number of moonshine cases held steady at about four hundred per year; fraudulent claims cases decreased in number if only because the war was now so far in the past. When Grover Cleveland was elected president, the Democratic congressmen from Tennessee urged that the Republican Meek be removed from office; when asked why he was unfit, they replied that Meek was charging the government for mileage while in fact he was using a free pass on the railroad. This complaint proved sufficient to effect his removal, although a Democratic auditor in the Treasury Department later admitted that Meek had been entitled to the mileage—that mileage was to be paid whether the attorney walked, rode his horse, took a ride in a friend's buggy, or used a railroad pass.[21]

Among those who complained to Attorney General Garland of Meek's conduct as U.S. attorney was J.C.J. Williams, who introduced himself as the man endorsed for Meek's position by the Democratic congressmen. Williams provided details of Meek's use of the railroad pass, then added that after all the facts were in he was sure "the President would not hesitate to order [Meek's] immediate removal." Williams was right: Cleveland was quick to order the Republican's ouster, and Williams became the new U.S. attorney. Williams was a thirty-eight-year-old native of Knoxville; his great-grandfather was the city's founder and his grandfather was a U.S. Senator. Like Wheeler, Williams was a poor correspondent. He did continue to handle impressive numbers of revenue cases; he also worked to expose and convict a ring of counterfeiters who were passing $1 notes that had been "raised" to twenties.[22]

A more flamboyant figure in the Cleveland years was the new Democratic marshal, Jo Jo Ivins. Congressman George G. Dibrell had suggested Ivins's appointment in a letter to the president, first mentioning Ivins's impressive credentials as a Democrat (he edited an influential party organ), then adding, "I admit that up to five or six years ago Ivins did at one time dissipate, but for the past four or five years he has completely reformed." The administration had a rare chance with Ivins—to use a reformed drinker to lead the fight against moonshine in east Tennessee. Ivins did receive the appointment, and he brought new vigor to the post of U.S. marshal. He first wrote to Attorney General Garland, asking permission to lead a large force into the southwest corner of the district to apprehend moonshiners: "The country is rough and in many parts almost inaccessible. My information is to the effect that the population is largely made up of violators, and that they will resist the officers by every possible means. . . . I am exceedingly anxious to succeed where others have failed."[23] With Garland's blessing and that of the secretary of the treasury, Ivins led a number of highly successful raids into Bledsoe and Rhea counties.

Tragically, after more than two years of energetic leadership in working to combat illicit distilling, Ivins succumbed to the old temptation and began to drink moonshine himself. At first, since he edited an important Democratic paper, and because he had a wife and seven children, he was given a second chance. He submitted an undated resignation the president might accept at any time that Ivins began to drink again. But he was unable to shake his habit, and soon his own bondsmen notified the various banks that they would no longer be responsible for Ivins's drafts as marshal. Unable to draw government funds and drunk during an entire four-week term of court, Ivins finally was replaced by a much less energetic officer, W. M. Nixon, who was thirty-six years old and had never held public office.[24]

Benjamin Harrison was never ashamed of being partisan, and when he assumed control of the executive branch in March 1889 he did not delay in removing the Democratic field officers of the Justice Department. To the post of U.S. attorney for eastern Tennessee, Harrison appointed H. B. "Bart" Lindsay. Lindsay was a native east Tennessean, a man who, although still in his early thirties, had held a number of offices including those of state legislator, district attorney, and U.S. commissioner. Lindsay's biographer noted that, as U.S. commissioner, "it fell his lot to conduct the preliminary examination of many mountaineers of Scott and adjoining counties who were suspected of moonshining."[25]

As U.S. attorney, too, Bart Lindsay would handle a large number of moonshine cases—the number reached an all-time high for the district in 1891, six hundred cases. A Justice Department examiner gave Lindsay high marks, although he complained of the difficulties of making an examination during the session of "a moonshine court, where the courtrooms, offices, halls, and steps were crowded with these moonshiners every day for three weeks." An assistant U.S. attorney, Henry M. Wiltse, aided Lindsay in his prosecutions.[26]

Like his predecessors, Lindsay tried a number of cases of counterfeiting. At the January term in 1890 he prosecuted William Downs for passing a counterfeit $20 greenback in the village of Sunbright in Morgan County; Downs was sentenced to two years in a federal penitentiary. At the next term of court Lindsay tried three more counterfeiters and was successful in all three prosecutions. These three counterfeiters received an average sentence of two years plus a nominal fine of $100.[27]

Although pension frauds were clearly on the wane in the 1890s, Lindsay did handle a few of these cases. The most important was *United States v. Marshall*. W. R. Marshall was a pension agent at Greenville, Tennessee; he forged papers purporting to prove that the son of Mrs. Nancy Davis had served in the Union army and been imprisoned at Andersonville. Although Marshall vigorously denied the forgery, Lindsay introduced a handwriting expert who testified that the handwriting on the papers was certainly Marshall's. Lindsay buttressed this testimony by showing that mistakes in spelling on the pension affidavits were duplicated in other samples of Marshall's writing. Marshall was found guilty and sentenced to the penitentiary.[28]

The U.S. marshal during the Harrison administration was W. S. Tipton. The Justice Department examiner was favorably impressed by Marshal Tipton: "He is a man of fine intelligence and good abilities, and when I saw the business done in this district and the hard characters, moonshiners, &c. the marshal has to handle, and the number of deputies he has to control, I knew the president had put the right man in the right place."[29]

One of Tipton's first actions as marshal was to undertake an extensive raid on illicit distilleries during a term of court. In the words of the *Knoxville Daily Journal*, "It has been the custom for moonshiners to get in lively work while federal court was in session and all the U.S. officers were supposed to be there." The first of Tipton's court-time raiding parties visited southeastern Monroe County, where they arrested twelve moonshiners, destroyed eleven stills, and seized one thousand gallons of contraband.[30]

But the extensive raids conducted during the tenure of Tipton and Ivins, and during the period of Raum's War, did not put an end to illicit distilling. It continued unabated until the early years of the twentieth century, when the annual number of cases in the district dropped to between one and two hundred. Statistics are scarcer for counterfeiting and fraudulent claims cases—in the U.S. attorneys' annual statistical reports these cases were included in a column labeled "Other." Judging from the correspondence of the attorneys and marshals, and a sampling of the Knoxville newspapers, it appears that the number of counterfeiting cases continued steady throughout the years 1870–1893. Pension and bounty fraud cases clearly declined, as might be expected since the war was by 1893 some thirty years in the past. On the other hand, the vigorous prosecutions of these frauds by U.S. attorneys certainly put the community on notice that applications for government claims were in fact carefully scrutinized and were not quickly and easily approved.

In short, the Justice Department efforts to "guard the Treasury" in eastern Tennessee had mixed success. The efforts were successful in that conviction rates were very high for all three classes of cases. The vigor with which U.S. attorneys and marshals pursued the offenders undoubtedly served as a deterrent to would-be moonshiners, counterfeiters, and fraudulent claimants. Government revenue tax receipts

In 1890, a Justice Department examiner said of Marshal W. S. Tipton: "When I saw the business done in this district and the hard characters, moonshiners, &c. the marshal has to handle, and the number of deputies he has to control, I knew the president had put the right man in the right place." From H. M. Wiltse, *The Moonshiners* (Chattanooga, 1895).

Table 4.1. Revenue Cases in Eastern Tennessee

Fiscal Year	Number of Cases	U.S. Attorney(s)	Cases in Entire United States
1870	63	Camp	2,272
1871	110	Camp	3,253
1872	147	Camp, Andrews	2,761
1873	135	Andrews	2,751
1874	253	Andrews	3,291
1875	252	Andrews	3,932
1876	370	Andrews	4,750
1877	287	Andrews	5,899
1878	512	Andrews	5,701
1879	367	Andrews, Wheeler	8,326
1880	491	Wheeler	6,341
1881	341	Wheeler	5,703
1882	425	Wheeler	4,611
1883	418	Wheeler, Meek	4,663
1884	465	Meek	5,026
1885	462	Meek	4,738
1886	557	Meek	6,243
1887	426	Meek, Williams	5,064
1888	330	Williams	6,097
1889	280	Williams, Lindsay	5,648
1890	462	Lindsay	6,720
1891	600	Lindsay	6,905
1892	427	Lindsay	4,137
1893	356	Lindsay	4,271

Sources: Statistics are from the *Annual Report of the Attorney General* for 1870–1893 (Washington, D.C.: GPO, 1870–1893); dates of appointment of U.S. attorneys are in the *Register of the Department of Justice* (Washington, D.C.: GPO, 1870–1891).

Note: The fiscal year ran from July to June.

increased each year, as more and more moonshiners decided to pursue their art legally. And yet the outright resistance to federal authority, and the great frauds upon the Treasury, continued at a very high level. As numbers of moonshine and counterfeiting cases remained high, it becomes clear that success was mingled with failure for the Justice Department in eastern Tennessee. Tennessee was by 1893 still isolated from the nation's social and economic mainstream. Although parts of east Tennessee were beginning to modernize, much of the mountainous region continued to live in the past, pursuing subsistence agriculture, following the old ways, and frustrating the best efforts of attorneys, marshals, and Treasury agents.

III

Once again, the pertinent questions in coming to a fuller understanding of federal law enforcement in eastern Tennessee involve the caliber of attorneys and marshals, the kind of help they did and did not receive from Washington, and the impediments they encountered in striving to enforce the federal laws.

In the three types of fraud considered here, successful detection and prosecution depended upon a constant and reliable flow of information to the U.S. attorney and marshal. But in only one case did the Justice Department hire a detective to do work in eastern Tennessee. More typical was the situation in the 1875 pension case of *United States v. Lyons*. Although prosecutor George Andrews was certain Lyons was guilty of gross frauds against the government, the requisite evidence proved elusive, and he asked Attorney General Pierrepont to send a detective. The attorney general responded, "In reply to your inquiry whether the investigation necessary can be made by some agent of this Department you are informed that it has no such agents." This answer was misleading. Although the department had no force of detectives, it could approve the temporary hire of a detective for particular cases, and in cases that involved the Treasury Department, as this one did, Secret Service operatives or other Treasury investigators might be detailed. But in this case, as in all too many others, the government lawyer was left to do his own detective work.[31]

R. M. Sherman was the one detective hired by the Justice Department, who worked in eastern Tennessee. Sherman arrived in November 1871 and stayed for several weeks, working to develop evidence in cases of bounty and pension frauds. He brought with him from Washington a tall stack of affidavits, applications, and other papers from the Pension Office. Sherman left this mass of documents and other evidence he worked up in Tennessee with the new U.S. attorney, George Andrews, and departed the state for another assignment. As the court term drew near, Andrews wrote Attorney General Akerman, asking that Sherman be present at the trial of the cases he had investigated. Akerman's reply was a little snide: "It occurs to me that with two qualified gentlemen [that is, Andrews and his assistant] to represent the Government professionally in east Tennessee there ought to be no need of further assistance." Andrews replied angrily that Sherman had simply dropped off the pile of documents without a word of explanation, and these hundreds of papers "could not be intelligently used by anyone who had not spent a large amount of time in arranging and digesting them," as Sherman had.[32]

Akerman was not the only Washington officer of the department to send snide letters to U.S. attorneys in Tennessee who asked for aid. In 1880 Xenophon Wheeler asked for clarification of a recent order from Attorney General Devens. In this order, Devens—desiring to experiment with leniency in the treatment of past offenders in moonshine cases, coupled with harsh treatment for new offenders—had instructed Wheeler to drop all pending moonshine cases on payment of costs. Wheeler explained to Devens that the moonshiners were so "incurably poor" that virtually none of them would be able to pay costs. The pardon clerk, Alexander T. Gray, answered for Devens: "It was presumed that you would be able to discriminate in the matter of payment of costs, and upon inquiry into the circumstances of parties, would know in what cases to require payment of the same."[33]

Indeed, seldom was a U.S. attorney or marshal able to obtain useful advice or instructions from the Justice Department. George Andrews's first letter to the department was tyical of the first letters of U.S. attorneys across the nation: "If there are general instructions as to the duties of my office . . . please have them forwarded." His request was ignored. Twelve months later Andrews was involved in an important revenue case and begged Attorney General Williams to "send authorities" on several important points. "I presume that you cannot undertake to make briefs for U.S. attorneys," wrote Andrews, "but these are important questions and a case of some importance, and . . . the libraries in this city are limited."[34] Once again, Andrews's request went unanswered.

A third request by Andrews for information and advice finally elicited a response from Attorney General Williams. To Andrews's request for instructions in a pension fraud case against a prominent Tennessean, Williams answered, "I must decline to express any opinion. . . . I must unless under very extraordinary circumstances leave the disposition of such matters to the United States attorneys." Occasionally, the attorneys general deigned to give advice, but almost always with great reluctance. When Marshal W. S. Tipton asked whether a deputy collector of internal revenue might also serve as a deputy marshal, W. H. H. Miller replied, "I am not in the habit of giving opinions on such questions but I know of no statute which would prevent his so acting." Similarly, when Marshal Nixon sent in an inquiry about inducements for the good conduct of prisoners, Attorney General Augustus Hill Garland sent him, not an answer, exactly, but a citation to a pertinent statute.[35]

On rare occasions the attorneys general could prove quite useful to their field subordinates. Andrews sent Devens a description of a pension case in which an agent had fraudulently withheld pension funds from a pensioner over a span of many years; Andrews worried that the agent would be protected by the statute of limitations. In response, Devens sent a copy of a recent federal case from western Pennsylvania in which the judge had held that "fraudulently withholding funds was continuous, and did not cease until the money was paid." Devens ended his letter with a positive instruction: "Prosecute."[36]

In 1872 Attorney General Williams wrote to Andrews, saying that he had just read a report on the Boyd cases and was impressed by the "strong evidence of his criminality." Williams continued, "You are expected by this Department to spare no pains to bring this Boyd and his confederates in crime to proper punishment." Andrews must have been flabbergasted to receive such clear instructions from his superior, but less than a month later Williams wrote that Boyd had asked for clemency—should his application be favorably considered? Andrews answered succinctly: "I consider him the most outrageous scoundrel that it was ever my lot to encounter. He has made a fortune out of the Government & out of the widows and orphans of east Tennessee. . . . I intend to convict him."[37] Williams answered, "Spare no pains to have him convicted."[38]

Attorney General George H. Williams. Convinced of the criminality of pension agent J. S. Boyd, he ordered the U.S. attorney to "spare no pains to bring this Boyd and his confederates in crime to proper punishment." Although Williams considered revoking his order less than a month later, Boyd was finally tried and convicted. Courtesy of U.S. Library of Congress.

If the Washington office of the Department of Justice offered only irregular and uneven support for its field officers in eastern Tennessee, it should also be pointed out that the U.S. Army played no role in the enforcement of federal laws in the district despite keen local resistance to Justice Department officers. In a few instances across the nation the army was used to assist in raids on illicit distilleries, notably in Georgia and South Carolina, and at least one solider, an army lieutenant, was killed in operations against moonshiners in Georgia. Only once was any military force used against moonshiners in eastern Tennessee, when Deputy Marshal George Larkin returned the fire of a mountaineer distiller, killing him. Arrested by state authorities in a remote county seat, Larkin heard the sheriff remark that a lynching would be almost unavoidable. The terrified deputy telegraphed Assistant U.S. Attorney John P. Smith in desperation, and Smith arranged for the governor to call out the Knoxville Rifles, a unit of the state militia. By the time the Rifles arrived the local citizens had calmed down, but the militia found Larkin shaking his head as if in a daze and recalling "the roar of the maddened mob thirsting for my life."[39]

But if the attorneys and marshals failed to benefit from the aid of the army (and there is no evidence that they sought its aid), they did receive the help of one other department of the government, the Treasury. All the cases considered here were handled by a partnership of the Departments of Justice and the Treasury. Moonshine cases, for example, ran a bewildering course from deputy marshal to revenue collector to U.S. attorney, then to a U.S. commissioner, and finally back to collector, marshal, and attorney. Generally, an informer, seeking to alleviate his own poverty by obtaining a government reward (paid by the Treasury Department), would approach a deputy marshal and give information. The deputy would report the case to a collector, who would investigate it. The collector reported to the U.S. attorney, who was to judge whether a conviction could be had. If the attorney chose to proceed, he would seek a preliminary hearing before a commissioner. The deputy marshal would make arrests, and the U.S. attorney or his assistant would finally try the case.[40]

The procedure was less circuitous for "raids." The deputy marshals were empowered to make immediate arrests of anyone caught distilling or in the vicinity of a still and were also charged with seizing the contraband whiskey and brandy. The deputy collectors seized or destroyed the stills. Also among members of the raiding parties were guides, local citizens who ran great personal risk by leading the party to illegal stills—all for a fee of $10.[41]

The aid that the Treasury Department gave to attorneys and marshals in eastern Tennessee was various. Treasury clerks were sent from Washington to testify in cases of bounty and pension frauds; the clerks provided crucial evidence by testifying that the fraudulent applications had actually been presented and paid. Collector of internal revenue Green B. Raum prepared and mailed to all U.S. attorneys a one-volume collection of the nation's revenue laws. This collection was particularly useful since U.S. attorneys were not provided with sets of the statutes until the mid-1880s, and, as George Andrews complained to his superiors, the law libraries in Knoxville were pitifully weak.[42]

Detectives of the Treasury Department's Secret Service were active at times in eastern Tennessee and helped to make up for the lack of Justice Department detectives. The Secret Service was particularly active in cases of counterfeiting. In pension cases, too, Treasury detectives were sometimes detailed. Andrews asked Attorney General Williams to hire a detective to develop the evidence in certain bounty and pension fraud cases; Williams relayed the request to Secretary of the Treasury George Boutwell. "The cases are of great magnitude," wrote the attorney general, "and for that reason, and on account of the intelligence, wealth, and prominence of some of the chief actors," it was imperative "that no efforts be spared to convict and make examples of the guilty parties." In the letter's closing sentence, Williams made it clear that if a detective was to be hired, the Treasury Department, and not Justice, must pay.[43]

Questions of just who should pay the expenses of detectives sometimes led to interdepartmental conflict. In July 1882 Xenophon Wheeler reported that he had several angry Secret Service agents on his hands. They had been investigating counterfeiting operations in the district, and their efforts had resulted in convictions. The agents asked that they be reimbursed for their expenses out of the marshal's funds and exhibited printed instructions from their superior saying that expenses must be paid by Justice Department officers. The marshal, however, had standing instructions from his own superior stating that Secret Service expenses must be paid by the Secret Service.[44]

Just as the provision of Treasury Department detectives sometimes alleviated the lack of Justice Department detectives, so instructions from the Treasury Department sometimes made up for the lack of attorney general's instructions. For example, the commissioner of internal revenue exercised a loose supervision of moonshine cases. In 1871 the commissioner frantically telegraphed U.S. Attorney Camp to halt all moonshine prosecutions because of adverse rulings of District Judge Trigg. Camp and the commissioner worked successfully to get some of the cases before Circuit Judge Emmons, whose construction of the revenue laws was firmer.[45]

The partnership between Justice and Treasury was made cumbersome by the steady stream of mail that passed between the various district and Washington offices of the two departments. U.S. attorneys corresponded with Treasury officials through the attorney general, and so, in a typical instance, Andrews wrote to Attorney General Williams asking for a Secret Service agent; Williams wrote to Treasury Secretary Boutwell relaying the request; Boutwell wrote to the chief operative of the Secret Service and then to Williams; and Williams finally sent the decision to Andrews. Documents from Treasury Department files were sent to the attorney general and then to the U.S. attorney for use as evidence; all too often in the flood of paperwork, the documents were mislaid or lost altogether. When Andrews wrote to Edwards Pierrepont asking for the pension file of Jesse M. Lyons, which was already in the hands of the Justice Department, a sheepish attorney general replied: "I have to inform you that the papers in the case of Jesse M. Lyons are out of place. I presume they will be found, but at the present I cannot send them. . . . You must have the case continued."[46]

One kind of help that the attorneys general did in fact provide for their subordinates in Tennessee was the appointment of assistant U.S. attorneys. Akerman commissioned George Andrews as Eldad Cicero Camp's assistant at a salary of $1,500, but added, "I am apprehensive that the funds at the command of this Department will not allow a permanent assistant in your district." Camp immediately returned Andrews's commission, "as he will not accept it"—the salary was too low. Camp suggested a salary of $2,500, since neither Andrews nor any other attorney would be willing to "neglect so seriously his own practice for $1500." The salary Akerman offered, concluded Camp, was "grossly inadequate." But Akerman remained steadfast: The department could not afford a larger salary.[47]

Finally, Augustus H. Pettibone, an attorney and a future congressman, agreed to accept the assistantship at $1,500. Attorney General Akerman expressed misgivings about whether the department could afford any assistant at any salary, and he made it clear that Pettibone's appointment was "revocable at any time, if the expense should not seem to be justified by the increased efficiency in the disposition of business." After a few years Circuit Judge Emmons urged the attorney general to raise Pettibone's salary, as otherwise he could not be expected to continue in office. In view of the overwhelming number of criminal cases in eastern Tennessee, added Emmons, it was particularly important to have a man "of local influence and social position." Attorney General Williams saw fit to increase the salary to $2,000, but Andrews, Pettibone, and Emmons continued to express dissatisfaction.[48]

Pettibone served almost ten years as assistant U.S. attorney. When he finally resigned, Devens appointed John P. Smith to replace him, at a pittance of $1,200 per year. Finally, Wayne MacVeagh approved an increased salary of $1,500, but only because Smith handled virtually all of the Knoxville business himself while U.S. Attorney Wheeler lived in the more relaxed, new court town of Chattanooga. Immediately, Smith asked MacVeagh for more—"The present rate of compensation is very much less than my services are worth." The district judge and U.S. attorney both supported Smith's request, but to no avail. When Smith left the service, H. M. Wiltse was hired as assistant U.S. attorney, and the salary reverted to $1,200. Wiltse pleaded for a fair compensation in view of "the vast volume of business" in the courts of eastern Tennessee, but he not only failed to receive a raise, the attorney general dispensed with his services in 1892, when Congress cut the appropriation for assistant attorneys from $125,000 to $100,000.[49]

If U.S. attorneys were hampered by uneven support from Washington in the matter of their assistants, they encountered an even greater obstacle in the form of local resistance to their enforcement of federal laws. Commissioner of Internal Revenue Green B. Raum, looking back on the first two years of his war on illicit distillers, noted that in east Tennessee and elsewhere in the southern highlands "Leading citizens were either directly interested in the business [of moonshining], or else were in active sympathy with the distillers, and the officers of the law have usually received but little aid or encouragement from the people in their efforts for the collection of the revenue and the arrest and punishment of offenders."[50] Raum also noted that the killing of a deputy marshal "scarcely creates a ripple on the surface of the public mind."[51]

Jess Carr, in his 1972 history of moonshining, *The Second Oldest Profession*, noted that illicit distillers had two chief methods of resisting the enforcement of the revenue laws. "The first was an agreement among moonshiners who operated closely enough geographically to assemble on short notice when the need arose and form a small guerilla band." As a veteran of many east Tennessee raiding parties put it, the moonshiners "give notice of our arrival as soon as we are seen, by the blowing of horns and the firing of guns." Occasionally, such raucous individuals were arrested and convicted of "obstructing officers in the discharge of their duty." The other method Carr cites of resisting the laws "was to secure neighborhood sympathy—silence or participation—regarding [the distiller's] illegal business." Any local citizen who did not approve of moonshining would be subjected to dire threats, and informers and witnesses often returned from the district court in Knoxville to find smoldering ashes where their barns once stood. One U.S. attorney noted, "It is frequently more difficult to get the witnesses than the defendant."[52]

The case of the notorious moonshiner Hut Amerine, whom Andrews sent to prison in 1872 for illicit distilling, was typical. Amerine returned home from his six months in the penitentiary and immediately resumed distilling. Andrews secured a new indictment, but from 1872 to 1878 the marshal was unable to effect an arrest. "He is a known desperado," reported Andrews, "and his neighbors are all, either in league with him or in fear of him."[53]

In pension fraud cases, too, the interests of the government suffered because the federal officers were seen as outsiders. The commissioner of pensions complained in a report to Congress that fraudulent pension applications were drawn up by members of close-knit communities, and the government, with its limited resources, could not make adequate investigations. The pension agent was the neighbor of the applicant and, of course, would be paid only if the application were successful. The examining surgeon was invariably "the neighborhood practitioner, whose professional and personal interest is with his neighbors . . . from whom he gains a livelihood, instead of with the government." Thus, concluded the commissioner, "every interest connected with the preparation of the case for adjudication—the claimant, his attorney, and the examining surgeon—is adverse to the government."[54]

If local sympathies were with moonshiners and dubious pension applicants, the question arises: How did the federal attorneys maintain in most years a conviction rate of 65 to 89 percent? An examiner of the

Department of Justice estimated that in moonshine counties "seven-eighths of the inhabitants . . . are connected with the illicit liquor business in some way." How then did the U.S. attorneys manage to convict hundreds of violators per year with only a dozen or so acquittals? The answer seems to lie in the composition of the petit juries. Unfortunately, little is known about such panels, but an enterprising reporter for the *Knoxville Daily Journal* did survey the members of several petit juries. He asked about age (almost all were in their forties or older), religion (overwhelmingly Baptist and Methodist), and occupation (nearly all were farmers). If the jurors were really devout Methodists and Baptists, it may not be surprising that they were willing to convict moonshiners, but if they were subsistence farmers, older men sympathetic to the old ways, it would seem that they should have been sympathetic to the moonshiners. A hint at the answer is given in the survey of two petit juries for July term, 1890, by the Knoxville reporter. Only in this survey did the reporter inquire as to county of residence. Although the twenty-four jurors hailed from eight different counties, not one came from the most moonshine-infested counties, such as Union, Rhea, or Bledsoe. It seems that, by securing jurors from towns and from the flatlands, the jury commission provided jurors who were willing to convict moonshiners.[55]

But even a willing jury could be stymied by bribed or fearful witnesses. It was not unusual for a U.S. attorney to report, as James Meek did in 1883: "I have had great trouble in convicting men from these [moonshine] counties, because of the intimidation of witnesses. It is spoken of as a disgrace, by men who live in these communities, and profess to be respectable and good citizens, for a witness to give evidence against this class of lawbreakers."[56]

In a poverty-stricken region such as the eastern district of Tennessee, criminal defendants or their friends could often successfully bribe jurors. In the first of the trials of the Boyd ring for fraudulent claims, two jurors refused to vote for conviction despite overwhelming evidence. The U.S. attorney was of the opinion that "the two were bought, beyond a doubt." When the prisoner was returned from Canada, Andrews began to hear reports that Boyd's friends were again preparing to engage in bribery and intimidation. "The fear that I have," wrote the attorney shortly before trial, "is of tampering with jurors and witnesses. Boyd's ring controls a large amount of money, and includes some of the most desperate men in the country." Fortunately, in the wake of Boyd's mock murder on the lonely mountainside, his community support waned as even his bondsmen disowned him, and the danger of juror or witness tampering diminished.[57]

In at least one instance a defendant attempted to bribe a Justice Department officer. In the revenue case of *United States v. Rader* the defendant walked into U.S. Attorney Bart Lindsay's office, dropped a $20 gold piece on the desk and left without saying a word. Lindsay went to the judge, handed him the coin, and said, "I don't know whether this is for you or me, Judge." Lindsay prosecuted Rader for attempted bribery, and an angry Judge Key sentenced Rader to two years in the penitentiary.[58]

In their mountain neighborhoods the illicit distillers turned to a number of forms of subterfuge to cloud the evidence of their guilt. If a stranger were found in the vicinity of a still, the moonshiner would force him to render some service, such as mixing the mash or chopping wood. As an east Tennessee revenue officer explained, "it is well-known that the law punishes those who work at an illicit distillery as well as those who operate one." Thus did moonshiners hope to silence would-be informers. Retailers of moonshine also resorted to subterfuge to hide the true nature of their sales. Commonly, they would have their customers, especially if strangers, place their money by an old stump and return later to find a jar of liquor. Or perhaps the liquor would be "loaned," with cash reimbursement later provided, when the loan was not repaid in kind. A moonshiner might sell a dozen apples at a very high price—and then throw in as a gift a bottle of apple brandy. Early in the 1870s these forms of deceit sometimes did work to secure the acquittal of a distiller or retailer, but as the years passed the courts were less and less deceived. In place of these kinds of subterfuge, the distillers came to rely on violence to protect themselves from the marshals and collectors.[59]

East Tennessee newspapers often decried the actions of U.S. attorneys and marshals. The *Knoxville Independent* complained in 1875 of the treatment of moonshiners: "When the court meets, the whole country having been scoured as if in pursuit of some beast of prey, there come up hundreds, all charged with every conceivable violation of the revenue laws. And here they are, some twenty, some fifty, some an hundred miles, and some even more miles than that, from their homes. . . . A more pitiable sight is not to be imagined."[60]

Local politicians often tried to exploit the moonshine issue in running for office. Looking back on two decades of revenue law enforcement, the *Knoxville Daily Journal* recalled in 1890, "These moonshiners from the mountains were voters. . . . Politicians promised them that they would have the [revenue] laws repealed if they would send them to Congress." Since a Republican Congress had passed the revenue laws, "more than one Democrat stormed the Gibraltar of east Tennessee Republicanism by attacking the internal revenue laws." But even the Republican representatives were not supportive of wholesale prosecutions of their constituents for moonshining. George Andrews wrote to Attorney General Pierrepont in 1876, "I see that our representatives are still much exercised in regard to prosecutions for violation of the revenue law in this district." The case of Eldad Cicero Camp, ousted by President Grant after Republican congressmen from Tennessee complained that he was bringing too many prosecutions for moonshining and pension fraud, was mentioned earlier. Later, Republican Congressman Leonidas C. Houk would seek to serve as something of a "pardon broker" for his constituents, asking the attorney general to drop a certain prosecution or to recommend a presidential pardon. Usually, however, the attorney general refused to accede to Houk's requests.[61]

The most important example of local resistance to federal authority in eastern Tennessee was the prosecution of federal officers by state and local authorities. We have seen the case of Deputy Marshal George Larkin, arrested by state authorities for killing a moonshiner—in this case the governor called out a unit of the militia. Larkin had been attempting to arrest the moonshiner when the moonshiner brandished a knife and advanced. Larkin drew his gun and fired twice. After intervention of the U.S. attorney, Larkin's case was removed to a federal court, in the wake of a recent Supreme Court case, *Tennessee v. Davis*. In the *Davis* case, which arose in the middle district of Tennessee, the Supreme Court held that where a U.S. officer was charged with a state crime committed in the line of duty, the case might be removed to a federal court. This decision greatly discouraged state officers from arresting federal officials. Earlier, U.S. attorneys had defended a deputy marshal from charges of false arrest, and a deputy collector from charges of brandishing a weapon.[62]

These cases of state-federal conflict in the 1870s were not confined to moonshining matters. In 1874 authorities in Union County arrested a Secret Service agent, J. E. Dyer, and charged him with passing counterfeit money. Assistant U.S. Attorney Pettibone reported to Washington that the charges against Dyer were wholly frivolous: "The whole proceeding is an infamous conspiracy, by which the state courts are used to defeat our operations." The local lawmen were friends and confederates of the counterfeiters Dyer had been investigating, and they had secured his indictment "for the purpose of rendering him infamous, and incompetent as a witness against them in the U.S. Circuit Court." Pettibone concluded that the counterfeiters were "reckless and desperate men" who wanted to see Dyer "sent to prison, driven away, or assassinated."[63]

Support from the Justice Department in Washington was sadly lacking in this case. Because U.S. Attorney Andrews and his assistant were busy at the federal court in Knoxville, Andrews hired local attorney A. L. Prosser to defend Dyer. Attorney General Williams, however, refused to approve payment for Prosser because, in the emergency, Andrews had failed to get advance departmental approval. Local Justice Department officials, however, exerted great effort to defend Dyer. Both Andrews and his assistant Pettibone provided legal aid; Andrews posted bail for Dyer with his own funds and provided a guard, without which "Dyer's life would not be safe." Chastising his superior for lack of support, Andrews wrote, "I propose to see [Dyer] through, if I have to do it at my own expense, as I have done thus far."[64]

In response to local resistance to federal laws, officials in Washington urged a vigorous enforcement program for the good of the various communities in east Tennessee. As Attorney General Devens put it in a letter to Andrews, "Where offenses of a particular class are so numerous and so sustained by the sentiment of the community, it is important that the prosecutions by the Government are speedy and successful," so as to encourage the community to discard its support of those who resisted federal laws. The commissioner of internal revenue noted that illicit distilling was bad not only because it defrauded the government of needed monies but because it encouraged growth of a "lawless spirit" among whole communities. This lawless spirit could be overcome by armed and experienced deputy marshals and deputy collectors, continued the commissioner. Overcoming resistance to federal laws, he concluded, "is in the interest of the Government, whose laws are violated and whose revenues are withheld; it is in the interest of the public, whose peace is disturbed and whose morals are debauched."[65]

But in spite of these declarations of a desire to improve the moral climate of communities in east Tennessee and to defend the power and prestige of the national government, the flow of funds needed to undertake such a project was irregular at best. Typical of dozens of telegrams was one sent by Marshal Thomas H. Reeves to the attorney general in July 1884, complaining that the court was in session but that there were no funds to pay its expenses. When his telegram went unanswered, Reeves sent another, as the court waited. Finally, there came an answer from Solicitor General Samuel F. Phillips. Reeves must use the proper forms: "To ask for money by telegraph is objectionable," and Reeves must pay for both telegrams out of his own pocket. Phillips's reply was borne by departmental telegram! Marshals Ivins and Tipton were likewise ordered to pay for telegrams themselves when they telegraphed for money during a court session.[66]

Ivins sent less pressing complaints by the U.S. mails. He once reported a visit by a delegation of jurors who demanded their pay, but he had no funds. On another occasion he complained that the delay of the appropriation "renders it almost impossible for my deputies to travel about and execute process, as travel in this mountainous country is expensive and ready funds are required to enable the men to move promptly." Altogether, concluded Ivins, the lack of funds was "seriously embarrassing" and a great hindrance to strict enforcement of the laws. In January 1887 he begged Attorney General Garland to see that the juror and witness funds were sent soon, "so as to enable me to meet the clamorous demands of the public creditors."[67]

W. M. Nixon spent a frustrating year as eastern Tennessee's federal marshal late in the Cleveland administration. In March 1888 he beseeched the attorney general to send the funds for court expenses quickly because the court was about to meet in Chattanooga. As the United States was already eleven months behind in paying jurors and witnesses, local merchants would be unwilling to provide room and board on credit, as they sometimes had in the past. If Garland would make the authorization in writing, Nixon would secure a personal bank loan to pay expenses, as Ivins had done repeatedly during his tenure. Soon after Garland received this letter, Congress prepared to pass a deficiency bill that would provide the needed funds. In the meantime, Garland asked Nixon "whether or not you cannot supply the witnesses and jurors with funds for their expenses in attendance upon the court." Nixon secured a bank loan, and the courts were able to proceed. Nixon later sought to be reimbursed for the interest charged by the bank but was refused. He was urged to re-read Garland's letter: "It was a suggestion to you to borrow money to meet the expenses of the Court . . . but nothing of an imperative nature was intended." In fact, the Department of Justice never paid the interest or bank fees of the many marshals who borrowed money to keep the courts running.[68]

This scenario repeated itself at the following two terms of court. Nixon wrote a number of letters, asking that the funds be sent immediately because there would be great hardship if "these poor mountain people are not able to collect their dues. They are a class who are unable to subsist at court" or even return home if unable to collect their fees. At the opening of court at Knoxville in July 1888 Nixon had five hundred witnesses in attendance but no funds. He risked a telegram: "Court commences today with full attendance. Witnesses unable to live here and unable to return home. . . . What shall be done?" No answer was forthcoming from the nation's capital, and Nixon and the court waited in frustration, while witnesses bedded down on the courthouse lawn or on the floor of the courtroom.[69]

Marshal W. S. Tipton had similar problems, with a court in session, hundreds of jurors and witnesses in attendance, and "my last dollar . . . expended." Tipton telegraphed yet another request for funds, asking consideration for the "poor people . . . who have no money to get home on." But the only reply Tipton received was a reprimand for wasting money by using the telegraph.[70]

If the marshals found their duties as the courts' financial officers irksome, how much more difficult was their role as supervisor of deputies. In the years of Raum's War and thereafter, U.S. marshals in the district had between thirty-five and forty deputy marshals, who were prime targets for the violence of east Tennesseans indicted for federal crimes. Attorney George Andrews reported to Devens: "There has been a good deal of armed resistance to officers in this district, and I want to put a stop to it. Nearly all of our officers have been shot at & several of them wounded. I sent three men to the penitentiary [in January 1878, for resisting a marshal], but there have been several similar assaults since."[71]

In August 1878 Andrews had to report the murder of John Cooper, "one of a party detailed to seize a still in Blount County." The raiding party had finally succeeded in locating Hut Amerine's well-hidden distillery; the actual raid began before daylight. Reported Andrews, "The persons in charge of the still retreated to the surrounding bushes, whence they immediately opened fire on the posse, who returned the fire as well as they could by the flashes of the guns." Deputy Marshal Snyder was shot through the hand, and the party returned to Knoxville for reinforcements. At sunrise the next day the party again reached the site, but the still had been carried away. While an examination was being made, the posse was fired upon from the bushes. Cooper was shot twice and died three hours later. His murderer was captured and, after a vigorous prosecution by the U.S. attorney, was sentenced to a jail term of twenty-two years.[72]

An 1879 report to Congress by Green B. Raum gives the story of violent resistance to revenue law enforcement in eastern Tennessee in concise form. In the fall of 1877, reported the commissioner, three informers had been killed, two of them in Grainger County. A couple of months later a gunfight between moonshiners and a raiding party resulted in two deaths, one a member of the party, named Cobb. In June 1878 a raiding party was fired upon, and the prisoners in tow were released. Seven weeks later, Cooper was killed, as narrated above. In March 1879 a raiding party was involved in a major gunfight, but, miraculously, no one was hurt. Two weeks later, a federal posse was fired upon, and a deputy collector was severely wounded. Thus in less than nineteen months in eastern Tennessee, three informers and two members of a raiding party were killed, while two officers were seriously wounded.[73]

Nor was violence toward U.S. officers confined to the period of Raum's War. In May 1887, for example, U.S. Attorney J.C.J. Williams reported to Washington the attempted assassination of two raiders. The two men were on a trip, attempting to make an arrest; they had passed the night near Nine Mile Post Office. In the morning they had proceeded four hundred feet down the road when they were fired upon from ambush. A deputy marshal was shot in both the hand and shoulder, while a deputy collector was shot in the arm. A year later, Marshal Nixon wrote to Garland, "I regret to report the assassination and murder of Deputy U.S. Marshal Thomas Goodson." Goodson had been en route to Lost Cove to summon two witnesses and to meet an informer when he was attacked with clubs and then shot twice in the head with his own pistol. His body was thrown into a sinkhole in a secluded, mountainous region and was found ten days later, after a diligent search. "The life of Deputy Goodson had been repeatedly threatened by the lawless offenders of this secluded mountain region," added Nixon, "but he heeded them not, proceeding fearlessly to execute his official duties wherever and whenever called."[74]

Less than a year later, Marshal Tipton, too, had to report the shooting of one of his deputies, who was "badly but not fatally hurt." Deputy Sam Hughes had been attempting to arrest two moonshiners; he demanded their surrender, but each aimed a gun at Hughes and ordered him away. Hughes stood firm, and, finally, one of the men fired. The shotgun blast hit the deputy in the left arm, breast, and gut. In March 1892 Deputy Marshal Charles K. Stuart joined the ranks of eastern Tennessee deputy marshals killed in the line of duty. Stuart was killed by a party of nine moonshiners when he refused to give up the prisoners in his custody.[75]

Faced with murder and maiming of deputy marshals and other members of the raiding parties, the attorneys general usually approved the offer of a reward of $250 or $500 for the arrest and conviction of the resisters. In several cases a sort of grudge match developed—Collector of Internal Revenue Cooper worked to arrest the murderers of his son Deputy John Cooper, while Deputy Marshal Sam Hughes went looking for Lum Averhart, who had severely wounded him. A U.S. commissioner warned Hughes that Averhart "has plenty of helpers and does not intend to give up; he swears he will kill you on sight." But virtually all of the men who shot federal officials were finally arrested, most of them by a regular posse of deputy marshals.[76]

Other impediments repeatedly cited by U.S. attorneys included certain rulings by federal judges that made convictions difficult or impossible to obtain. For example, in 1887 Commissioner of Pensions John C. Black wrote the attorney general in exasperation. Pension cases in eastern Tennessee, he reported, "are being 'knocked endwise', many of them, under the rulings of the Judge. I have the honor to request that a continuance be taken in every case." The commissioner cited the case of *United States v. Butler* as an example. Judge David Key had ruled that the forgery of an endorsement upon a government check was no crime under the federal statutes. Noted a disgusted Commissioner Black, "If this be the law every substantial safeguard against fraud . . . is removed."[77]

In this case of *United States v. Butler*, the defendant, Richard H. Butler, had been indicted for cashing a pensioner's $1,443 check by forging the endorsement. During the trial, Black reported, "the city and the court room swarmed with the paid heelers and strikers of R. H. Butler." One man admitted to a Justice Department examiner that "he was a paid witness by Butler to testify as might be necessary in Butler's behalf." Black came to the conclusion that "the accused has enlisted in [his] behalf the sympathy of the community as well as that of the Judge." Judge Key held that, although forging a government check was a crime, forging an endorsement was not the same thing, and U.S. Attorney Williams was not able to secure a conviction.[78]

Nor was the *Butler* case an isolated example. In some cases in the late 1880s Key ruled that, although certain fees were prohibited to pension agents, gifts were not prohibited—thus was the door left open for veiled extortion by pension agents. In another instance a former assistant U.S. attorney, Pettibone, now a member of Congress, sought to arrange a nolle prosequi for his constituent, pension agent T. J. Berry. Prosecutor J.C.J. Williams agreed to dismiss the case if Berry would pay costs. Berry declined to accept the proposition, Williams reported, "preferring to take his chances for acquittal under the liberal holdings of the court." Berry made a wise choice. Key ruled that the U.S. attorney could try only one indictment at a time and could not introduce evidence from the other, closely related, cases. Berry was not convicted.[79]

Key was not the only judge to provoke the ire of U.S. attorneys and Treasury officials. In 1871 the commissioner of internal revenue asked the attorney general to order a continuance in all eastern Tennessee revenue cases because of adverse rulings of District Judge Trigg. As U.S. Attorney Camp explained to the solicitor general, Trigg had ruled that "in retailing cases the party, before he can be guilty, must be proved to have followed retailing as a means of livelihood." Furthermore, under Trigg's construction of the law, only the owner of a still could be guilty of distilling, and only the owner of the whiskey could be guilty of retailing: Paid employees were not subject to prosecution. Camp succeeded in getting these questions before Circuit Judge Emmons, who corrected most of Trigg's unfortunate rulings. But Camp was still dissatisfied, for Emmons ruled that while employees of an illicit distillery might be tried for distilling, the prosecutor must prove that the employee acted "with the knowledge that the principal has not complied with the law." Camp believed that it was clear that "guilty knowledge" was not required.[80]

Supported by Trigg's and Emmons's rulings, dozens of defendants submitted affidavits declaring that they had been mere employees and were unaware of the distiller's transgressions. Camp complained to his superiors in Washington: "Were ever such obstacles interposed to defeat the

U.S. attorney in such cases? If a party being present aids in killing he is guilty as a principal of murder. If he is present & distills whiskey [as a hired hand] he is liable only as an aider & then only in case you prove a guilty knowledge."[81] In spite of the adverse rulings, Camp's record shows few acquittals, "for the reason that even juries cannot accept Judge T's law."[82]

In counterfeiting cases, too, U.S. attorneys had problems with judges' rulings. In *United States v. Snodderly* George Andrews convinced the counterfeiter Snodderly to turn state's evidence; in return, Andrews promised that he would have to pay only a moderate fine with no jail sentence. Judges Trigg and Emmons disapproved of Andrews's bargain, saying that one who turned state's evidence was always entitled to an absolute discharge. But Andrews told the attorney general that because Snodderly was "a prominent man in the community I was determined that he should not go absolutely unpunished." Trigg refused to honor Andrews's arrangement with the defendant unless the attorney general approved his course. Accordingly, the U.S. attorney had to write George H. Williams asking him to "relieve the court from unpleasant responsibility" by backing the agreement with Snodderly. Williams sent the requested letter, and Snodderly was then ordered to pay his fine.[83]

The bulk of the cases considered here were heard by two men, District Judges Connally F. Trigg, who served from 1862 to 1880, and David M. Key, who served from 1880 to 1894. Both men were exceptionally lenient judges. Their leniency, however, was confined to revenue cases. The long prison sentences handed down for men such as Boyd who made fraudulent claims, or for those who resisted marshals or passed counterfeit money, show that their leniency was not invariable. But Trigg's biographer noted that, regarding the sentencing of moonshiners, "a more unpleasant duty could not have been imposed, and he did not enjoy it. Some said that his kindness of heart led him to be too lenient with the unfortunate, and generally ignorant men, who were constantly infringing the severe laws."[84] And Judge Key's leniency can be seen by the fact that when he announced his retirement he received a lengthy petition from the moonshiners of east Tennessee begging him to stay on.[85]

Under both Trigg and Key a first offense against the revenue laws usually resulted in a suspended sentence, or, occasionally, a fine of $100 and a jail term of one month. For subsequent offenses the fines generally ranged from $100 to $200, and the jail term from one to three months, although even in these subsequent offenses the judge sometimes suspended sentence.[86] A departmental examiner in 1893 inquired into sentencing in eastern Tennessee revenue cases; his report is the basis for Table 4.2.

But the data in Table 4.2 is even more revealing when it is noted that, of the 537 cases in which the judge handed down a prison sentence, sentence was suspended in 245 cases. Or, as the examiner pointed out to the attorney general, the average sentence actually imposed in the 569 convictions (which included a high percentage of repeat offenses) was less than twenty-seven days. "The light sentences imposed in this district do not in any way reflect upon the U.S. attorney's zeal and energy as a prosecutor." Instead, the examiner blamed the judge: "While it would seem that U.S. Judges in districts in which illicit manufacture of liquor is carried on should know what is demanded in the interest of justice in cases coming before them, yet this is one of several districts in which moonshining . . . is getting worse year by year, and I believe it to be so on account of the light punishments afforded on conviction being obtained."[87]

In short, a violator of federal law in eastern Tennessee had good reason to be optimistic about avoiding a prison sentence. If unable to silence informers or witnesses, he could probably depend on the leniency of the court, especially if his was a first offense. But even a month or two in prison was, as Examiner W. E. Hazen put it, "an enforced but not altogether disagreeable vacation." Assistant U.S. Attorney Wiltse, looking back in 1895 on his service as a federal prosecutor, recalled that the average prisoner was an impoverished mountaineer who had never been out of his own county. The journey to the penitentiary in Ohio or New York "was, therefore, the great event of his life, and the pleasure of it seemed to completely overpower all sense of remorse and shame."[88]

The widespread poverty in east Tennessee affected not only federal criminals, but deputy marshals and U.S. commissioners as well. Since these men, with the U.S. attorney and marshal, received fees when cases were brought but otherwise received none, they were constantly accused of bringing frivolous cases merely to earn fees. And in a few instances such accusations appear to have been well founded. Among the letters of complaint that the Justice Department received was one from Republican Congressman Houk, written in August 1875. Houk admitted that he was not on good terms with the U.S. attorney, but he swore that,

Table 4.2. Sentencing in Revenue Cases in Eastern Tennessee, 1891–1892

Number of Cases	Sentence
377	1 month
40	2 months
101	3 months
9	6 months
10	1 year or more
32	No prison sentence

Note: Based on Examiner Hazen to Miller, January 27, 1893, in the Year Files, Records of the Department of Justice, Record Group 60, National Archives.

in east Tennessee, Justice Department officers "prowl over the country, making arrests and seizures" in crimes of a strictly "technical nature." Circuit Judge John Baxter made a more credible report early in 1880, when he reported that he suspected that certain commissioners and deputy marshals were in collusion to increase their fees by frivolous prosecutions. Attorney General Devens immediately sent an examiner to investigate Baxter's suspicions.[89]

The Washington office of the Justice Department soon instructed the deputy marshals and commissioners to refuse to proceed in any case until they had secured the approval of the U.S. attorney. Deputy marshals were also ordered always to take prisoners before the nearest commissioner for preliminary hearing, in order to reduce mileage fees. Baxter insisted that the latter order be revoked, however: "It would not be prudent, in all cases, for officers making arrests to take the accused before the nearest commissioner. To do so would invite rescues and provoke breaches of the peace."[90]

Serious charges against Justice Department officers in the district were made by the commissioner of internal revenue in 1885. The charges stated that Deputy Marshal Sam Watts and Commissioner William C. Emmerts were guilty of manufacturing fictitious cases. "It is represented," wrote the internal revenue commissioner, "that persons are hired to allow themselves to be prosecuted." Thus the defendant earned money in the case, as did the witnesses, deputy marshal, and federal commissioner, who earned fees for the preliminary investigation.

When the witness provided only worthless evidence, the case was dismissed, to no one's detriment but the government's.[91]

U.S. Attorney Meek investigated the charges; he found that, although frivolous cases had been brought, neither Watts nor Emmerts was guilty of wrongdoing. "I think that Watts has been misled by parties who wanted to be witnesses," reported Meek. For example, witness J. L. Murray earned a tidy sum by testifying as a witness in nine preliminary hearings "and did not prove a single material fact in any one of them." But since Watts and Emmerts were guilty at least of gullibility, Meek asked their suspension. In cases such as these the witness approached the deputy marshal, whispering of his complete knowledge of local moonshining but saying that he did not want to testify. A subpoena followed, and a preliminary hearing where the witness was suddenly struck by dense ignorance—but nevertheless earned his fees.[92]

In 1892 Attorney General William H. H. Miller wrote angrily to U.S. Attorney Bart Lindsay, returning a commissioner's financial account that Lindsay had approved. "It is amazing to me that you should have approved such an account," fumed Miller; there was clear evidence of fraud and fee making. Of the 104 cases heard by the commissioner, seventy-seven were dismissed at the preliminary hearing. Miller noted that the same families seemed to have alternated their roles—"the defendant of today is the witness of tomorrow"—and thus did the families seek fraudulently to supplement their incomes. "These cases would never have reached the preliminary hearing stage," Miller asserted, "if you had done your duty in the premises."[93]

Lindsay answered, "To this last language I would be inclined to object if I did not know that you believed such [criticism] was justifiable and necessary in order to obtain the best administration of affairs in our department." Lindsay now promised a full explanation, "leaving it to you to modify or add . . . such remarks as may seem just to myself." Lindsay's explanation was similar to that of Meek; namely, that informers promised to work to secure convictions but then gave no useful information at the preliminary hearing. Lindsay had instructed the deputies and commissioners to be more suspicious and to get a sworn statement from a would-be witness before agreeing to summon him. As to the "fee fiend" witnesses, Lindsay had been working against them for some time. "I have sent four men to the penitentiary upon this charge . . . and three more for perjury—for first swearing men [into court] and then swearing them out." Two more perjury trials were pending. Lindsay's letter of explanation ended by touching upon a weakness of departmental administration—the lack of regular reports by field officers.[94] "I suppose if I had made these explanations some time ago I would not have been blamed as I have been; but . . . I had only done my duty in the extraordinary efforts I have made to punish persons guilty of these frauds, and I did not feel like firing long letters and reports into your office, constantly calling attention to what *I* had done."[95] Miller, after his harsh letter to Lindsay, was kind enough to withdraw his earlier criticism and commend the U.S. attorney for prosecuting those who made false witness fee claims against the government.[96]

The accusations against Justice Department officers for fee making soon meant that they were being watched all too closely by the department's examiners and the Treasury auditors. In a typical instance, Attorney General Garland wrote Ivins asking whether it had really been necessary to spend $801 taking eleven prisoners (with five guards) to the penitentiary at Albany, New York. Were five guards really necessary? Did they follow the shortest route? After a long exchange of letters, Garland approved the marshal's account for $773—a savings of $28, which came out of Ivins's pocket. Similarly, Examiner Ira Baker reported to Garland in 1888 that Marshal Nixon was too extravagant in his charging of fees. For instance, Nixon charged for several consecutive days of "endeavoring to arrest," when no arrests were made. Nixon's deputies not only charged fees for bringing a prisoner before a commissioner, they took a second deputy along as a "guard," and the guard charged fees, too.[97]

Nixon was quick to respond to the charges. "The topography of the country is rough, frequently nigh impassible," and was populated by those who "impede and obstruct the officers of the Government."[98] Nixon added that he suspected the department's examiners thought "that the defendants are but to be visited," that they "are anxious to be arrested, and readily submit to being brought out of their mountain fastnesses, from among their friends and sympathizers." Actually, it took days to locate defendants, and only by traveling in pairs could the deputies be relatively safe. "If the examiner would take one of these trips, the experience would change his opinion of the necessity of such expenses."[99]

Generally, the marshals performed well in spite of being the target of

When U.S. Attorney H. Bart Lindsay's failure to correspond with Washington led to a serious misunderstanding, he explained to the attorney general sheepishly: "I did not feel like firing long letters and reports into your office, constantly calling attention to what *I* had done." From *Tennesseans* (N.p.: Speed Publishing, 1901–1902); courtesy of Lawson McGhee Public Library, Knoxville.

much ill will and even the targets of desperate gunmen. With the exception of Ivins's eventual return to drinking, none served with dishonor, and even Ivins remained extraordinarily popular after his removal. Ivins and Tipton were the most active and aggressive marshals; S. P. Evans, T. H. Reeves, and W. M. Nixon were quieter men, although they, too, performed well. How were the marshals selected in eastern Tennessee? The recommendation of congressmen from the Volunteer State was essential, although the president considered the recommendations of other prominent men as well. Marshal S. P. Evans, appointed in 1869, was selected largely because he was a crippled soldier. A captain in a company of Union troops from Tennessee, Evans had lost a leg while leading a charge, and was in 1869 a poor man, "totally unable . . . to perform the ordinary labors of life." Evans had picked up valuable experience as a county sheriff during the four years after the war. T. H. Reeves, Garfield's choice for marshal, was an attorney and, like Evans, also benefited from his record as a Union soldier from Tennessee. W. M. Nixon, who served only one year late in the Cleveland administration, was a young man who had never held elective office; he was a businessman and, as his congressman reported to Garland, "a fit representative of the young conservative Democracy of Tennessee who feel that they should be recognized."[100]

Marshals Ivins and Tipton were selected primarily because they edited important party newspapers. Ivins edited a Democratic journal, the *Athens Weekly Post*, while Tipton edited a Republican paper, the *Cleveland Weekly Herald*. One of Tipton's references urged that in view of the importance of his paper he should be rewarded "in some way besides a little one horse post office." Another letter suggested, "To give him the office [of marshal] would greatly aid him in making his paper a power in our next canvas, & if he don't get something, I am satisfied the paper is compelled to be neglected."[101]

Investigating the background of the hundreds of men who served as deputy marshal in eastern Tennessee in the late nineteenth century would be an overwhelming task. Each marshal had from thirty-five to fifty deputies; Marshal Ivins reported that his deputies were "first class men, of good social standing at home, nearly all of them having enjoyed the confidence of their neighbors as sheriffs, deputy sheriffs, and constables." Examiner W. E. Hazen was somewhat less positive in his appraisal of the deputy marshals: "In this District in which are many miles of mountains and on each mountain many "moonshiners," the work of deputy marshals is arduous and dangerous and no marshal could surround himself with a force of efficient deputies of high mental and moral attainments."[102] Instead of deputies of high mental and moral character, reported the examiner, Marshal Tipton appointed men who were well acquainted with the region's geography, "who are inured to the hardships of mountain ranging and are fearless as to personal safety." In spite of the fact that "the position of Deputy Marshal is not held in high repute by the neighborhood people," virtually all of Tipton's deputies had proved themselves to be good officers, in the opinion of Examiner Hazen.[103]

The position of U.S. attorney was generally reserved for those who had campaigned vigorously for the national administration, often as a presidential elector. Of the six attorneys and three assistants who served in this period, one had a law degree; this was H. M. Wiltse who served as assistant attorney during the Harrison administration. Three others, James Meek, Xenophon Wheeler, and Assistant U.S. Attorney Pettibone, had bachelor's degrees. Four of the attorneys brought experience as local district attorneys (called "attorneys general" in Tennessee). Andrews, Lindsay, Pettibone, and Williams had served as district attorney general, while Lindsay also benefited from his experience as one of eastern Tennessee's roughly thirty U.S. commissioners. But aside from questions of education and experience, what kinds of background did the Justice Department lawyers share?[104]

Nearly all were Union veterans. One exception was James Meek, who had been a Unionist legislator in Tennessee; he was tried by the Confederates for treason and sent south to a prison camp. Another trait that binds together the attorneys and many marshals is the fact that, in this poverty-ridden district of eastern Tennessee, they were comfortable, even wealthy men, active in the business community. Eldad Cicero Camp, for example, was not only a Knoxville atttorney; he was active in the chamber of commerce, a stockholder in several banks and director of the Third National Bank, and "one of the largest owners of realty" in east Tennessee. He was also president of the Coal Creek Coal Company, the Virginia-Tennessee Coal Company, the Knoxville Acetylene Company, and the Marble City Improvement Company. He was active in the National Rivers and Harbors Association, and "through his efforts" the Southern Railway built lines connecting Knoxville to the coalfields.[105]

Xenophon Wheeler was director of the Chattanooga Savings Bank, the

Chattanooga Building and Loan Association, the Richmond Spinning Mill, Chattanooga Coffin and Casket, and the Columbian Iron Works. Wheeler's successor James Meek was director of a bank and a railroad company; his biographer wrote that Meek worked his way from schoolmaster to wealthy capitalist by being an energetic lawyer, a wise investor, and a sound corporate director. Marshal Nixon was president of the Board of Trade of Chattanooga, director of the First National Bank, founder of the Athens Woolen Mill, and interested in the North Athens Cotton Mill, the Athens Land Company, and the Starr Mountain Iron Company. Bart Lindsay served as director of the First National Bank at Knoxville and was a corporate lawyer for the Aluminum Corporation of America. Assistant U.S. Attorney Wiltse was president of a real estate development company, manager of an electric company, and secretary of the Iron, Coal, and Manufacturer's Association. Others not included in this list owned and operated smaller businesses—Ivins and Tipton had their newspapers, for example, and Andrews had the most prosperous law practice in the region. It is revealing that these men, who were attempting to lead east Tennessee into the mainstream of the modern U.S. economy, found themselves opposed in the courtroom to the poverty-bound representatives of an older, subsistance-farming culture.[106]

As might be expected from a crew of corporate investors and directors, the attorneys and marshals were involved in various charitable ventures in their neighborhoods. A biographical sketch of Eldad Cicero Camp notes that "at his own expense he maintained a shelter for unfortunate women on Jackson Avenue" in Knoxville. Both Lindsay and Wheeler were cofounders and generous supporters of Knoxville's public library, while Camp, Andrews, and Lindsay were naturalists and worked for conservation of the natural resources of the Smokies. But most interesting of all, in light of the thousands of moonshine prosecutions, was the involvement of many Justice Department officers with the local temperance movement. Camp maintained a large scrapbook, which he shared with community leaders, on the subject of "temperance and wine," and he was active in Knoxville's temperance society. Ivins was selected as marshal largely because he was a reformed drinker and was "at the head of the temperance reformers." One congressman, in recommending Ivins, asserted, "He has done more for the cause of temperance in east Tennessee over the past four years than any man there." As noted above, however, Ivins fell back into his old habits.[107]

One of the most important temperance reformers in east Tennessee was Assistant U.S. Attorney A. H. Pettibone. Pettibone worked for an amendment to the Tennessee Constitution invoking prohibition. Soon after leaving the assistant attorney's office, he wrote a political essay on the subject of temperance, which was printed and distributed as a broadside headed "Attention Republicans!"

> What are the evils of whiskey? My God! what are they not? I see this as a criminal lawyer. I know, as probably the one man in Tennessee who has prosecuted more men and drawn more indictments than any man now living. . . . I was ten years engaged in prosecuting at the federal court in Knoxville and two years as attorney general. I have prosecuted as many as 5,000 different persons, and whiskey was almost always the devil that was behind the scene.[108]

According to Pettibone, whiskey was the one thing "which piles up the taxes, fills the jails, the poor houses, the hospitals! Jurors' fees, witnesses' fees, sheriffs' fees, doctor bills!" The former prosecutor urged Tennesseans to go beyond controlling and taxing, and enact outright prohibition.[109]

Pettibone was not the only Justice Department official to go beyond his duties as a prosecutor to reach out by the printed word to the people of his district. It has already been mentioned that Ivins and Tipton were newspaper editors; Assistant U.S. Attorney H. M. Wiltse, too, served a stint as editor (his paper was the *Chattanooga Commercial*), and James Meek was a stockholder in a Republican organ. The editorial writings of these men were influenced by the duties they performed for the Justice Department. As Wiltse recalled, it was not uncommon for a deputy marshal to visit a newspaper office and write an account of recent raids, including numerous tales of derring-do by government officers.[110]

When J. S. Boyd wrote to President Grant denouncing the government and its officers and claiming that he was the "innocent victim of the wiles of a lot of negroes & ignorant mountaineers," George Andrews sought permission to have the letter published: "I consider [it] not only wonderful in its impudence and rascality but very valuable in view of the prosecutions we have had against that scoundrel Boyd." Although Acting Attorney General Bristow was dubious, he gave Andrews permission, if "the publication of this letter would be of advantage in any way to the Government." Andrews accordingly made the letter public and thus worked to erode the strong public support Boyd had so long enjoyed.[111]

In the nineteenth century only two books were written about moonshiners and moonshining in the United States, and the authors of both were active in federal law enforcement in eastern Tennessee. George Wesley Atkinson wrote an 1881 book titled *After the Moonshiners*; he had the book published anonymously, signing it only "by One of the Raiders." Atkinson was a deputy collector of internal revenue, and as such he participated in dozens of raids in the district of eastern Tennessee. *After the Moonshiners* was an adventure book, full of tales of intrepid marshals and collectors. Atkinson emphasized the determination of Green B. Raum, the support of Attorney General Devens, and the skill and bravery of the deputy marshals. Under his anonymous byline, Atkinson could include himself as a particularly valiant raider. Shortly after the book was published, Attorney General MacVeagh secured Atkinson's appointment as the marshal for West Virginia—another hotbed of illicit distilling. Atkinson's career finally took him to West Virginia's governor's mansion.[112]

The other book, called simply *The Moonshiners*, was written by Assistant U.S. Attorney Wiltse and published at his expense in 1895. Why did Wiltse write his book? In part because "little is heard of [the raiders] by the public except when they engage in some tragic incident, encounter some startling adventure, or make a seizure or arrest of unusual importance. And yet some of their raids which are never heard of involve the greatest difficulties and hardships."[113] The tone of *The Moonshiners* is markedly sympathetic to the illicit distillers whom Wiltse prosecuted in the early 1890s. "The moonshiner is not," wrote Wiltse, "the hopelessly bad man that he is ordinarily portrayed to be." When he considers the morality of his actions, "he considers the laws which he violates unjustifiable abridgements of his natural personal rights, and rights of property." The moonshiner believed that it was better to violate an unjust law than to let his wife and children go hungry, Wiltse concluded.[114]

Wiltse's book alternates between stories of brave deputy marshals and stories of sympathetic moonshiners. At the book's end, however, the author pointed out that the nation was moving forward, and progress would wipe away the old ways. Wiltse wrote that the moonshiner "must understand that by reason of the mighty march of civilization, the advance of nineteenth century progress, soon to be taken up by the twentieth century, he will be early forced to abandon his occupation." Finally, Wiltse addressed the moonshiners directly, and his tone hardened: "Your deeds of cruel and cowardly assassination . . . are almost without parallel of cruelty in the annals of the most savage and degraded peoples. . . . You skulk, you hide, you crawl, you fire from ambush. . . . Reform! gentlemen! reform at least in this, or the tears of widows will burn into your soul and the cries of orphans will ring in your ears throughout the never ending ages of eternity."[115]

In a few instances eastern Tennessee's Justice Department officials supplemented their role as publicists with lobbying efforts of various kinds. George Andrews explained to the attorney general that he feared to proceed in several pension fraud cases: "Judge Trigg's sympathies and associations are such that I very much dislike to try such cases before him." Andrews asked that "Justice Swayne, or any other Supreme or Circuit Judge" be asked to come hear the cases. Circuit Judge Emmons refused to come because the government paid his expenses only for the regular terms of his court. Emmons was angry at the government's refusal to pay for an office for him at Knoxville; as Andrews reported, Emmons "says he cannot use his bedroom at the hotel for an office, strewing his books about the floor, and piling them upon the bed. The Judge uses a good many books, and I agree that he ought to be provided with an office."[116]

Andrews soon sent the attorney general and Senator George F. Edmunds (chairman of the Senate Judiciary Committee) a manuscript of a proposed bill that would provide payment of the expenses of circuit judges when detailed to hear special cases. "The government loses in delay and expense every year ten times what it would cost to pay the expenses of . . . Judges on such trips," argued Andrews. When, nine months later, no action had been taken, Andrews had the proposed bill printed and sent copies to the attorney general. With the Boyd trial approaching, and Judge Trigg in sympathy with "old families" such as Boyd's, Andrews urged the bill be passed; failure of passage would "decrease respect for Federal power in Tennessee." Three months later Andrews sent yet another letter urging congressional action. By this time the Boyd trial was over, but Judge Emmons fortunately had agreed to hear the case with or without government payment of his expenses.[117]

In 1874 a comptroller in the Treasury Department ruled that marshals should receive a lump sum of $2 for serving writs, regardless of miles traveled or expenses incurred. Andrews wrote to Washington, urging that Congress overrule the comptroller. Two dollars was inadequate compensation, Andrews reasoned, "for a service which may involve a ride of several days through the mountains, with a chance of being shot at into the bargain"; soon, no one would be willing to serve as deputy marshal. In this case Andrews did not have to engage in extensive congressional lobbying, as the attorney general worked out an acceptable agreement with the Treasury Department whereby marshals might be reimbursed for "endeavoring to arrest."[118]

Marshals Ivins and Tipton each visited the department's Washington office during their tenure, seeking advice on reducing expenses. Specifically, they were concerned with a practice whereby prisoners were surrendered by their bondsmen to the nearest deputy marshal shortly before the term of court. The marshal was then required to deliver the defendant to court, which was often more than a hundred miles away over rough mountain roads—at government expense. But the marshals were told to work out their own solutions.[119]

In fact, throughout the late nineteenth century U.S. attorneys and marshals in eastern Tennessee made up for a lack of instructions from Washington by devising elaborate plans of their own and by issuing explicit instructions to deputy marshals and commissioners. Ivins, for example, in the matter of bondsmen surrendering their prisoners, ordered his deputies to put such prisoners into the local jail and await the call of the court. Presumably, this would discourage defendants from seeking free transportation. U.S. Attorney Lindsay, too, devised some money-saving plans. Under his predecessors, witnesses in all criminal cases were brought to the court town on the first day of the term. Lindsay instead made a detailed schedule for each term, in consultation with the judges, and ordered the attendance of witnesses only as called for by the schedule. He thus saved the government thousands of dollars in witness per diem fees.[120]

George Andrews took it upon himself to revise instructions received from Washington. In a circular letter to all U.S. marshals, Attorney General Williams had ordered them always to take prisoners before the nearest commissioner. Andrews urged the deputy marshals to ignore the order when necessary; as he explained to Williams, in the rough and violent areas of eastern Tennessee "there are localities where an examination could not be free from the danger of rescue or a mob. . . . It is of great importance that the proceedings be had and bail taken before a commissioner who is not the nearest neighbor of the criminal."[121]

Unhappy with both of the two district judges he encountered during his tenure, Andrews was satisfied with Circuit Judges Emmons and Baxter, who were not local men and were thus firmer. Satisfied that Baxter was not "soft" on moonshine, Andrews worked with him to devise an experiment in sentencing. Accordingly, explained Andrews to the attorney general, he had instructed the deputy marshals and commissioners not to bring any revenue cases for violations committed before "the adjournment of the session of court just closed." The idea, he wrote to Washington, "is to let by-gones go, and try whether a vigorous enforcement of the law upon recent offenders" would be effective. Attorney General Devens approved the plan, and in the first year the number of prosecutions for revenue law violations dropped from 512 to 367. But soon the number rose again, and the plan was thus not effective.[122]

Even assistant U.S. attorneys became instructors of the deputy marshals; Assistant John P. Smith wrote Deputy John C. Campbell, warning him to desist from the practice of arresting the same individual for different instances of retailing. "In the U.S. Courts," wrote Smith, "any number of sales constitutes only one offense." Marshal Ivins, disgruntled by the assistant attorney's issuing orders to his deputy, complained to Washington. When the practice Smith suggested was followed, Ivins contended, retailers sold liquor unimpeded after their first arrest while free on bond, since subsequent arrests were not permitted. Finally, U.S. Attorney Meek entered the controversy and told the attorney general that Ivins's contention was "exaggerated." If a retailer continued to sell after his arrest, such facts would be brought out at the trial, and he would be sentenced more severely.[123]

The most remarkable examples of U.S. attorneys and marshals issuing instructions to deputy marshals and commissioners were the carefully printed instructions issued by George Andrews in 1875, and by J. J. Ivins in 1886. In a pamphlet titled "Instructions to United States Commissioners," Andrews provided both general and specific orders. The commissioners were not, by allowing vast numbers of cases, to turn the federal courts "into engines of oppression and malice," nor should they litter the docket books with "trashy and insignificant cases of [technical] violations of the law." Although the statute of limitations was five years, cases should be brought only if: (1) the offender was still violating the laws; and (2) proof still existed sufficient to win the case. In cases where the defendant was an intimidating person and the witnesses seemed reluctant, the commissioners should require witnesses as well as the defendant to post bond. Finally, Andrews instructed the commissioners to follow the language of the statute as closely as possible in framing complaints. All of these instructions worked directly to keep the numbers of convictions high and to reduce the number of cases that would later have to be dismissed.[124]

Marshal Ivins prepared a pamphlet for the instruction of his forty deputies. In the face of the violence commonly offered to his men, Ivins wrote, "you are required to treat all prisoners humanely while in your custody and on no occasion will you hurt one save in self-defense. . . . In no case are you justified in taking a human life except in self-defense."[125] Although arrest warrants were usually required before a prisoner could be apprehended, they could be dispensed with if a man was caught in actual violation of law. Arrests must not be made at church or on Sunday, and "the use of intoxicating liquors is strictly forbidden."[126]

The success of the Justice Department in protecting the Treasury in the southern highlands was mixed. Between 1870 and 1893 the department handled nearly ten thousand cases of fraudulent claims, counterfeiting, and illicit distilling and retailing. The conviction rates achieved were high—often close to 90 percent. But the numbers of such cases did not readily decline in the nineteenth century. The one factor that cannot be easily measured is the extent to which U.S. attorneys and marshals prevented even greater frauds by their vigorous prosecution of cases. Certainly, the enforcement program was vigorous enough to prevent many of the more timid or marginally law-abiding citizens from filing false claims, passing bogus currency, or making or selling white lightning.

The obstacles to a successful program of prosecutions were many. National public opinion was indifferent to the kinds of cases being tried in eastern Tennessee. The recurring lack of funds made the government appear indecisive in its desire to punish wrongdoers, as did the leniency of the district judges in revenue cases, and the rarity of clear and decisive instructions from the attorney general hurt. The resistance of the mountain communities, which included gunplay, made the jobs of the attorneys and marshals more difficult. All in all, federal officials in eastern Tennessee did a good job in difficult circumstances. The deputies acted with restraint and bravery when fired upon by counterfeiters or moonshiners, and several gave their lives or were maimed in the federal service. The marshals attempted to alleviate the lack of funds by securing personal bank loans and trying to arrange credit or a place to sleep for jurors and witnesses. Faced with the refusal of most attorneys general to issue instructions, U.S. attorneys and marshals regularly gave instructions of their own.

But though it was true, as Attorney Wiltse tried to tell the moonshiners, that nineteenth-century progress marched steadily onward, it was impossible to force east Tennessee to fit the mold of a modern, progressive United States. To the extent that the federal attorneys and marshals failed, they failed because they were battling a symptom of poverty, and they had no weapons to fight the disease—nor were they called upon to do so. Such practices as adulterating coinage and distilling beverages unhampered are as old as civilization itself, and the government officers undertook a monumental task in attempting to modify such ancient practices, especially in the poor, isolated, mountainous region of east Tennessee.

5

The Anteroom to Statehood The Justice Department in Arizona Territory

I

The professed policy of the U.S. government toward the territories was to prepare them for admission to the Union so that they might receive the same rights and powers enjoyed by the states. The judges, attorneys, and marshals appointed by the president for service in the various territories were expected to aid local authorities in establishing law and order, to help the territory grow in such a way that it fit the mold of the states, and in short to help the territory prepare itself for full membership in the Union.[1]

In Arizona Territory federal officers faced an overwhelmingly difficult task. Arizona in 1870 had only a scattered population, was undeveloped, relatively lawless, and very far from being ready for statehood. With some ninety-six hundred residents in the 1870 census, Arizona ranked forty-fifth of the forty-six states and territories as to population. Even the frontier territory of Montana had twice the population of Arizona, while Utah Territory was nine times as populous. Arizona was still largely undeveloped a decade later. The 1880 census ranked Arizona last of the states and territories in value of manufactures, and second to last in the value of farm products. Arizona's only claim to economic importance was her production of precious minerals; here the territory ranked seventh in the nation.[2]

There were no railroads in Arizona in 1870, while roads and stage lines were few and rude. Although the census listed nineteen hundred school-age children, there were no nonsectarian public schools in the territory. As was the case with Utah, many easterners had reason to feel that Arizona was out of conformity with the rest of the United States. Not only were public schools absent, but the preponderance of bachelors meant that the traditional American family had not taken root. Men outnumbered women four to one in Arizona. Furthermore, Anglo-Americans were completely outnumbered by Indians and Mexican-Americans. By the 1880s Mormons and Chinese immigrants provided further diversity not usually appreciated by leaders of the territory or by eastern politicians. Thomas Jefferson's ideal society of sturdy yeoman farmers certainly did not develop; the only farmers in Arizona were members of certain Indian tribes and a small number of Mexican-Americans.[3]

Yet Arizona grew quickly. Its population quadrupled between the 1870 and 1880 censuses, then more than doubled by 1890. From all over the United States, people arrived to participate in the development of what was perceived as the nation's last frontier. Arizona settlers gave up the comforts of the East to make their fortunes in this raw territory. When rich gold and silver strikes proved elusive, Arizonans turned to another obvious source of money: the federal government. One could make money honestly from the government by holding office or contracting to supply the Indian reservations or army outposts. One could also steal from the federal government through embezzlement, fraudulent land claims, trespass on federal lands, robbing the mails, or direct theft of government property.

All of these kinds of crimes, and more, would receive the attention of the federal attorneys and marshals in Arizona. Over the two decades beginning in 1870, the territory's U.S. attorneys handled a large number of federal criminal cases. Arizona ranked seventh in the nation in number of criminal cases per capita. It was not an atypical day when Arizona's federal marshal telegraphed Washington in 1878, "Five stage robberies, mail and express, last ten days. Called on from all over territory to act." The high crime rate in Arizona was inevitable given the fact that the territory was full of ambitious men, some of whom had begun a criminal career before coming to the territory, and because the isolation and sparseness of population meant that many crimes would go unwitnessed. In addition to working to punish mail robbers, Justice Department officers in Arizona also worked to prevent smuggling across the Mexican border, to prevent illegal immigration of Chinese, to guard federal land from timber thieves, and to punish fraudulent army contractors. Although the kinds of cases were varied, federal prosecutors by their actions simultaneously sought to protect the interests of the federal government and to help prepare Arizona for eventual statehood.[4]

Many cases involved the Apache Indians. U.S. attorneys and marshals performed a wide range of tasks, including both defense and prosecution of Indian murderers, prosecution of whites who murdered Indians, and prosecution of whites who traded illegally with the Indians. "Apache" is a label pinned by whites to several distinct groups of Indians who were tied together more by common language than by closely related societies. The Apache groups subsisted by hunting, raising crops, and raiding their enemies to take cattle or other goods. These people did not submit readily to white domination, and the practice of raiding Indian neighbors was soon expanded to include raids on the whites who were encroaching on their traditional lands.[5]

Arizona was divided into three judicial districts in the charge of district judges appointed by the president to four-year terms. Sitting together, the three judges constituted the territorial supreme court. In 1871 the First District Court met at Tucson, the Second at Arizona City, and the Third at Prescott and Phoenix. As in Utah, the district judges heard territorial as well as federal cases. But in Arizona locally elected officers were permitted to try the territorial cases, while the U.S. attorney and marshal were restricted to federal cases.[6]

The U.S. attorney in 1870 was Converse Willard Chamberlin Rowell. Rowell was a native of Vermont who had moved to California in 1850. Joining the California Infantry during the Civil War, he was dismissed from the service in 1863 for disobeying orders. By 1864 Rowell was practicing law in Arizona, and, in the last days of President Andrew Johnson's administration, he received the appointment as the territory's federal attorney. Forty-three years old when he assumed office, Rowell had previously served as justice of the peace and member of the territorial legislature.[7]

C.W.C. Rowell found his first years as U.S. attorney exceedingly difficult. Early in his tenure he had to complain regularly to Washington about the failure of U.S. Marshal Edward Phelps to do his duty. Phelps seemed to have little interest in the office, and Rowell found himself without funds and without any way to have served the process of the court. Finally, the *Arizona Miner* reported that Phelps had "skedaddled into Mexico with funds belonging to his country and countrymen." Arizona's territorial delegate secured the appointment of his friend Isaac Q. Dickason to replace Marshal Phelps. Dickason was a successful man who had made his money by prospecting and speculating in mining lands.[8]

The ambitious Dickason hoped that the marshalship would not only bring him honor, but a good income as well. He very quickly found, however, that the fees were small, while serving process in Arizona was expensive, and, like Phelps, he soon lost interest in his position. Although Dickason's deputies served some process of the courts, U.S. interests suffered, and Rowell had to send regular complaints to Washington.[9]

Some of the earliest cases to occupy Rowell involved the trade of private citizens with Arizona's Indians. Rowell prosecuted these traders for violation of the Intercourse Acts, which provided that only federal Indian agents and their designees could trade with reservation Indians. Such cases were locally unpopular, since Arizonans believed that everyone should have an opportunity to make a profit by such trade. The only kinds of Indian trade cases that had the support of the local citizens were prosecutions for selling liquor to the Indians; most citizens of Arizona believed that Indians' drinking led to their acts of violence against whites. Such acts of violence seemed increasingly common in 1870 and 1871.[10]

A federal judge for Arizona later recalled that he and other citizens of Arizona believed that "the Apache was indeed the scourge of the Southwest"; certainly, "no traveler, no prospector or miner, no trader or lonely ranchman was ever safe during the early years of the American settlement of Arizona." Indeed, the Arizona legislature in 1864 had called for a war of extermination against the Apaches. In 1871 a committee of the legislature, including a future U.S. marshal, memorialized Congress for aid in killing the Apaches. "Our citizens have been murdered on the highway," reported the committee, and "some of the most fertile portions of our territory are being abandoned by the settlers, on account of the repeated and destructive raids of the Apache Indians."[11]

Meanwhile, some five hundred members of the Arivaipa band of Western Apache made peace with Lieutenant Royal A. Whitman of Camp Grant, who ordered them to camp nearby. Whitman gave the Indians a chance to earn food and clothing by doing agricultural work. But soon after they had encamped near Camp Grant, a series of raids on isolated white settlers began. It will never be known whether the Indian raiders were from among those who had surrendered to Whitman. Certainly, the citizens of Tucson believed that they were, and Tucsonians resolved to take action to prevent further depredations.[12]

On April 30, 1871, a party of forty-six Hispanos and Anglos, along with ninety-two Papago Indians, left Tucson under the leadership of William H. Oury and Jesús M. Elías. Attacking the Indian camp early in the morning, the party killed Apache adults and children who were present; a few Indian children were spared, and sold or given away. None of the Tucson group was seriously hurt, while estimates of Indian deaths range from forty to 128, nearly all women and children. Leader W. H. Oury later recalled, "By eight o'clock . . . our tired troops were resting and breakfasting on the San Pedro, a few miles above the post in the full satisfaction of a work well done."[13]

Although Rowell was aware of the massacre—as were all Arizona residents—he did not take any action until finally, three months later, Attorney General Akerman wrote, sending army reports of the slaughter and directing Rowell to "make every exertion to bring to justice the parties guilty of the outrage." Rowell replied that any attempt to prosecute the Camp Grant murderers would fail, since everyone in Pima County had either been involved in the raid in some way or was in hearty sympathy with the raiders. Akerman cannot have been heartened by Rowell's closing remark: "I will try but do not censure me if I fail."[14]

A month later Rowell was still trying to prepare an indignant Akerman for failure. A full investigation and a fair jury would be impossible, explained Rowell, "as everybody is interested in one way or another with suppressing the truth." Rowell knew by common report who had been involved, but common report is not useful evidence. "The difficulties I labor under in trying to enforce the U.S. laws here, are greater than you can imagine. . . . Still I will try the best I can to get justice done." Rowell asked the attorney general what charge should be made against the Camp Grant murderers.[15]

Both the attorney general and President Grant were of the opinion that the Camp Grant massacre was "purely murder," and that the perpetrators should be tried for murder. Rowell did not want to intrude on the jurisdiction of the local prosecutor, and he made clear the federal nature of the case by seeking indictments for the murder of Indians who were in the custody of the U.S. Army. Rowell succeeded in getting his friend Andrew H. Cargill a seat on the federal grand jury, and Cargill served as its secretary. At Rowell's instigation, Cargill spread the rumor that if indictments were not found President Grant would declare martial law and have the raiders tried by the military, which would likely have resulted in conviction and severe punishment. The ploy worked, and the grand jury reluctantly returned indictments against some one hundred individuals. But Rowell again reported to the Justice Department, "I have very little hope of convictions."[16]

The case of *United States v. Sidney R. DeLong et al.* came to trial in Tucson on December 6, 1871; all the defendants pled not guilty. The taking of testimony occupied five days. Rowell succeeded in getting two participants in the massacre to testify as to the facts in exchange for their names being dropped from the indictment. Rowell called Lieutenant Whitman, who testified that the Indians were in the custody of the United States, that they had only a few bows and arrows and no guns, and that they stayed near their camp and were not guilty of outrages upon Arizona citizens. A doctor testified as to the brutality of the attack upon the Indian camp, which had included rape and mutilation of the victims.[17]

The defense produced hats and boots that allegedly had belonged to citizens killed in Apache raids; defendants testified that these had been found at the Indians' encampment near Camp Grant. Other defendants testified that it was common practice to fit out parties "both civilian and military" to fight Indians. Rowell asked sarcastically if it was common practice to attack Indians who were in the direct custody of a detachment of the U.S. Army. But a juror demanded to know if the Indians at Camp Grant were under actual military guard, and Whitman was forced to admit that they were not.[18]

Closing arguments of the lawyers occupied one and a half days; Judge John Titus then gave his charge to the jury. To kill those who engage in unlawful depredations, Titus told the jury, would not be murder. On the frontier, "the resident is not bound to wait until the assassin, savage or civilized, is by his hearth or at his bedside. . . . He may anticipate his foe and quell or destroy him to secure his own personal safety." While easterners were protected by "a numerous population and adequate police," in Arizona, where citizens were few and scattered, "the citizen must take care of himself." Finally, denouncing the national government itself, the federal judge declared that if the government allowed one class of persons to prey upon another, then the injured class had the right to fall back upon "its natural right of self-defence." In Arizona, said Titus, "that[,] I charge you is the law."[19]

Given this charge by the federal judge, it is surprising that it took the jury as long as nineteen minutes to deliberate and find the defendants not guilty. Arizonans were jubilant, Rowell was not surprised, and Akerman, his faith in the goodness of human nature already weakened by the Ku Klux Klan, shook his head in amazement. Rowell was in a weak position, with officials in Washington disappointed and the citizens of Tucson hating him. Charges were made that he had offered to dismiss a minor criminal case against a defendant if the defendant would hire Rowell as counsel in a civil case. Rowell defended himself by saying that the two cases were unrelated and denying that it was an instance of veiled extortion, but, with no supporters in Arizona or Washington, Rowell was soon replaced by a new U.S. attorney. Rowell's career was not ruined, however. Moving away from Tucson, he set up a law practice in Arizona City and was soon elected district attorney for Yuma County by a landslide vote.[20]

Rowell was replaced by James E. McCaffry, a thirty-nine-year-old attorney who had come to Arizona during the Civil War as a member of the California Column of Union volunteers. McCaffry had held a number of posts including clerk of the legislature, territorial attorney general, and assistant U.S. attorney in certain cases under Rowell. His service as one of two chief defense lawyers in the Camp Grant case apparently was not held against him in Washington. At least he was well respected locally—the *Arizona Miner* praised him for nobly defending the persecuted Camp Grant defendants.[21]

McCaffry's tenure in office was notable chiefly for his prosecution of those who sold spirituous liquors to the Indians. By prosecuting such offenders vigorously, McCaffry hoped to prevent the kind of Indian raids that had led to the Camp Grant massacre. "We constantly see Indians in a state of intoxication," he reported to the attorney general, and he worried that this would contribute to the disruption of peace and order in Arizona. McCaffry achieved a strong record for conviction of violators of the Intercourse Acts.[22]

McCaffry's time was also occupied by problems with the marshalship of the territory. Isaac Q. Dickason still was nominally marshal, although he rarely applied for funds from Washington and rarely offered to spend funds for the good of the Arizona courts. When Arizona citizens complained to Washington that Dickason was a drinker and a gambler and an unworthy marshal, Attorney General George H. Williams asked McCaffry for his opinion. McCaffry replied that Dickason did gamble, although that was not the problem. He did drink, but "Mr. Dickason is not considered a drunkard." The real problem was that he was not really interested in being marshal. Soon after the attorney general chastised Dickason for neglecting his duties, the marshal abandoned his office, went north on a prospecting trip, and was never heard from again. Dickason was one of several early Arizona marshals who showed little interest in the office, did not serve long, and left office without properly settling his financial accounts.[23]

At about the time of Dickason's resignation, problems also arose in the U.S. attorney's office. Few records exist to explain just what happened, but in May 1875 McCaffry received a blunt letter from Attorney General Pierrepont: "I enclose herewith a copy of the order of the President suspending you from the office of Attorney of the United States for Arizona Territory." The new U.S. attorney arrived in the territory and called on McCaffry to confer about certain cases then in progress, but reported, "I found him in a condition totally unfit for the transaction of business," a condition from which he might never recover. A few months later McCaffry was dead; the coroner reported that he had died of a concussion received during a fall. The *Arizona Weekly Miner* reported that McCaffry had died "demoralized by drink." The paper went on to say that despite his drinking he had been universally hailed as an excellent attorney, and indeed it is remarkable that almost no complaints about McCaffry are in the Justice Department files—this was rarely the case for any territorial attorney or marshal.[24]

Finally, the department did manage to secure the services of an attorney and marshal who were interested in a long and faithful service. U.S. Attorney Everett B. Pomroy, a young Californian, arrived at his post in Arizona in June 1875 and served seven years. U.S. Marshal Crawley P. Dake took office in 1878 and served a full four-year term. A Union veteran of Gettysburg and the Wilderness, Dake had been severely wounded in the hip during the war and was still crippled by this injury. In postwar Michigan he had been a minor Republican leader and a federal revenue officer. On receiving the marshal's appointment, Dake and his wife and children moved to Arizona; Dake remained in the territory until his death in 1890. Assisting him was his chief deputy, Joseph W. Evans, who had gained valuable experience as a special agent of several express and stagecoach companies.[25]

One of the most important classes of case handled by Pomroy and Dake involved individuals who recruited and trained, within Arizona, armed bands for the purpose of attempting to join a revolution against the Díaz government of Mexico. Marshal Dake and Deputy Evans organized a major expedition against these bands, especially the group led by Brijido Reyes. Reyes's group numbered about seventy, but Dake complained that whenever he got within striking distance the group scattered. The marshal's posse quickly spent the $1,200 authorized by the attorney general; Dake soon wrote asking for another $2,000. The expense would help maintain friendly relations between the United States and Mexico, Dake urged. Already, he and Evans had received "very complimentary" letters from the governor of the Mexican state of Sonora thanking them for their help in tracking down the revolutionaries.[26]

Sonorans grew increasingly angry at the bands of revolutionaries. Reyes's men held the Mexican town of Magdalena hostage until they were given $4,000; Reyes laughingly told the townspeople that he was more a highwayman than a revolutionary. Soon, he was wanted by the Sonoran courts for robbery and by the federal courts of Arizona for violation of the United States' Neutrality Acts. Reyes regularly crossed the border between Sonora and Arizona. Finally, after two weeks of chasing the revolutionary bandits, Dake managed to arrest one of Reyes's chief lieutenants and nine of his followers. Pomroy tried the ten for organizing an expedition on U.S. soil for the invasion of Mexico; for this violation of the Neutrality Acts, the defendants received a fine of $200 each and were sent for a two-year sentence to the Detroit House of Corrections. Dake and Evans did much to create good feeling between the United States and Mexico; this was fortunate, given the sore trials to which U.S. relations with Mexico were soon subjected.[27]

The problems were, at the time, called the "cowboy troubles" and would soon capture the attention of the U.S. public, anger Mexican authorities, and involve President Chester Arthur in Arizona's law enforcement. The cowboy troubles were a time of rampant criminal activity that began with an epidemic of stagecoach robberies. Since the robberies usually involved the U.S. mails as well as bullion, most of these crimes were both federal and territorial. Detecting and capturing the dozens of stage robbers who preyed upon the mails in 1878 and 1879 was difficult, Dake reported, because they were not individual robbers but "appear to act in concert." Governor Anson P. K. Safford urged that the highwaymen "be swept from the face of the earth as remorselessly as the most ferocious wild beast." Marshal Dake asked the attorney general to provide the needed financial support, as "there is a great state of excitement throughout the territory in consequence of the frequent robberies and the success of the desperadoes."[28]

Dake managed to capture many of the mail robbers, while Pomroy's prosecutions usually resulted in convictions and heavy jail sentences. But all too often the mail robbers escaped from rude frontier jails and headed across the border into Sonora. The *Arizona Miner* was prophetic when it warned, "Mexico will soon object to being overridden with people belonging to the United States whose hands are fresh stained with the blood of their fellow man." But the stage robberies of 1878 and 1879 were just the beginning.[29]

Attorney General Wayne McVeagh first heard of the disorders in April 1881; he then asked U.S. Attorney Pomroy to investigate the "gang of desperadoes called cowboys." Pomroy wrote back, explaining that the brigands were men "who subsist by rapine, plunder and highway robbery, and whose amusements are drunken orgies and murder." More specifically, the "cowboys" were organized groups of outlaws who stole cattle, smuggled cattle and horses, robbed stagecoaches, and generally made their living by crime. They found it advantageous to operate in an area where the boundaries of four jurisdictions—Arizona, New Mexico, Sonora, and Chihuahua—came together.[30]

A few months after McVeagh's letter the depredations of the outlaw gangs seemed to be growing worse. Arizona's Governor Frederick A. Trittle wrote to Washington reporting that "robbery, murder, and resistance of law have become so common that they have ceased to cause the least surprise." Marshal Dake said that he was sending out ever-larger posses to capture the robbers, but that the expense was going to be enormous. Dake's chief deputy reported the deaths of many Mexican citizens at the hands of U.S. desperados, adding, "If the cowboys are not suppressed soon these depredations will occasion serious international trouble," since Mexican officials were becoming incensed. Dake, Deputy Evans, and Governor Luís Torres of Sonora continued to be in constant communication, ignoring the regular channels of diplomacy.[31]

The most famous event in this carnival of disorder in Arizona was the shoot-out at the O.K. Corral in the boomtown of Tombstone. Historians such as Daniel Boorstin have long reveled in the ambiguity of "good guy" and "bad guy" on the western frontier. The lawmen Wyatt and Virgil Earp seem incongruous to the twentieth-century mind because they were at once peace officers and the gambling frequenters of saloons. This combination would not have seemed so strange in nineteenth-century Tombstone. The Earps were well respected in their adopted home; they carefully pursued political success within the Republican party, made judicious real estate investments, and cultivated the friendship of some of the town's leading citizens, including John P. Clum, mayor and editor of the *Tombstone Epitaph*. Clum later recalled that Wyatt Earp was "my ideal of the strong, manly, serious and capable peace officer."[32]

Virgil Earp was a regular deputy U.S. marshal under Crawley P. Dake; he was also police chief of Tombstone. Wyatt Earp, too, had served as one of Dake's deputies, and Morgan Earp had done some work as a federal deputy marshal as well. Facing the Earps in the O.K. Corral shoot-out were five members of the Clanton gang of cattle rustlers. Deputy Marshal Wyatt Earp had earned the enmity of the Clantons when he visited their ranch and recovered several mules stolen from the U.S. Army. Later events had only worsened the bad feeling between Wyatt Earp and the Clantons. On the day of the shoot-out members of the Clanton gang were heard to say that they would shoot any Earp on sight. As the town's chief peace officer, Virgil Earp attempted to disarm the Clanton gang under ordinances that prohibited carrying weapons within the city limits. Unsuccessful in these efforts, the Earps finally confronted the Clantons with weapons drawn, and the ensuing gunfight resulted in the deaths of three of the five members of the Clanton gang.[33]

Some have said that the trouble between the Clantons and the Earps was purely personal and that the shoot-out at the O.K. Corral was really an assassination. Defenders of the Earps have said that they acted properly, as local peace officers, to disarm known criminals who were making threats and illegally carrying guns within the town limits. The truth is that a variety of factors motivated the Earps, and the shoot-out was a mixture of proper law enforcement, local power struggle, and personal quarrel.[34]

Justice Department records suggest an additional dimension to the fight at the O.K. Corral. Early during the cowboy troubles, federal attorneys and marshals in Arizona were repeatedly instructed to restore order in the territory. U.S. Attorney Everett B. Pomroy had reported to Washington that, although most of the outlaws' crimes were not federal but territorial (murder, assault, highway robbery, and cattle rustling), the local Justice Department officers should get involved anyway. "The territories are," Pomroy wrote, "wards of the Government . . . and they naturally look to the General Government for assistance and support." Furthermore, the cowboy troubles were likely to disrupt U.S. relations with Mexico. For these reasons Pomroy and Dake involved themselves in local actions against the gangs.[35]

When President Chester Arthur asked the attorney general to urge Marshal Dake to take vigorous action against the "cowboys," Dake telegraphed back proudly: "My deputies at Tombstone have struck one effectual blow to that element, killing three out of five." In another report Dake supplied more details: "The Earps have rid Tombstone and neighborhood of this outlaw element. They killed several cowboys in Tombstone recently." At a hearing before the local magistrate on a charge of murder, Dake continued, "my deputies were vindicated and publicly complimented for their bravery in driving this outlaw element from this part of our territory." The shoot-out had sent an important signal to all of the brigands, Dake concluded, and "hereafter my deputies will not be interfered with in hunting down stage robbers, mail robbers, cattle thieves, and all that class of murdering *banditti* on the border." Dake was disappointed to find, however, that few Arizonans applauded the work of his deputies, the Earps.[36]

The cowboy troubles were not yet over. One month after the Tombstone shoot-out, President Arthur, in a message to Congress, reported on Arizona's lawless condition and urged legislators to define as new federal crimes any actions that might lead to international border troubles with neighboring countries. Arthur also suggested that Congress rescind its prohibition of the use of the army as a posse, a prohibition made by a Democratic Congress tired of army involvement in southern election cases. If Congress wished, such a rescinding could be applied to the territories only, Arthur added. In Arizona Territory, "from sparseness of population . . . it is often quite impracticable to summon a civil posse."[37]

Wyatt Earp, seated second from left, with a number of his cronies, shortly before he moved to Tombstone, Arizona. Marshal Dake wrote proudly to Washington, "My deputies at Tombstone have struck one effectual blow" to the lawless element at the O.K. Corral, "killing three out of five" of the Clanton gang. Courtesy of Arizona Historical Society.

When Congress still had not acted five months later, Arthur sent a second message urging action. Finally, a congressional committee told Arthur that special legislation was not needed; the president clearly had the power to use the army to suppress disorder in the territories. The federal government accordingly began supplying Dake with troops as well as dollars in some instances.[38]

On May 3, 1882, Crawley P. Dake reported the daring nighttime stage robbery along the Black Canyon line. Four or five men had stopped both the stage going toward Phoenix and the stage returning from that city. One of the men wounded by the robbers was a deputy U.S. marshal who was a passenger on one stage. The double robbery in Black Canyon spurred Arthur to action again; this time, he issued a proclamation preliminary to declaring martial law in Arizona, since "it has become impracticable to enforce . . . the laws of the United States within that territory." The president ordered the outlaw bands to "disperse and retire peaceably to your respective abodes" within twelve days. Stage robberies seemed to fall off, and Arthur never declared martial law. Under the leadership of Dake and his chief deputy, Joseph W. Evans, with large sums of money supplied by Washington and the occasional use of troops to aid the marshal, the cowboy troubles had largely passed by 1883.[39]

Dake's four-year term as marshal expired in July 1882. Letters from members of Congress urged that he be reappointed in view of his largely successful work in moving against the "cowboys," but Dake made it clear that he did not want a second term. Meanwhile, Pomroy received one of those abrupt telegrams from the attorney general: "It is intimated to the Department that you have resigned. Is such the case? If not, your resignation of the office of U.S. Attorney for the Territory of Arizona, will be accepted." Pomroy responded, "The language of your telegram is unusual and may not have been properly sent." He quoted the telegram in full, but Attorney General Benjamin H. Brewster assured him that there had been no mistake. The department was unhappy at the fact that Pomroy was counsel for a firm that was going to be sued by the federal government; if he remained in office as U.S. attorney, the government would have to hire special counsel for the lawsuit.[40]

Zan L. Tidball was appointed marshal in July 1882, while at about the same time James A. Zabriskie received his commission as U.S. attorney. Zabriskie had received a bachelor's degree at Columbia University and then studied law in California with Stephen J. Field. A California volunteer during the Civil War, Zabriskie served at Yuma, Arizona, and also in western Texas. Settling at El Paso, young Zabriskie served as assistant U.S. attorney for western Texas and as a local prosecutor. Coming to Arizona as a Treasury Department official in 1878, he entered private practice in the territory, accepting many court-appointed cases defending indigent Hispanos.[41]

Much of the work of Zabriskie and Tidball involved cleaning up the disasters left behind by dishonest federal officials. Two of these cases were suits against the bondsmen of Marshals Isaac Q. Dickason and Wiley W. Standefer. Both men had left office without settling their accounts; little progress was possible in the suits against the bondsmen, because several had left the territory and the others did not seem to have very much money. The United States won the suit against the bondsmen of Dickason but had trouble collecting; the case against the bondsmen of Standefer was continued from term to term.[42]

Zabriskie was also detailed to investigate one of hundreds of the nation's Star Route cases of fraud by contractual mail carriers. Zabriskie functioned as a detective as he investigated the mail route between Tres Alamos and Clifton. The mail carrier had submitted a petition, allegedly signed by persons along the route, asking for more frequent mail service (with the attendant increase in pay for the carrier). Zabriskie's investigation showed that the route received very little mail, did not warrant increased service, and that the petition was fraudulent. His investigations were used in the Star Route prosecutions, but the government was not successful in court.[43]

The fraud case that most interested Zabriskie was the case of Indian Agent Joseph C. Tiffany at the San Carlos Reservation. A federal grand jury investigated the reservation in the fall of 1882. The grand jurors reported to Judge Wilson W. Hoover that "fraud, peculation, conspiracy, larceny, plots and counterplots, seem to be the rule of action upon this reservation." The jurors little suspected when they first convened "that they were about to open a Pandora's box of iniquities seldom surpassed in the annals of crime." Zabriskie asserted proudly that the labors of the grand jury "will live in the recollections of the people here through all time." Both the attorney and the grand jury were incensed at Tiffany not only because he embezzled many thousands of dollars in cash and property but because the Indians were hungry, ill clothed, and increasingly upset with the government and with life on the reservation. Tiffany and his cronies could easily be responsible for renewed Indian wars, Zabriskie concluded.[44]

The case went to trial at the fall term of 1883. Zabriskie was confident of victory until Tiffany spirited away the chief prosecution witness, got him drunk, and sent him into Sonora, where the yellow fever was raging. The witness was never heard from again and reportedly died of the fever. Zabriskie was forced to dismiss the case against Tiffany. Tiffany meanwhile embarked on a wide-ranging program of character assassination aimed at prosecutor Zabriskie. He appeared before a committee of the House of Representatives that was investigating the Justice Department, accusing Zabriskie of prosecuting frivolous cases to make fees, citing his own dismissed case as an example. In an interview with the *Philadelphia Times,* which was copied by many national papers, Tiffany charged that the U.S. attorney had secured the indictment by "procured" testimony of "scalawags" and "gutter snipes." In the Philadelphia paper the interview ran under the headline "A District Attorney's Doings. Some Account of the Dishonest and Blackmailing Schemes of Zabriskie, Who Still Remains in Office."[45]

Zabriskie was infuriated and tried to get himself summoned to appear before the House committee before which Tiffany had testified. The committee, a majority Democratic, refused to subpoena Zabriskie. Instead he submitted a sworn affidavit answering Tiffany's charges, but the affidavit was ignored.[46]

Zabriskie tackled another tough opponent in his prosecution of Charles H. Lord, of the powerful Lord and Williams Company, for "timber trespass," the unauthorized cutting of timber on federally owned land. This case had its origin when Lord and Williams contracted to supply the Southern Pacific Railroad with twenty thousand cords of mesquite and catsclaw at $4 per cord. The company had caused about forty-five hundred cords to be cut before Marshal Tidball stepped in and took possession. Lord and Williams hired seven lawyers who began constructing a legal case and lobbying in Washington. The lawyers argued that mesquite and catsclaw were not timber, but fuel. Timber was what was used to build the structure of houses and ships. But Zabriskie countered that if the public lands were denuded of the only wood upon them they would be worthless for bona fide settlers, and Arizona would remain an undeveloped, underpopulated territory undeserving of statehood.[47]

In the criminal case for timber trespass Lord was found guilty. As Marshal Tidball confided to the attorney general, the verdict was a surprise to everyone, "not because the evidence of guilt was lacking" but because Lord was socially prominent. Lord and Williams engaged in civil suits attempting to regain possession of the wood, including a suit against the U.S. marshal, but to no avail. Marshal Tidball took steps to sell the wood, now deemed the property of the federal government. But because the wood was stacked along the tracks of the Southern Pacific Railroad, it had value only if the railroad would agree to transport it for the buyer. This the railroad was not disposed to do. The Southern Pacific announced that it might be interested in buying the wood, but only if the price were very low. The railroad agent wrote Tidball teasingly, "If you know what the department expects to do about [the wood] in case we do not take it, please let me know."[48]

Federal timber policy as interpreted by the secretary of the interior was in flux in this period. In 1882 the secretary dumbfounded federal officials in Arizona by declaring that mesquite was so soft that it was not timber. He also ruled that when federal law said that timber on mineral lands might be cut for "domestic consumption," this meant that citizens could cut the timber or have it cut for use anywhere within the territory. Previous rulings had interpreted "domestic consumption" as meaning "use on the mineral lands from which the wood was cut." Fortunately for Zabriskie, the secretary modified these rulings so that mesquite was again declared to be timber, and timber cut on mineral lands must be used for mining purposes.[49]

The number of timber trespass cases continued to increase in the 1880s. Zabriskie viewed himself as protector of future settlers who would want to buy federal lands with the accompanying timber; to allow woodcutters to denude the public lands of their timber "would be a crime against civilization." Nevertheless, many Arizonans did not like the timber cases since wood was scarce and constantly needed. "You can therefore see," Zabriskie wrote the attorney general, "the difficulties under which we labor here in our efforts to make the government respected and respectable." Zabriskie added that the Vulture Mine had just advertised its willingness to buy thirty thousand cords of wood. "This will be cut on government land, of course."[50]

The attorney general replied, "I had hoped that the conviction of Dr. C. H. Lord . . . would deter evil disposed persons from depredating upon the public lands. This, however, appears not to be the case." A discouraged attorney general ended by instructing Zabriskie to "prosecute only cases of clear guilt, but prosecute all such."[51]

Among the other cases handled by Zabriskie during his service as U.S. attorney were cases of smuggling cattle, making a fraudulent land claim, and selling liquor to the Indians. Also, he prosecuted a number of newly arrived Mormon settlers for polygamy and defended an Indian agent who had ejected white squatters from a reservation.

With the election of Grover Cleveland to the presidency, Democratic politicians in Arizona began to look for faults among the Republican federal officeholders. Tidball was berated for the fact that he was behind in his accounting reports; he resigned shortly thereafter. In his place, Cleveland appointed William Kidder Meade, who had spent the last fourteen of his thirty-four years in Arizona. Meade had served in both houses of the legislature as well as a term as deputy sheriff of Pinal County. The new marshal was also a wholehearted Democrat.[52]

U.S. Marshal William K. Meade was a former member of the territorial legislature and a former deputy sheriff. A fourteen-year resident of the territory prior to his appointment, Meade was a wholehearted Democrat. Courtesy of Western History Collections, University of Oklahoma Libraries.

The new attorney for Arizona was Owen T. Rouse, a graduate of the College of Law at Cleveland, Ohio. He had practiced law ten years and had served in the state senate in Missouri. Rouse moved his family to Arizona on receipt of Cleveland's appointment in the fall of 1885.[53]

Unfortunately for Rouse, Marshal Meade immediately conceived a dislike for him. One cause was the fact that a close personal friend of Meade had been an unsuccessful candidate for the attorney's job. Soon the marshal was complaining to Attorney General Garland that Rouse "has managed to make himself ridiculous before the court," and was "the laughing stock of the bar." When Garland asked the opinion of Judge William H. Barnes, Barnes reluctantly admitted that Rouse's first year in office had been largely unsuccessful. A departmental examiner looking into Rouse's performance found that the root of the problem seemed to be that the rules of procedure in Arizona were very much different from those back east. Nevertheless, Rouse "is not an orator, nor is he conversant with criminal law."[54]

Garland went so far as to ask one of Rouse's friends in Congress to secure his resignation so as to prevent the ugly necessity of a removal. But Rouse now began to fight back. Writing to the chairman of the Senate Judiciary Committee, Rouse reported that he had been about to resign because of the poor compensation but now meant to fight to stay on. "When my term of office is closed, I expect to return home a wiser, but not much wealthier man than when I came here." He was a victim of factional politics, contended Rouse, and, considering the expense he had incurred in moving his family to Arizona, he deserved at least to finish out his four-year term. Members of the Tucson bar soon sent a petition to Cleveland, and, later, one to Garland, urging that Rouse be retained. Rouse's performance as prosecutor continued to improve, and in April 1893 he was appointed to one of Arizona's federal judgeships.[55]

As U.S. attorney, Rouse prosecuted a wide variety of criminal cases. Rouse also was attorney for the defense in the case of *Arizona v. Hambleton*. B. E. Hambleton was a mounted inspector of the Customs Service. He had seized some cigars smuggled into the United States by D. M. Kahler, station agent at Nogales for the Sonora Railroad Company. Kahler finally paid the duty and took his cigars but was heard to mutter that Nogales was too small for him and Hambleton to live in at the same time. In a second argument over the importation of Mexican cattle into the United States via the Sonora Railroad, Kahler attacked Hambleton, and Hambleton shot and killed him. Local sentiment was against the customs agent, Rouse wrote the attorney general, since Nogales was a hotbed of smuggling. In the first trial the jury was hopelessly deadlocked, but in a second trial in November 1887 Rouse secured Hambleton's acquittal.[56]

Rouse's most important actions as U.S. attorney in Arizona had to do with a new period of trouble between Indians and whites beginning in 1885. Chiricahua Apaches under Geronimo left the San Carlos Reservation, while other Apaches fled the White Mountain Reservation. Historians agree that the Indians had justification for their renewed violence against whites. Many of the Indian agents had embezzled funds and supplies, leaving the Indians short of food and other necessities. Also, the discovery of coal and copper on some reservation lands meant that the reservations were soon being overrun by anxious white miners. Geronimo in particular caught the attention of the newspaper-reading public back east, and the solicitor general soon asked Rouse to look discreetly into the matter of alleged crimes committed by Geronimo and his band and to begin to make a list of witnesses to any such crimes. "It is not desirable that anyone but yourself should know the result or purpose of your inquiry," he added.[57]

Rouse sent in the report of robberies and murders committed by Geronimo's followers but cautioned that questions of jurisdiction were far from clear. Congress had passed new laws regarding jurisdiction of Indian crimes, and the Supreme Court had not yet interpreted these laws. It was uncertain whether the cases should be tried in tribal, territorial, or U.S. courts. But the attorney general replied firmly that "the number and character of offenses committed are such, that proper steps should be taken to bring these offenders to trial for their crimes." Questions of jurisdiction would be left to the judges.[58]

Congress had recently passed the Major Crimes Act of 1885, which called for the trial of Indians accused of serious crimes in the territories before "Territorial Courts." Attorney Rouse was of the opinion that Congress was unaware of the ambiguity it created in giving jurisdiction to "Territorial Courts." Did Congress mean the U.S. district courts established for the territories? Or did Congress mean the county courts established by the legislature and presided over by federally appointed judges? Although both sets of courts had the same presiding judges, the other officers of court were different, and the courts had separate records and separate rules of procedure. Judge William W. Porter called it a "vexed question" but agreed with Rouse that Congress must have intended that the U.S. district courts try the cases.[59]

The Arizona case that finally settled the question was the murder trial of Gonshayee. Gonshayee and his followers killed an Indian and a federal official on their White Mountain Reservation, then fled the reservation and killed a number of white citizens. The prosecution was for Gonshayee's murder of rancher William Deal, which took place off the reservation. Gonshayee was convicted in the district court, and he petitioned the U.S. Supreme Court for a writ of habeas corpus.[60]

Rouse sent his arguments to the solicitor general for use in preparing the United States' brief. Rouse contended that, although the Major Crimes Act spoke vaguely of "Territorial Courts," it must mean the district courts. Several of Arizona's counties were covered with reservations, and it would bankrupt the counties to require their officers to arrest and try all Indians who committed serious crimes. In fact, federal law prohibited local law officers from even entering reservations—how could they serve process? Although the Major Crimes Act said that Indians would be tried under "territorial law," Rouse believed that this simply meant that, since the United States had no murder statutes, the district courts should follow territorial laws specifying procedure and punishment.[61]

The U.S. Supreme Court heard *Gon-shay-ee, Petitioner* quickly, and in April 1889 Attorney General William H. H. Miller relayed the news to Rouse by telegram: "Supreme Court has decided the district court, as a United States court, had no jurisdiction." Miller ordered Rouse and Meade to take immediate steps to have all Indians convicted of major crimes in Arizona's district courts brought back from their imprisonment in Detroit. The reasoning behind the justices' decision was that the intent of Congress was to have Indians subject to the same laws as whites. Since white murderers were tried by county courts, Indians should be too. The justices claimed that they were looking out for the Indians' rights: A defendant should have the right to be tried near his home by a county court and not be dragged away to a distant district court. It is far from clear, however, that an Indian defendant would receive any special benefit by being tried before a jury made up of the neighbors of the white murder victim.[62]

Rouse was incredulous and sent in more arguments to the attorney general, asking how the Court could possibly have made this decision. But Miller answered by telegraph, "All you suggest . . . was fully presented and considered." The marshal began making arrangements to bring dozens of Indian convicts back from the Detroit House of Corrections. When Rouse asked if the marshal might turn some of the defendants over to territorial authorities for retrial, the attorney general answered that this would not be proper. But if Rouse wanted to let the territorial authorities know when and where the Indian prisoners would finally be freed, this would be permissible. One of the prisoners retried by local authorities was the Apache Kid. On being returned from Detroit, the Apache Kid was tried by local officers for assault with intent to kill; he was convicted but soon escaped and continued his life of crime. He was never recaptured.[63]

After serving four years as U.S. attorney, Rouse was replaced by Harry R. Jeffords. As a Republican in Mississippi, Jeffords had worked assiduously for free voting and fair elections. He moved to Arizona in 1884 in hopes of improving his health; he was thirty-four years old at the time of his appointment. Jeffords had served as a state senator in Mississippi and as district attorney in Arizona. He was widely respected in the territory, and even Democrats hailed his appointment as a good one.[64]

U.S. Attorney Jeffords's greatest role in Arizona history came with his investigation of the Wham robbery of May 11, 1889. Paymaster Joseph W. Wham of the U.S. Army had been traveling to the various forts in Arizona, paying the men in cash, as was the custom. Wham's retinue included ten privates, a sergeant, and a clerk. En route from Fort Grant to Fort Thomas, the party stopped when they noticed large boulders in the road. A band of robbers immediately opened fire on the soldiers. Although Wham and his men attempted to shoot back, most of them were quickly injured, and they retreated a distance away from the wagon. The robbers stole the moneybags containing more than $28,000. It was the most daring, most successful, most remunerative robbery ever committed in Arizona.[65]

All federal army and legal officers wanted to secure swift, decisive punishment of the robbers, to defend the honor of the army and of the nation, and to prevent similar robberies of the large sums of money carried by army paymasters. Jeffords and Marshal Meade went to work on the case, and Meade soon arrested a number of suspects in the Gila

Site of Wham robbery, twenty-four hours after the crime. Such lonely stretches of road, running through vast and isolated territory, made highway robbery all too easy. The raid on army paymaster Wham and his small contingent of soldiers is arguably the most daring heist ever committed in Arizona. Courtesy of Arizona Historical Society.

valley. The trial of the Wham robbers, *United States v. Cunningham et al.*, began on November 12, 1889.[66]

Paymaster Joseph Wham was the chief witness. He testified that he had seen several of the seven defendants in Tucson since the robbery, and he identified two of them in open court. On cross-examination, however, he was forced to admit that he "wasn't positive about" earlier identifications. Wham also testified that some of the stolen gold dollars had had a strange, whitish cast to them, and that he had recently received some of these same whitish dollars at a store near the homes of the defendants. Jeffords submitted some of this money as evidence.[67]

The defense attorneys responded that it was ridiculous to imagine that Wham could actually identify certain gold dollars as being from his moneybags. They also produced a witness who swore that he had seen the ringleader, Mark Cunningham, on the far side of the territory at the time of the robbery. Jeffords forced this witness, William Brown, to repeat his story in endless detail and succeeded in getting him to stumble and contradict himself. After two and a half days of testimony the case went to the jury, which quickly returned a verdict of not guilty. The presiding judge later remarked that it was clear that at least some of the seven defendants were guilty, but the testimony of William Brown had made the jury uncertain. The attorney general remarked that "the result is a great disappointment to the department," and he backed Jeffords's decision to try the crucial witness William Brown for perjury. Two years later certain amateur detectives suggested that other men were guilty of the Wham robbery, but though the army and Justice Department looked into the matter, the case was too old and the evidence ambiguous. No one was ever punished for the crime.[68]

The Harrison administration had allowed Democratic Marshal William K. Meade to remain in office, fearing that a change could delay or otherwise affect the Wham trial. But on the close of the trial he was replaced by Robert H. Paul. Paul had lived an adventurous life. As a cabin boy on a whaler, Paul had been around the world twice, visiting New Zealand, South Africa, Siberia, and Tahiti. He was severely wounded when a whale tossed his little boat into the air. As a young man, he was sheriff of Calaveras County, California, in its "lawless times." In Arizona he served as a guard and detective for Wells, Fargo and for the Southern Pacific Railroad, working closely with Wyatt Earp and Bat Masterson in stage robbery cases. After serving a couple of terms as sheriff of Pima County, Paul received President Harrison's appointment as marshal.[69]

Paul was widely endorsed for the marshalship. Many were of the opinion that in his service as agent for Wells, Fargo and Southern Pacific, and as sheriff of Pima County, he was responsible for "the early capture or flight of the hard characters who formerly cursed this country with their presence." Attorney Jeffords declared that "his detective ability is miraculous in its character, and the great strength of physique enables him to run down and trace any trail which he may once strike."[70]

Among the more interesting cases handled by Marshal Paul and Attorney Jeffords were prosecutions under the Chinese Exclusion Acts. Congress had first limited Chinese immigration in 1882, when it passed a law that prohibited immigration of Chinese laborers for ten years, provided for deportation of illegal Chinese immigrants to the country from which they came, and prohibited state and federal courts from admitting the Chinese to citizenship. Chinese immigrants who were not laborers could enter the country only after presenting a certificate from the Chinese government attesting to their status. Later laws were even more stringent, extending the restrictions past the initial ten-year period. In passing the Chinese Exclusion Acts, Congress was motivated by a belief that the Chinese were too different from other residents ever to be assimilated into U.S. culture. The Chinese Exclusion Acts were a way of keeping unwanted diversity out of the Union.[71]

In Arizona about one in twenty-five residents was Chinese in 1880. The Chinese were seen by many Arizonans as gamblers, opium smokers, and prostitutes. A classic expression of racism against the Chinese is found in a *Tombstone Epitaph* article of 1882, a supposed description of the typical Chinese resident: "He is a heathen, a devourer of soup made from the fragrant juice of the rat, filthy, disagreeable, and undesirable generally, an incumbrance that we do not know how to get rid of." To some Arizona employers, however, the Chinese were a godsend, since they worked for low wages in mines, on the railroads, and on the newly developing irrigated farms of the territory.[72]

The first Arizona case under the Exclusion Acts was heard in July 1890. As provided by law, the hearing was before a U.S. commissioner and not the district court. Jeffords being ill, Assistant U.S. Attorney Calvert Wilson tried this first case of twenty-four Chinese who had come to Arizona to work. Wilson proved that the twenty-four had come from China aboard a steamer, and that on arrival in San Francisco Bay they had been transferred to another ship that carried them to the Sonoran port of Guaymas. From there they had traveled overland and entered Arizona illegally. The Chinese immigrants, through an interpreter, admitted to the facts of the case, but their court-appointed attorneys argued that since they had come to the United States from Mexico they could only be deported to Mexico—not to China.[73]

Assistant Attorney Wilson countered by saying that since the immigrants were in continual, unbroken transit from China they should be deported to China. The presiding commissioner agreed and ordered the aliens' deportation to China. The attorneys for the Chinese applied to Judge Joseph H. Kibbey of the Second District Court for a writ of habeas corpus. Counsel for both sides repeated their previous arguments. Calvert Wilson also asserted that the law provided no appeal from the commissioner's decision, and because the Chinese were aliens they were not entitled to the benefit of the writ of habeas corpus. Judge Kibbey agreed that the commissioner's decision was final, and Marshal Paul took the twenty-four to San Francisco, where they were put on a boat bound for the Orient.[74]

Soon, Jeffords was handling a dozen Chinese Exclusion cases each month. In the case of two immigrants, Ah Lem and Ah Chew, the commissioner declared that because the two men had lived for a time in Mexico they should be deported to Mexico. Accordingly, a deputy marshal escorted them to Nogales, where he put them across the line. U.S. customs officials complained bitterly of this action, pointing out that there was nothing to prevent Ah Lem and Ah Chew from quickly crossing back into the United States. The Justice Department then directed the marshal to take the more expensive course of putting the Chinese on a steamer at Yuma bound for Guaymas in southern Sonora. It was believed that this would discourage the return of those who were deported to Mexico.[75]

Like his predecessors, Jeffords handled a large number of cases for timber trespass. Although he had no trouble winning the conviction of small operators, when he tried to prosecute large companies and their managers Jeffords ran into trouble. In the case of *United States v. D. D. Ross* Jeffords tried an individual who cut or caused to be cut over 2 million board feet of lumber from federal lands near Willcox. This lumber was cut for the Copper Queen mining company, which was also sued by the government for the value of the timber cut. The defendant, Daniel Ross, argued that the woodcutting was permitted because the land was "mineral land" in the meaning of the law. He pointed out that the wood had been cut within "the California Mining District."[76]

Jeffords responded that the California Mining District was only a paper entity, a region that included some mineral land and much land that was valuable only for grazing or lumbering. He also pointed out that D. D. Ross and the other cutters had not only sold lumber to the Copper Queen Mining Company (perhaps permissible if the land cut over was really mineral land) but had also sold to general lumber merchants. These Copper Queen cases dragged on for many years. U.S. attorneys were forced to dismiss *United States v. D. D. Ross* twice because the juries appeared to be biased. Not until 1902 was the matter finally settled; Ross and Copper Queen won their cases.[77]

Jeffords had a full caseload in 1890 and 1891. He tried individuals for illegally fencing the public lands, tried a receiver of the U.S. Land Office for extortion, and tried another federal employee for defaulting. He prosecuted a number of Mormons for polygamy. He tried William Brown twice for perjury in the Wham trial, but the juries hung both times. While preparing for a third Brown perjury trial, Jeffords's old illnesses, including Bright's disease, returned, and the attorney died suddenly on April 2, 1891.[78]

Just how successful were the federal attorneys, marshals, and other officers in bringing calm, law, and order to the western frontier? As was the case in east Tennessee, the answer is mixed. There were some major failures. The inability of U.S. attorneys to win convictions in the Camp Grant case, the Copper Queen timber trespass cases, and the Wham robbery case was disappointing, particularly since the cases received widespread publicity within the territory and showed Arizonans that spectacular crimes could easily go unpunished. These trials also were widely reported back east, reinforcing in many people's minds the idea that Arizona was a lawless place far from ready for statehood. On the other hand, important victories were won, including the timber case against prominent merchant Charles H. Lord, the Neutrality Act cases against Brijido Reyes's followers, and scores of mail robbery and cattle-smuggling cases in the period of the cowboy troubles. Indian massacres did not again occur, and the number of stage robberies was much decreased by 1892—although such robberies still occurred four or five times per year. And while some of the well-known timber trespass cases were not successfully concluded, the overall conviction rate was high for this class of offense.

Looking at the conviction rate in Arizona, it is clear that federal prosecutors there did much better than in the other territories. The conviction rate in federal cases in New Mexico was an abysmal 15 percent, while in Wyoming the rate was 27 percent. Arizona's conviction rate was a highly respectable 64 percent. Against the forty-six states and territories, Arizona ranks eleventh as to conviction rate, higher than the apparently law-abiding states of Ohio, Pennsylvania, and Maine. So, despite a few major failures, federal law enforcement officers did achieve an admirable record for convictions. As in northern Mississippi, so in Arizona the record was one of a large number of cases and a high conviction rate. Arizona was at once a relatively lawless region, and a territory where federal law enforcement officers were doing their jobs successfully.[79]

II

As in the other states and territories, U.S. attorneys and marshals in Arizona often sought instructions from Washington. As officials of the national administration, they wanted to make certain they were following administration policy. But the attorney general, often preoccupied with cases before the Supreme Court or involved in administering the appropriation for federal courts, was extremely reluctant to give general or specific instructions.

When Marshal Robert H. Paul wanted to know if he should offer a reward for the capture of a defaulting official of the U.S. Land Office, Attorney General Miller replied, "It is thought best to give no present instructions." U.S. Attorney Jeffords asked for advice regarding the Wham case but was told, "It is impossible for the Department to give much advice to the United States Attorneys for the reason that our time is so taken up with matters immediately surrounding us." James A. Zabriskie needed advice on what to do with the wood that had been cut by Charles H. Lord. The Justice Department replied that he should act to protect the interests of the government. Zabriskie bristled. "It is to be presumed that I would do this to the best of my ability irrespective of any instructions on the subject." The case was novel, and he could not be guided by precedent. Zabriskie finally managed to get instructions as to the disposition of the wood.[80]

The inability to secure instructions was common to attorneys and marshals across the United States. What really sets Arizona apart in this respect is the fact that, while the Justice Department was reluctant to instruct its field officers, the attorneys and marshals were not left to "grope on." The reason for this is that nearly all of the cases handled by Arizona's federal law officers involved some department of the federal government other than Justice. The War Department was interested in Wham. The Customs Service was concerned about the Chinese cases and the defense of Inspector Hambleton against murder charges. The Indian service was interested in the Camp Grant and Tiffany cases. The Treasury Department worried about defaulting and embezzling officers. The General Land Office watched fraudulent land claim cases and cases of illegal fencing of public lands. The Post Office Department was concerned about the robbery of mail stages.

So, while the Department of Justice did send a number of letters to

Arizona declining to give advice, it also sent many letters that contained clear instructions. In a case of fraud by army contractors Attorney General Devens wrote to U.S. Attorney Pomroy, "The case is regarded by the War Department as an aggravated one, and you will prosecute these men with vigor, that an example may be made of them." In a case involving white settlers who were plundering the Pima Indians' water supply Attorney General Miller wrote to Harry R. Jeffords, enclosing a letter of the secretary of the interior and adding, "You will observe that the Secretary of the Interior considers the affair of some importance and shows some anxiety that it should not be allowed to drag." And in a timber trespass case involving the Silver King Mining Company Attorney General Garland passed on to U.S. Attorney Rouse the secretary of interior's belief that "this is a case demanding prompt and energetic action."[81]

The most detailed exchange of opinions and instructions involved the timber depredation cases. Federal attorneys in Arizona were glad that the interior secretary was interested in these cases, but they were also concerned that the secretary was interposing hardships in their prosecutions. In 1884 the secretary of interior received complaints that too many timber trespass cases were being brought in Arizona, and he asked Attorney General Brewster to prohibit all timber cases that did not originate with a timber agent of the Interior Department.[82]

Zabriskie answered patiently that "we have not had a timber agent stationed here for many a year. There is absolutely no one here to look after the interests of the Government except the U.S. Attorney and Marshal." The last timber agent had been very cozy with timber interests and had shown little interest in prosecution; now he had disappeared. "I desire to know," continued Zabriskie, "if we are to sit idly by and witness these depredations and not be permitted to arrest the progress of this vandalism?" A new timber agent was soon dispatched to the territory, and the cases moved forward.[83]

Receiving some direction from the various departments in Washington was a substantial help to the attorneys and marshals in Arizona. Another kind of help that arrived from the nation's capital was authorization for the offer of rewards. Federal officials in Arizona had great confidence in the utility of reward offers. In the East local police and patriotic citizens could usually gather the evidence necessary to advance criminal cases; in Arizona something more was needed. Police were few in number, and most crimes were committed in isolated lo-

When the attorney general asked U.S. Attorney James A. Zabriskie to move more cautiously in timber depredation cases, Zabriskie grew angry: "I desire to know if we are to sit idly by and witness these depredations and not be permitted to arrest the progress of this vandalism?" Courtesy of Arizona Historical Society.

calities where there were few witnesses. By offering rewards, law officers could in effect contract out investigative work—amateur lawmen would undertake to gather evidence and make an arrest. Governor John P. Hoyt asked the attorney general to offer a reward for the arrest and conviction of a mail robber, explaining that this "would lead some good detective to come here and carefully work up the cases."[84]

The attorney general was often willing to offer rewards. William H. H. Miller offered a $500 reward for the arrest and conviction of the Wham robbers. Rewards of $100 to $500 were also offered for a number of mail robbers, and for escaped federal prisoners. Sometimes the attorney general attempted to get other departments to supply the rewards. In 1890 Attorney General Miller declined to authorize a reward for the arrest of an extortionist in the General Land Office, because that office's commissioner refused to supply the money. In another case Attorney General Devens refused to agree to the offer of a reward but managed to get the postmaster general to agree to pay $1,000 for the hire of a detective.[85]

The direct hiring of detectives and other experts was not as common as the offer of rewards but still was helpful to attorneys and marshals in a number of cases. Detectives were hired to work up the evidence in the Wham case, in the case of an embezzling Indian agent, and in a number of cases of selling liquor to the Indians. In other cases surveyors were hired to prove various kinds of encroachments on public lands, including timber trespass and illegal fencing. Mineral experts were hired to assist in a number of prosecutions. In *United States v. D. D. Ross* the defendant claimed that his timber cutting was done on mineral lands and was therefore permitted under law. The U.S. attorney hired a local prospector to examine the land and testify as to its lack of valuable minerals. When the attorney found that the land was being minutely examined by the defendant's experts, he hired a nationally renowned geologist and mineralogist. And finally, the federal attorney paid an assayer who testified as to the worthlessness of ore taken from the cut-over land.[86]

U.S. attorneys often received permission from Washington to hire translators for trials. In Arizona a wide variety of language skills was called for, and translators in Navajo, Apache, Spanish, and Chinese were all hired from time to time by the Justice Department. For *United States v. Gon-shay-ee,* no English-to-Apache translator could be found. U.S. Attorney Rouse therefore hired two translators, one skilled in English and

Spanish and the other in Spanish and Apache. As the Apache witnesses testified, the first interpreter translated their words into Spanish, while the second translated the Spanish into English. It made for a difficult trial, but, as in so many cases in Arizona, the interpreters' services were essential. Another kind of expert service provided by the Justice Department was the hire of stenographers to report certain trials. Stenographic reports could mean the difference between success and failure if a case had to be tried a second time, or if a case were appealed.[87]

U.S. attorneys in Arizona enjoyed a larger staff of assistants than did other attorneys across the nation—usually, an office clerk and two or more assistant attorneys. This was not a case of the sympathetic generosity of the attorney general who approved their hire, however. Federal law stated that across the United States the maximum amount of fees that could be earned by a U.S. attorney was $6,000 per annum. The two exceptions to this ceiling were the territories of Arizona and New Mexico, where the maximum was $3,500. In his annual report the attorney general repeatedly pointed out this injustice to federal attorneys in the Southwest. There seemed to be no logical reason for the difference; perhaps Congress believed that in these "empty territories" no attorney could legitimately earn more than $3,500 per annum.[88]

The law provided that any fees above the attorney's maximum might be used for the hire of clerks or assistant attorneys. Since the Arizona attorneys quickly reached their maximum level of fees, they were happy to accept assistant attorneys who earned no salary but collected the fees that were above the U.S. attorney's maximum. So Arizona's attorneys enjoyed the services of a clerk, special attorneys to assist in important cases such as Wham and *Gon-shay-ee,* and regular assistants. But the attorneys general were not always quick to approve the hire of regular assistants. When the question of an assistant attorney for the Third District came up, Charles Devens wrote to U.S. Attorney Pomroy that the law provided "but one Attorney for the United States in your Territory," and Pomroy must attend the court despite "personal inconvenience." Pomroy answered patiently that in Arizona "the distances are great and the means of travel rude in the extreme." The distance from the court at Tucson to the one at Prescott was three hundred miles over rough stage and wagon routes; travel was slow and very expensive. It was a physical impossibility to appear in every court and commissioner's hearing in all three districts, Pomroy concluded, and Devens finally approved hire of an assistant.[89]

Field officers of the Justice Department in Arizona could also count on the U.S. Army; there were more than two thousand troops stationed at a dozen outposts in the territory. Army garrisons guarded prisoners who seemed likely to try to escape, and prisoners sentenced to die or to very long sentences were termed "desperate" and were often sent temporarily to Fort Whipple (near Prescott) or Fort Lowell (near Tucson). This guard service was particularly useful since breaking out of Arizona's rude frontier jails was relatively easy. But imprisonment at a fort of the U.S. Army was not invariably secure. In June 1877 two mail robbers sentenced to life imprisonment and being kept at Fort Whipple escaped. They had been at the fort, the marshal reported, because he did not have the funds to take them to San Quentin prison.[90]

Marshal Dake asked the attorney general if he might enlist the aid of the army in capturing Brijido Reyes's band of revolutionaries. Attorney General Devens replied that, although Reyes's followers formed a military unit, in the eyes of the law they were simply violators of the Neutrality Acts and must be captured by a civilian posse. This was especially clear since Congress in 1879 had prohibited the use of the army in a marshal's posse. Dake proceeded to use a civilian posse to capture Reyes's followers but explained to the attorney general that expenses were extraordinarily high since Dake was "deterred from using the military to the extent I would have wished." The army did guard the prisoners after Dake had effected their capture.[91]

During the cowboy troubles of 1881, many Arizonans despaired of receiving adequate protection from either local or federal law enforcement officers and begged the government to use the army to pursue and capture the outlaws. The *Prescott Arizonian* proclaimed that "the robbers must be put down. If the civil officers cannot do it, the military can." The newspaper suggested that prominent citizens lobby the War Department so that General Orlando B. Willcox would be authorized "to rid the territory of the scoundrels." Secretary of the Interior Henry M. Teller wrote to President Arthur describing the lawlessness of the gangs, then argued, "The most prompt and certain means of ridding the Territory of this reckless and utterly abandoned class is to cause the cavalry branch of the United States Army to follow them to their bitter end."[92]

The Arthur administration finally agreed to the idea of having the army back up Justice Department officers in Arizona, and Lieutenant H. P. Blocksom of the Sixth Cavalry soon wrote to Deputy Marshal Joseph W. Evans, who was on the border directing operations against the "cowboys." His men were ready to aid Evans in moving against any of the outlaws, including Billy the Kid who had been spotted recently near Fort Bowie. But in all operations "the subservience of the Military to the Civil Authority will be *strictly observed*."[93]

This strict separation of civil and military officers was at the heart of the procedures worked out between Dake, Evans, the army officers, and Attorney General McVeagh. The army provided Indian scouts who were experts at trailing, while the marshal supplied horses for the scouts. The Indian scouts were deemed nonmilitary and actually served as a part of the posses led by Dake and Evans. The soldiers themselves, however, followed the posse at a discreet distance of about a quarter-mile. In the event of a gun battle the posse fell back to join the troops, and the troops, finding themselves under fire, joined in the battle in order to defend themselves. The marshal and the army officers thus observed a neat if superficial observance of the separation of military and civil spheres.[94]

By the middle and late 1880s the army was rarely involved in aiding Justice Department officers except in the matter of guarding prisoners. The U.S. attorneys did handle some cases that involved the military. In one instance the U.S. attorney worked on the case of the murder of one soldier by another; in another instance the federal attorney defended a military officer from assault charges after the officer had ejected a drunken civilian from an army canteen. Once, a Justice Department employee stirred up the anger of the War Department: James A. Zabriskie was so enthusiastic in his prosecution of timber thieves that he brought a case against an army officer for cutting firewood on a military reservation. Attorney General Brewster admitted that this woodcutting was of dubious legality, but the cutting of wood for fuel on military bases "is a custom that has long been practiced and one that seems proper." Zabriskie was persuaded to dismiss the case.[95]

Justice Department officials in Arizona were fortunate to receive these various kinds of aid from the Justice and other departments of the administration since they faced a number of very serious obstacles to the performance of their duties. As in Tennessee, Utah, and Mississippi, so in Arizona many observers spoke of a kind of rebellious spirit toward the government. Governor Trittle reported to the president that the territory was in a state of "insurrection" during the cowboy troubles, and that insurrection was not confined to the outlaws. Citizens in southern Arizona often refused to serve on posses, and merchants happily bought stolen or smuggled cattle. U.S. attorneys often had trouble getting juries to take federal criminal cases seriously. "*Here* crimes against the government are not regarded by the people in the light people in the states regard crimes," reported attorney Owen T. Rouse. "Here nearly every person is against the government."[96]

Part of the reason for the opposition of many Arizona citizens to federal prosecutions is the fact that many of the federal officers were outsiders newly arrived in the territory. As Acting Governor John J. Gosper put it, "A very strong prejudice exists in this territory against so-called 'carpet-bag' officials, and a spirit of distrust and uncertainty exists in the minds of our citizens in the case of . . . officials coming into their midst from abroad." The *Arizona Miner* looked forward to the eventual "emancipation of the people of Arizona from the rule of imported officials who come here . . . to earn rewards for dirty political services performed in other states and territories."[97]

U.S. District Judge Richard E. Sloan later recalled, "There was . . . a difference in the attitude of the average citizen of the territory toward the enforcement of the criminal laws of the United States and those of the Territory." Sloan was sure that it was "much easier to obtain convictions in the Territorial district courts for offenses against the Territory than it was to obtain convictions in the United States District Courts for offenses against the United States." One reason for this was that Arizonans were more interested in enforcing "laws of their own making" than laws passed by the Congress "in which they have no voice."[98]

Another reason was that the very nature of federal cases meant that they were locally unpopular. The Camp Grant trial was an early example of a prosecution that pitted the federal attorney against the entire community. A few days after the trial Rowell reported that "the case seemed to be an arraignment of the Government for failure to protect the people from Indians instead of the trial of the case as charged." Rowell was burned in effigy by the citizens of Tucson for his role in the trial. The clerk of the grand jury (who had pushed the indictments through) was fired from his mercantile job with Lord and Williams, "as they said the feeling was so strong they would lose business by keeping me." Rowell declared, "The utmost hostility is shown against me personally for trying to perform my duties faithfully in the interest of the government."[99]

Arizona newspapers were quick to denounce federal officers. Reporting the Camp Grant trial, the *Arizona Citizen* was of the opinion that, "but for U.S. District Attorney Rowell's fearful lying about what could be proven against the Camp Grant Massacre parties, a grand jury would not have been called to investigate the matter." Given the result of the trial, however, "as a liar he was only a temporary success in this instance." Turning to Andrew H. Cargill, the *Citizen* wrote that Rowell "had to assist him a Grand Juror whose name is synonymous with everything that is low and despicable, and who has been expelled from the employ of respectable men and firms, and who stands lower in the public estimation than any man here."[100]

Rowell undoubtedly expected to stir up less controversy with his defense of a federal Indian agent who had seized the merchandise of a trader selling goods on a reservation, in violation of the Intercourse Acts. But the federally appointed governor of the territory, A.P.K. Safford, condemned the action against the trader and urged him to take legal action against Rowell and the Indian agent. When Rowell lost the case the *Arizona Citizen* praised the court's decision under the headline "The Rights of the People." The newspaper believed that Rowell had been working to limit the "rights of the people" to trade freely with the Indians, although, clearly, it was Congress who had limited this freedom by providing for the system of licensed Indian traders.[101]

Rowell's successor James McCaffry began prosecution of the Goldwater Brothers, a trading company, for falsely claiming that army property they were transporting had been lost in an Indian attack. McCaffry was prepared to prove that Goldwater Brothers actually had these goods in its possession. But finally, he decided to dismiss the case since no Arizona jury would find for the federal government. If the case were to go to trial, the defense would claim that the goods had been lost in an Apache raid, and the U.S. attorney would be in the awkward position of defending the Apaches' reputation while attacking that of the whites. "So general is the impression here that the officers of the Government attempt to fasten upon white men the atrocities of the Apaches," McCaffry explained, that the defense would appeal "with irresistible force to the sympathy of those who have frequently seen the accumulations of a lifetime swept away in a moment by the Indians." Both the attorney general and the secretary of war reluctantly approved the dismissal of the case.[102]

Marshal Dake found that many Arizonans would not serve on his posses, and that a number of southern Arizona's best citizens were trading contentedly with the outlaws. "Another trouble and the *greatest* one that has existed," Dake wrote to the Justice Department, "is that some of my Deputies in the southern part of the Territory have been driven from, or compelled to leave the Territory to save their lives."[103]

Even timber cases aroused "great excitement" in towns such as Tucson. Although James Zabriskie and other attorneys wanted to protect federal lands from a denuding that would leave them worthless, Arizona citizens needed fuel and timber, and often the federal lands were the only ones left that had not been cut over. Furthermore, there was a great deal of money to be made by timber trespass, for lowly woodcutters, middlemen, and powerful miners and merchants. Zabriskie repeatedly reported that the whole community was against the federal officers, but "all we ask is that the Government will stand by us." In the trial of Dr. Charles H. Lord for woodcutting, the seven defense attorneys won points with the jury by using "abusive epithets and ridicule" of the U.S. officers.[104]

The secretary of the interior followed a number of U.S. Attorney Rouse's timber cases very closely. In the prosecution of those who cut timber for the Silver King Mining Company, the secretary admitted that it would be very difficult to win convictions since "nearly every person within a twenty mile radius is directly or indirectly dependent upon [Silver King] for 'bread and butter'." Other federal officials in Tucson wrote to Washington, praising the work of the government attorneys in these timber cases, where they faced the "active opposition of nearly everyone of influence" and often succeeded despite "a hostile public opinion, born of lawlessness peculiar to this border country." The timber cases remained unpopular throughout the period. Reporting a timber trespass case that was being investigated in 1888, the *Tombstone Prospector* noted sarcastically, "It is to be presumed that some poor devil has built a house out of pine logs which a good Lord provided for his necessities, but which our great and just government says thou shalt not steal."[105]

Not only in prosecuting but in serving as defense lawyers for federal officers, the U.S. attorneys were excoriated by the community. When Rouse was assigned to defend Customs Inspector Hambleton from murder charges, he found that opinion in Nogales was overwhelmingly against the inspector because the border town was "a hotbed of smuggling." Indeed, Rouse was unable to secure an acquittal by a Nogales jury; after a mistrial in that town he secured a change of venue and won Hambleton's release.[106]

In defending army officers from prosecutions and lawsuits arising out of their ejecting trespassers from Indian reservations, federal attorneys faced a formidable task. Army officers were difficult to defend, a U.S. attorney told the attorney general, since "all the white men who protect the Indians in this territory incur the prejudice and frequently the animosity of a large number who compose the jurors." An army officer, writing to Washington about another ejectment case, explained that juries in Arizona disliked the army not only because it defended the Apaches, but because the army ejected go-getters who squatted on Indian lands or tried to trade illegally on the reservation. In his own case, arising out of an act of ejection, Captain Lewis Johnson explained to the attorney general that he was fearful because "it will come up before an *Arizona* jury, proverbially not kindly disposed toward Army officers."[107]

Another difficulty faced by U.S. attorneys and marshals in performing their official duties was the fact that, because of factional politics and a lack of uniform policy, their fellow federal officers could often be as great a problem as biased juries. So, for example, in prosecution of the Camp Grant case, which was supported by the president and the attorney general, the federally appointed governor testified for the defense at the December 1871 trial. Governor A.P.K. Safford was sworn and told the court that "the country is very unsafe and has been so at all times." He testified that the army had given him arms that were to be used by civilians to fight the Apaches. By his testimony the governor made it seem clear that citizens' Indian fighting was both necessary and sanctioned by the army. And while Lieutenant Royal A. Whitman testified that Eskiminzin's Indians were not guilty of outrages, other soldiers testified that Indians could and did sneak away for raids. And, of course, the federal judge's remarkable charge to the jury dashed any small hope Rowell might have had for a guilty verdict.[108]

Nor was the Camp Grant trial the only case wherein a governor worked against the U.S. attorney. The case of the interloping Indian trader being prosecuted by Rowell was mentioned above; the governor in this case publicly defended the rights of the trader and urged the man to take legal action against Rowell. And when Owen T. Rouse dismissed certain cases of selling liquor to the Indians, Governor Conrad M. Zulick "publicly abused" the new U.S. attorney at great length on the streets of Tucson.[109]

Lesser federal officials, too, worked against marshals and attorneys. The clerk of one of the district courts wrote to the attorney general, claiming that in the recent Copper Queen timber trespass case twenty-six of the thirty men summoned by Marshal Paul to serve on the grand jury were from Bisbee and very much in the sway of the powerful company. Paul, in reply, sent a documented statement proving that not one of the grand jurors was from Bisbee. The clerk was politically motivated, reported Paul.[110]

One of the most politically active Democrats in the territory was Marshal W. K. Meade. Meade urged President Cleveland to remove the Republican Attorney Zabriskie, saying that "should Col. Zabriskie be allowed to act for the government" in the case of a defaulting Indian agent "the case is lost." While Zabriskie did soon leave office, Meade was chagrined to see President Cleveland pass over Mark A. Smith for the attorneyship and appoint Rouse instead. Meade sent a half-dozen letters to Washington documenting Rouse's "complete incompetence," but to no avail. After enduring nearly four years of Meade's backbiting, Rouse telegraphed the attorney general, "I tender my resignation. No one can discharge the duties of the office properly and pleasantly with Meade as Marshal." This kind of political infighting did nothing to strengthen efforts at federal law enforcement in Arizona.[111]

Another thing that made justice difficult to achieve in Arizona was a prevailing racism among jurors and occasionally among the government lawyers. Achieving a conviction in the Camp Grant case was an impossible task because of the feelings of Arizona settlers against the Apaches. Judge Sloan recalled that "to the early settler the Apache was a devil incarnate without any human quality"; the Tucson jury was predictably indisposed to convict those who had murdered "devils incarnate." Eskiminzin foresaw the truth a few days after the massacre, when he told the army officers that "I do not expect ever to see any of them punished, for they will never punish a white man for killing an Indian." And though Attorney Rowell prosecuted the case as vigorously as he could, the defense delighted in pointing out that Rowell, too, had attended citizens' meetings where future civilian scouting parties against the Apaches had been planned.[112]

At the request of the Indian service, Jerry Millay served as special assistant U.S. attorney to defend two Papago Indians from murder charges. He found the defense very difficult because of "a strong public sentiment" against Indians A second special attorney was detailed to defend Indian murderers in 1888. He reported to the Justice Department that he had won an acquittal in twelve of the fourteen cases. But he, too, found the cases difficult. The Indians "have unpronounceable names and look alike, and an extra degree of care is required" to keep from mixing up the defendants.[113]

Prosecuting a case of selling liquor to the Indians, Owen T. Rouse won the goodwill of the jury but lost his case in his closing statement. Rouse's only witnesses to the sale of liquor were two Indian women. In his summation Rouse remarked, "I do not blame you at all for not believing Indian testimony. I would not believe any of them under oath." And presiding Judge Richard E. Sloan was sure that the main reason the United States lost the Wham case was that the chief prosecution witnesses were black soldiers who had accompanied Wham.[114]

Attorneys and marshals were constantly berated by their superiors in Washington for failing to follow the proper forms and file the necessary reports. When Marshal Dake was chastised for not submitting his weekly financial reports, he defended himself by pointing out that he had deputies all over the territory; "they are away from mail or telegraphic communication for months at a time." He could not report their expenses until he heard from them. Dake had done his duty, he reported, as far as "the facilities of a frontier country" would allow. When, during the cowboy troubles, the delay in submitting weekly reports led to delay in receiving funds for his deputies, Dake complained, "It is unfortunate that we live in a country where the law does not seem to provide for such emergencies." From time to time Dake was so far behind in his reports that he was accused of financial irresponsibility.[115]

The poor facilities for communication and travel mentioned by Dake were a constant problem for both marshals and attorneys. During a period of rampant mail robberies, Devens telegraphed Dake, "Do not understand why you do not reply to my telegram this morning." Dake finally answered by pointing out that the only telegraph in the territory available to him was the military telegraph, which was not always open to civilian use, and on the day in question the wire was down. "In fact I might say that the mails & telegraph lines in this Territory are things not much to be depended upon."[116]

When Attorney General Miller frantically telegraphed, asking the U.S. attorney why he had not sent his brief for a Supreme Court hearing, Jeffords replied helplessly that he could not send the brief because floods had cut mail service with the outside world. Similarly, during the cowboy troubles, Dake telegraphed asking the attorney general to wire any information that had recently been sent by mail, since "owing to washouts on the railroad no eastern mail received here for past ten days."[117]

When the attorney general criticized Marshal Tidball for sending a five-page telegram and ordered him to use the mails, Tidball declined to accept the order. "Owing to the lack of transportation facilities" and a slow mail service that took at least two weeks to reach Washington, "it becomes a frequent and almost absolute necessity to employ the telegraph as a means of protecting the interests of the Department of Justice." But the telegraph was not without its problems. It was subject to the whims of the military that ran it in the 1870s, and even when Western Union began public operations the service was unreliable. And, as a Justice Department examiner reported to the attorney general, the Western Union offices were "exceedingly lax in discipline." On several occasions, the examiner explained, important departmental communications "became common report in the community" in a very short time.[118]

Official travel of the marshal and attorney also caused problems. Marshal Dickason complained in 1871 that "an officer of the General Government can ill afford to perform the duties and services here for the same pecuniary compensation that would be paid for the same service in the Atlantic States." Hotels, meals, and fares in Arizona cost twice as much as in the eastern states, but the fee schedule for both areas was the same. U.S. Attorney Rowell reported that to go from his home in Arizona City to the court at Tucson cost $110 each way, and his board while at Tucson was $10 per week. Rowell was rapidly losing interest in the office, since "my fees scarcely pay my expenditures."[119]

Attorneys general often noticed that court expenses were high in Arizona, and they sometimes criticized the marshal for extravagance. But the roving departmental examiners stated in their reports that the high costs of justice in Arizona were related to the high cost of travel and the necessity of frequent telegraphing. One examiner reported that in any case involving Indians it was necessary for the marshal to incur great expense by going to the reservation, escorting the Indians to court, and later escorting them back home. This kind of expense had no counterpart in the East, but, if the Indians traveled to court on their own, "outrages and loss of life would doubtless occur by a conflict between the races."[120]

Examiner Frank B. Crosthwaite feared that the failure of the United States to cover adequately the expenses of witnesses hurt the chances of the government in criminal cases. Crosthwaite cited the case of a witness, living in Globe, summoned to appear in court at Phoenix. The witness paid $33.10 in railroad fares and $14 for meals. His total reimbursement allowed by law was five cents per mile, for a total of $15.60. This witness paid $31.50 out of his own pocket for the privilege of testifying in a U.S. court. Other witnesses had to come to court by stage because their home was not served by a railroad; the stagecoach fare was always at least fifteen or twenty cents per mile, but still the government paid only five cents per mile, which was expected also to cover meals.[121]

Many witnesses got around this problem by ignoring the subpoena. The court then issued a citation for contempt, the marshal brought the witness into court (paying his fare along the way), and, on pleading poverty, the witness was discharged from contempt. This kind of procedure caused great delay in the prosecution of federal criminals, and Crosthwaite estimated that the practice was costing the government $5,000 per year. He pointed out that the government would actually save money if it would only raise the five cents per mile rate.[122]

Efforts of the federal officers to enforce the laws in Arizona were hampered on many occasions by a lack of funds. On some occasions the marshal was so far behind in his weekly financial reports that the first comptroller of the Treasury refused to honor his drafts for more funds. Very often, however, the attorney general returned the marshal's request, saying that "no money can be advanced to you for the payment of jurors or witnesses, the appropriations for these expenses being exhausted." In response, the marshal could either avoid all further expense until the next fiscal year or attempt to run the courts on credit. Neither action helped secure victories in the federal courts. Attorney Rowell recalled that "I ran the courts on credit the first year," but then court funds were advanced by private citizens. Five years later Marshal Wiley W. Standefer complained that the United States had paid nothing to help run the courts, and the expenses "were sustained by citizens of the District."[123]

One way of running the courts on credit was for the marshal to print up "vouchers" for jury or witness service, which would be paid after Congress made a deficiency appropriation. Discouraged jurors and witnesses sometimes sold their vouchers at a one-quarter to one-half discount. Treasury officials in 1881 tried to halt this speculation in Justice Department vouchers by refusing to pay them except to the original holder, but Marshal Dake persuaded them to abandon this policy. In many cases the vouchers were not held by speculators, Dake explained, but by innkeepers who had accepted them in exchange for jurors' room and board.[124]

Jurors and witnesses were never happy at being paid by vouchers, and several times the attorneys complained that the voucher system was hampering efforts to win indictments and convictions. At the recent term of court, U.S. Attorney Pomroy reported, grand jurors "refused to serve on the grounds that they hold certificates for pay due them for serving as long ago as two years." Even when the grand jury was empaneled it was totally uncooperative, "solely because of this financial embarrassment." Much of Marshal George Tyng's dissatisfaction with his position was related to the fact that he was overwhelmed with requests to pay stale accounts for juror and witness fees. "The *uncertainty* and smallness of payment for time and travel are doing much to defeat the ends of justice in Arizona," Tyng pointed out.[125]

The Justice Department, too, was flooded with requests for payment by disgruntled jailers, guards, doctors, and stenographers. Nor did the department always understand that everything cost more on the frontier. When court reporter Bryan W. Tichenor submitted his bill for making a transcript in the Hambleton murder case, the attorney general cut the fee in half. Tichenor responded that he presumed the attorney general's figure "was arrived at by computation according to the prevailing rate for somewhat similar service at Washington." In Arizona stenographic services cost much more, just as the cost of living was higher. Besides, Tichenor was the territory's only stenographer. In fact, Tichenor told the attorney general that he would not serve the government again until he received a favorable answer—which never came.[126]

Two years later the attorney general was astounded to receive the $1,640 bill of a Los Angeles stenographic firm for making a transcript of the Wham trial: "Why was a Los Angeles firm employed? Was no one in Arizona capable?" U.S. Attorney Jeffords replied that Tichenor was capable but no longer interested in serving the government.[127]

Attorneys and marshals often considered their salaries and fees, and wondered if they were really willing to serve the government for such a pittance. For special assistant attorneys, the Justice Department followed the ill-advised policy of discussing compensation only after the case was concluded. Regular U.S. attorneys sometimes received special legal fees for cases that were outside their normal duties, and these fees, too, were determined only after the case was disposed of. It is certain that the attorneys general who set the fees were completely unaware of the typical fees earned by frontier lawyers. The federal government won few friends in the legal profession as it set fees for its attorneys' services.

Assistant Attorney Jerry Millay was hired to defend fourteen Indians from charges of murder; the cases were especially difficult because of the ill feeling of the white community, but Millay won the release of all twelve of the defendants who pled not guilty. Millay asked $1,362 in compensation, but the attorney general approved his account for $300. When Attorney Zabriskie was hired as a special attorney to defend the marshal from a $10,000 lawsuit filed by a woodcutter for false arrest, he found that the Tombstone Milling and Mining Company was vitally interested in the case and had "gained control of the jury." After a long trial the government lost the case; Zabriskie appealed to the territorial Supreme Court and won a reversal of the lower court decision. Zabriskie billed the government for $2,800 but he, too, was paid $300.[128]

Compared with the keen competition for the attorney and marshal positions in many of the states, it is interesting to see how many of the officers in Arizona expressed mixed feelings at the time of their appointment. On accepting the marshalship in 1878, Crawley P. Dake told the attorney general, "I shall give the office a fair trial, and hope for the best." If he could not make a living out of the marshalship, Dake concluded, "I shall have to let somebody else try it." Four years later Dake telegraphed, "Commission having expired, do not seek reappointment. The office is thankless and unprofitable." U.S. Attorney Rouse almost resigned because of the low income; he remained in office only because he wanted to fight Meade's charges of incompetence. Meanwhile, two of Rouse's assistant attorneys resigned because of the low pay; as one of them put it, "I cannot afford to hold the position." Rouse complained, "They can make more money by taking the side against the government."[129]

But it was the marshals who were in the greatest financial danger in Arizona, as in the states. The marshal was advanced money—up to

$20,000 at a time—and he made the day-to-day decisions as to how the money should be spent. His accounts were regularly audited by the U.S. attorneys, the judges, the Washington office of the Justice Department, roving examiners, and by the Treasury Department itself. If any of the marshal's expenditures were deemed improper or exorbitant, the amount was disallowed, and the marshal was forced to pay the expense out of his own pocket. Further, unless the marshal kept exquisitely detailed accounts and receipts as he spent the money advanced from the Treasury, he could later be accused of misuse or even theft of government funds.

Marshal Dake was faced with an enormous program of expenditures in attempting to bring the cowboy troubles to an end. He was an extraordinarily careful and foresighted marshal. He bombarded the attorney general with estimates of expenses, then asked, "What amount will be allowed?" The attorney general usually began by answering: "In this matter I have no instructions to give," and the details were left to Dake. Dake would then delay incurring heavy expense while he again asked for authorization. The attorney general would be more specific in the second letter, saying, "All reasonable expense which you may incur . . . for the arrest of the desperadoes who infest the borders of Arizona and New Mexico, will be allowed by this Department."[130]

By obtaining such general authorizations and by repeatedly making it clear that expenses would be heavy, Dake was able to prevent heavy losses in the auditing of his accounts. As he explained to the attorney general, he was more than willing to advance money to break up the cowboy threat "if there will be no doubt of the payment of the same in the future." Dake was an energetic marshal, but after he left office his reputation remained under a cloud. His accounts were delinquent at the time he resigned, and he had great difficulty tracking down his former deputies to get receipts since many had left the territory.[131]

When Dake prepared to make a major assault on the cowboy outlaws in the fall of 1881, he asked Deputy Joseph W. Evans to prepare an estimate of expenses. "Men who are worth having cannot be had for less than $10.00 per day and expenses," began Evans. In addition to the men's daily pay was the expense of horses, saddles, pack animals, carbines, pistols, and ammunition. The posse must contain at least thirty citizens, and Evans added that one Arizona citizen "is worth many Indians or soldiers in fighting." Spies should also be hired to infiltrate the outlaws' organizations. In short, concluded Evans, the expense of the operation would be $30,000. The attorney general had rarely received such a huge request for funds, and Dake and Evans had to await a special congressional appropriation before proceeding. But the enormous expense did have the desired effect.[132]

The isolation of the frontier meant that federal judges and attorneys were hampered by the lack of law books. Judge John Titus praised the appointment of James McCaffry as U.S. attorney: "Nearly all of the law books in private hands in Arizona belong to his well selected library." But when, in one of his first letters to the attorney general, McCaffry outlined a legal argument, he mentioned a number of Supreme Court cases and apologized that he could not cite them by page and volume—there were no *United States Reports* in Tucson.[133]

Soon, Attorney General Williams, a westerner himself, had a set of the reports shipped to Arizona. Judge Titus wrote that he was glad; "I shall most cheerfully hail and acknowledge this valuable addition to our legal resources as soon as the same shall be realized." The arrival of the books was greatly delayed because they were shipped first to Pueblo, Colorado, where the express company discovered that there was no rail or stage route from Colorado to Arizona. Somehow by 1874 the set found its way into the territory. But not until 1882 did a copy of the revised statutes reach Arizona.[134]

Rarely was there orderly transition from one U.S. attorney to another or from one marshal to another. Marshals abandoned their posts, and attorneys died in office or left the territory in disgust. Marshal George Tyng replaced the vanished Isaac Q. Dickason; Tyng complained that opportunities to learn about the duties and routine of a marshal "are in this frontier country rare and difficult." Attorney Everett B. Pomroy arrived in the territory only to find his predecessor near death. "I am unable to procure any records, documents, or papers pertaining to the office, or any information relating to the business thereof." When Pomroy was abruptly asked to resign seven years later, he had little interest in helping his successor get started in the office. Zabriskie reported that he and the new marshal, Zan Tidball, had to "grope our way in darkness without the light of precedent or any evidence as to the status of any matter connected with the prosecution of United States cases."[135]

Deputy marshals presented special problems. Although most marshals reported that the deputies were brave and loyal, the deputies usually had no business sense whatever. They repeatedly failed to get receipts for their expenses, while in two instances deputies illegally pursued criminals into the states and brought them back to Arizona without due process. The kind of men who were willing to serve as deputies, reported Marshal Tyng, were "men of less than average information" who required highly detailed instructions in order to do any job properly. Some deputies do seem to have been poorly chosen. Deputy E. M. Mills was sent to deliver a subpoena in the William Brown perjury case; on finding that the witness had moved away from the address given on the subpoena, Mills tossed the document into the empty house through an open window. The witness, of course, never saw his subpoena, and the government lost the case. An examiner reported that Mills "is a hard worker, an intelligent deputy and a republican but nevertheless a dishonest man." Mills was dismissed and later prosecuted.[136]

Deputies such as Mills were the exception, however. Most deputies served well and deserve much credit for moving successfully against dangerous men including mail robbers, smuggling cattlemen, and Mexican revolutionaries. In at least two instances U.S. deputy marshals in Arizona Territory were killed in the line of duty.[137]

Deputies and marshals were not opposed only by desperate criminals. They sometimes found themselves directly opposed to local law enforcement officers. When the Riverside stage was robbed in 1882, one Redfield was arrested by Sheriff A. J. Doran and charged with highway robbery. Doran later recalled that ten days after the arrest he and his deputies were approached by Deputy U.S. Marshal Joseph W. Evans, "known as a determined and fearless man," and his federal posse made up of nine "noted gunmen." Evans demanded the prisoner Redfield, who was wanted for mail robbery, but Doran was sure the local jury was more likely to convict than the federal jury and refused to give up the prisoner. Evans's posse and the sheriff and his deputies stared at each other for several tense minutes, both refusing to back down. Only the discovery of Redfield hanging in his cell (whether from suicide or lynching is unclear) prevented conflict between the two groups.[138]

Similarly, in the Lord and Williams timber case Deputy Evans was guarding the disputed wood as it lay stacked along the tracks of the Southern Pacific. When the local sheriff arrived with a writ giving custody of the wood to Lord and Williams pending litigation, Evans and his men drew their revolvers and ordered the sheriff away. Evans and one other deputy were taken before the county court on a charge of contempt, from which the U.S. attorney successfully defended them. In many other cases marshals and attorneys were sued or prosecuted for their official actions. In Rowell's case involving a man trading illegally with the Indians, the defendant took Governor Safford's advice and sued Rowell and the Indian agent for the value of merchandise that was seized. And in an 1884 timber case woodcutters in the employ of the Tombstone Milling and Mining Company sued Marshal Tidball for $10,000 for false arrest, averring that their cutting had been done legally. Zabriskie saw that the purpose of the suit was to intimidate the federal officers. These kinds of cases were never successful in this period in Arizona but served to harass the federal officers and add to their already heavy caseload.[139]

In some instances local and federal authorities worked together in a friendly way. Many cases were at once local and federal: Stage robberies, for example, usually involved both the local offense of highway robbery and the federal offense of mail robbery. The cattle rustlers in the period of the cowboy troubles were guilty both of stealing cattle and of smuggling stolen cattle across the Mexican border. In many instances the territory and the federal government offered rewards jointly, while in others the federal marshals and the county sheriffs coordinated their efforts to make arrests. In the town of Tombstone the cowboy lawlessness grew so great that townspeople contributed $5,000 toward the arming of a citizen's group of "rangers" that was put in the charge of Deputy U.S. Marshal John H. Jackson. Among their accomplishments, this band protected Wyatt and Virgil Earp on the day of the O.K. Corral shoot-out, guarding against their being lynched by friends of the Clantons.[140]

Community opposition to federal law enforcement took its most serious form when it involved tampering with witnesses and juries, and intimidating potential witnesses. Marshal Tidball received dozens of letters giving details of illegal woodcutting on federal lands, "but most of the complaints made in writing are anonymous, the writers expressing fear to disclose their names lest they may in some way be injured in person or estate." Although Tidball could initiate cases on his own complaint, it did not bode well when cases began with the reports of fearful and anonymous witnesses. Marshal Paul reported that he had been vis-

U.S. Marshal Zan L. Tidball received dozens of reports of illegal timber cutting, but he noted that "most of the complaints . . . are anonymous, the writers expressing fear to disclose their names lest they may in some way be injured in person or estate." Courtesy of Arizona Historical Society.

ited by a man who knew the identity of several stage robbers who had plundered the U.S. mail, but the witness refused to give information because he lived on an isolated ranch and feared that if he did so neither his life nor his property would be safe. Nor was fear restricted to potential witnesses. Governor Frederick Trittle complained to President Arthur in 1882 that "the people have lost confidence in law and government, and many fear to trust their lives in any posse." It was difficult to hope for successful law enforcement when "the citizens are so intimidated that few of them dare to express an opinion adverse to lawlessness and crime."[141]

Jury tampering and biased juries were problems that continued to dog U.S. attorneys throughout this period. In the timber cutting case of *United States v. D. D. Ross* prosecuting attorney Harry R. Jeffords was hampered by the fact that nearly all the jurors depended on mining for their livelihood and, since the plundered timber had been used in mining, were reluctant to bring back a conviction. The government did lose the case, although jurors' sympathies toward mining was only one explanation for the defeat. A special timber agent who was present to observe the trial later heard several of the jurors bragging about "how much they had received from . . . the Copper Queen Mining Company for bringing in this verdict."[142]

After the Wham trial Attorney General Miller noted that the evidence had been overwhelmingly in favor of conviction, the charge of the judge was fair, and yet the jury had returned an acquittal after a very short deliberation. Miller was quick to suspect jury tampering. Jeffords agreed that jury tampering had probably occurred, although perhaps more telling was the fact that even before the trial began the defendants and their friends had been indicted for "attempting to induce witnesses not to testify" and "attempting to induce witnesses to testify falsely."[143]

The most outrageous obstruction of justice occurred in the trial of Indian Agent Tiffany for embezzlement. The defendant got the chief prosecution witness drunk and sent him off to die in a region ravaged by a yellow fever epidemic. Tiffany then circulated the rumor that Marshal Tidball had spirited the witness away, and Tiffany's friends stood on the street corners offering a reward to anyone who would find the witness and bring him to the courthouse. The U.S. attorney was forced to dismiss the charges.[144]

Defendants had other methods of attempting to change the outcome of a trial. Owen T. Rouse reported that essential records "frequently disappear from the records of the court," and defendants even stole documents from his desk. In the first trial of Customs Inspector Hambleton for murder, Rouse had to report that the "smuggling interests" had intimidated Hambleton's bondsman to the point that he withdrew from the bond; fortunately, Hambleton eventually found another bondsman.[145]

In 1884 the Tombstone Milling and Mining Company used its influence to gain the appointment of one P. L. Peel as U.S. commissioner. Soon thereafter Deputy Marshal Evans brought nineteen woodcutters into Tombstone for a preliminary examination before Peel. The charge was cutting wood on nonmineral federal lands; the wood was clearly destined for Tombstone Milling and Mining. Commissioner Peel met the deputy marshal on the streets of Tombstone and denounced him "in a very violent and boisterous manner." A large crowd gathered, and Evans began to fear that the citizens would attempt to release the woodcutters. He therefore took them to Tucson for their preliminary hearing. Peel later repeated his performance, and Evans again took his prisoners to Tucson.[146]

Anonymous complaints and clippings from the *Tombstone Republican* soon reached the attorney general, charging that Evans was seeking to increase his income by dragging his prisoners far away from their homes, thus collecting higher fees for mileage. Evans, Tidball, and Zabriskie all sent their explanations to the attorney general. Tidball urged Attorney General Brewster not to be misled by the stories from the *Tombstone Republican*, since that paper, like Commissioner Peel, was "under the thumb of the Tombstone Mill and Mining Company, whose tyrannical hand rests upon the entire community." His only goal, Tidball assured Brewster, was to do his duty "without fear or favor."[147]

Despite the many obstacles that hindered marshals and attorneys, these federal officials were able to achieve a remarkably high rate of convictions. In spite of jury tampering, intimidation of witnesses, biased juries, lack of funds, and woefully inadequate communications, Arizona's conviction rate was higher than that of any other territory except Washington and higher than that of most of the states. A possible explanation for the high conviction rate would be that judges, sympathizing with members of the local community, handed down such lenient sentences that jurors did not hesitate to convict.

This, however, was not the case in Arizona Territory. Judges, appointed almost without exception from the East, showed little sympathy for the criminals who appeared in their courts, and few sentences handed down in Arizona's district courts seem lenient by modern standards. Among cases of mail robbery sentences of five to ten years were common, and life sentences were imposed with regularity. In cases of selling liquor to the Indians typical sentences ranged from six months to two years, plus a fine. Embezzlement cases involved a sentence of at least one year per count and a fine equal to the amount embezzled. The soldiers of fortune in Brijido Reyes's band were convicted of violating the Neutrality Acts, fined $200 each, and sent to the Detroit House of Corrections for two years.[148]

Federal efforts to bring law and order to Arizona were also helped by the fact that the wheels of justice could turn quickly. Arizona justice was usually "swift and sure." The deputy U.S. marshal made an arrest two days after the Casa Grande stage was robbed in the late 1880s; the prisoner was carried to a federal district court that was in session, where he was quickly tried. Within seven days from the time of the robbery the prisoner was on his way to the federal penitentiary at Alcatraz with a life sentence. Similarly, when a large number of Mormon settlers moved to Arizona in 1884, five of them were, "within a few days after their arrival," indicted for polygamy, arrested, tried, and sentenced. Three of the five received a stiff sentence of three and a half years' imprisonment and a heavy fine.[149]

Federal Judge A. W. Sheldon was in many ways typical of the federal judges who served in this period. As Joseph Miller recorded in *Arizona: The Last Frontier*, Sheldon was unpopular with defendants and with many attorneys. "He seemed to think his mission was to enforce the law and rid Arizona of criminals," wrote Miller, and this perceived mission explained "the severity of his judgements which were rarely tempered with mercy."[150]

Given that the judges deserve a good deal of the credit for the successful program of law enforcement in Arizona, how much credit do the attorneys and marshals deserve for the high conviction rate? What was the caliber of the federal law officers?

Most of the U.S. attorneys in Arizona were appointed for political reasons; many of them had campaigned vigorously for their party, and many had served as delegates to the national convention where they supported the victorious candidate. Attorneys McCaffry, Zabriskie, and Jeffords had had experience as federal or local prosecutors before taking office as Arizona's U.S. attorney. Rowell had served as a justice of the peace.[151]

The marshals, too, had usually performed important political services before their appointments. The first few marshals considered here clearly did not perform well. Although none "milked the office for all it was worth," at least two disappeared without settling their accounts, thus leaving to the U.S. attorneys the unpleasant duty of suing the marshals' bondsmen. Marshal George Tyng served honestly and efficiently but for only eleven months, and Francis H. Goodwin did not serve much longer. Among the marshals, Goodwin and Paul had been sheriffs, while Tidball had garnered valuable experience as a postal inspector and Justice Department agent. Dake and Meade also had had some pertinent experience, Dake as an internal revenue collector and Meade as the superintendent of Arizona's penitentiary at Yuma.[152]

What of the accusation constantly made by many Arizonans to the effect that federal marshals and attorneys were "carpetbag" officials who had no real interest in the progress of the territory? The *Phoenix Daily Herald* came to the conclusion that "the Washington authorities will learn by experience that instead of seeking to discharge a personal obligation to some petty politician by appointing him to an office," they should appoint local men who cared for the future of the territory. The records show that such charges were usually false. Of the fourteen attorneys and marshals considered here, only four were appointed from outside the territory, and at least two of these chose to remain in Arizona after their service to the Justice Department had ended.[153]

The key to understanding the problems of lawlessness in Arizona Territory has to do with the fact that nearly all the Anglo-Americans who were there in the 1870s and 1880s were relative newcomers who were interested in making money. Doubtless, the "Gilded Age" was a period when men all across the nation wished to make substantial fortunes, but in Arizona men often became obsessed with their financial goals. Most Arizonans had given up a great deal, forsaking the more comfortable and settled areas of the country, and often had used all their fortune to move to the Southwest and set themselves up as prospectors, cattlemen, or merchants. As the small operators often were crushed by larger businesses in mining, ranching, and mercantile pursuits, many turned to the federal government to seek their fortune. As Examiner Crosthwaite put it in his report to the attorney general, "there seems to be a general feeling in Arizona that any excuse for a charge or claim against the United States is warranted no matter what are the means or methods adopted to swell the account."[154]

It became the duty of the U.S. attorneys to fight frivolous or unfounded claims against the government. The desire to make money led citizens to plunder the Indian reservations of minerals or water, to overcharge the army for supplies, and to strip the public lands of their timber. For the more daring entrepreneurs, dealing in stolen Mexican cattle or even robbing the mails became potentially profitable ventures.

Acting Governor John J. Gosper discerned the problem in an 1882 letter to Marshal Dake. The citizens of Arizona, wrote Gosper, "in their mad career after money, have grossly neglected local self-government." It was useless to hope for punishment of stage robbers or cowboy rustler-smugglers by local authorities, for, "partaking of the general reckless spirit of accumulation of money and property," they winked at crime and were bribed into protecting the criminals. Those local merchants who were most interested in low prices for their wholesale purchases gladly bought stolen merchandise, including goods intended for soldiers or Indians, without asking any questions. The root of Arizona's problems, according to Zabriskie, was "fanatical avarice."[155]

The marshal and his deputies worked to bring order and respect for the law to Arizona, but they labored with little help from the citizens. U.S. Attorney McCaffry reported that he could prosecute cases of selling liquor to the Indians only when he split his fees with the chief witness—otherwise the witnesses believed that testifying was not worth their time, and they kept their knowledge to themselves. Marshals, too, had problems in securing the cooperation of citizens. In the eastern states a marshal could summon a posse of law-abiding citizens who would help him enforce the law. In Arizona, the marshals found, citizens were loath to serve because such service was dangerous and there was no money in it—only the ridiculously low fee provided by the Justice Department fee bill. As General William Tecumseh Sherman wrote to Attorney General Brewster, it was idle to think that rough miners and cowhands would risk their lives for small fees to help the marshal bring in desperate smugglers. Sherman believed the matter was so serious that only the army could make arrests and serve process.[156]

As attorneys, marshals, governors, generals, and judges wrote to the president and attorney general asking for help in Arizona, they did not merely report violation of the law. After Judge Charles Silent reported a wave of mail robberies in 1878, he added, "if not for these troubles a bullion production of from five to twenty millions per annum could have been reasonably expected." The judge asked that the marshal be adequately supported with funds, since "this absolute lawlessness is paralyzing business and checking the progress of the territory." Acting Governor Gosper asked that the marshal be authorized to pay all necessary expenses of posses, because "outlawry . . . is causing great injury to the business interests of our growing territory." During the cowboy troubles, Dake reported that the stage robberies had made Arizonans so fearful that they would no longer travel for business reasons or ship goods or money. "The effect upon business is so damaging it is almost beyond description," the marshal concluded.[157]

Marshals and attorneys joined to an extent in this "mad career after money." They seem to have been motivated not only by a desire to earn their salary and fees and uphold the honor of the federal government; they were interested in fostering a calm and prosperous business climate.

Marshal Francis H. Goodwin found that Arizona in the early 1870s was not yet booming. His method of making his fortune was to hold as many offices as possible. Among the offices he held, many of them simultaneously, were those of legislator, sheriff, U.S. consul at Nogales, probate judge, deputy marshal and marshal, deputy collector of customs, court crier, clerk of the Pima Board of Supervisors, and deputy collector of internal revenue. At the same time he also practiced medicine. As economic opportunities in the territory increased, Goodwin engaged in stock raising, farming, and mercantile pursuits.[158]

Early marshals I. Q. Dickason and W. W. Standefer were so prosperous as miner and cattleman, respectively, that they had little interest in the marshalship. Dickason was named by an Arizona newspaper as one of the wealthiest men in the territory, while Standefer raised cattle as well as sheep on a huge ranch in the Williamson Valley.[159]

Other federal officers managed to pursue their business interests and their Justice Department duties simultaneously with no noticeable detriment to either. Zabriskie founded a syndicate for speculation in Mexican lands, was secretary of the Arizona and Mexico Railroad, was a

In his reports of lawlessness in Arizona in the late 1870s, U.S. Marshal Crawley P. Dake concluded: "The effect upon business is so damaging it is almost beyond description." Courtesy of Western History Collections, University of Oklahoma Libraries.

successful rancher, and made astute mining investments. Zabriskie and Tidball together were directors of a mining company. Marshals Meade and Paul made modest fortunes in mining, although Paul lost his in an ill-advised gravel mine investment.[160]

The go-getting attorneys and marshals prosecuted those who violated federal criminal law and constantly asked for more help from Washington, warning of the effect of crime on the territory's economy. In a number of instances the attorneys and marshals made special lobbying efforts to win some concession from Washington. The most common kind of lobbying involved petitioning for the removal of one of the federal judges. Zabriskie and Tidball sent repeated warnings to the Justice Department about Judge Wilson Hoover; they believed that he had been "improperly and unlawfully influenced in certain important cases," including the embezzlement case of Indian agent Tiffany. After both marshal and attorney journeyed to Washington to demonstrate their concern, an agent of the department was dispatched to Arizona to investigate. The agent agreed with Zabriskie and Tidball. Hoover had "prostituted his high office to personal and selfish ends" by borrowing money from litigants before his court. The judge was quickly removed from office.[161]

Jeffords and Meade lobbied vigorously for the removal of Judge W. H. Barnes as the trial of the Wham robbers approached. Barnes was a personal friend of several of the Wham defendants, Jeffords reported, and he had made questionable statements in their favor from the bench. The two men apparently got a federal grand jury involved in the removal effort; the jurors wired Attorney General Miller in September 1889, asking Barnes's removal. Even paymaster Wham involved himself in the lobbying, asking not only for Barnes's removal but demanding a new assistant attorney. Finally, the efforts of Jeffords, Meade, Wham, and the grand jurors had the desired effect, and Barnes was replaced by Judge Richard E. Sloan.[162]

Several of the Arizona officers of the Justice Department used their influence to change federal land and timber policy in Washington. Spearheading these efforts was James A. Zabriskie. In April 1882 Zabriskie reported that rumors were rife in the territory that the secretary of the interior and the attorney general were both indignant at the Arizona timber cases and believed them to be harassing prosecutions. Zabriskie declared that he could not believe the rumors and asked permission to issue a public denial. The attorney general assured him that the rumors were false and sent printed statements of the Interior Department's timber policy and the permission to use the papers *"as you see fit."*[163]

When the interior secretary ruled that mesquite was too thin and soft to be classified as timber, Zabriskie emphatically disagreed. Mesquite was the hardest wood known, he told the attorney general. It was used for many purposes in Arizona including the framing of buildings. "No bona fide settler will care to pre-empt land when all the wood for fuel, farming, and building purposes is cut from it." Zabriskie believed that under the secretary's ruling the big companies in Arizona would soon strip the land. "I ask whether this is to be the course of action by the government, or whether we are to be protected from such a fate." The attorney asked Attorney General Brewster to take the question up with the interior secretary. Brewster did so and won a retraction. On reading the secretary's new instructions, Zabriskie announced that he heartily approved of them; they would "meet the requirements of the case."[164]

In weighing the success or failure of the Justice Department's efforts to bring law and order to Arizona, we have several measures that might be used. As mentioned above, a number of spectacular cases were lost, but on the other hand a number of very important cases were won for the government as well. Judging by the conviction rate, the efforts of federal law officers in Arizona were an unqualified success, as Arizona ranked near the top of all states and territories for achieving a high conviction rate. Overall numbers of cases per capita, however, indicate that not much progress was made: These numbers held steady throughout the two decades after 1870.

The kinds of cases being tried did change. Mail robbery and other postal cases, for example, made up 17 percent of the U.S. attorney's work load in the early 1870s; this figure dropped to less than 3 percent by the late 1880s. Numbers of "miscellaneous cases" rose from 44 percent of the caseload to 75 percent in the same period. The chief reason for this change was a great increase in the number of timber trespass cases. Federal attorneys would continue to try large numbers of these cases into the early twentieth century, when the conservation movement led to the founding of the U.S. Forest Service. Under Forest Service management, federal lands might be grazed or the timber harvested, but only under scientifically controlled conditions and only after the collection of fees. By 1890 the number of federal cases per capita remained high, but Arizona was no longer a region of life-threatening mail robberies and the "insurrection" of smuggling cowboys. The era of the Camp Grant massacre and the shoot-out at the O.K. Corral was over, and no similarly lurid events took their places. Never again would the U.S. president call upon Arizonans to "retire peaceably to their abodes."[165]

In fact, Arizona was becoming so law-abiding and prosperous that Congress soon was giving serious consideration to statehood. One great impediment was the fact that the territory tended to vote Democratic, and the Republican Senate therefore delayed. The greatest opponent of Arizona statehood was Republican Senator Albert J. Beveridge. A proponent of U.S. colonial expansion into the Caribbean and the Pacific, Beveridge believed firmly in the superiority of Anglo-American culture. As historian Howard R. Lamar put it, Beveridge came away from a whirlwind tour of Arizona believing that "the Spanish-speaking citizens of the Southwest were at best second-class citizens—passive, pliant, and uneducated." They were too different and clung to their own language, law, and customs.[166]

Beveridge also objected to the presence of Mormons, another group that he believed was un-American, in Arizona. In short, according to Lamar, Beveridge believed the Southwest "was still a backward and underdeveloped colonial area." Many other prominent politicians, including President Theodore Roosevelt, agreed. The struggle for Arizona statehood, concluded Lamar, was the "familiar struggle of a region acting to resist outside authority which was attempting to standardize and force conformity."[167]

Arizona was never forced to conform absolutely to the model of the eastern states. Still, serious congressional discussions of the statehood issue dragged on for more than a decade after the turn of the century. By the time of Arizona's admission to the Union, Anglos outnumbered Hispanics, Mormon polygamy was at an end, the growing of crops was under way, public schools and universities were prospering, and many towns had paved streets, streetcars, and electric streetlights. The U.S. attorneys and marshals deserve a good deal of the credit for preparing Arizona for statehood. They had helped guide the territory not only to a condition of relative peace, they had also helped Arizona meet the minimum standards of conformity that would allow admission to the Union.

Only in 1912 did both houses of Congress agree that Arizona was ready for statehood. It was the last territory of the continental United States to enter the Union. Arizona endured a long territorial apprenticeship; a teenager who was sixteen years old when Arizona became a U.S. possession would have been eighty at the time of statehood. But on February 14, 1912, Arizonans forgot their bitter feelings and joined enthusiastically the Union of states.

6

Conclusion

Our in-depth look at federal law enforcement in four varied judicial districts provides an opportunity to assess larger questions of national governance, federalism, and criminal law in the late 1800s. Historians have often studied aspects of U.S. criminal law; the overwhelming emphasis has been upon enforcement of state and local laws. This is perhaps as it should be, since a great majority of U.S. criminal cases are for violation of state laws. Among the excellent recent studies of criminal law are Edward L. Ayers's *Vengeance and Justice: Crime and Punishment in the Nineteenth-Century American South* and Samuel E. Walker's *Popular Justice: A History of American Criminal Justice*. These two authors describe a number of trends at the state and county levels that were duplicated in the enforcement of federal criminal law.[1]

In studying the nineteenth-century South, Ayers is most interested in the widespread violence of the region, which supported a high crime rate. This same trend kept federal attorneys busy prosecuting cases of resisting arrest in eastern Tennessee and organized violence against blacks in northern Mississippi. Not only was violence not roundly condemned in the South, it was sometimes looked upon with public favor. In many local cases, Ayers notes, a murder or assault defendant was acquitted by a friendly jury and left the courthouse with increased popularity and respect. Violation of federal law, too, could increase one's respect in the community. Public support of moonshining and ballot box stuffing in the South hindered U.S. attorneys and marshals in the late nineteenth century. In the western districts the Camp Grant murderers and the Mormon polygamy convicts were raised to heroic status, making a successful federal law enforcement program difficult.[2]

Samuel E. Walker points out that, throughout U.S. history, crime has been what legislative bodies make it. Thus, in addition to prosecuting murderers and robbers, state and county governments have used the criminal justice system to suppress "political dissidents, radical and religious minorities, or simply different cultural lifestyles by the majority." Certainly, the Mormons believed they were being persecuted by federal attorneys because they were Mormons; Mississippi Democrats were sure they were the victims of a Republican administration that wanted to suppress its opponents. The Chinese in Arizona knew of no basis for their trials except their race and nationality, while Tennessee mountaineers felt the foundation of the cases against them was the government's disdain for their life-styles and preference for the large distilling companies. Walker finds citizen resistance a widespread problem for local prosecutors; commonly, the state courts turned to the solution of lenient sentencing, which helped to prevent acquittals. We have seen that in Mississippi and Tennessee mild sentencing was employed to achieve this same effect.[3]

Walker discusses some trends that were different from those seen at the federal level and, in so doing, raises some interesting questions of federalism. He points out that local sheriffs, judges, and police were often under the control of the numerically most powerful local group. Thus, if the Ku Klux Klan were locally strong, its members would not be prosecuted for murder; if labor unions were locally powerful, the sheriff and police would support strikers and harass Pinkertons and strikebreakers. In federal cases, on the other hand, the groups that were most powerful nationwide controlled the prosecutions; this meant that a powerful outside force came into conflict with a locally powerful state or county power structure. Resistance and strife were the inevitable result.[4]

This resistance was sometimes demonstrated by individuals, sometimes by the state and county officers themselves. Many of the cases considered in the preceding pages were brought for activity that was both a state and federal crime. Klansmen and ballot box stuffers in Mississippi violated state statutes dealing with assault and election fraud but were not prosecuted by the state officers. During the cowboy troubles in Arizona, the stage robbers and cattle rustlers violated territorial law as well as certain federal laws (mail robbery and smuggling), but the federal government usually showed much more energy in bringing the outlaws to justice. In Utah the marshals were harassed, spied upon, and even assaulted by local law enforcement officers, while federal attorneys angered territorial officials by prosecuting Mormons under their own territorial laws designed to punish sexual sins. In Tennessee local sheriffs and prosecutors who were friends of the violators of federal law brought harassing and frivolous prosecutions for the purpose of delay; they also were quick to try to prosecute federal officers who killed or wounded moonshiners or counterfeiters.

The United States' system of federalism long served as a shield for minority rights. If a group were unable to achieve its ends in one arm of the federal system, it could try another. For example, prior to the Civil War abolitionists fared badly in seeking favorable action from Congress and the federal courts, but they enjoyed some success at the state level. Many state judges in the North moved to protect fugitive slaves and whites who harbored them. Similarly, antebellum southerners by 1860 believed that Congress and the federal judiciary would not protect their interests, and they seceded from the Union, determined to rely upon the state governments for protection. In the 1870s, if a black defendant were denied his rights in a state court, he could successfully seek redress at the federal level. But in the wake of the Civil War the national government reigned supreme, and state and local officers were unable to do much beyond harassment and delay. While it is true that southern states, in their new constitutions after 1890, were able to circumvent black voting, the federal Enforcement Act program in the South had died of other causes at least six years earlier. Throughout the late 1800s official actions of state, county, and city officers were not able to stymie federal prosecution in the areas of the four case studies.[5]

We have examined the history of emphatic resistance to federal laws in four judicial districts. Were these districts unique in their resistance? Were the laws violated in these districts the only laws that incited citizen resistance? The answer to both of these questions is clear: There was widespread resistance to a variety of federal laws in the late nineteenth century.

The pattern of resistance to the Enforcement Acts, for example, was repeated over and over in districts across the southern states. But Justice Department employees in the North also exerted great effort to enforce these election laws, often with much popular opposition. In New York City, Marshal George Sharpe worked to prevent fraud in congressional and presidential elections. The extent of his operations can be seen in a letter to Attorney General Akerman in which he tells what kinds of arms and ammunition he hopes to borrow from the U.S. Army for use in the 1870 election: "Colt's or Remington's short barrel revolvers, of caliber not less than 44 or 36 are to be preferred. . . . Five thousand may be required, also the same number of holsters and belts. I have also to request that 200,000 rounds of ammunition . . . and 200 rounds of assorted howitzer ammunition, may be held by the Ordnance Officer in this city, subject to my order."[6] Sharpe's thousands of deputies prevented much fraud in 1870, but they must have been disappointed in the results of the election: The Democrats won handily. Soon after the election federal officers in New York were responsible for the removal of hundreds of names of deceased or fictitious persons from the voter rolls.

In the West the Enforcement and Civil Rights Acts were used experimentally to protect the Chinese from mob violence and thus restore order in a number of cities. Attorney General Akerman and President Grant urged the Justice Department officers in California to use the Enforcement Acts to protect the Chinese from organized bands of anti-Chinese whites. Fifteen years later cases from the district of Oregon involved the violent expulsion of Chinese from three towns. The U.S. attorney secured the conviction of several individuals in 1886 but soon lost his zeal because of new rulings of the U.S. Supreme Court.[7]

Violations of the internal revenue laws by moonshiners were particularly prevalent in the districts of West Virginia, Kentucky, western North Carolina, and northern Georgia, as well as eastern Tennessee, but violations were common in dozens of judicial districts. Urban moonshiners were active in cities ranging from New York to Chicago to San Francisco. Atkinson, in *After the Moonshiners,* devotes a chapter to federal efforts to stop the practice of illicit distilling in New York City, and gunplay in the metropolis was, according to Atkinson, as common as in the southern highlands.[8]

But while the North did experience widespread violation of federal law and occasional bouts of serious resistance by citizens, it is undeniable that the most severe problems for federal law enforcement arose in the South and West. Here the number of criminal cases per capita was very much higher. Here violence and intimidation of attorneys, marshals, jurors, and witnesses was the greatest. Consider the district of New Hampshire: In the twenty years after 1870 U.S. attorneys there handled a mere 277 criminal cases, or eight cases per 10,000 persons over the whole period.[9] But even in the larger and more urban states of the North the number of federal cases was small, as can be seen by referring to Table 6.1.

There are a number of plausible reasons for the greater number of federal criminal cases and the greater resistance to federal laws in the South and West. One is the fact that Congress aimed certain laws particularly at the South or West—these laws sought to stifle heterogeneity and create a calm and uniform business climate across the United States. If congressmen could prevent race war in Mississippi, cotton production would remain high, as would Mississippians' orders for northern manufactured goods. If congressmen could move against the Mormon economic domination of Utah, a new wave of entrepreneurial immigrants could move to the territory. If mountaineer distillers could be suppressed, they could be made to give in to the "mighty march of civilization" (in prosecutor H. M. Wiltse's words) and become wage laborers in the coal mines or on the railroads; meanwhile, the large distilleries of Kentucky and Tennessee would continue to grow. From Arizona, governors, attorneys, and marshals reported that if not for the wave of lawlessness "a bullion production of from five to twenty millions per annum could have been reasonably expected."[10]

Another reason for the higher federal crime rate in the south and west is the fact, often noted by contemporary observers, that firearms were common and physical force less unacceptable in the southern and western United States. A U.S. attorney in Kentucky reported that, in the South, "there exists a public sentiment which justifies the taking of a human life upon very small pretext." In attempting to explain to northern congressmen the violent elections in the South, U.S. Attorney Thomas Walton of Mississippi explained that firearms were ubiquitous: "It is the greatest place on the face of the earth for pistols." Pistols were commonly brought into use to frighten black voters, punish white Republican voters, and resist U.S. marshals.[11]

Observers of society on the western frontier made the same comment. From Arizona, one newcomer wrote, "Six shooters [are] part of a man's dress here." The violence of the West has resulted in the elevation of Wyatt Earp and Doc Holliday to mythic proportions; while movies and novels are often far from true to life, the myths are based firmly on the reality of the pervasive violence of much of the western frontier. And in Appalachia, according to historian William L. Montell, there developed a "subculture of violence" in which aggression and force were "natural responses to threats, insults, and displays of weapons." In this violent subculture, acts of coercion were committed without guilt, "for the act is not considered wrong by group standards."[12]

Local public opinion hampered federal attorneys and marshals in the South and West. In the South citizens harkened to Thomas Jefferson and believed "the less government the better." Concepts of state's rights were still strong in the South, and local communities looked askance at efforts by federal prosecutors to try citizens for their violent acts at election time, or distillers for failing to pay an oppressive new tax. If the local citizens' actions were criminal at all, the cases should be tried in state courts. Public opposition to federal laws was aided by community leaders who spoke out publicly against their enforcement, and by local newspaper editors who printed articles denouncing judges, attorneys, and marshals.

The Jackson, Mississippi, *Weekly Clarion* marshaled public opinion against the Ku Klux Klan prosecutions as it told how the defendants "had been kidnapped from their quiet homes, leaving their crops to the mercy of the grass, and their wives and little ones unprotected." In the wake of the Camp Grant trial, the *Arizona Citizen* tried to sap U.S. Attorney

Table 6.1. Cases per 10,000 Persons, 1871–1890, Selected States and Territories

Pennsylvania	8.4
Ohio	9.8
Illinois	16.0
New York	17.4
Mississippi	51.2
Tennessee	105.6
Arizona	114.0
Utah	159.8

Source: Annual Report of the Attorney General for 1871–1890 (Washington, 1871–1891), Table B in each volume.

Rowell's little remaining community support by urging that the "universally despised" prosecutor be "tarred and feathered and escorted out of town on a lively cactus."[13]

During the Ku Klux prosecutions in Alabama, former president Zachary Taylor's son wrote articles that appeared in the *Montgomery Advertiser* in which he denounced the federal court officials as "corrupt and drunken conspirators whose vulgarity and venality have made the United States a by-word of reproach and disgust among the nations." The presiding judge was sure that the purpose of such newspaper articles was to "create a public panic which will demoralize jurors and witnesses in coming trials." U.S. Attorney John Minnis struck back by writing and publishing a long pamphlet titled "Ku Klux in Alabama." Even though he was being denounced by well-respected men, Minnis in his pamphlet said that he could not forget the dying shrieks of the Klan's victims or forget the plight of their widows and orphans. He reminded his readers that, unlike the Klansmen, the black victims did not have the benefit of trial by jury, defense counsel, and appeal prior to their "punishment." Minnis concluded by directly asking his audience for support: "I beg you to think of this calmly and seriously; do not be guided by passion and prejudice, do not let us make any more mistakes."[14]

All across the South and West influential local leaders denounced the Justice Department officers. Tennessee congressional candidates based their campaigns on attacks on the revenue officers and prosecutors. In Utah the vast majority of the people, including church leaders, legislators, town officers, and newspaper editors, denounced the federal government and its efforts to attack the institution of plural marriages. From Arizona leaders did call for federal efforts to bring law and order to the territory; nevertheless, citizens chaffed at particular prosecutions. They believed the Camp Grant massacre had been caused by the army's failure to protect citizens; the prosecution of the hundred defendants was seen as a cruel and unfounded action. Timber trespass prosecutions in Arizona were similarly despised by local citizens, who could not understand why the federal government did not wish them to have the materials they needed to build the territory.

Many residents of the western territories attempted to justify their resistance to federal prosecutors by pointing out that judges, attorneys, and marshals were nonresidents who did not have the interest of the territory at heart. Newspapers in Arizona, Utah, and elsewhere across the West objected to the harsh and greedy "carpetbag" officials. Howard R. Lamar has written that federally appointed officers of the territories were "political hacks, defeated congressmen, or jobless relatives of congressmen and cabinet members." These kinds of assessments are generally too harsh to apply to the Justice Department officials in Utah and Arizona. In Utah most of the attorneys and marshals *were* appointed from outside the territory. Under the circumstances, the federal government certainly was not going to appoint Mormons to the attorney and marshal positions; it is doubtful that Mormons would have been much happier if the appointments had gone to Gentile residents of Utah. None of the attorneys or marshals in Utah disgraced their office, although Marshal Dyer and Attorney Peters had weaker records than the others. Prosecutors Carey, Dickson, and Varian made impressive records under difficult circumstances.[15]

In Arizona local appointments were much more common; in fact, only four of the fourteen attorneys and marshals considered here were appointed from outside the territory. Several of the early Arizona marshals did perform poorly and showed little interest in the office. With these exceptions, the Justice Department officers served with distinction, and men such as James A. Zabriskie and Harry R. Jeffords compiled strong records against much opposition. Nevertheless, complaints about "outsider" federal officials continued to be made and lessened the citizens' respect for the federal courts. Although western congressmen proposed bills that would have required the appointment of territorial officers from within the territory, the Republican Senate invariably failed to agree. One Senate report pointed out that "it often happens that schemes exist in the territories, or a certain policy prevails that Congress is anxious to suppress," and local appointees would be more likely to support than oppose such "schemes." Although the Senate report was probably referring to polygamy, the assertion had equal validity when applied to such practices as citizens' Indian fighting, timber trespass, and illegal trading with the Indians.[16]

Another inherent problem of enforcing federal laws in the western states and territories was the typically high costs of travel, food, and lodging, and of legal services. The attorney general and Treasury officers, whether through ignorance or economic necessity, refused to pay prevailing rates when hiring special attorneys, detectives, or stenographers. Furthermore, Congress had created a national "fee bill" for the payment of fees and mileage to jurors, witnesses, marshals, and deputy marshals. The fee bill provided five or six cents per mile for travel expenses; in the West travel by stagecoach cost twenty-five cents per mile. Jurors and witnesses paid the difference out of their own pockets—and were unlikely to be favorably inclined toward the government's case. A congressional investigation turned up the case of one juror who traveled over 400 miles to court, taking jobs at ranches along the way to pay his expenses. His reimbursement covered only a fraction of his costs. The attorney general reported to Congress that many cases in the West failed because of the ill will of the witnesses[17]

These kinds of problems were less severe in the South. The fee bill was adequate there, as may be seen by the eastern Tennessee schemes whereby mountaineers worked hard to be summoned as witnesses so they could earn fees. Communication facilities were better in most parts of the South; Mississippi, for example, had a good system of railroads connecting most towns. In the mountains of Tennessee travel was often more difficult; the greatest problem was the fact that the marshal and a deputy or two were often required to go on horseback deep into the moonshiners' communities, facing immense personal danger. In the flatlands of the South one common problem was that opponents of the Enforcement Acts usually controlled the telegraph. Attorneys in Mississippi often used the mails even when time was of the essence so that important information would not be leaked to the enemy. In South Carolina military officers helping the Justice Department sent all messages in a code they called "Choctaw," again with the purpose of preventing Klansmen from intercepting messages.[18]

One would be hard pressed to cite examples of fully successful programs of federal law enforcement in the late nineteenth century. Everette Swinney, in his 1966 dissertation "Suppressing the Ku Klux Klan," maintains that enforcing of the Enforcement Acts between 1871 and 1874 was a success, because the Klan was destroyed.[19] Of course, achieving the Klan's demise *was* an important victory. But fierce race riots and massacres followed within a year of the peace of 1874, and, in the larger perspective of the whole of the late nineteenth century, the Enforcement Act program was a signal failure in the South. Free elections, two-party politics, and black participation disappeared from most parts of the region. Of the four areas examined in this book, Mississippi was left the furthest from the U.S. norm. Unindustrialized, nonurban, and stricken by poverty, Mississippi was left with weak public schools, a one-party system of politics, a very small electorate, and a quasi-official caste of second-class citizens that made up a majority of the population.

Efforts to end frauds upon the Treasury in the southern highlands were also largely unsuccessful. Despite the high conviction rate, the number of cases did not readily decline, nor were the mountainous regions of east Tennessee quickly integrated into the dominant branch of U.S. economic and social life. Tennessee and Mississippi are indicative of Justice Department efforts in many other areas of the South. No Enforcement Act program was really successful, nor was there any region where attorneys, marshals, and revenue agents won a decisive and enduring victory over illegal distilling.

Arizona presents a somewhat more cheerful case. Although the number of federal cases per capita remained steady into the twentieth century, Arizona did become an area more clearly deserving of statehood. Public lands cases, including timber trespass, kept the total number of cases high, but Arizona had been delivered from its earlier existence as a land of Indian massacres, shoot-outs between citizens and lawmen, thrice-weekly stage robberies, and presidential pleas for order. But the clearest case of success was the program to end polygamy and theocracy in Utah Territory.

Why did the Department of Justice fail in so many instances, and why were there so many instances of success mixed with failure (high conviction rates with continued violations of the law)? And why did the Department find some success in Arizona and Utah?

We will briefly review the obstacles encountered by the officers of the Justice Department. First of all, the attorneys general were overworked individuals who gave the greatest attention to their roles as attorney before the Supreme Court and writer of opinions for the president and cabinet members. Only rarely did they take time to ascertain what important cases were being tried by the U.S. attorneys or to offer help or advice to their subordinates in the field. The 1883 letter of Solicitor General S. F. Phillips to the U.S. attorney for Nevada was similar to hundreds of other letters sent during the period. The attorney had asked for instructions as to certain important cases in his district; Phillips replied,

"You are informed that this Department has no specific instructions to give U.S. Attorneys as to the discharge of their duties, it being supposed that they are competent to discharge the duties of the office, otherwise they would not be appointed."[20]

All too often, even in extraordinarily important cases, government lawyers were rebuffed in their efforts to secure advice or instructions. In his prosecution of Brigham Young for murder and lewd and lascivious cohabitation, George Caesar Bates complained of receiving no help from Washington, "and I am left to grope on."[21] While, of course, the federal attorneys were expected to be competent to try cases on their own, it is unfortunate that they usually did so with no direction from Washington. The attorneys general continued to cling to the ideal of lawyering as a solitary and independent profession, while Justice Department field officers saw the need for a true bureaucracy, with information regularly flowing between the court towns and Washington, and with the head of the department issuing clear and firm instructions.

The lack of supervision by the attorney general meant that the Justice Department had no uniform policy. In South Carolina, for example, Enforcement Act cases were dismissed by the hundreds, while in Mississippi they were tried. In Arkansas election crimes were often ignored altogether. If in any type of case a U.S. attorney developed a particularly successful program for securing convictions, his techniques were not shared with other federal prosecutors, both because he might not report his successes to the attorney general, and because the attorney general did not pass information on to his subordinates.

United States attorneys who wondered what the administration's policy was found more answers in city newspapers than in letters from their superior in Washington. The *Washington Chronicle*, mouthpiece of the Grant administration, wrote that the national government must "bring Utah into harmony with our political and social system, and lay the foundation of a respectable state." The national party platforms also spoke of policy matters. The Republican platform in 1888 hinted that the government should, in all the territories, foster the growth of population, material resources, and "public intelligence and morality." When all four measures were sufficiently strong, the territory should be admitted to the Union. The 1876 Republican platform urged that the national government work to secure "the supremacy of American institutions in all the territories." In other platforms the Republicans spoke of protecting black rights and restoring the purity of the southern ballot box. The Democratic platforms called for "a free ballot and a fair count"; the party wanted a prohibition of the use of "troops and deputy marshals" to surround the ballot boxes. The Democrats in their platforms also stated that the internal revenue taxes had been passed as "war taxes" and should be used only for "war purposes."[22]

U.S. attorneys and marshals did receive some guidance from departments other than Justice. The two districts considered here where local Justice Department officers received a steady stream of advice and instructions from Washington were Tennessee and Arizona. The reason for this is that the Tennessee cases involved the Treasury Department, while Arizona cases involved the Departments of War, Treasury, Interior, State, and Post Office. If the attorney general would not send instructions, the other cabinet secretaries would. In Utah and Mississippi there was no executive department that was specifically interested in polygamy or Enforcement Act cases, respectively. The U.S. president sometimes showed a strong interest in these two kinds of cases, and Congress often did—but rarely did the attorney general.

The dean of historians of federal administrative history, the late Leonard D. White, devotes only a few sentences to the attorney generalship in his study *The Republican Era*. White did say that the attorney general was hampered in his more important duties by pleas for jobs, pleas for dismissal of cases, and pleas for pardons. And, as Robert M. Goldman notes in his dissertation on the Department of Justice and southern voting rights after 1876, "between 1884 and 1893 the correspondence of the Attorney General's office is replete with vouchers and requests for funds for such items as desk lamps, bookcases, fire escapes for courthouses, and spittoons."[23]

Similar administrative burdens were placed upon the attorney general by Congress in its calls for information. In response to congressional requests, Garland's annual report for 1885 included, in addition to reports of business in the federal courts: lists of pardons granted; lists of prisons in which federal prisoners were incarcerated; lists of assistant U.S. attorneys and their salaries; and reports on the District of Columbia Reform School, the Justice Department library, and ill and insane convicts. The attorneys general also had to report the department's expenditures to Congress in minute detail. In 1875, for example, Edwards Pierrepont included in his annual report these expenses, among others, for the Washington office:

Soap $10.05
Matches 1.00
Feather Dusters 9.00
Mucilage 2.00
Roach Powder .25
6 Quarts Ink 3.50
2 Pairs Cuspidors 7.00[24]

Because of the constant press of demands upon the attorney general by Congress and officers of the executive branch, the supervision and instruction of attorneys and marshals was neglected.

The failure of Congress to make appropriations adequate for the enforcement of the laws was also unfortunate. Thus we have the ludicrous situation of U.S. marshals taking out loans in their own name, even mortgaging their property, to provide funds to keep the courts running. They worked to find places for impoverished jurors and witnesses to sleep, and they printed payment vouchers—which they hoped local merchants would honor. But delay and postponement, and disgruntled jurors and witnesses, were unavoidable and made the federal government appear weak and indecisive.

Leonard D. White again sheds some light on the situation: Throughout the period "the business of the Departments constantly increased with the rise of population and the flow of legislation, but its effective discharge was half-paralyzed by the reluctance of Congress to provide adequate staff."[25] Less than a year after the creation of the Department of Justice, Attorney General Akerman wrote to a U.S. attorney, "It is my individual opinion that the judicial and professional force of the Government might be advantageously doubled in most parts of the country. But such does not seem to be the judgement of Congress."[26] In Table 6.2 we can trace the growth of the Justice Department by decades. Although in the twenty years after 1874 the criminal case load trebled, the department's staff grew slowly.

Moreover, the salaries provided for U.S. attorneys and marshals were terribly small. The attorneys, for instance, were paid an annual salary of $250 plus fees; the marshals earned $200 and fees. An unhappy Akerman wrote, "I know of no work for the public good which is so ill paid."

Attorney General Amos T. Akerman saw that one of the Justice Department's greatest problems was understaffing. "The judicial and professional force of the Government might be advantageously doubled in most parts of the country. But such does not seem to be the wisdom of Congress." Courtesy of U.S. Library of Congress.

Table 6.2. Growth of the Justice Department

Fiscal Year	Criminal Cases Tried	U.S. Attorneys and Assistants	Cases Per Prosecutor
1874	6,018	135	45
1884	12,542	141	89
1894	21,744	177	122

Sources: Annual Report of the Attorney General (Washington, D.C.: GPO, 1874, 1884, and 1894); *Register of the Department of Justice* (Washington, D.C.: GPO, 1874, 1884, and 1894).

Note: The numbers in the assistant attorney column are the totals of those who served as regular assistant U.S. attorneys in any given year; the number of individuals who served at any one time was probably 25 percent smaller.

Akerman recommended doubling the fee structure, doubling the salaries in small districts, and quadrupling the salary in large districts. Year after year, his successors recommended that the fee structure be dropped, and the attorneys and marshals be paid an adequate annual salary. As Edwards Pierrepont put it, "there is as much impropriety in paying United States Attorneys as they are now paid, as there would be in paying district judges the same way."[27]

The fee system of paying commissioners, attorneys, and marshals meant that these positions would pay well only if large numbers of cases were brought. While the attorneys general, seeking to reduce expenses, urged that "a few cases that really result in conviction" would do more to achieve respect for the law than "a vast number of cases where no convictions can be had," the experiment was rarely tried. Augustus Hill Garland wrote that in Utah "the practice of polygamy may be more successfully met by the conviction of large offenders than by the conviction of every offender in the community." But if the U.S. attorney were to try only ten "large offenders," he would, for these ten difficult cases, receive $200. The attorney was more fairly compensated if he tried a hundred relatively easy cases and made $2,000. None of the U.S. attorneys grew rich, however, as any fees above the amount of $6,000 per year ($3,500 in Arizona and New Mexico) were returned to the Treasury. Only in 1896 did Congress finally dismantle the hated fee system and initiate payment by salary.[28]

In searching for the causes of failures of the Justice Department enforcement programs, the federal courts must not be overlooked. Federal courts in this period staggered under extremely heavy caseloads. With a thousand cohabitation cases tried in Utah, a thousand election cases in northern Mississippi, and ten thousand cases of fraud tried in eastern Tennessee, the courts' work load grew almost unmanageable. In other districts the point of unmanageability was in fact reached. With more than four hundred Enforcement Act cases pending in Columbia, South Carolina, Akerman reported to Congress, "With the caution and deliberation which the law wisely observes in criminal proceedings, it is obvious that the attempt to bring to justice even a small portion of the guilty . . . must fail, or the judicial machinery of the United States must be increased. If it takes a court one month to try five offenders, how long will it take to try four hundred already indicted and many hundreds more who deserve to be indicted?"[29]

Akerman finally directed the dismissal of most of the cases in South Carolina, so that in fiscal 1873 there were in South Carolina fourteen convictions under the Enforcement Acts, four acquittals, and 536 cases dismissed. In 1883 Attorney General Brewster, seeing that many district courts were unable to handle the mass of cases, proposed a long and detailed law for the consideration of Congress. Brewster envisioned new rules under which trials might be "shorn of the technical objections and numberless dilatory motions that can now be interposed to prevent a speedy trial upon the merits." But Brewster's bill was not enacted, and the district courts continued to have problems hearing all the cases on their calendars.[30]

Although the attorney general's annual report warned Congress that the judiciary was overworked, the number of new judicial districts added did not nearly keep pace with the rise in numbers of cases. Most commonly, Congress simply added new court towns, an action that did nothing to relieve the judges and U.S. attorneys of their burdens but, on the contrary, added the necessity of regular travel to their duties. But the creation of new meeting places for the courts pleased voters in towns such as Aberdeen, Mississippi, and Chattanooga, Tennessee. In 1891 Congress at last aided the federal judiciary in a real way, as it added a tier of courts of appeals, appointed new judges, and rearranged the jurisdiction of the district and circuit courts.[31]

One remedy that was adopted by judges in northern Mississippi, eastern Tennessee, and elsewhere was the practice of holding quick trials and handing down mild sentences. It was not uncommon for Judge Robert A. Hill to hold fifteen jury trials per day at Oxford. The sentencing was so mild that the jurors did not balk at returning quick verdicts of guilty, and the defense lawyers did not insist on long, protracted trials. Typically, a ballot box stuffer would plead not guilty and produce two witnesses. The U.S. attorney would produce a few witnesses; the jury would retire for twenty minutes and return a guilty verdict. Judge Hill would then impose a $25 fine. In eastern Tennessee the courts operated in a similar manner, although, because so many suspended sentences were handed down, a very large proportion of defendants simply pled guilty. The Knoxville court typically disposed of ten to fifteen jury trials per day. The imposition of severe sentences in either district undoubtedly would have led to more elaborate defense strategies and more cautious juries.[32]

The lack of a Justice Department detective force impeded efforts to enforce the federal laws. Only rarely was the local hire of detectives approved, and even then the hire was temporary. If a case involved the Post Office or Treasury Department, postal inspectors or Secret Service agents were sometimes detailed to make investigations. But in other kinds of cases the U.S. attorneys were the only field investigators available. As Justice Joseph Story wrote prior to the Civil War, Congress seemed "to have forgotten that such a thing as an internal police or organization is necessary. . . . I believe in my conscience many members imagine that the laws will execute themselves." Decades later, congressmen were still passing new criminal laws without providing the means for detecting and prosecuting violators.[33]

Sometimes, instead of using detectives, the Justice Department simply offered a reward for information. Usually, however, such rewards were offered for information as to the whereabouts of an individual already indicted. In the case of murderers of deputy marshals a reward was usually offered for the apprehension of the murderer, especially in the 1880s and 1890s, but if the deputy was only injured, no reward offer was made. Rare and sporadic use of detectives and occasional offers of rewards did little to insure a vigorous federal law enforcement program.[34]

The failure of both the Congress and the attorney general adequately to support U.S. attorneys and marshals in their execution of the laws is crucial to a full understanding of the enforcement of federal laws in the late nineteenth century. But are these factors sufficient to explain the recurring lack of real success in such law enforcement?

Without a doubt, the element most important in hampering the attorneys and marshals was local resistance. Homer Cummings, who while U.S. attorney general wrote a history of the attorney general's office from 1787 to 1937, discusses the prevalence of local resistance throughout the nation's history: "The enforcement of laws is always delicate as well as difficult. Particularly in the field of federal legislation, laws do not find places upon the statute books until the social conditions which they are designed to remedy have become fixed. Even where the justice of legislation is apparent, large groups whose daily lives are entwined with existing conditions constitute an influential opposition."[35]

Our four cases studies bear witness to Attorney General Cummings's words. Racial customs in Mississippi, the poverty and folk culture of Tennessee, and celestial marriages in Utah were firmly entrenched when Congress passed laws designed to alter the society of those regions. Hatred of the Apache and a desire to make money from the government had become characteristic of the population in Arizona before the attorneys and marshals set out to try to enforce the federal laws. Congressmen grossly overestimated their own powers if they imagined that a few statutes would make whites in Mississippi respect black political equality or make devout Mormons quickly renounce their families. Laws cannot alter a community's folkways unless the community is ready for change.

The scholar who coined the term *folkways* was William Graham Sumner, who was writing in the late nineteenth century. By folkways, Sumner meant mass phenomena that are "uniform, repeated, and widely concurred in" in a given community. Sumner also coined the term *mores,* which are folkways that have taken on a philosophy of right living and thus have become the correct "life policy" for a group of people. Sumner maintained that U.S. society has two ways of attempting to change mores: preaching and legislation. Both usually fail. The reformer who wanted to get a law passed to abolish some perceived evil was "only a mischief-maker," according to Sumner. Changes that are opposed to mores are very difficult to effect and generally can be accomplished only over a long period of time. Interestingly, among the examples of well-entrenched mores cited by Sumner were polygamy, race relations in the South, and practices related to alcohol and its regulation.[36]

In Tennessee, Arizona, Utah, and Mississippi the field officers of the Justice Department encountered citizens who were not willing to abandon their entrenched folkways. Even those who favored change were fearful of their neighbors and therefore fearful of testifying. From northern Mississippi Marshal Pierce reported to Washington that witnesses were so frightened that he had to "take them by force." From Utah the marshal reported that he had to round up unwilling witnesses "like a lot of wild cattle." In Tennessee witnesses feared barn burnings or even assassination, and the U.S. attorney noted that it frequently was "more difficult to get the witness than the defendant." In Arizona witnesses sent anonymous letters reporting violations of federal law but were afraid to do anything more to aid the government. Defendants were often highly successful in hiding themselves with the help of their neighbors. In Utah a number of church leaders, including President John Taylor, successfully avoided arrest on the underground. In northern Mississippi J. E. Gillenwater hid near Corinth and surrounded himself with loyal friends who shot at marshals and killed men who informed on him. The moonshiner Hut Amerine succeeded in avoiding arrest for many years and killed more than one man who came too near.[37]

The power of the communities that opposed the federal laws meant that lying could be acceptable behavior for witnesses, and obstruction acceptable for jurors. The words of U.S. Attorney James Meek, although describing the situation in east Tennessee, are also descriptive of other areas of the country: "It is spoken of as a disgrace, by men who live in these communities, and profess to be respectable and good citizens, for a witness to give evidence against . . . lawbreakers."[38]

In Mississippi the trial of Aleck Page's murderers was made a mockery when scores of white women (the mothers, wives, and sisters of the twenty-eight defendants) testified either that their kinsman had been sick in bed the night of the crime or had been sitting up with a sick family member. Threats of violence against witnesses and federal officers could quickly work to stop a prosecution. Attorney General Miller reported in 1889 that in many regions of the country prosecutions could not proceed; the danger to witnesses and jurors was so great that "it would be simply inhuman to enforce their attendance." Miller added, "In certain localities no occupation is so dangerous as a faithful performance of duty by United States Marshals."[39]

Why did Justice Department officers in Mississippi, Arizona, and Tennessee, and in other districts across the nation, fail to win great victories in their programs of federal law enforcement? Fearful witnesses, biased jurors, violent defendants, local "spotters" who watched the marshal, overworked courts, inadequate appropriations, and taciturn attorneys general—all contributed to the failures and disappointments. In Utah a number of factors led to the genuine success of Justice Department officers. The army gave its aid throughout the latter part of the century; all U.S. presidents vowed to do their part to crush polygamy. National public opinion was always antipolygamy even in the 1850s, and such sentiments grew to a fever pitch by the 1880s. Money for detectives was provided—$200 in 1879, $600 in 1884, and $5,000 in 1886.[40]

But what of citizen resistance in Utah? Did the Justice Department officers not encounter spotters, unwilling witnesses, and unsympathetic jurors? They did, but Congress provided the weapons needed to overcome these problems. In Utah, in fact, all three branches of the federal government joined together in a concerted effort to do whatever necessary to end polygamy and theocracy. Another reason the federal government was successful in its program in Utah was the fact that Utah was not yet a state. According to the Constitution and various Supreme Court cases interpreting the Constitution, Congress has almost unlimited powers to govern the territories. Niceties of states' rights, and even certain kinds of citizens' rights, need not be observed in the case of territories.[41]

In Utah, when simple prosecution did not work, Congress passed increasingly harsh laws, thus giving the U.S. attorneys and marshals the weapons they needed to fight the Mormons. Justices of the Supreme Court gave their aid as well, in several important decisions. If Mormon jurors would not convict, they would be barred from juries in cohabitation trials. If the church leadership showed no signs of weakening, the government would disincorporate the church and seize its property. If local government were sympathetic to the church, Congress would appoint a commission to reorganize political participation in the territory, disfranchising first polygamists and later preparing to disfranchise all church members. These draconian federal policies led to a successful

Justice Department enforcement program. Such harsh actions could not have been easily taken in the states of the Union, particularly in the absence of strong national public opinion in favor of black political participation, say, or the enforcement of the government tax on liquors. Congress could have used harsh power to enact legislation aimed at general lawlessness in the western territories, but it rarely did so. Both congressional opinion and public opinion were aroused to a fever pitch over polygamy but showed only "concern" for Arizona's mail robbery and timber trespass.

Federal prosecutors in Utah and Arizona benefited from having judges appointed from back east. These men were quite willing to move forcefully against the established institutions of the territories. In Mississippi and Tennessee, on the other hand, local men such as Judges Hill, Trigg, and Key were in hearty sympathy with their neighbors and were incapable of harshness to ballot box stuffers or moonshiners. As Professor Henry R. Glick put it in his book *Courts, Politics, and Justice*, "since judges often are products of the same environment as their court, the link between their background and the local culture is often very strong and has a clear effect on judicial decision making."[42] Historian Kermit L. Hall has made the same point in his excellent studies of federal judges. An important part of the founding fathers' balance between state and federal powers was the fact that federal judges reflected local values. But their reflection of local values was detrimental to federal law enforcement programs.[43]

Of course, the U.S. attorneys and marshals were generally local men, too (although not in Utah). Yet we see little sympathy on their part for their neighbors who violated the laws. One reason for this, of course, is that because of the fee system they would have no income if they did not prosecute cases and work for convictions. Also, unlike the district judges, they could be removed if they did not do their duty in enforcing the laws firmly. And because they served only short, four-year terms, they were likely to be in step with the administration that appointed them. In many districts the judges were from an earlier era and had little sympathy with new congressional enactments—Judge Hill, for example, who served almost until the end of the century, had been appointed in 1866 by Andrew Johnson and had scant interest in black voting rights or the survival of the Mississippi Republican or Greenback parties.

What happened after 1893 to the four jurisdictions that form the focus of this book? Arizona experienced ups and downs in the years after statehood. The era of World War I brought a large number of new jobs in copper mining, cotton production, and irrigated farming. No new wave of lawlessness interfered with this economic prosperity. The decade of the 1920s included a sharp economic downturn with a corresponding loss of jobs. With the entry of the United States into World War II, the state's economy began to boom again, and, interestingly, Arizona returned to the old frontier days' reality of a federal government that was central to the region's economic life. Army forts, prisoner camps, Japanese-American internment camps, and arms factories—all brought new economic opportunity to the state. Arizona has continued to become more typical of the U.S. norm. It is now 80 percent urban, 91 percent white, and features factories, mining, agriculture, and a bounteous timber production from national forest lands. As one historian has concluded, "by 1970 Arizona was squarely in the mainstream of American life."[44]

Utah experienced a similar history. Two years after the territory's admission to the Union, Utah residents demonstrated their patriotism and nationalism by a particularly enthusiastic support of the Spanish-American War. In 1916 the state elected its first non-Mormon governor. As in Arizona, the post–World War I era brought a sharp economic downturn that included an outmigration of people. And as with Arizona, the industrial boom of World War II helped the state enormously as the federal government aided in locating steel plants and other war factories there; manufacturing employment increased 120 percent. Even after the war, uranium, missiles, and the space program helped maintain the state's flourishing economy. By 1970 Utah was 74 percent Mormon, down from more than 90 percent one hundred years earlier. But, as in 1870, the national government continued to be central to Utah's history; today the largest employer in the state is the federal government.[45]

The Tennessee case study mentioned the beginnings of the state's integration into the national economy. Between 1870 and 1893 railroads were built at a rapid pace, and attorneys, marshals, and other eager citizens were investing heavily in coal, iron, steel, and woolen mills. The economic growth and diversification continued into the twentieth century. Today Tennessee is characterized by textile manufacturing, coal mining, and the production of hardwood products. Agribusiness has become the rule, particularly large-scale production of tobacco and cattle. Certainly, Tennessee is no longer unacquainted with the progress experienced by other areas of the country. The poor farmer striving to keep his family alive by raising a little corn, a few chickens, and some apples and peaches, has become rare. Nevertheless, Tennessee's mountain culture has proved deep-rooted, and violations of the federal revenue laws are still being prosecuted, albeit on a much smaller scale, in the district of eastern Tennessee.[46]

In the early twentieth century Mississippi remained far apart from the U.S. norm. Overwhelmingly rural, dependent upon one crop, populated by impoverished whites and a majority population of stifled blacks, and with no urban culture to speak of, it would be difficult to name a state further removed from the economic and social realities of the other forty-seven. Gradually, in the second half of the twentieth century, change has come. Sharecropping has given way to corporate agriculture, while soybeans and cattle have challenged cotton for primacy. Timber production is important, and industrial plants are common—although most manufacturing jobs are in low-paying industries such as apparel and wood products. The U.S. attorneys and marshals of the 1960s helped bring racial progress to the state, while by 1980 Mississippi's demographics were not so incredibly different from those of the other states. In 1880 Mississippi was 3 percent urban and 42 percent white; one hundred years later the state was 47 percent urban and 64 percent white. As historian John R. Skates has observed, trends in Mississippi since 1940 have served to "remold it in the national image."[47]

As the nineteenth century drew to a close, the Justice Department began to be in danger of being overwhelmed by the caseloads in federal courts. In the years after 1893 Congress passed new criminal statutes at an ever-increasing rate. The courts in the 1870s had kept their work loads manageable by sidestepping the new role Congress had given them for the enforcement of the rights of national citizenship. Although many Congressmen shared James A. Garfield's determination "to see to it that, hereafter, personal rights are placed in the keeping of the nation," the Supreme Court declined to admit that the federal courts should protect the basic rights of all citizens. Unless a case involved racial bias, state action, and a right specifically guaranteed by the Constitution, the

Supreme Court left citizens to attempt to enforce their civil rights in state courts.[48]

Nevertheless, the number of different kinds of federal cases being heard in the federal courts increased dramatically. In fact, in the first half of the twentieth century Congress began taking ever-greater interest in the matter of crime, including crimes that had traditionally been state offenses. In an increasingly mobile society, Congress moved to punish prostitution, kidnaping, and larceny by prescribing punishments for "crossing state lines" in the commission of such crimes. In addition to this use of the Constitution's interstate commerce clause, Congress used its power to tax in an effort to move against other undesirable practices: The National Firearms Act of 1934 and the Marijuana Tax Act of 1937 placed prohibitive taxes on the sale of machine guns and marijuana, respectively. The most important new class of criminal cases came with Prohibition and the passage of the Eighteenth Amendment and the accompanying Volstead Act. In the three years after 1918 the number of federal criminal cases increased two and a half times.[49]

U.S. attorneys, marshals, and judges faced crowded dockets as they began to prosecute cases of liquor sales, kidnaping, bank robberies, and interstate automobile theft. With these increased work loads, patchwork repairs to the federal criminal justice system would prove inadequate. Among the patchwork repairs made were the hire of increasing numbers of assistant attorneys and the occasional division of a judicial district into two new districts. Two new structures did move the Justice Department away from mere patchwork repair and proved enormously helpful to the field officers of the Department of Justice: Already mentioned was the 1891 creation of a new tier of courts of appeals and the appointment of new federal judges to help lighten the judicial work load; but undoubtedly, the greatest factor in making possible the successful prosecution of large numbers of federal criminal defendants was the development of a large and specialized Justice Department bureaucracy in the twentieth century.[50]

In 1909 the Justice Department organized a Bureau of Investigation, which finally provided detectives other than the U.S. attorneys. The bureau grew slowly in size and power—not until the 1930s were its detectives allowed to carry arms or to make seizures and arrests. But soon, the Federal Bureau of Investigation had a highly professional, nationwide network of agents skilled at detecting crime, locating guilty parties, and working up strong evidence for use in court. J. Edgar Hoover, director of the bureau, knew that laboratories and investigators were not enough to combat resistance to federal law, and he developed great skill as a publicist and molder of public opinion. Soon, at the forefront of the nation's heroes were the "G-men," or FBI agents. The fact that Justice Department officers were heroes would mean more local cooperation and less resistance to federal criminal law enforcement.[51]

Also much improved was the situation of U.S. attorneys. By the 1960s and 1970s these federal prosecutors were no longer left to guess as to proper U.S. policy. The central Justice Department bureaucracy has written and published hundreds of books for government attorneys and marshals, conveying general and specific advice. One of the most useful is titled *Ethics and Professional Conduct for the Federal Attorney,* containing clearly stated rules followed by lucid commentary. Among the nuts-and-bolts discussions are sections dealing with "Initiating and Declining Prosecution," "Selecting Charges," and "Entering into Plea Agreements." For specific kinds of cases, specific publications are provided. A good example is *Federal Prosecution of Election Offenses*, which includes sections on "Election Day Procedures," "Timing and Objectives of Election Fraud Investigations," and the "Departmental Prosecutive Policy."[52]

In comparison with modern federal law officers, U.S. attorneys and marshals in the years 1870 to 1893 labored under severe handicaps, and emerge from this study as remarkable men. Against great odds they worked to enforce the nation's laws. When they saw the need for a new law they lobbied Congress. When the attorney general ignored them they persevered and wrote again. If Congress made no appropriation, they advanced their own funds or secured a bank loan in their own names. They guided cases to the U.S. Supreme Court, earning at most 20 or 30 dollars for such important cases. If they saw that public opinion was not with them, they made speeches and wrote pamphlets, broadsides, letters to the editor, even books. To the extent that federal laws were enforced at all in the nineteenth century, these men deserve the credit. Failures of the Justice Department are not attributable to its field officers. Congress and the attorney general prescribed tasks for these men but usually failed to supply the needed tools, especially as public opinion failed to support vigorous federal action. In the case of Utah, public opinion did allow for a successful enforcement program. In Arizona violation of federal laws remained widespread, but at least calm order prevailed, and the territory was soon deemed ready for statehood. In northern Mississippi and eastern Tennessee the partial victory afforded by a high conviction rate was the best that could be achieved without additional legislation, a supportive bureaucracy, generous appropriations, and the firm interest of the American people.

Notes

The following abbreviations are used throughout the notes:

AF	Appointment Files, Records of the Department of Justice, Record Group 60, National Archives
E&C	Executive and Congressional Letterbooks, Records of the Department of Justice, Record Group 60, National Archives
INST	Instruction Books, Records of the Department of Justice, Record Group 60, National Archives
J&C	Letters to Judges and Clerks, Records of the Department of Justice, Record Group 60, National Archives
RDC	Records of the District Court for Northern Mississippi, Federal Records Center, East Point, Georgia
RDJ	Records of the Department of Justice, Record Group 60, National Archives
SCF/AZ	Source-Chronological File for Arizona Territory, Records of the Department of Justice, Record Group 60, National Archives
SCF/ETN	Source-Chronological File for Eastern Tennessee, Records of the Department of Justice, Record Group 60, National Archives
SCF/NMS	Source-Chronological File for Northern Mississippi, Records of the Department of Justice, Record Group 60, National Archives

SCF/UT Source-Chronological File for Utah Territory, Records of the Department of Justice, Record Group 60, National Archives

YF Year Files, Records of the Department of Justice, Record Group 60, National Archives

Chapter 1: The Department of Justice and Federal Law Enforcement

1. *Historical Statistics of the United States: Colonial Times to 1970* (Washington, D.C.: GPO, 1975), 8, 512, 517 and passim, 543, 580, 606, 666, 731.

2. Morton Keller, *Affairs of State: Public Life in Late Nineteenth-Century America* (Cambridge, Mass., 1977); Stephen Skowronek, *Building a New American State: The Expansion of National Administrative Capacities, 1877–1920* (New York, 1982); William Edward Nelson, *The Roots of American Bureaucracy, 1830–1900* (Cambridge, Mass., 1982).

3. Everette Swinney, "Suppressing the Ku Klux Klan: The Enforcement of the Reconstruction Amendments, 1870–1874" (Ph.D. diss., University of Texas, Austin, 1966); Robert J. Kaczorowski, *The Politics of Judicial Interpretation: The Federal Courts, Department of Justice, and Civil Rights, 1866–1876* (Dobbs Ferry, N.Y., 1985).

4. For studies of early federal criminal law enforcement, see Dwight F. Henderson, *Congress, Courts, and Criminals: The Development of Federal Criminal Law, 1801–1829* (Westport, Conn., 1985); and Stanley W. Campbell, *Slave Catchers: Enforcement of the Fugitive Slave Law, 1850–1860* (Chapel Hill, N.C., 1970).

5. See, e.g., Douglas F. Dowd, "A Comparative Analysis of Economic Development in the American South and West," *Journal of Economic History* 16 (1956): 558–74; Willard Hurst, "The Uses of Law in Four 'Colonial States' of the American Union," *Wisconsin Law Review* (1945): 577–92.

6. *Compendium of the Tenth Census* (Washington, D.C.: GPO, 1882).

7. *Biographical Directory of the American Congress, 1774–1971* (Washington, D.C.: GPO, 1971), 21–24, 47, 198–253; Leo Pfeffer, *This Honorable Court* (Boston: Beacon Press, 1965), 427.

8. Stanley P. Hirshon, *Farewell to the Bloody Shirt: Northern Republicans and the Southern Negro, 1877–1893* (Bloomington: Indiana University Press, 1962), 226–35.

9. *Annual Report of the Attorney General* (Washington, D.C.: GPO, 1871–1891). Table B of these reports each year gave the number of criminal cases disposed of by district. I added together the number of cases for all years for each region,

then divided by the population figures given in the 1882 *Compendium of the Tenth Census: Population.*

10. Samuel Walker, *Popular Justice: A History of American Criminal Justice* (New York, 1980), 103–20.

11. *Annual Report of the Attorney General* (Washington, D.C.: GPO, 1876–1885). Each year, Table B of these reports gave the number of convictions, acquittals, and dismissals in each judicial district.

12. Judiciary Act of 1789, 1 Statutes at Large 73; Homer Cummings and Carl McFarland, *Federal Justice: Chapters in the History of Justice and the Federal Executive* (New York, 1937), 142–46.

13. James D. Richardson, comp., *A Compilation of the Messages and Papers of the Presidents, 1789–1908* (N.p.: Bureau of National Literature and Art, 1909), vol. 1, 577, vol. 2, 314, 453, 527, vol. 4, 415; Cummings and McFarland, 142–60.

14. Cummings and McFarland, 142–46.

15. *Congressional Globe*, 41st Congress, 2d sess., 3034–39, 3065–67; Act of August 2, 1861, 12 Stat. 285; The Department of Justice Act, 16 Stat. 162 (1870).

16. *Congressional Globe*, 41st Congress, 2d sess., 3034–39, 3065–67.

17. *Dictionary of American Biography,* 1st ed. (1964), vol. 1, 133; *Nation*, June 23, 1870, 397; William S. McFeely, "Amos T. Akerman: The Lawyer and Racial Justice," in *Region, Race, and Reconstruction: Essays in Honor of C. Vann Woodward,* ed. J. Morgan Kousser and James M. McPherson (New York, 1982), 395–415.

18. *New York Times*, August 1 and December 2, 17, and 20, 1873; "Expenditures in the Department of Justice," House Report 610, 43d Congress, 1st sess., Serial Set vol. 1625; William S. McFeely, *Grant* (New York, 1981), 390–92; Sidney Teiser, "Life of George H. Williams: Almost Chief Justice," *Oregon Historical Quarterly* 47 (1946): 255–80, 417–40.

19. *New York Times*, May 25, 1875; Lewis A. Leonard, *Life of Alphonso Taft* (New York, 1920), 155–81.

20. Stephen Cresswell, "The Attorney Generalship of Charles Devens," *Hayes Historical Journal* 3, no. 6 (1982): 32–45.

21. Benjamin H. Brewster to President Arthur, October 31, 1881, Arthur Papers, Library of Congress; Arthur to Wayne MacVeagh, November 11, 1881, Arthur Papers; MacVeagh to Arthur, November 8, 1881, Arthur Papers; *New York Times*, March 6 and November 12, 1881.

22. *Annual Report of the Attorney General* for 1883, 23–30; Cummings and McFarland, 253–61.

23. *New York Times*, January 8, 1885, February 17 and August 17, 1886, February 2 and May 25, 1887; Leonard Schlup, ed., "Augustus Hill Garland: Gilded Age Democrat," *Arkansas Historical Quarterly* 40 (1981): 338–46; Robert M. Goldman, "'A Free Ballot and a Fair Count': The Department of Justice and the Enforcement of Voting Rights in the South, 1877–1893" (Ph.D. diss., Michigan State

University, East Lansing, 1976), 192–220. Goldman asserts that Garland did not disown the enforcement program.

24. Maria Margaret Quinn, "William Henry Harrison Miller: Attorney General of the United States, 1889–1893" (Ph.D. diss., Catholic University of America, Washington, D.C., 1965), 2–9; *New York Times*, March 5, 1889.

25. 16 Stat. 162 (1870).

26. C. Vann Woodward, "Government by Gaslight," *New York Times Book Review*, March 30, 1958, pp. 3, 26.

27. "Methods of Transacting the Public Business," Senate Report 507, 50th Congress, 1st sess., 1–60, Serial Set vol. 2521–22 (1888).

28. Amos T. Akerman to C. F. Whitely, November 9, 1871, Akerman Letterbooks, Alderman Library, special collections, University of Virginia.

29. "Walt Whitman," *Funk & Wagnalls New Encyclopedia*, vol. 25, 108 (1971); Cindy Sondik Aron, *Ladies and Gentlemen of the Civil Service: Middle-Class Workers in Victorian America* (New York, 1987).

30. *Annual Report of the Attorney General* for 1873 and 1893; Goldman, "'A Free Ballot and a Fair Count'," 278; *Register of the Department of Justice* (Washington, D.C.: GPO, 1871, 1891); "Employees in the Department of Justice," Senate Exec. Doc. 82, 44th Congress, 1st sess., Serial Set vol. 1664 (1876).

31. *Register of the Department of Justice* for 1874 and 1883; *Annual Report of the Attorney General* for 1883, p. 40; Aron, 90–96.

32. Akerman to John M. Montgomery, August 21, 1871, Akerman Letterbooks.

33. Akerman to J. A. Minnis, July 7, 1871, INST; G. Wiley Wells to Attorney General Williams, September 28, 1874, SCF/NMS.

34. Attorney General Devens to Senator John Morgan, April 30, 1870, E&C.

35. Anonymous to Devens, August 8, 1879, Devens Papers, Hayes Presidential Center, Fremont, Ohio.

36. Akerman to C.W.C. Rowell, August 22, 1871, INST.

37. Devens to the U.S. attorneys, April 5, 1877, INST.

38. *Annual Report of the Attorney General* for 1877, pp. 4, 6–7.

39. Garland to the U.S. marshals, April 6, 1885, INST.

40. Walter Van Dyke to Attorney General Pierrepont, telegram, April 14, 1876, SCF for California; L. D. Latimer to Benjamin H. Bristow, April 20, 1872, SCF for California; L. D. Latimer to Williams, February 27, 1873, SCF for California.

41. *Annual Report of the Attorney General* for 1878, p. 18.

42. William F. Holmes, "Moonshining and Collective Violence: Georgia, 1889–1895," *Journal of American History* 67 (1980): 589–611.

43. C. Vann Woodward, *The Burden of Southern History*, rev. ed. (Baton Rouge, 1968).

44. Patricia Nelson Limerick, *The Legacy of Conquest: The Unbroken Past of the American West* (New York, 1987).

Chapter 2: Enforcing the Enforcement Acts in Northern Mississippi

1. Richard N. Current, "Carpetbaggers Reconsidered," in E. C. Rozwenc, *Reconstruction in the South* (Lexington, Mass.: D. C. Heath, 1972), 88–105.

2. William C. Harris, *The Day of the Carpetbagger: Republican Reconstruction in Mississippi* (Baton Rouge, 1979); Allen W. Trelease, *White Terror: The Ku Klux Klan Conspiracy and Southern Reconstruction* (New York, 1971).

3. William Gillette, *Retreat from Reconstruction, 1869–1879* (Baton Rouge, 1979), 1–25, 186–210; William Gillette, *The Right to Vote: Politics and the Passage of the Fifteenth Amendment*, 2d ed. (Baltimore, Md.: Johns Hopkins University Press, 1969); John and La Wanda Cox, "Negro Suffrage and Republican Politics: The Problem of Motivation in Reconstruction Historiography," *Journal of Southern History* 33 (1967): 303–30.

4. Act of May 31, 1870 (First Enforcement Act), 16 Statutes at Large, 140–46.

5. Act of February 28, 1871 (Second Enforcement Act), 16 Stat. 433.

6. Act of April 20, 1871 (Ku Klux Act), 17 Stat. 13.

7. *United States v. Reese,* 92 U.S. 214 (1876); Robert M. Goldman, "'A Free Ballot and a Fair Count': The Department of Justice and the Enforcement of Voting Rights in the South, 1877–1893" (Ph.D. diss., Michigan State University, East Lansing, 1976), 9–43; Robert J. Kaczorowski, *The Politics of Judicial Interpretation: The Federal Courts, Department of Justice, and Civil Rights, 1866–1876* (Dobbs Ferry, N.Y., 1985), 200–17.

8. *United States v. Cruikshank et al.,* 92 U.S. 542 (1876); Goldman, "'A Free Ballot and a Fair Count'," 9–43; Kaczorowski, 128–32, 205–17.

9. *Ex Parte Yarbrough,* 110 U.S. 651 (1884); Goldman, "'A Free Ballot and a Fair Count'," 9–43.

10. Statistics are taken from the *Annual Report of the Attorney General* (Washington, D.C.: GPO, 1871–1892), Table B for each year. Kermit L. Hall, "Political Power and Constitutional Legitimacy: The South Carolina Ku Klux Klan Trials, 1871–1872," *Emory Law Journal* 33 (1984): 936–51; Peggy Lamson, *The Glorious Failure: Black Congressman Robert Elliot and the Reconstruction in South Carolina* (New York: Norton, 1973), 129ff.; Everette Swinney, "Suppressing the Ku Klux Klan: The Enforcement of the Reconstruction Amendments, 1870–1874" (Ph.D. diss., University of Texas, Austin, 1966), 205–34.

11. *Compendium of the Tenth Census: Population* (Washington, D.C.: GPO, 1882).

12. *Illustrated History of Los Angeles County, California* (Chicago: Lewis Publishing, 1889), 190–93.

13. *Vicksburg Times and Republican*, July 1, 1871. The verbatim transcript of proceedings in this habeas corpus case of *Ex Parte Walton et al.* can be found in

U.S. Congress, Joint Select Committee to Inquire into the Condition of Affairs in the Late Insurrectionary States, "Report . . ." (Washington, 1872), vol. 12, 934–87.

14. Joint Select Committee, "Report"; *Vicksburg Times and Republican*, July 4 and 6, 1871.

15. *Oxford Falcon*, July 7, 1871; *Vicksburg Times and Republican*, July 7, 1871.

16. *Vicksburg Times and Republican*, July 7 and 8, 1871.

17. Minute Books, April 5 and August 29, 1872, Docket numbers 473, 482, and 483, RDC.

18. Wells to Akerman, December 11, 1871, SCF/NMS; Joint Select Committee, "Report," vol. 12, 1154–60.

19. Harris, 650–90; Gillette, *Retreat*, 150–65; Vernon Lane Wharton, *The Negro in Mississippi, 1865–1890* (New York, 1965), 181–98; William S. McFeely, *Grant* (New York, 1981), 419–25.

20. Harris, 650–90; Wharton, 181–98.

21. Adelbert Ames to President Grant, September 8, 1875, E&C.

22. Pierrepont to Grant, September 12, 1875, E&C; Ames to Pierrepont, September 11, 1875, printed in *New York Times*, September 21, 1875.

23. John R. Lynch, *The Facts of Reconstruction* (New York: Neale Publishing, 1913), 150–51; Gillette, *Retreat*, 150–65; McFeely, *Grant*, 419–25.

24. *Jackson Weekly Clarion*, October 20, 1875; *New York Times*, October 10, 1875; U.S. Senate, "Mississippi Election of 1875" [Boutwell Report,] Senate Report 327, 44th Cong., 1st sess. (1876), vol. 1, 473–74; vol. 2, 1801–18 (hereafter "Mississippi Election of 1875").

25. "Mississippi Election of 1875," vol. 2, Appendix, 92.

26. Ibid., vol. 1, 473–74; vol. 2, 1801–18.

27. Ibid., vol. 2, 1801–18.

28. *Illustrated History of Los Angeles County*, 190–93.

29. For a typical report by Whitfield as a private citizen, see Whitfield to Pierrepont, November 6, 1875, SCF/NMS.

30. See Whitfield's bulky file in the Appointment Files, RDJ. E. R. Bliss to Pierrepont, telegram, March 21, 1876, AF; J. T. Harrison to Pierrepont, telegram, March 24, 1876, AF; J. L. Morphis to President Hayes, July 17, 1877, Hayes Papers, Hayes Presidential Center, Fremont, Ohio.

31. Dunbar Rowland, *Courts, Judges, and Lawyers of Mississippi, 1798–1935* (Jackson, 1935), 250; "Mississippi Election of 1875," vol. 1, 47.

32. These particulars are taken from a file of affidavits of witnesses examined by the July 1876 grand jury, filed at July 1876 in SCF/NMS.

33. Ibid. at July 8, 1876.

34. Walton to Attorney General Taft, September 13, 1876, SCF/NMS.

35. Pierce to Taft, September 13, 1876, SCF/NMS.

36. U.S. Senate, "Denial of the Elective Franchise in Mississippi in 1875 and 1876," S. Misc. Doc. 45, 44th Cong., 2d sess. (1877), 974–75, 993 (hereafter "Denial 1875 and 1876").

37. Walton to Taft, telegram, September 18, 1876, SCF/NMS; Walton to Attorney General Devens, October 4, 1877, and April 23, 1878, SCF/NMS; Robert A. Hill to Devens, August 26, 1878, SCF/NMS; J. L. Morphis, September 19, 1878, SCF/NMS.

38. Rowland, *Courts, Judges, and Lawyers,* 260; Greene C. Chandler, *Journal and Speeches of Greene Callier Chandler* (privately printed, 1953), 6, 103, 154. See also the file for Chandler in AF. Chandler to Devens, December 15, 1878, SCF/NMS.

39. Albert D. Kirwin, *Revolt of the Rednecks: Mississippi Politics, 1876–1925* (New York, 1965), 3–28; Chandler to Devens, December 15, 1878, SCF/NMS. The numbers of cases tried, and numbers of convictions, are based on the *Annual Report of the Attorney General* for 1871–1892, Table B for each year.

40. Docket Book, 1881, Docket numbers 1785 and 1786, RDC; Final Record Book Number 5, p. 217, RDC.

41. Chandler to Devens, December 13, 1880, SCF/NMS; Chandler to Devens, January 7, 1881, SCF/NMS.

42. Justus D. Doenecke, *The Presidencies of James A. Garfield and Chester A. Arthur* (Lawrence, 1981), 105–26; Willie D. Halsell, ed., "Republican Factionalism in Mississippi," *Journal of Southern History* 7 (1941): 84–101; Willie D. Halsell, "James R. Chalmers and 'Mahoneism' in Mississippi," *Journal of Southern History* 10 (1944): 37–58.

43. Halsell, "Chalmers," 37–58; *Oxford Falcon*, November 2, 1882.

44. Halsell, "Chalmers," 53; Doenecke, 116–18.

45. Brewster to George F. Edmunds, December 30, 1882, E&C.

46. Based on the *Annual Report of the Attorney General* for 1878–1886, Table B for each year.

47. *Oxford Eagle*, June 12, 1883.

48. Ibid.; Chandler to Brewster, July 9, 1883, SCF/NMS; Brewster to Chandler, July 16, 1883, INST.

49. Chandler, *Journal and Speeches*, 155.

50. Affidavit of J. W. Youngblood, June 29, 1885, AF for J. L. Morphis; John M. Allen to Garland, July 15, 1885, AF for G. C. Chandler.

51. John M. Allen to Garland, July 15, 1885, AF for G. C. Chandler.

52. *New York Times*, September 11, 1885.

53. *Biographical and Historical Memoirs of Mississippi* (Chicago: Goodspeed, 1891), 964–65; Rowland, *Courts, Judges, and Lawyers,* 161.

54. James Chenway to Garland, October 21, 1887, YF; Thomas B. Hardin to Garland, November 28, 1887, YF; S. E. Kercheval to Miller, April 16, 1890, YF.

55. *New York Times*, September 26 and 27, and October 6, 1889.

56. Application of H. C. Niles, April 15, 1889, AF.

57. Niles to Miller, December 31, 1889, YF.

58. Burton to Miller, January 11 and February 8, 1890, YF.

59. Niles to Miller, June 25, 1890, YF.

60. Niles to Miller, August 20, 1890, YF.

61. Miller to Niles, July 5 and August 27, 1890, YF.

62. *Annual Report of the Secretary of War* (Washington, D.C.: GPO, 1870–1877).

63. Ibid., vol. 1, 37 (1870); vol. 1, 62–64 (1871); vol. 1, 92–94 (1872).

64. Pierce to Akerman, May 23, 1871, SCF/NMS; Akerman to Pierce, May 31, 1871, INST; Solicitor General Bristow to Pierce, June 14, 1871, INST.

65. A. P. Huggins to Akerman, June 14, 1871, SCF/NMS; U.S. House of Representatives, "Correspondence Between the War Department and Colonel Emory," House Exec. Doc. 209, 42d Cong., 2d sess. (1872), 30–32; James E. Sefton, *The United States Army and Reconstruction* (Westport, Conn., 1980), 224.

66. Sefton, 231.

67. Wells to Williams, April 18, 1872, SCF/NMS; Wells to Williams, July 8, 1872, SCF/NMS.

68. Pierce to Williams, July 13, 1872, SCF/NMS.

69. Act of June 17, 1878 (Army Appropriations Bill), 13 Stat. 145; 16 Opin. 162–64.

70. Pierce to Akerman, June 24 and July 12, 1871, SCF/NMS; Akerman to Pierce, July 25, 1871, INST.

71. Akerman to Wells, August 15, 1871, INST; Wells to Akerman, August 21, 1871, SCF/NMS.

72. Wells to Williams, March 9, 1872, SCF/NMS.

73. Akerman to E. P. Jacobsen, July 11, 1871, INST.

74. Ibid.

75. Devens to Luke Lea, April 11, 1877, INST; Akerman to James Jackson, November 20, 1871, Akerman Letterbooks, Alderman Library, University of Virginia; Akerman to Wells, telegram, July 8, 1871, INST.

76. Wells to Williams, telegram, July 1, 1874, SCF/NMS; Williams to Wells, telegram, July 2, 1874, INST; Williams to Wells, November 13, 1873, INST.

77. Williams to Pierce, January 26, 1875, INST; Wells to Williams, December 15, 1874, SCF/NMS; Williams to Wells, December 19, 1874, INST.

78. Devens to Walton, May 7, 1878, INST; Solicitor General Phillips to Chandler, December 24, 1879, INST; Devens to the U.S. attorneys, November 22, 1880, INST.

79. "The Inflation of the Attorney General," *Nation*, October 1, 1874, pp. 214–15.

80. *New York Times*, September 5, 1876; Brewster to J. L. Morphis, November 2 and 3, 1882, INST; Devens to southern U.S. attorneys, November 17, 1880, INST.

81. *Annual Report of the Attorney General* for 1876, p. 13.

82. Ibid. for 1878, p. 18; and for 1880, pp. 16–19.

83. Ibid. for 1889, pp. xiv–xv.

84. Akerman to Foster Blodgett, November 8, 1871, Akerman Letterbooks.

85. Several good studies of native Mississippi Republicans have appeared. See, e.g., David H. Donald, "The Scalawag in Mississippi Reconstruction," *Journal of Southern History* 10 (1944): 447–60.

86. L.Q.C. Lamar to Pierrepont, May 18, 1876, AF; the text of Walton's speech is given in an unidentified newspaper clipping, filed at September 1876, SCF/NMS.

87. Walton to Devens, November 23, 1877, SCF/NMS.

88. Application of G. C. Chandler, July [n.d.] 1891, AF.

89. Chandler, *Journal and Speeches*, 227.

90. Ibid., 157–63.

91. Ibid.

92. Niles to Miller, March 11, 1889, AF; Halsell, "Republican Factionalism," 90; "Denial 1875 and 1876," 998; Pierce to Akerman, July 12, 1871, SCF/NMS.

93. Wells to Solicitor General Bristow, telegram, November 17, 1871, SCF/NMS; Joint Select Committee, "Report," vol. 12, 1154–56; *Harper's Weekly* 16 (January 27, 1872): 73, and 16 (October 19, 1872): 805.

94. Wells to Williams, March 5, 1872, SCF/NMS.

95. Chandler to Devens, December 15, 1878, SCF/NMS.

96. Pierce to Taft, August 21, 1876, SCF/NMS; Pierce to Taft, telegram, November 9, 1876, SCF/NMS; Pierce to Taft, November 17, 1876, SCF/NMS.

97. *New York Times*, November 16, 1876.

98. Devens to Pierce, July 10, 1877, INST; Pierce to Devens, July 13, 1877, SCF/NMS. Pierce's authorship of the letter is probable because it is unlikely that two politically active residents of Oxford (population 1,500), with initial "P," were in Memphis at the same time, writing letters about the election.

99. *New York Times*, October 9, 1875; Memo of G. C. Chandler, November [n.d.] 1882, SCF/NMS.

100. "Mississippi Election of 1875," vol. 1, 50.

101. Ibid., 50–66.

102. *Memphis Daily Appeal*, June 27, 1874.

103. *Jackson Weekly Clarion*, July 6, 13, and 20, 1871.

104. Wells to Williams, November 7, 1873, SCF/NMS; Henry B. Whitfield to Wells, December 9, 1874, SCF/NMS.

105. *Jackson Weekly Clarion*, July 20, 1871.

106. Unidentified clipping in Morphis to Brewster, August 21, 1882, SCF/NMS.

107. Morphis to Brewster, August 21, 1882, SCF/NMS; Burton to Miller, January 11, 1890, YF.

108. Joint Select Committee, "Report," vol. 12, 1160; Wells to Williams, telegram, January 2, 1873, SCF/NMS; Wells to Williams, January 2, 1873, SCF/NMS.

109. Joint Select Committee, "Report," vol. 12, 1149; "Equality Before the

Law" to Wells, March 28, 1874, SCF/NMS; Wells to Williams, April 2, 1874, SCF/NMS; W. F. Dowd to Pierrepont, September 7, 1875, SCF/NMS; Henry B. Whitfield to Pierrepont, March 25, 1876, AF.

110. A. P. Huggins to Akerman, June 28, 1871, SCF/NMS; Pierce to Akerman, September 7, 1871, SCF/NMS.

111. Pierce to Akerman, May 23, 1871, SCF/NMS.

112. Wells to Akerman, telegrams, July 15 and September 18, 1871, SCF/NMS; Sefton, 223; Solicitor General Bristow to Wells, telegram, September 19, 1871, INST.

113. Joint Select Committee, "Report," vol. 11, 298, vol. 12, 1161.

114. Ibid.

115. Wells to Akerman, August 21, 1871, SCF/NMS; *Oxford Falcon*, November 17, 1871; Joint Select Committee, "Report," vol. 12, 1165.

116. Pierce to Williams, October 27 and November 1, 1873, SCF/NMS; Wells to Williams, telegram, August 9, 1873, SCF/NMS; *Jackson Weekly Clarion*, August 14, 1873.

117. A. P. Huggins to Williams, December 13, 1873, SCF/NMS; F. J. Reed to Taft, September 3, 1876, SCF/NMS; Pierce to Taft, November 17, 1876, SCF/NMS.

118. Chandler to Brewster, October 11, 1884, YF.

119. Minute Book Number 6, p. 190, RDC.

120. Pierce to A. J. Falls, February 10, 1873, SCF/NMS; Pierce to Williams, June 25 and September 28, 1874, SCF/NMS.

121. Chandler to Devens, December 13, 1880, SCF/NMS; Chandler to Brewster, December 22, 1882, SCF/NMS.

122. Walton to Taft, July 16, 1876, SCF/NMS; W. Cavett to Taft, August 23, 1876, SCF/NMS.

123. *Aberdeen Weekly,* quoted in *Oxford Eagle*, January 16, 1879.

124. Pierce to Akerman, August 21, 1871, SCF/NMS; Akerman to Pierce, August 28, 1871, INST.

125. Drew L. Kershen, "The Jury Selection Act of 1879: Theory and Practice of Citizen Participation in the Judicial System," *University of Illinois Law Forum* (1980): 707–82.

126. *Oxford Eagle*, January 16, 1879.

127. "Denial 1875 and 1876," 346; Morphis to Brewster, August 21, 1882, SCF/NMS; Act of June 30, 1879 (Judiciary Appropriation Bill), 21 Stat. 43; Chandler to Brewster, December 22, 1882, SCF/NMS.

128. Dunbar Rowland, *Mississippi: Comprising Sketches of Counties, Towns, Events* (Atlanta: Southern Historical Publishing Association, 1907), vol. 1, 863–64; *Biographical and Historical Memoirs of Mississippi,* 926–28; Biographical Sketch of R. A. Hill, unsigned typescript, Subject Files, Mississippi Department of Archives and History.

129. *Biographical and Historical Memoirs of Mississippi,* 926–28.

130. Minute Books, 1872–1874, RDC.

131. Ibid., 1872–1883, RDC. The case mentioned that resulted in a prison sentence is Docket Number 454.

132. *U.S. v. Willis Younger et al.,* Minute Book and Final Record Book (1874), Docket Number 548, RDC.

133. *U.S. v. W. E. Weaver et al.,* Docket Book and Final Record Book (1881), Docket Number 1792, RDC.

134. A. P. Huggins to Akerman, June 28, 1871, SCF/NMS; Akerman to E. P. Jacobsen (U.S. attorney for southern Mississippi), August 18, 1871, Akerman Letterbooks.

135. Wells to Williams, April 2, 1872, SCF/NMS; Devens to Chandler, January 22, 1879, INST; Chandler to Devens, January 25, 1879, SCF/NMS; Devens to Chandler, January 28, 1879, INST.

136. Chandler to Devens, January 19, 1881, SCF/NMS; Devens to Chandler, January 25, 1881, INST; Chandler to Brewster Cameron, December 4, 1882, SCF/NMS.

137. Hill's newspaper letters are contained in two clippings, dated September 9 and 20, 1875, in the R. A. Hill Subject File, Mississippi Department of Archives and History. The newspapers are not identified. Similar unidentified clippings are in Hill to Williams, September 18, 1874, SCF/NMS. Akerman to Hill, September 12, 1871, Akerman Letterbooks.

138. Hill to Bristow, September 18, 1871, and May 13, 1872, Bristow Papers, Library of Congress.

139. Hill to MacVeagh, August 19, 1881, SCF/NMS; MacVeagh to Hill, August 25, 1881, J&C.

140. Hill to Harrison, April 30, 1889, Harrison Papers, Library of Congress; Hill to Miller, August 3, 1889, YF.

141. Kaczorowski, 68, 71; Kermit L. Hall, "The Civil War Era as a Crucible for Nationalizing the Lower Federal Courts," *Prologue* 7 (Fall 1975): 177–86.

142. The best exploration of the ultimate failure of Reconstruction is Gillette, *Retreat.*

143. Wharton, 206.

144. Ibid., 206–207.

145. *New York Times*, February 24, 1892.

146. James D. Richardson, comp., *A Compilation of the Messages and Papers of the Presidents, 1789–1908* (N.p.: Bureau of National Literature and Art, 1909), vol. 9, 55–56.

147. Ibid.

148. *New York Times*, September 11, 1885. Of course, Mississippi voters did have some choices—in primary and some general elections. But this does not lessen the truth of the statement that Mississippi was left far out of the national political mainstream.

149. C. Vann Woodward, *The Strange Career of Jim Crow*, 3d rev. ed. (New York: Oxford University Press, 1974), 175; *Statistical Abstract of the United States, 1982–83* (Washington, D.C.: GPO, 1982), 488. For an intelligent treatment linking Mississippi's past and present, see Walter Lord, *The Past that Would Not Die* (New York: Harper and Row, 1965).

Chapter 3: One Man, One Wife
Combating Polygamy in Utah Territory

1. G. D. Watt, ed., *Journal of Discourses* (Liverpool: F. D. Richards, 1854–1886), vol. 10, 329. On Utah's Mormon history generally, see Nels Anderson, *Desert Saints: The Mormon Frontier in Utah* (Chicago, 1942); Leonard J. Arrington, *Great Basin Kingdom: Economic History of the Latter-day Saints, 1830–1900* (Lincoln: University of Nebraska Press, 1966); John R. Wunder, "Freedom from Government. Case Study: The Mormon Frontier Experience," in Carl Ubbelohde and Jack R. Fraenkel, eds., *Values of the American Heritage: Challenges, Case Studies, and Teaching Strategies* (n.p., 1976), 74–108.

2. C. Peter Magrath, "Chief Justice Waite and the 'Twin Relic': *Reynolds v. United States,*" *Vanderbilt Law Review* 18 (1965): 515.

3. The Utah district courts were established by the Act of September 9, 1850 (Utah Territory Organic Act), 9 Statutes at Large 453, 455–56. See also the Act in Relation to Marshals and Attorneys, 1852 Utah Laws 56–58.

4. Morrill Act, 12 Stat. 501 (1862).

5. Alan E. Haynes, "The Federal Government and its Policies Regarding the Frontier Era of Utah Territory, 1850–1877" (Ph.D. diss., Catholic University, Washington, D.C., 1968), 167.

6. James B. McKean to Attorney General Williams, November 12, 1873, SCF/UT; *New York Times*, October 18, 1873.

7. Charles H. Hempstead to Attorney General Akerman, January 20, 1871, SCF/UT.

8. Later, a new U.S. attorney (George Caesar Bates) claimed that McKean had no right to appoint an ad interim U.S. attorney, and a number of gullible writers have believed him. McKean's justification can be found in Section 1875 of the Revised Statutes.

9. Orson F. Whitney, *Popular History of Utah* (Salt Lake City, 1916), 269.

10. Charles Hempstead et al. to Attorney General Akerman, February 13, 1871, SCF/UT.

11. Orson F. Whitney, *History of Utah* (Salt Lake City, 1893), vol. 2, 586–87.

12. An Act in Relation to Crimes and Punishments, Section 33, 1852 Utah Laws 122.

13. J. H. Wickizer to Attorney General Akerman, September 20, 1871, SCF/UT; Edward B. McKean to U. S. Grant, October 9, 1871, SCF/UT; George Caesar Bates to Benjamin H. Bristow, October 25, 1871, Bristow Papers, Manuscripts Division, Library of Congress.

14. George Caesar Bates to Benjamin H. Bristow, October 25 and November 25, 1871, Bristow Papers.

15. George Caesar Bates to Attorney General Akerman, telegram, December 1, 1871, SCF/UT.

16. George Caesar Bates to Attorney General Akerman, telegram, December 7, 1871, SCF/UT; Akerman to Bates, telegram, December 19, 1871, INST; Akerman to Bates, December 20, 1871, INST.

17. *Salt Lake Tribune*, January 6, 1872; Anderson, 269–73.

18. Brigham Young to Willard Young, January 26, 1872, in Dean C. Jessee, ed., *Letters of Brigham Young to his Sons* (Salt Lake City: Deseret Book, 1974), 174–75.

19. Attorney General Akerman to George Caesar Bates, December 20, 1871, INST.

20. George Caesar Bates to Attorney General Akerman, December 4, 1871, SCF/UT; Bates to Akerman, December 10, 1871, SCF/UT; Bates to Akerman, telegram, January 4, 1872, SCF/UT; Bates to George H. Williams, December 16, 1871, SCF/UT.

21. Robert N. Baskin, *Reminiscences of Early Utah* (Salt Lake City, 1914), 55–58; Attorney General Williams to George Caesar Bates, March 2, 1872, INST; *Salt Lake Tribune*, March 16, 1872; George Woods to U.S. Grant, April 18, 1872, SCF/UT.

22. George Caesar Bates to Benjamin H. Bristow, January 7, 1872, Bristow Papers.

23. *Clinton et al. v. Englebrecht,* 80 U.S. 434, 440–43, 447–49 (1871).

24. Act of January 19, 1855, 1855 Utah Laws 87; see also *Ferris v. Higley,* 87 U.S. 375, 382–84 (1874); James B. Allen, "The Unusual Jurisdiction of County Probate Courts in the Territory of Utah," *Utah Historical Quarterly* 36 (1968): 132–42; Raymond T. Swenson, "Resolution of Civil Disputes by Mormon Ecclesiastical Courts," *Utah Law Review* (1978): 573–95; Earl S. Pomeroy, *The Territories and the United States, 1861–1890: Studies in Colonial Administration* (Seattle, 1969), 58–61. A good study of the ecclesiastical courts is found in Edwin Brown Firmage and Richard Collin Mangrum, *Zion in the Courts: A Legal History of the Church of Jesus Christ of Latter-day Saints, 1830–1900* (Urbana, 1988).

25. William Carey to Attorney General Williams, November 7, 1873, SCF/UT. Carey's name is often spelled "Cary" in the records.

26. James D. Richardson, ed., comp., *A Compilation of Messages and Papers of the Presidents,* 1789–1908 (Washington, N.p.: Bureau of National Literature and Art, 1909), vol. 7, 208–10.

27. Act of June 23, 1874 (Poland Act), 18 Stat. 253; *Congressional Record*, 43rd Congress, 1st sess., vol. 2, 4466–75, 5417–18.

28. *Salt Lake Tribune*, June 24, 1874; Philip Emerson to Attorney General Williams, June 25, 1874, SCF/UT; William Carey to Williams, December 29, 1874, SCF/UT; D. P. Wheedon to Williams, December 14, 1874, SCF/UT.

29. Attorney General Williams to William Carey, December 22, 1874, INST; Carey to Williams, December 30, 1874, SCF/UT.

30. William Carey to Attorney General Williams, December 29, 1874, SCF/UT.

31. James L. Clayton, "The Supreme Court, Polygamy, and the Enforcement of Morals in Nineteenth-Century America: An Analysis of *Reynolds v. United States,*" *Dialogue: A Journal of Mormon Thought* 12, no. 4 (1979): 49.

32. A copy of the transcript of the second *Reynolds* trial is filed with Sumner Howard to Attorney General Taft, July 26, 1876, SCF/UT. *Salt Lake Tribune*, December 10 and 11, 1875; *Deseret News*, December 10 and 11, 1875.

33. *Reynolds* trial transcript in Howard to Taft, July 26, 1876, SCF/UT.

34. Sumner Howard to Attorney General Taft, July 26, 1876, SCF/UT; Devens's brief is in the U.S. Supreme Court Records and Briefs series for *Reynolds v. United States,* 98 U.S. 145 (1879). *United States v. Reynolds,* 1 Utah 319 (1876).

35. Magrath, 507–43; Clayton, 46–61; Ray Jay Davis, "Plural Marriage and Religious Freedom: The Impact of *Reynolds v. United States,*" *Arizona Law Review* 15 (1973): 287–306; Ray Jay Davis, "The Polygamous Prelude," *American Journal of Legal History* 6 (1962): 1–27.

36. *Reynolds v. United States,* 98 U.S. 145 (1879).

37. Sumner Howard to Attorney General Devens, July 10, 1877, SCF/UT; *Salt Lake Tribune*, May 12 and 30, 1876.

38. See, e.g., William Wise, *Massacre at Mountain Meadows* (New York: Crowell, 1976); Juanita Brooks, *The Mountain Meadows Massacre* (Norman: University of Oklahoma Press, 1962).

39. Whitney, *History of Utah*, vol. 2, 781–829. Young had been willing to supply an affidavit for the first trial, but Carey went ahead with his plans to implicate church leaders in the murder. Anderson, 185–95.

40. Philip Van Zile to Attorney General Devens, August 21, 1878, SCF/UT; *Miles v. United States,* 103 U.S. 304 (1880); Anderson, 308–10.

41. For briefs and transcripts of the trial, see the U.S. Supreme Court Record and Briefs series for 103 U.S. 304.

42. Philip Van Zile to Attorney General Devens, July 14, 1879, SCF/UT; *Miles v. United States,* 103 U.S. 304 (1880).

43. Philip Van Zile to Attorney General Devens, July 11, 1879, SCF/UT.

44. Act of March 22, 1882 (Edmunds Act), 22 Stat. 30–32.

45. *Provo Territorial Enquirer*, December 2, 1882; Philip Van Zile to Attorney General Brewster, December 19, 1882, SCF/UT; Anderson, 313.

46. Philip Van Zile to Attorney General Brewster, December 19, 1882, SCF/UT; Brewster to Van Zile, June 29, 1883, INST; James Staunton's memo to the attorney general, February 13, 1884, SCF/UT; S. F. Phillips's memo to the attorney general, undated (c. February 1884), SCF/UT. The Utah commissioners also submitted a proposed oath to the attorney general.

47. Whitney, *History of Utah*, vol. 2, 541–42; *History of the Bench and Bar of Utah* (Salt Lake City, 1913), 140–41.

48. Alexander Ramsey to Attorney General Brewster, August 14, 1883, SCF/UT; A. B. Carlton to Brewster, January 13, 1885, YF.

49. *Murphy v. Ramsey,* Defendant's brief at 8–9, 12, 16. This brief (Dickson's) is filed in the SCF/UT with letters of January 1884.

50. *Murphy v. Ramsey,* Defendant's brief at 20, 23–27.

51. The Defendant's brief prepared by Attorney General Brewster and Solictor General Phillips is in the U.S. Supreme Court Records and Briefs series, for *Murphy et al. v. Ramsey et al.,* 114 U.S. 15. *Murphy et al. v. Ramsey et al.,* 114 U.S. 15 (1884).

52. Whitney, *Popular History*, 377; Melvin L. Bashore, "Life Behind Bars: Mormon Cohabs of the 1880s," *Utah Historical Quarterly* 47 (1979): 22; Richard D. Poll, "The Political Reconstruction of Utah Territory, 1866–1890," *Pacific Historical Quarterly* 27 (1958): 120; Allen L. Shepherd, "Gentile in Zion: Algernon Sidney Paddock and the Utah Commission," *Nebraska History* 57 (1976): 361; Davis, "The Polygamous Prelude," 10; Charles A. Cannon, "The Awesome Power of Sex: The Polemical Campaign Against Mormon Polygamy," *Pacific Historical Review* 43 (1974): 62. My own objection to the term *crusade* is double-faceted. First, to speak of a crusade beginning in 1884 implies that federal officers were suddenly seized by a zealous, crusading spirit, when actually their zeal tended to be uniform over time. Second, a crusade is a struggle between two parties, each of which has a religious motivation. As I make clear in the text, I do not believe the religious motivations of federal officials were very important.

53. Act of June 23, 1874 (Poland Act), Section 4, 18 Stat. 253; Act of March 22, 1882 (Edmunds Act), section 5, 22 Stat. 32.

54. Baskin, 212–13; Whitney, *History of Utah*, vol. 2, 278–300.

55. Varian's brief is enclosed in C. S. Varian to Attorney General Garland, March 18, 1885, YF. The brief is quoted at 9–11, 16. C. S. Varian to Attorney General Brewster, January 25, 1885, YF.

56. *Clawson v. United States,* 114 U.S. 55 (1885).

57. C. S. Varian to Attorney General Garland, September 5, 1885, YF; George F. Edmunds to Garland, October 27, 1885, YF; W. H. Dickson to Garland, November 11, 1885, YF. For further information about Dickson's resignation, see W. H. Dickson to Garland, March 1, 1887, AF; and A. G. Norrell to Garland, March 10,

1887, AF. Joseph Outhwaite to Garland, April 7, 1887, AF; A. G. Thurman to Garland, April 5, 1887, AF; *National Cyclopaedia of American Biography* (New York: White, 1891–1984), vol. 21, 380.

58. "Suppression of Polygamy in Utah," House Report 2735, 49th Congress, 1st sess. (1886); Act of March 3, 1887 (Edmunds-Tucker Act), 24 Stat. 635–41.

59. Anonymous to Cleveland, April 16, 1887, AF; G. A. Jenks to George Peters, September 3, 1887, INST; Jenks to Peters, September 9, 1887, INST; Peters to Jenks, September 17, 1887, YF; Jenks to Peters, September 24, 1887, INST; Attorney General Garland to Peters, October 10, 1887, INST; Garland to Henry W. Hobson, October 10, 1887, INST; Hobson to Garland, October 31, 1887, YF.

60. Henry W. Hobson to G. A. Jenks, October 31, 1887, YF.

61. Ibid.

62. Attorney General Garland to George Peters, November 22, 1888, INST; Henry W. Hobson to Garland, November 28, 1888, YF; *Salt Lake Tribune,* February 13, 1889.

63. Wilford Woodruff to William Atkin, November 24, 1887, typescript in the collections of the Utah Historical Society, original at the Huntington Library.

64. *Annual Report of the Attorney General* for 1890 (Washington, D.C.: GPO, 1890): Exhibit Q is Varian's report on the church property cases. See also Arrington, 365–79; Frank H. Dyer to C. S. Varian, June 12, 1890, YF.

65. G. A. Jenks to Henry W. Hobson, December 14, 1888, INST; Hobson to Jenks, December 14, 1888, YF.

66. George Peters to G. A. Jenks, December 20, 1888, YF.

67. Defendant's brief at 32, *The Late Corporation of the Church of Jesus Christ of Latter-day Saints v. United States,* 136 U.S. 1 (1890). The brief is included in the U.S. Supreme Court Records and Briefs series.

68. *The Late Corporation of the Church of Jesus Christ of Latter-day Saints v. United States,* 136 U.S. 1, 1–36 (1890).

69. *History of the Bench and Bar*, 213–14; Whitney, *History of Utah*, vol. 2, 542–43.

70. The U.S. Supreme Court upheld the Idaho Test Oath Act (a statute requiring a would-be voter to take an oath that he was not a member of any organization that taught polygamy) in *Davis v. Beason,* 133 U.S. 333 (1890).

71. Anderson, 324–25; Arrington, 377–78; Whitney, *Popular History*, 488.

72. Attorney General Miller to C. S. Varian, November 8, 1890, INST.

73. C. S. Varian to Attorney General Miller, November 13, 1890, YF.

74. Baskin, 246.

75. George L. Wood to Attorney General Akerman, August 29, 1871, SCF/UT; M. T. Patrick to Attorney General Williams, April 16, 1872, SCF/UT.

76. *Salt Lake Tribune*, June 9, 1874.

77. Ibid., and June 12, 1874; *Deseret News*, August 11, 1874; Attorney General Williams to William Carey, February 5, 1875, INST; Carey to Williams, February 15, 1875, SCF/UT; Williams to Carey, telegram, July 23, 1874, INST.

78. Sumner Howard to Attorney General Taft, telegram, February 21, 1877, SCF/UT; Taft to William Nelson, February 23, 1877, INST.

79. Sumner Howard to Attorney General Devens, July 28, 1877, SCF/UT; Devens to Howard, August 3, 1877, INST.

80. Elwin A. Ireland to Attorney General Garland, March 22, 1886, YF; O. W. Chapman to C. S. Varian, November 1, 1889, INST; Attorney General Miller to Varian, February 20, 1890, INST.

81. *Annual Report of the Attorney General* for 1878, 12; Philip Van Zile to Attorney General Devens, July 11, 1879, SCF/UT; Devens to Van Zile, July 19, 1879, INST; Van Zile to Devens, July 29, 1879, SCF/UT.

82. W. H. Dickson to Attorney General Brewster, August 26, 1884, YF; Brewster to Dickson, November 18, 1884, INST; Dickson to Brewster, February 8, 1885, YF.

83. Elwin A. Ireland to Attorney General Garland, November 2, 1885, YF; Ireland to O. W. Powers, August 4, 1885, YF; Garland to Ireland, November 11, 1885, INST; Garland to Frank H. Dyer, November 6, 1886, INST; Garland to W. H. Dickson, January 25, 1887, INST.

84. William McKay to Attorney General Garland, May 13, 1886, YF; W. H. Dickson to Garland, May 27, 1886, YF.

85. Sumner Howard to Attorney General Taft, May 27, 1876, SCF/UT; Attorney General Devens to Van Zile, April 5, 1878, INST.

86. George Caesar Bates to Attorney General Williams, December 16, 1871, SCF/UT; Bates to Williams, January 4, 1872, SCF/UT; Bates to Attorney General Akerman, January 4, 1872, SCF/UT; Attorney General Devens to Philip Van Zile, April 5, 1878, INST.

87. Attorney General Garland to Elwin A. Ireland, November 11, 1885, INST.

88. Attorney General Pierrepont to William Carey, November 2, 1875, INST.

89. Jacob Boreman to William Carey, November 10, 1875, SCF/UT.

90. Attorney General Miller to C. S. Varian, November 8, 1890, INST; Henry W. Hobson to William H. H. Miller, March 28, 1889, YF.

91. C. S. Varian to Attorney General Miller, September 1, 1892, YF; Brief for the plaintiff, *Murphy v. Ramsey,* 114 U.S. 15 (1884), in U.S. Supreme Court Records and Briefs series; Affidavit of Jeter Clinton, May 11, 1889, AF. For Van Zile's publications, see *A Catalog of Books Represented by Library of Congress Printed Cards* (New York: Rowman and Littlefield, 1968), vol. 156, p. 65.

92. Pomeroy, *The Territories*, 62–79.

93. Internal memo prepared by Henry Hodges, January 24, 1876, SCF/UT; Attorney General Devens to William Nelson, December 6, 1877, INST; Attorney General Garland to Frank H. Dyer, June 13, 1887, INST.

94. Vernal A. Brown, "The United States Marshals in Utah Territory to 1896" (M.S. thesis, Utah State University, Logan, 1970), 95–155.

95. Charles H. Hempstead to Attorney General Akerman, January 20, 1871, SCF/UT; George Caesar Bates to Benjamin H. Bristow, January 7, 1872, Bristow Papers, Library of Congress; Sumner Howard to Attorney General Devens, September 29, 1877, SCF/UT; C. S. Varian to Attorney General Garland, September 5, 1885, YF.

96. Charles H. Hempstead et al. to Attorney General Akerman, February 13, 1871, SCF/UT; Affidavit of George R. Maxwell, January 2, 1873, SCF/UT.

97. Elwin A. Ireland to Attorney General Garland, telegram, May 11, 1886, YF; Ireland to Garland, April 7, 1886, YF.

98. Philip Van Zile to Attorney General Devens, April 4, 1878, SCF/UT; Statement of George R. Maxwell, January [n.d.] 1876, SCF/UT.

99. Edward B. McKean to Attorney General Williams, November 7, 1873, SCF/UT; Elwin A. Ireland to Attorney General Garland, March 4, 1886, YF; Attorney General Brewster to Ireland, April 29, 1884, INST.

100. Statement of George R. Maxwell, January [n.d.] 1876, SCF/UT; Elwin A. Ireland to Attorney General Garland, March 15, 1889, AF; W. H. Dickson to Garland, March 1, 1887, AF.

101. Baskin, 217–18, Whitney, *Popular History*, 415; Howard Roberts Lamar, *The Far Southwest, 1846–1912: A Territorial History* (New Haven, 1966), 397.

102. *Deseret News*, September 14, 1884; Baskin, 229–30.

103. *Deseret News*, November 23 and December 14, 1885; *Salt Lake Tribune*, January 18 and 25, 1886; Baskin, 223–29.

104. Baskin, 223–29.

105. Edward B. McKean to Attorney General Williams, November 12, 1873, SCF/UT; Sumner Howard to Attorney General Devens, July 28, 1877, SCF/UT. On Morrisite schism, see Anderson, 223–26.

106. Elwin A. Ireland to Attorney General Garland, November 11, 1885, YF; Whitney, *Popular History*, 420–21; Baskin, 222–23; Lamar, *Far Southwest, 397.*

107. Whitney, Popular History, 432–33; Baskin, 219–22.

108. George Caesar Bates to Benjamin Harris Bristow, December 1, 1871, Bristow Papers, Library of Congress; Philip Van Zile to Attorney General Devens, July 11, 1879, SCF/UT; W. H. Dickson to Attorney General Brewster, February 8, 1885, YF.

109. Thomas G. Alexander, "Charles S. Zane, Apostle of the New Era," *Utah Historical Quarterly* 34 (1966): 292; Irma Watson Hance and Virginia Picht, *The First Seventy-five Years* (Salt Lake City: First Unitarian Church, 1966), 12.

110. W. H. Dickson to Attorney General Garland, May 27, 1886, YF; Baskin, 216.

111. J. Cecil Alter, *Utah, the Storied Domain: A Documentary History of Utah's Eventful Career* (Chicago, 1932), 384; Brown, 98–104.

112. *Deseret News*, December 14, 1882; William Carey et al. to U. S. Grant, telegram, March 17, 1875, SCF/UT.

113. Philip Van Zile, "The Twin Relic" (n.p., n.d. [c. 1880]), in the Philip Van Zile Scrapbook, special collections, Harold B. Lee Library, Brigham Young University.

114. W. E. Curtis to Philip Van Zile, December 28, 1880, Van Zile Scrapbook.

115. *Ogden Daily Herald*, quoting the Chicago *Inter-Ocean*, October 10, 1882.

116. Anonymous, "The Mormon Endowment House! Graphic Exposure of the Treasonable Institution Where Polygamous Marriages are Solemnized, by an Eyewitness" (Salt Lake City, 1879). Copy inscribed by Van Zile at Hayes Presidential Center, Fremont, Ohio.

117. *Deseret News*, July 27, 1886; *Salt Lake Herald*, July 28, 1886.

118. Quotations from *Desert News*, July 27, 1886; the pamphlet appeared as William H. Dickson, "Solid Facts from a Loyal Man" (Salt Lake City, n.d. [1886]), 3.

119. *Annual Report of the Attorney General* for 1875–1888.

120. Richardson, vol. 7, 208–10, 606; vol. 8, 11, 184, 361.

121. Orma Linford, "The Mormons, the Law, and the Territory of Utah," *American Journal of Legal History* 23 (1979): 213–35; Firmage and Mangrum, 174–77.

122. *United States v. Cannon,* 116 U.S. 55 (1885).

123. Ibid., at 66.

124. Ibid., at 66.

125. Firmage and Mangrum, 177.

126. *United States v. Orson P. Arnold,* unpaged trial transcript, in *Territorial Case Files of the U.S. District Court of Utah*, National Archives micropublication 1401, reel 1, case file 39.

127. Ibid.

128. See, e.g., Firmage and Mangrum, 175.

129. *United States v. Arnold,* transcript.

130. Firmage and Mangrum, 209.

131. Many aspects of the federal enforcement program in Utah remain unclear. Certainly, the existence of homeless, hungry women and children has not been demonstrated; it is not clear what factors were most instrumental in preventing this kind of homelessness and hunger. It is hoped that this book, as well as the ones by Firmage and Mangrum and others, will provide a foundation for future historians who will look in detail at the records of the one thousand actual court cases. Such a study would tell us more about the differences between evidence in polygamy cases and that used in cohabitation trials, the conviction rate in this class of case, average sentencing, and the prevalence of the practice of dividing offenses into chronological periods so that multicount indictments resulted from a man's continuing cohabitation with one set of plural wives. Unfortunately, the official trial records that remain do not usually include information about judgment and sentencing; newspaper records could be used to supplement the official records.

Chapter 4: Guarding the Treasury in the Southern Highlands

Federal Law Enforcement in Eastern Tennessee

1. Sam McDowell, ed., *East Tennessee History: Reprinted from Goodspeed's History of Tennessee* (Hartford, 1978), 3; Xenophon Wheeler to Attorney General Devens, November 18, 1880, SCF/ETN.

2. *East Tennessee Historical and Biographical* (Chattanooga, Tenn.: A. D. Smith, 1893), 113–21.

3. J.C.J. Williams to Attorney General Garland, August 5, 1885, YF. Historians have written almost nothing about counterfeiting in the United States, but see H. C. Whitely, *In It* (Cambridge, Mass., 1894). Whitely was chief of the Secret Service; his book emphasizes counterfeiting in New York City.

4. *Annual Report of the Commissioner of Pensions* (Washington, D.C.: GPO, 1872), 18–21.

5. Ibid. The prosecutions were under Sections 5421 and 5438 of the Revised Statutes.

6. Joseph Dabney, *Mountain Spirits* (New York, 1974), 74; *Annual Report of the Commissioner of Internal Revenue* (Washington, D.C.: GPO, 1875), v–vi.

7. Henry M. Wiltse, *The Moonshiners* (Chattanooga, 1895), 19, 92, 206–209; *Annual Report of the Commissioner of Internal Revenue* for 1891, 44–45.

8. *Register of the Department of Justice* (Washington, D.C.: GPO, 1871); William T. Hale, *A History of Tennessee and Tennesseans* (Chicago, 1913), vol. 6, 1112; John Trotwood Moore, *Tennessee: The Volunteer State* (Chicago, 1923), 931–35; *National Cyclopaedia of American Biography* (New York, White, 1891–1984), vol. 1, 478.

9. *Annual Report of the Attorney General* for 1870 (Washington, D.C.: GPO, 1871); Benjamin Bristow to E. C. Camp, October 24, 1871, INST.

10. W. G. Brownlow, R. R. Butler, and Horace Maynard to President Grant, October 16, 1871, AF.

11. Camp to Benjamin Bristow, telegram, October 28, 1871, SCF/ETN; Camp to President Grant, November 11, 1871, AF; Attorney General Akerman to Camp, November 6, 1871, INST.

12. John W. Green, *Bench and Bar of Knox County, Tennessee* (Knoxville, 1947), 76; Moore, vol. 2, 24–25. Hale, vol. 6, 1547.

13. George Andrews to Attorney General Williams, January 26, 1872, SCF/ETN; Andrews to Williams, September 11, 1872, SCF/ETN.

14. Andrews to Williams, September 11 and November 12, 1872, SCF/ETN; *Knoxville Daily Press and Herald*, January 19, 1873.

15. *Knoxville Daily Press and Herald*, January 22 and 24, and February 1, 1873.

16. Ibid.

17. Affidavits of Frank Hybergen et al., December 30, 1873, L. C. Houk Papers, McClung Collection, Lawson McGhee Public Library, Knoxville.

18. Andrews to Attorney General Pierrepont, with enclosed letter from Samuel N. Newton, August 2, 1875, SCF/ETN.

19. George Wesley Atkinson, *After the Moonshiners, by One of the Raiders* (Wheeling, 1881); U.S. Congress, Senate, "Salaries of Revenue Officers," Senate Exec. Doc. 23, 46th Cong., 1st sess. (1879), 11.

20. Zella Armstrong, *History of Hamilton County and Chattanooga, Tennessee* (Chattanooga: Lookout Publishing, 1931), vol. 1, 470. The data from the annual statistical reports are contained in the tables of the *Annual Report of the Attorney General*. Attorney General Brewster to Wheeler, March 9, 1882, INST; William A. Maury to Wheeler, October 5, 1882, INST.

21. William S. Speer, *Sketches of Prominent Tennesseans* (Nashville: A. B. Tavel, 1885), 568–70; Leigh Chalmers to Attorney General Garland, January 18, 1886, YF; File of letters discussing Meek, c. March and April 1885, AF; Comptroller Johnson to Attorney General Garland, July 1, 1886, YF.

22. J.C.J. Williams to Attorney General Garland, April 17, 1885, AF; Green, *Bench and Bar*, 140–41; J.C.J. Williams to Garland, August 5, 1885, YF.

23. G. G. Dibrell to Garland, April 25, 1885, AF; J. J. Ivins to Garland, August 11, 1885, YF.

24. Ivins to Examiner Nightingale, October 30, 1886, YF; Nightingale to Garland, November 5, 1886, YF; J. R. Neal to Garland, August 13, 1887, AF.

25. Hale, vol. 6, 1806–1807; Green, *Bench and Bar*, 160–62; Robert M. McBride and Dan M. Robinson, *Biographical Directory of the Tennessee General Assembly* (Nashville: Tennessee State Library and Archives, 1979), vol. 2, 533.

26. Examiner Staub to Attorney General Miller, April 23 and May 2, 1890, YF.

27. *Knoxville Daily Journal*, January 23 and July 26, 1890.

28. Ibid., January 16, 1891.

29. Examiner Staub to Attorney General Miller, April 23, 1890, YF.

30. *Knoxville Daily Journal*, July 24, 1891.

31. Attorney General Pierrepont to Andrews, July 10, 1875, INST.

32. Attorney General Akerman to Andrews, January 8, 1872, INST; Andrews to Akerman, January 5, 1872, SCF/ETN.

33. Alexander T. Gray to Wheeler, September 24, 1880, INST.

34. Andrews to Akerman, January 1, 1872, SCF/ETN; Andrews to Attorney General Williams, December 20, 1872, SCF/ETN.

35. Attorney General Williams to Andrews, July 2, 1872, INST; Attorney General Miller to Tipton, April 7, 1890, INST; Garland to W. M. Nixon, October 21, 1887, INST.

36. Attorney General Devens to Andrews, September 25, 1877, INST.

37. Attorney General Williams to Andrews, July 10, 1872, INST; Williams to

Andrews, August 7, 1872, INST; Andrews to Williams, August 12, 1872, SCF/ETN.

38. Attorney General Williams to Andrews, August 17, 1872, INST.

39. U.S. Congress, House, "George T. Larkin," House Exec. Doc. 402, 51st Cong., 1st sess. (1890), Serial Set vol. 2752; *Annual Report of the Commissioner of Internal Revenue* for 1881, vii–viii; Jess Carr, *The Second Oldest Profession: An Informal History of Moonshining in America* (Englewood Cliffs, N.J., 1972), 33–39.

40. Wiltse, 56–64.

41. Ibid.

42. *Annual Report of the Commissioner of Internal Revenue* for 1879, v–vi; Attorney General Williams to Andrews, September 4, 1872, INST.

43. Attorney General Williams to Secretary Boutwell, January 30, 1872, E&C.

44. Wheeler to Attorney General Brewster, July 18, 1882, SCF/ETN.

45. E. C. Camp to Benjamin Bristow, October 11, 1871, SCF/ETN.

46. Pierrepont to Andrews, January 11, 1876, INST.

47. Akerman to E. C. Camp, May 4, 1871, INST; Camp to Benjamin Bristow, June 12, 1871, SCF/ETN; Camp to Akerman, April 29, 1871, SCF/ETN; Akerman to Camp, September 9, 1871, INST.

48. Akerman to Andrews, December 27, 1871, INST; H. H. Emmons to Attorney General Williams, April 2, 1874, SCF/ETN; Williams to A. H. Pettibone, May 22, 1874, INST.

49. Attorney General Devens to John P. Smith, November 18, 1880, INST; John P. Smith to Attorney General Brewster, July 28, 1884, SCF/ETN; Henry Hodges to Brewster, September 5, 1884, YF; H. M. Wiltse to Attorney General Miller, May 1, 1890, YF; Miller to Lindsay, November 10, 1892, INST.

50. *Annual Report of the Commissioner of Internal Revenue* for 1878, iv–v.

51. Ibid.

52. Carr, 33; Wiltse, 92; Andrews to Pierrepont, June 8, 1875, SCF/ETN.

53. Andrews to Devens, August 12, 1878, SCF/ETN.

54. U.S. Congress, House, "Views of the Commissioner of Pensions Upon the Adjudication of Pension Cases," House Misc. Doc. 29, 45th Cong., 2d sess. (1878), Serial Set vol. 1815, 4–5, 8.

55. *Knoxville Daily Journal*, January 16 and 25, 1890.

56. James Meek to Attorney General Brewster, July 2, 1883, SCF/ETN.

57. Andrews to Attorney General Williams, August 12, 1872, SCF/ETN.

58. *Knoxville Daily Journal*, July 18, 1891.

59. Atkinson, 23; Wiltse, 18–26.

60. Undated clipping from the *Independent*, enclosed in Andrews to Pierrepont, August 5, 1875, SCF/ETN.

61. *Knoxville Daily Journal*, January 13, 1890; Andrews to Pierrepont, February 16, 1876, SCF/ETN.

62. U.S. Congress, House, "George T. Larkin," 3–8; *Tennesee v. Davis,* 100 U.S.

257 (1880); Attorney General Williams to Andrews, May 6, 1873, INST; N. T. Beal to Akerman, November 7, 1871, SCF/ETN.

63. A. H. Pettibone to Attorney General Williams, July 14, 1874, SCF/ETN.

64. Andrews to Attorney General Williams, February 25, 1874, SCF/ETN.

65. Devens to Andrews, July 20, 1878, INST; *Annual Report of the Commissioner of Internal Revenue* for 1877, xxx–xxxii, and for 1879, iv–v.

66. S. F. Phillips to T. H. Reeves, July 16, 1884, INST.

67. Ivins to Garland, September 8, 1886, and January 7, 1887, YF.

68. Nixon to Garland, March 22 and 28, 1888, YF; Garland to Nixon, April 3, 1888, INST; William Maury to Nixon, June 9, 1888, INST.

69. Nixon to Garland, July 2 and 9, 1888, YF.

70. Tipton to Miller, July 19, 1889, YF.

71. Andrews to Devens, August 12, 1878, SCF/ETN.

72. Ibid.

73. U.S. Congress, Senate, "Salaries of Revenue Officers," 11–14.

74. J.C.J. Williams to Commissioner of Internal Revenue Miller, May 27, 1887, YF; N. Gregg to Commissioner Miller, May 27, 1887, YF; Nixon to Garland, December 17, 1888, YF.

75. Tipton to Attorney General Miller, August 21, 1889, YF; H. C. Evans to Miller, August 23, 1889, YF; Tipton to Miller, telegram, March 4, 1892, YF; Tipton to Miller, March 9, 1892, YF; Wiltse, 81–83.

76. A. H. Faulkner to Sam Hughes, February 3, 1890, YF.

77. Commissioner of Pensions Black to Garland, January 21 and March 11, 1887, YF.

78. Ibid.

79. Ibid.; J.C.J. Williams to Garland, February 28, 1887, YF.

80. E. C. Camp to Solicitor General Bristow, October 11, 1871, SCF/ETN.

81. Ibid.

82. Ibid.

83. Andrews to Attorney General Williams, August 1, 1874, SCF/ETN; Williams to Andrews, August 5, 1874, INST.

84. Moore, vol. 2, 238–39; *Knoxville Daily Journal*, January 13, 1890.

85. David M. Abshire, *The South Rejects a Prophet: The Life of D. M. Key* (New York, 1967), 221.

86. These statements are based on a broad sampling of issues of the *Knoxville Daily Journal* and the *Knoxville Daily Press and Herald*, from throughout this period. The newspapers usually provided little more than the name of the case, the charge, and the sentence.

87. Examiner Hazen to Miller, January 27, 1893, YF.

88. Ibid.; Wiltse, 69–87.

89. L. C. Houk to Pierrepont, August 4, 1875, SCF/ETN; John Baxter to Devens, January 31, 1880, SCF/ETN; Devens to Baxter, February 19, 1880, J&C.

90. John Baxter to Attorney General MacVeagh, October 1, 1881, SCF/ETN.

91. Commissioner Miller to Garland, April 4, 1885, YF.

92. James Meek to Garland, April 14, 16, and 25, 1885, YF; Wiltse, 27–31.

93. Attorney General Miller to Lindsay, February 25, 1892, INST.

94. Lindsay to Miller, February 29, 1892, YF.

95. Ibid. (emphasis in original).

96. Miller to Lindsay, March 2, 1892, INST.

97. Garland to Ivins, February 23, 1887, INST; Examiner Baker to Garland, April 12, 1888, YF.

98. Nixon to Garland, July 4, 1888, YF.

99. Ibid.

100. A. M. Cate to Horace Maynard, March 19, 1869, AF; McDowell, 5, B23, B53; *Knoxville Daily Journal*, January 18, 1890; T. H. Reeves to William Rule, Rule Papers, McClung Collection, Lawson McGhee Public Library, Knoxville; J. R. Neal to Garland, August 13, 1887, AF.

101. J. W. Nightingale to Garland, November 5, 1886, YF: M. T. Fouts to H. C. Evans, January 17, 1889, AF for Tipton; W. H. Murphy to H. C. Evans, January 14, 1889, AF for Tipton.

102. Ivins to Garland, January 7, 1887, YF; Examiner Hazen to Miller, January 30, 1893, YF.

103. Examiner Hazen to Miller, January 30, 1893, YF.

104. These statements are based upon the same biographical sources cited for each of these men in Section II of this chapter.

105. Moore, vol. 4, 931–35; *National Cyclopaedia*, vol. 1, 478.

106. Armstrong, vol. 1, 470; *East Tennessee Historical and Biographical*, 311–12, 405; Speer, 568–70; J. R. Neal to Garland, August 13, 1887, AF; McBride and Robinson, vol. 2, 533; Hale, vol. 6, 1806–1807.

107. Moore, vol. 4, 931–35; McBride and Robinson, vol. 2, 533; Armstrong, vol. 1, 470; G. G. Dibrell to Garland, April 13, 1885, AF.

108. A. H. Pettibone, "Attention Republicans!" broadside, undated, McClung Collection, Lawson McGhee Public Library, Knoxville.

109. Ibid.

110. James Meek to President Harrison, April 3, 1889, AF; Wiltse, 51.

111. Andrews to Benjamin H. Bristow, June 8, 1872, SCF/ETN; Bristow to Andrews, June 11, 1872, INST.

112. Attorney General MacVeagh to Atkinson, May 16, 1881, INST.

113. Wiltse, 5, 90.

114. Ibid.

115. Ibid., 211–17.

116. Andrews to Benjamin H. Bristow, August 12, 1872, SCF/ETN; Andrews to Attorney General Williams, November 12, 1872, SCF/ETN.

117. Andrews to Attorney General Williams, February 3 and November 25, 1873, and March 2, 1874, SCF/ETN.

118. Andrews to Attorney General Williams, October 11, 1874, SCF/ETN. Congress at first agreed that a $2 lump sum was adequate payment, but it later reversed itself.

119. Ivins to Garland, December 18, 1886, YF; Tipton to Miller, August 19, 1890, YF.

120. Ivins to Garland, June 4, 1886, YF; Examiner Staub to Miller, May 2, 1890, YF.

121. George Andrews to Attorney General Williams, February 15, 1875, SCF/ETN.

122. Andrews to Devens, July 23, 1878, SCF/ETN.

123. John P. Smith to John C. Campbell, June 18, 1885, YF; Ivins to Garland, June 24, 1885, YF; Meek to Garland, July 4, 1885, YF.

124. George Andrews, "Instructions to United States Commissioners," pamphlet enclosed in Andrews to Pierrepont, August 5, 1875, SCF/ETN.

125. Examiner Chalmers to Garland, January 18, 1886, YF, enclosing Ivins's printed instructions to his deputies.

126. Ibid.

Chapter 5: The Anteroom to Statehood
The Justice Department in Arizona Territory

1. Earl S. Pomeroy, *The Territories and the United States, 1861–1890: Studies in Colonial Administration* (Seattle, 1969), ix–5.

2. *Historical Statistics of the United States: Colonial Times to 1970* (Washington, D.C.: GPO, 1975), 24–37; *Compendium of the Tenth Census: Manufactures* (Washington, D.C.: GPO, 1882), 5, 67; and *Agriculture* (Washington, D.C.: GPO, 1883), 4; and *Precious Metals* (Washington, D.C.: GPO, 1885), 359.

3. T. A. Larson, "Women's Role in the American West," *Montana: The Magazine of Western History* 24 (Summer 1974): 2–11; John R. Wunder, "Law and the Chinese on the Southwest Frontier, 1850–1902," *Western Legal History* 2 (1989): 139–58. The best studies of territorial Arizona are found in Howard Roberts Lamar, *The Far Southwest, 1846–1912: A Territorial History* (New Haven, 1966); and Jay J. Wagoner, *Arizona Territory, 1863–1912: A Political History* (Tucson, 1970). An important book dealing with federal law enforcement in this region is

Larry D. Ball, *The United States Marshals of New Mexico and Arizona Territories, 1846–1912* (Albuquerque, 1978).

4. *Annual Report of the Attorney General* (Washington, D.C.: GPO, 1871–1891); Crawley P. Dake to Charles Devens, telegram, August 19, 1978, SCF/AZ.

5. "Apache Indians," in Howard R. Lamar, ed., *Reader's Encyclopedia of the American West* (New York: Harper and Row, 1977), 34–37; Angie Debo, *A History of the Indians of the United States* (Norman: University of Oklahoma Press, 1970), 267–83.

6. *The District Courts of the Territory of Arizona* (Phoenix: Arizona Statewide Archival and Records Project, 1941), 1–10, 32–37.

7. Biographical file of C.W.C. Rowell, Arizona Historical Society, Tucson.

8. M. F. Pleasants to Edward Phelps, September 9, 1870, INST; *Arizona Miner*, February 24, 1871.

9. I. Q. Dickason to Akerman, April 14, 1871, SCF/AZ; Rowell to Amos T. Akerman, August 7, 1871, SCF/AZ.

10. Rowell to Akerman, August 4, 1871, SCF/AZ; Rowell to George H. Williams, February 5, 1872, SCF/AZ.

11. Richard E. Sloan, *Memories of an Arizona Judge* (Stanford, 1932), 140–41; Wagoner, 22, 103–4.

12. James R. Hastings, "The Tragedy at Camp Grant in 1871," *Arizona and the West* 1 (1959): 146–60; Patricia Nelson Limerick, *The Legacy of Conquest: The Unbroken Past of the American West* (New York, 1987), 259–60.

13. Hastings, quotation at 153.

14. Akerman to Rowell, July 13, 1871, INST; Rowell to Akerman, August 7, 1871, SCF/AZ.

15. Rowell to Akerman, August 11, 1871, SCF/AZ.

16. Akerman to Rowell, August 28, 1871, INST; Andrew Hays Cargill, "The Camp Grant Massacre: Reminiscences of Andrew Hays Cargill, 1907," *Arizona Historical Review* 7 (1936): 73–79.

17. Two different, summarized transcripts of the trial exist. The transcript made by Andrew H. Cargill is filed with Rowell to Akerman, December 22, 1871, SCF/AZ; the other transcript was printed in the *Daily Alta Californian*, February 4, 1872.

18. See note 17, supra.

19. Ibid.

20. *Arizona Citizen*, January 20, 1872; Rowell to Williams, January 20, 1872, SCF/AZ; Ball, 68–70.

21. James E. McCaffry biographical file at Arizona Historical Society, Tucson; *Arizona Miner*, January 6, 1872. McCaffry's name is also regularly spelled "McCaffrey" and "McCaffery."

22. Clement H. Hill to McCaffry, June 13, 1872, INST; Williams to McCaffry, July 13, 1872, INST; McCaffry to Williams, December 13, 1872, SCF/AZ.

23. McCaffry to Williams, September 13, 1873, SCF/AZ; Ball, 64–78.

24. Pierrepont to McCaffry, May 19, 1875, INST; Everett B. Pomroy to Pierrepont, June 21, 1875, SCF/AZ; *Arizona Weekly Miner*, January 7, 1876.

25. Francis Blake to H. F. Page, November 21, 1879, AF for Pomroy; G. L. Seligmann, "Crawley P. Dake, U.S. Marshal," *Arizoniana* 2 (1961): 13–14; "J. W. Evans," in *A Historical and Biographical Record of the Territory of Arizona* (Chicago, 1896), 441–42.

26. Dake to Devens, telegrams, September 1 and 9, 1880, SCF/AZ. Reyes's first name is also sometimes given as "Brigata."

27. *San Francisco Chronicle*, August 27, 1880; *Tucson Citizen*, September 4, 1880; Dake to Devens, October 21, 1880, SCF/AZ.

28. Dake to Devens, telegram and letter, August 19, 1878, SCF/AZ; Wagoner, 113.

29. *Arizona Miner*, August 31, 1878.

30. McVeagh to Pomroy, April 14, 1881, INST; Pomroy to McVeagh, June 23, 1881, SCF/AZ.

31. U.S. Congress, House, "Lawlessness in Arizona," House Exec. Doc. 188, 47th Cong., 1st sess. (1882), 2 (hereafter "Lawlessness in Arizona"); Dake to McVeagh, May 30, 1881, SCF/AZ; Evans to Dake, June 30, 1881, SCF/AZ.

32. Daniel Boorstin, *The Americans: The Democratic Experience* (New York: Random House 1973), 34–41; Henry P. Walker, "Retire Peaceably to Your Homes: Arizona Faces Martial Law, 1882," *Journal of Arizona History* 10 (1969): 1–18; Odie B. Faulk, *Tombstone: Myth and Reality* (New York, 1972), 129–59; John P. Clum, *It All Happened in Tombstone* (Flagstaff, 1965), quotation at 8.

33. Faulk, 129–59; Clum, 1–12; Zoe A. Tilghman, *Spotlight: Bat Masterson and Wyatt Earp as U.S. Deputy Marshals* (San Antonio, 1960).

34. Faulk, 129–59; Clum, 1–12.

35. McVeagh to Pomroy, April 14, 1881, INST; Pomroy to McVeagh, June 23, 1881, SCF/AZ.

36. Dake to S. F. Phillips, telegram, December 8, 1881, SCF/AZ; Dake to Phillips, December 3, 1881, SCF/AZ.

37. James D. Richardson, comp., *A Compilation of the Messages and Papers of the Presidents, 1789–1908* (N.p.: Bureau of National Literature and Art, 1909), vol. 8, 53–54.

38. Walker, "Retire Peaceably," 17.

39. Dake to Brewster, telegram, May 3, 1882, SCF/AZ; Richardson, vol. 8, 122–23.

40. T. W. Ferry to Brewster, June 2, 1882, AF for Dake; Brewster to Pomroy, April 25, 1882, INST; Pomroy to Brewster, April 27, 1882, SCF/AZ.

41. *Portrait and Biographical Record of Arizona* (Chicago, 1904), 650–52.

42. Morris Goldwater to Brewster, June 2, 1882, SCF/AZ; Brewster to Zabriskie, June 21, 1882, INST.

43. Brewster to Tidball, October 27, 1882, INST; Homer Cummings and Carl McFarland, *Federal Justice: Chapters in the History of Justice and the Federal Executive* (New York, 1937), 253–61.

44. John G. Bourke, *On the Border with Crook* (New York: Scribner's, 1891), 438–40; Zabriskie to Brewster, October 23, 1882, SCF/AZ; Ball, 168–70.

45. Tidball to Brewster, October 7, 1883, SCF/AZ; Zabriskie to Brewster, February 11, 1884, SCF/AZ; clippings from *Philadelphia Times*, no date, enclosed in the latter letter; Tidball to William Springer, February 10, 1884, SCF/AZ.

46. Brewster to Tidball, February 20, 1884, INST.

47. Zabriskie to Brewster, January 29, 1882, SCF/AZ.

48. Tidball to Brewster, October 7, 1883, SCF/AZ; Tidball to Garland, October 30, 1885, SCF/AZ.

49. Brewster to Zabriskie, June 1, 1882, INST; S. F. Phillips to Zabriskie, telegram, October 13, 1882, SCF/AZ.

50. Zabriskie to Brewster, no date [c. May 1882], SCF/AZ.

51. Brewster to Zabriskie, March 24, 1884, INST.

52. Garland to Tidball, June 24, 1885, INST; *Historical and Biographical Record*, 508–509; *Alexandria Gazette*, December 13, 1884; *Arizona Citizen*, September 16, 1898.

53. *Historical and Biographical Record*, 537–38; Rouse's application, March 13, 1885, AF for Rouse.

54. Meade to Garland, January 25, 1888, YF; Barnes to Garland, June 8, 1886, AF for Rouse; D. A. Fisher to Garland, February 18, 1886, YF.

55. Rouse to F. M. Cockrell, June 9, 1886, YF; members of the Tucson bar to Cleveland, telegram, July 10, 1886, AF for Rouse; members of the Tucson bar to Garland, January 17, 1887, AF for Rouse.

56. Rouse to Garland, March 2, 1887, YF; Rouse to Garland, May 2, 1887, YF; Rouse to Garland, December 29, 1887, YF.

57. Lamar, *Far Southwest*, 473–74; G. A. Jenks to Rouse, September 29, 1886, INST.

58. Garland to Rouse, November 5, 1886, INST.

59. Erwin C. Surrency, *History of the Federal Courts* (New York, 1987), 100; Act of March 3, 1885, 23 Stat. 385; Rouse to Garland, November 28, 1888, YF; W. W. Porter to Garland, May 25, 1888, YF.

60. Rouse to Garland, November 28, 1888, YF.

61. Ibid.; Rouse to Garland, February 18, 1889, YF.

62. *Gon-shay-ee, Petitioner*, 130 U.S. 343 (1889); Miller to Rouse, telegram, April 15, 1889, INST. See also *Ex Parte Crow Dog*, 109 U.S. 556 (1883), and *Captain Jack, Petitioner*, 130 U.S. 353 (1889).

63. Rouse to Miller, telegram, April 16, 1889, YF; Miller to Rouse, telegram,

April 17, 1889, INST; Miller to Rouse, May 2, 1889, INST; Wagoner, 302–303.

64. Jeffords to John W. Noble, March 6, 1888, AF for Jeffords; *Arizona Weekly Gazette*, March 21, 1889; *Arizona Republican*, April 4, 1891.

65. *United States v. Mark Cunningham et al.*, transcript, filed at November 12, 1889, YF.

66. O. W. Chapman to Meade, July 25, 1889, INST; Jeffords to Miller, November 3, 1889, AF for Meade; Ball, 176–80.

67. *United States v. Mark Cunningham et al.*, transcript, filed at November 12, 1889, YF.

68. Ibid.; Sloan, 88–89.

69. *Arizona Daily Citizen*, March 26, 1901; Robert H. Paul biographical file, Arizona Historical Society, Tucson; Paul to Miller, January 16, 1890, AF for Paul.

70. Thomas Hughes to Miller, October 28, 1889, AF for Paul; Jeffords to Miller, October 4, 1889, AF for Paul.

71. Act of May 6, 1882, 22 Stat. 58; Act of September 13, 1888, 25 Stat. 476; Leonard W. Levy, ed., *Encyclopedia of the American Constitution* (New York: Macmillan, 1986), s.vv. "Chinese Exclusion Act."

72. Wunder, "Law and the Chinese," 140; *Tombstone Epitaph*, February 13, 1882, quoted in Wunder, "Law and the Chinese," 139.

73. Wilson to Miller, July 12, 1890, YF.

74. Ibid.

75. R. H. Paul to Miller, October 3, 1890, YF; Jeffords to Miller, September 12, 1890, YF.

76. John Noble to Miller, May 16, 1890, YF; Thomas F. Wilson to Miller, November 29, 1890, YF.

77. Thomas F. Wilson to Miller, November 29, 1890, YF; *United States v. Copper Queen Mining Co.*, 185 U.S. 495 (1902).

78. *Arizona Republican*, April 4, 1891.

79. *Annual Report of the Attorney General* for 1876–1885. Table B in each report has the number of cases, as well as the number of convictions, acquittals, and dismissals.

80. Miller to Paul, September 23, 1890, INST; O. W. Chapman to Jeffords, September 14, 1889, INST; Zabriskie to Brewster, January 29, 1882, YF.

81. Devens to Pomroy, January 8, 1879, INST; Miller to Jeffords, telegram, January 20, 1891, INST; Garland to Rouse, November 25, 1887, INST.

82. Brewster to Zabriskie, July 12, 1884, INST.

83. Zabriskie to Brewster, July 26, 1884, SCF/AZ.

84. John P. Hoyt to Devens, September 9, 1878, SCF/AZ.

85. Miller to Paul, September 23, 1890, INST; Miller to Meade, May 14, 1889, INST; Devens to Dake, September 20, 1878, INST.

86. Thomas F. Wilson to Miller, November 29, 1890, YF; William Stone to Miller, November 25, 1890, YF.

87. *United States v. Gon-shay-ee*, transcript, filed in W. W. Porter to Garland, June 18, 1888, YF.

88. See, e.g., *Annual Report of the Attorney General* for 1884, 12.

89. Devens to Pomroy, March 23, 1879, INST; Pomroy to Devens, April 25, 1879, SCF/AZ.

90. Dake to Devens, August 19, 1878, SCF/AZ.

91. Devens to Dake, telegram, August 28, 1880, INST; Dake to Devens, October 21, 1880, SCF/AZ.

92. *Prescott Arizonian*, July 12, 1879; U.S. Congress, House, "Lawlessness in Parts of Arizona," House Exec. Doc. 58, 47th Cong., 1st sess. (1882), 2 (hereafter "Lawlessness in Parts of Arizona").

93. H. P. Blocksom to J. W. Evans, June 16, 1881, SCF/AZ (emphasis in the original).

94. Ibid.; Major James Biddle to Evans, June 16, 1881, SCF/AZ; MacVeagh to Dake, July 1, 1881, INST.

95. Brewster to Zabriskie, May 15, 1884, INST.

96. "Lawlessness in Arizona," 1–4; Rouse to F. M. Cockrell, June 9, 1886, YF (emphasis in the original).

97. Report of Gosper to the secretary of the interior, 1882, quoted in Wagoner, 181; *Arizona Miner*, February 3, 1872.

98. Sloan, 92.

99. Rowell to Akerman, December 22, 1871, SCF/AZ; Cargill, 78.

100. *Arizona Citizen*, January 20 and 27, 1872.

101. Ibid., February 10, 1872.

102. McCaffry to Williams, August 24, 1872, SCF/AZ; Williams to McCaffry, September 26, 1872, INST.

103. Dake to Brewster, June 24, 1882, SCF/AZ (emphasis in the original).

104. Tidball to Brewster, October 7, 1883, SCF/AZ; Zabriskie to Brewster, telegram, April 25, 1882, SCF/AZ.

105. H. L. Muldrow to Garland, November 22, 1887, YF; C. E. Daily to Brewster, June 23, 1882, AF for Zabriskie; *Tombstone Prospector,* quoted in Flagstaff *Arizona Champion*, September 15, 1888.

106. Rouse to Garland, March 2, 1887, YF.

107. Thomas F. Wilson to Miller, March 19, 1892, YF; Lewis Johnson to Miller, March 5, 1892, YF (emphasis in the original).

108. *United States v. DeLong*, filed with Rowell to Akerman, December 22, 1871, SCF/AZ.

109. Rowell to Akerman, August 4, 1871, SCF/AZ; Rouse to F. M. Cockrell, March 13, 1886, AF for Rouse.

110. Paul's defense is found in Lewis Wolfley to Miller, January 10, 1891, AF for Paul.

111. Meade to Leigh Chalmers, September 17, 1885, AF for Zabriskie; Rouse to

Miller, telegram, May 24, 1889, AF for Rouse.

112. Sloan, 146; Cargill, 77; *Daily Alta Californian*, February 4, 1872.

113. Millay to Brewster, February 4, 1884, SCF/AZ; Joseph Campbell to Garland, June 13, 1888, YF.

114. D. A. Fisher to Garland, February 18, 1886, YF; Sloan, 89–90.

115. Dake to S. F. Phillips, October 5, 1881, SCF/AZ; Dake to Devens, May 17, 1879, SCF/AZ; Dake to MacVeagh, September 14, 1881, SCF/AZ.

116. Devens to Dake, telegram, May 16, 1879, INST; Dake to Devens, May 16, 1879, SCF/AZ.

117. Jeffords to Miller, March 6, 1891, YF; Dake to MacVeagh, telegram, August 5, 1881, SCF/AZ.

118. Tidball to Brewster, November 3, 1882, SCF/AZ; Howard Perry to Brewster, March 31, 1883, SCF/AZ.

119. Dickason to Akerman, August 14, 1871, SCF/AZ; Rowell to Akerman, December 22, 1871, SCF/AZ.

120. Tidball to Brewster Cameron, September 10, 1883, SCF/AZ; S. E. Kercheval to Miller, April 9, 1892, YF.

121. Crosthwaite to Miller, June 30, 1890, YF.

122. Ibid.

123. John Goode to Meade, April 20, 1886, INST; Rowell to Akerman, September 9, 1871, SCF/AZ; W. W. Standefer to Taft, July 22, 1876, SCF/AZ.

124. Dake to MacVeagh, June 3, 1881, SCF/AZ.

125. Pomroy to Taft, December 13, 1876, SCF/AZ; Tyng to Williams, August 21, 1874, SCF/AZ (emphasis in the original).

126. Tichenor to Garland, February 2, 1888, YF.

127. Bill of Longley Brothers, January 1, 1890, YF; Miller to Jeffords, August 15, 1890, INST.

128. Millay to Brewster, October 23, 1883, SCF/AZ; Zabriskie to Garland, December 14, 1885, YF.

129. Dake to Devens, August 15, 1878, SCF/AZ; Dake to Brewster, telegram, June 21, 1882, AF for Dake; Rouse to A. H. Buckner, March 24, 1886, AF for Rouse; Rouse to Garland, January 23, 1888, AF for Rouse.

130. Dake to Devens, telegram, July 15, 1880, SCF/AZ; S. F. Phillips to Dake, September 27, 1881, INST; MacVeagh to Dake, June 15, 1881, INST.

131. Dake to Devens, September 16, 1879, SCF/AZ.

132. Evans to Dake, September 5, 1881, SCF/AZ; S. F. Phillips to Dake, October 17, 1881, INST.

133. Titus to Williams, July 16, 1872, AF for McCaffry; McCaffry to Williams, July 12, 1872, SCF/AZ.

134. John Titus to E. Babcock, November 8, 1873, SCF/AZ; Zabriskie to Brewster, August 23 and October 3, 1882, SCF/AZ.

135. Tyng to Williams, June 27, 1874, SCF/AZ; Pomroy to Pierrepont, June 21, 1875, SCF/AZ; Zabriskie to Brewster, no date [c. November 1882], SCF/AZ.

136. S. F. Phillips to Tidball, March 7, 1885, INST; W. A. Smith to Garland, October 26, 1885, YF; Tyng to Williams, September 28, 1874, SCF/AZ; F. B. Crosthwaite to Miller, June 20, 1890, YF.

137. Dake to Devens, September 5, 1878, SCF/AZ; Dake to Devens, February 29, 1880, SCF/AZ.

138. A. J. Doran, "Interesting Reminiscences," *Arizona Historical Review* 1 (October 1928): 59.

139. Zabriskie to Brewster, April 22, 1882, YF; Benjamin Morgan to McVeagh, April 22, 1882, YF; Akerman to Rowell, August 23, 1871, INST; Zabriskie to Garland, December 14, 1885, YF.

140. John Gosper to McVeagh, August 18, 1881, SCF/AZ; Wagoner, 203; "Lawlessness in Parts of Arizona," 4–5; Clum, 16–17.

141. Tidball to Brewster, March 17, 1884, SCF/AZ; "Lawlessness in Arizona," 1–2.

142. Jeffords to Miller, November 29, 1890, YF; R.J.H. Hartman to J. W. Noble, December 3, 1890, YF.

143. Miller to Jeffords, December 23, 1889, INST; Jeffords to Miller, November 3, 1889, AF for Meade.

144. Tidball to Brewster, October 7, 1883, YF; Affadavit of Zan Tidball, March 10, 1884, SCF/AZ.

145. Rouse to A. H. Buckner, March 24, 1886, YF; Rouse to Garland, December 29, 1887, YF.

146. Tidball to Brewster, May 3, 1884, SCF/AZ; Zabriskie to Tidball, April 30, 1884, SCF/AZ; Evans to Tidball, April 25, 1884, SCF/AZ.

147. See n. 146, supra.

148. Garland to Meade, April 28, 1888, INST; Tidball to Brewster, July 11, 1883, SCF/AZ; Dake to Devens, July 14, 1879, SCF/AZ; Flagstaff *Arizona Champion*, December 8, 1888; C. A. Tweed to Pierrepont, October 26, 1875, SCF/AZ; Dake to Devens, October 21, 1880, SCF/AZ.

149. Doran, 60–61; Wagoner, 184.

150. Joseph Miller, *Arizona: The Last Frontier* (New York, 1956), 173.

151. *Arizona Citizen*, February 10, 1872; *Portrait and Biographical Record*, 650–52; *Arizona Republican*, April 4, 1891; C.W.C. Rowell biographical file at Arizona Historical Society, Tucson.

152. W. V. Whitmore, "Francis Henri Goodwin, M.D.," unpublished typescript in Francis Henri Goodwin Papers, Arizona Historical Society, Tucson. *Arizona Daily Citizen*, March 26, 1901; D. B. Parker to Chester Arthur, June 13, 1882, AF for Tidball; *Arizona Citizen*, September 16, 1898.

153. *Phoenix Daily Herald*, February 10, 1886.

154. Crosthwaite to Miller, June 30, 1890, YF; Limerick, 44, 77.

155. Gosper to Dake, November 28, 1881, in "Lawlessness in Parts of Arizona," 2–3; Zabriskie to Brewster, August 14, 1882, SCF/AZ.

156. McCaffry to Williams, December 13, 1872, SCF/AZ; W. T. Sherman to Brewster, telegram, April 12, 1882, SCF/AZ.

157. Silent to Devens, September 6, 1878, SCF/AZ; Dake to Devens, September 5, 1878, SCF/AZ.

158. Whitmore; *Arizona Citizen*, October 15 and November 19, 1870; *Arizona Miner*, September 14, 1872.

159. *Arizona Miner*, July 10, 1869; *Arizona Weekly Miner*, August 6, 1875.

160. *Portrait and Biographical Record*, 650–52; prospectus of Wedge Mining Company, with C. E. Dailey to Brewster, October 24, 1884, YF; *Arizona Daily Citizen*, March 26, 1901; *Cochise Record*, December 12, 1884.

161. Brewster to Zabriskie, November 21, 1882, INST; Brewster Cameron to B. H. Brewster, March 13, 1883, SCF/AZ; Howard Perry to Brewster, March 17, 1883. On the record of the territorial judiciary, see John D. Guice, *Rocky Mountain Bench: The Territorial Supreme Courts of Colorado, Montana, and Wyoming, 1861–1890* (New Haven, 1972) and Kermit L. Hall, "Hacks and Derelicts Revisited: American Territorial Judiciary, 1789–1959," *Western Historical Quarterly* 12 (1981): 273–89. For an example of negative treatments of the territorial judiciary, see Lawrence M. Friedman, *A History of the American Law* (New York, 1973), 326–28.

162. Jeffords to Miller, telegram, September 30, 1889, Wham case file in AF; members of the grand jury to Miller, telegram, September 30, 1889, Wham case file in AF; J. W. Wham to Miller, telegram, August 7, 1889, Wham case file in AF.

163. Zabriskie to Brewster, telegram, April 30, 1882, YF; S. F. Phillips to Zabriskie, September 8, 1882, INST (emphasis in the original).

164. Zabriskie to Brewster, August 2, 1882, YF; Zabriskie to Brewster, October 21, 1882, SCF/AZ.

165. *Annual Report of the Attorney General* for 1871–1890, Table B for each year.

166. Wagoner, ix; Lamar, *Far Southwest*, 491–92.

167. Lamar, *Far Southwest*, 491–97 (first quotation at 491, second at 497).

Chapter 6: Conclusion

1. Edward L. Ayers, *Vengeance and Justice: Crime and Punishment in the Nineteenth-Century American South* (New York, 1984); Samuel E. Walker, *Popular Justice: A History of American Criminal Justice* (New York, 1980).

2. Ayers, 1–10.

3. Walker, *Popular Justice,* 11–34.

4. Ibid., 103–23.

5. William Edward Nelson, *The Roots of American Bureaucracy: 1830–1900* (Cambridge, Mass., 1982), 157. After 1884 a few Enforcement Act cases were tried in the South, but, certainly, the "enforcement program" there was dead.

6. George Sharpe to Akerman, October 22, 1870, SCF for southern New York.

7. Akerman to W. G. Morris, July 29, 1870, INST; H. J. May to Garland, June 17, 1886, YF; Lewis L. McArthur to Garland, March 9, 1887, YF.

8. George Wesley Atkinson, *After the Moonshiners, by One of the Raiders* (Wheeling, 1881).

9. *Annual Report of the Attorney General* for 1871–1890 (Washington, D.C.: GPO, 1871–1891), Table B in each volume. Per capita figures were calculated by dividing numbers of criminal cases by the population figures given in *Compendium of the Tenth Census: Population* (Washington, D.C.: GPO, 1882). Note that these are not annualized per capita figures but are total numbers of cases per 10,000 persons over twenty years.

10. James D. Richardson, comp., *A Compilation of the Messages and Papers of the Presidents, 1789–1908* (N.p.: Bureau of National Literature and Art, 1909), vol. 7, 606 (on immigration to Utah); Henry M. Wiltse, *The Moonshiners* (Chattanooga, 1895), 211–12; Charles Silent to Charles Devens, September 6, 1878, SCF/AZ.

11. Robert J. Kaczorowski, *The Politics of Judicial Interpretation: The Federal Courts, Department of Justice, and Civil Rights, 1866–1876* (Dobbs Ferry, 1985), 95 (first quotation); U.S. Congress, Senate, "Mississippi Election of 1875," Senate Rep. 327, 44th Cong., 1st sess. (1876), 50–51 (second quotation).

12. Henry P. Walker, "Retire Peaceably to Your Homes: Arizona Faces Martial Law, 1882," *Journal of Arizona History* 10 (1969): 3; William L. Montell, *Killings: Folk Justice in the Upper South* (Lexington, 1986), xv.

13. *Jackson Weekly Clarion*, July 20, 1871; Tucson *Arizona Citizen*, January 20, 1872.

14. *Montgomery Advertiser,* quoted in Richard Busteed to George H. Williams, March 29, 1872, SCF for middle Alabama; John A. Minnis, "Ku Klux in Alabama: Address of John A. Minnis, Charges of Hon. Richard Busteed" (Montgomery, Ala., 1872), 4, 23.

15. Howard Roberts Lamar, *The Far Southwest, 1846–1912: A Territorial History* (New Haven, 1966), 13 (quotation). See also Howard R. Lamar, "Carpetbaggers Full of Dreams: A Functional View of the Arizona Pioneer Politician," *Arizona and the West* 7 (1965): 187–206; Lawrence M. Friedman, *A History of the American Law* (New York, 1973), 326–28. Among the works that have aimed to rehabilitate the judiciary are John D. Guice, *Rocky Mountain Bench: The Territorial Supreme Courts of Colorado, Montana, and Wyoming, 1861–1890* (New

Haven, 1972); and Kermit L. Hall, "Hacks and Derelicts Revisited: American Territorial Judiciary, 1789–1959," *Western Historical Quarterly* 12 (1981): 273–89.

16. Senate report quoted in Earl S. Pomeroy, "Carpet-baggers in the Territories: 1861 to 1890," *The Historian* 2 (1939): 55.

17. U.S. Congress, House, "Jurors and Witnesses in the Territories," House Rep. 1288, 46th Cong., 2d sess. (1880), 1.

18. Akerman to General Alfred H. Terry, November 18, 1871, Akerman Letterbooks, special collections, Alderman Library, University of Virginia.

19. Everette Swinney, "Suppressing the Ku Klux Klan: The Enforcement of the Reconstruction Amendments, 1870–1874" (Ph.D. diss., University of Texas, Austin, 1966), 205, 233–34, 268.

20. S. F. Phillips to Trenmore Coffin, April 13, 1883, SCF for Nevada.

21. George Caesar Bates to George H. Williams, January 4, 1872, SCF/UT.

22. *Washington Chronicle,* quoted in *Deseret News*, February 9, 1873; Kirk H. Porter and Donald B. Johnson, comps., *National Party Platforms, 1840–1960* (Urbana, University of Illinois Press, 1961), 54ff., 66, 81.

23. Leonard Dupee White, with Jean Schneider, *The Republican Era, 1869–1901: A Study in Administrative History* (New York, 1958), 1–19; Robert M. Goldman, "'A Free Ballot and a Fair Count'" (Ph.D. diss., Michigan State University, East Lansing, 1976), 296.

24. *Annual Report of the Attorney General* for 1875, 32–63; and for 1885, Exhibits K, M, N, O, and P.

25. White and Schneider, 1.

26. Akerman to Noah Davis, March 23, 1871, INST.

27. *Annual Report of the Attorney General* for 1870 (1871), 2; and for 1875, 6.

28. Devens to all U.S. attorneys, November 22, 1880, INST; Garland to Elwin A. Ireland, November 11, 1885, INST.

29. *Annual Report of the Attorney General* for 1871 (1872), 7.

30. *Annual Report of the Attorney General* for 1873, 28; and for 1883, 23.

31. Act of March 3, 1891, 26 Stat. 826; Homer Cummings and Carl McFarland, *Federal Justice: Chapters in the History of Justice and the Federal Executive* (New York, 1937), 525–26.

32. Statements regarding the daily caseloads at Oxford and Knoxville are based on the Minute Books of the District Court for the Northern District of Mississippi, at the Federal Records Center at Atlanta, and a wide sampling of Knoxville newspapers throughout the period.

33. Quoted in Cummings and McFarland, 470.

34. Cummings and McFarland, 366–83.

35. Ibid., 510–11.

36. William Graham Sumner, *Folkways: A Study of the Sociological Importance of Usages, Manners, Customs, Mores, and Morals* (Boston: Ginn, 1906), 55, 77, 94 (first quotation), 113 (second quotation), 350.

37. James Meek to Attorney General Brewster, July 2, 1883, SCF/ETN. For discussion of Gillenwater, Taylor, and Amerine, see supra, Chapters 2, 3, and 4, respectively.

38. James Meek to Brewster, July 2, 1883, SCF/ETN.

39. *Annual Report of the Attorney General* for 1889, xv; for a discussion of the trial of Page's murderers, see supra, Chapter 2.

40. See supra, Chapter 3.

41. U.S. Constitution, Article IV, Sec. 3, cl. 2; *First National Bank v. County of Yankton,* 101 U.S. 129 (1880).

42. Henry R. Glick, *Courts, Politics, and Justice* (New York, McGraw-Hill, 1983), 244.

43. Kermit L. Hall, "The Civil War Era as a Crucible for Nationalizing the Lower Federal Courts," *Prologue* 7 (Fall 1975): 177–86.

44. Harwood P. Hinton, "Arizona," in Howard R. Lamar, ed., *Reader's Encyclopedia of the American West* (New York: Harper and Row, 1977), 43.

45. Leonard J. Arrington, "Utah," in Lamar, ed., *Reader's Encyclopedia of the American West*, 1208–11.

46. Robert E. Corlew, "Tennessee," in David C. Roller and Robert W. Twyman, eds., *Encyclopedia of Southern History* (Baton Rouge: Louisiana State University Press, 1979), 1196–97.

47. *Historical Statistics of the United States: Colonial Times to 1970* (Washington, D.C.: GPO, 1975), 30; *Statistical Abstract of the United States, 1987* (Washington, D.C.: GPO, 1986), 20; *Statistical Abstract of the United States, 1982–83* (Washington, D.C.: GPO, 1982), 32; John R. Skates, "Mississippi," in Roller and Twyman, eds., *Encyclopedia of Southern History*, 832–34.

48. Kaczorowski, 163.

49. Arthur C. Millspaugh, *Crime Control by the National Government* (Washington, D.C.: Brookings Institution, 1937), 50–54; Erwin C. Surrency, *History of the Federal Courts* (New York, 1987), 106.

50. Surrency, 49–57; see Stephen Skowronek, *Building a New American State: The Expansion of National Administrative Capacities, 1877–1920* (New York, 1982), for a discussion of stopgap repairs to the bureacracy.

51. Cummings and McFarland, 366–83; Walker, *Popular Justice*, 161–264.

52. *Ethics and Professional Conduct for the Federal Attorney* (Washington, D.C.: GPO, 1983); *Federal Prosecution of Election Offenses*, 4th ed. (Washington, D.C.: GPO, 1984).

Selected Bibliography

Books, Theses, and Dissertations

Abshire, David M. *The South Rejects a Prophet: The Life of D. M. Key*. New York: Prager, 1967.

Alter, J. Cecil. *Utah, the Storied Domain: A Documentary History of Utah's Eventful Career*. Chicago: American Historical Society, 1932.

Ames, Blanche Butler. *Chronicles from the Nineteenth Century: Family Letters of Blanche Butler and Adelbert Ames*. Clinton, Mass.: Colonial Press, 1957.

Anderson, Nels. *Desert Saints: The Mormon Frontier in Utah*. Chicago: University of Chicago Press, 1942.

Aron, Cindy Sondik. *Ladies and Gentlemen of the Civil Service: Middle-class Workers in Victorian America.* New York: Oxford University Press, 1987.

Arrington, Leonard J. *Great Basin Kingdom: Economic History of the Latter-day Saints, 1830–1900*. Lincoln: University of Nebraska Press, 1966.

Atkinson, George Wesley. *After the Moonshiners, by One of the Raiders*. Wheeling; W.Va.: Frew and Campbell Steam Book, 1881.

Ayers, Edward L. *Vengeance and Justice: Crime and Punishment in the Nineteenth-Century American South*. New York: Oxford University Press, 1984.

Ball, Larry D. *The United States Marshals of New Mexico and Arizona Territories, 1846–1912*. Albuquerque: University of New Mexico Press, 1978.

Bancroft, Hubert Howe. *History of Utah*. San Francisco: History, 1889.

Baskin, Robert N. *Reminiscences of Early Utah*. Salt Lake City: privately printed, 1914.

Braeman, John. *Before the Civil Rights Revolution: The Old Court and Individual Rights*. New York: Greenwood Press, 1988.

Brown, Vernal A. "The United States Marshals in Utah Territory to 1896." M.S. thesis, Utah State University, Logan, 1970.

Caldwell, Joshua. *Sketches of the Bench and Bar of Tennessee*. Knoxville: Ogden Brothers, 1898.

Campbell, Stanley W. *Slave Catchers: Enforcement of the Fugitive Slave Law, 1850–1860*. Chapel Hill: University of North Carolina Press, 1970.

Carr, Jess. *The Second Oldest Profession: An Informal History of Moonshining in America*. Englewood Cliffs, N.J.: Prentice-Hall, 1972.

Clum, John P. *It All Happened in Tombstone*. Flagstaff, Ariz.: Northland Press, 1965.

Cummings, Homer, and Carl McFarland. *Federal Justice: Chapters in the History of Justice and the Federal Executive*. New York: Macmillan, 1937.

Current, Richard N. *Those Terrible Carpetbaggers*. New York: Oxford University Press, 1988.

Dabney, Joseph. *Mountain Spirits*. New York: Scribners, 1974.

Davison, Kenneth. *The Presidency of Rutherford B. Hayes*. Westport, Conn.: Greenwood Press, 1972.

Doenecke, Justus D. *The Presidencies of James A. Garfield and Chester A. Arthur*. Lawrence: Regents Press of Kansas, 1981.

Dwyer, Robert Joseph. "The Gentile Comes to Utah: A Study in Religious and Social Conflict (1862-1890)." Ph.D. diss., Catholic University, Washington, D.C., 1941.

Faulk, Odie B. *Tombstone: Myth and Reality*. New York: Oxford University Press, 1972.

Firmage, Edwin Brown, and Richard Collin Mangrum. *Zion in the Courts: A Legal History of the Church of Jesus Christ of Latter-day Saints, 1830–1900*. Urbana: University of Illinois Press, 1988.

Foner, Eric. *Reconstruction: America's Unfinished Revolution, 1863–1877*. New York: Harper and Row, 1988.

Friedman, Lawrence M. *A History of the American Law*. New York: Simon and Schuster, 1973; 2d ed., 1986.

Gillette, William. *Retreat from Reconstruction, 1869–1879*. Baton Rouge: Louisiana State University Press, 1979.

Gillis, Norman E. *Biographical and Historical Memoirs of Mississippi*. N.p.: privately printed, 1962.

Goldman, Robert M. "'A Free Ballot and a Fair Count': The Department of Justice and the Enforcement of Voting Rights in the South, 1877–1893." Ph.D. diss., Michigan State University, East Lansing, 1976.

Green, John W. *Bench and Bar of Knox County, Tennessee*. Knoxville: Archer and Smith, 1947.

———. *Law and Lawyers: Sketches of the Federal Judges of Tennessee*. Jackson, Tenn.: McCowat-Mercer Press, 1950.

Guice, John D. *Rocky Mountain Bench: The Territorial Supreme Courts of Colo-*

rado, Montana, and Wyoming, 1861–1890. New Haven, Conn.: Yale University Press, 1972.

Hale, William T. *A History of Tennessee and Tennesseans*. 8 vols. Chicago: Lewis, 1913.

Harris, William C. *The Day of the Carpetbagger: Republican Reconstruction in Mississippi*. Baton Rouge: Louisiana State University Press, 1979.

Haynes, Alan E. "The Federal Government and its Policies Regarding the Frontier Era of Utah Territory, 1850–1877." Ph.D. diss., Catholic University, Washington, D.C., 1968.

Henderson, Dwight F. *Congress, Courts, and Criminals: The Development of Federal Criminal Law, 1801–1829*. Westport, Conn.: Greenwood Press, 1985.

A Historical and Biographical Record of the Territory of Arizona. Chicago: McFarland and Poole, 1896.

History of the Bench and Bar of Utah. Salt Lake City: Inter-state Press Association, 1913.

Kaczorowski, Robert J. *The Politics of Judicial Interpretation: The Federal Courts, Department of Justice, and Civil Rights, 1866–1876*. Dobbs Ferry, N.Y.: Oceana Publications, 1985.

Keller, Morton. *Affairs of State: Public Life in Late Nineteenth-Century America*. Cambridge, Mass.: Harvard University Press, 1977.

Kilts, Clair T. "A History of the Federal and Territorial Court Conflicts in Utah, 1851–1874." M.A. thesis, Brigham Young University, Provo, Utah, 1959.

Kirwin, Albert D. *Revolt of the Rednecks: Mississippi Politics, 1876–1925*. New York: Harper and Row, 1965.

Lamar, Howard Roberts. *The Far Southwest, 1846–1912: A Territorial History*. New Haven, Conn.: Yale University Press, 1966.

Larson, Gustive O. *The "Americanization" of Utah for Statehood*. San Marino, Calif.: Huntington Library, 1971.

Leonard, Lewis A. *Life of Alphonso Taft*. New York: Hawke, 1920.

Limerick, Patricia Nelson. *The Legacy of Conquest: The Unbroken Past of the American West*. New York: W. W. Norton, 1987.

Lynch, James Daniel. *The Bench and Bar of Mississippi*. New York: Hale and Son, 1881.

McDowell, Sam, ed. *East Tennessee History: Reprinted from Goodspeed's History of Tennessee*. Hartford, Ky.: privately printed, 1978.

McFeely, William S. *Grant*. New York: Norton, 1981.

Miller, Joseph. *Arizona: The Last Frontier*. New York: Hastings House, 1956.

Montell, William L. *Killings: Folk Justice in the Upper South*. Lexington: University Press of Kentucky, 1986.

Moore, John Trotwood. *Tennessee: The Volunteer State*. Chicago: Clarke, 1923.

Mulder, William, and A. Russell Mortensen, eds. *Among the Mormons: Historic Accounts by Contemporary Observers*. New York: Knopf, 1958.

Nelson, William Edward. *The Roots of American Bureaucracy, 1830–1900*. Cambridge, Mass.: Harvard University Press, 1982.

Nevins, Allan. *Grover Cleveland: A Study in Courage*. New York: Dodd, Mead, 1932.

Pomeroy, Earl S. *The Territories and the United States, 1861–1890: Studies in Colonial Administration*. Seattle: University of Washington Press, 1969.

Portrait and Biographical Record of Arizona. Chicago: Chapman Publishing, 1904.

Quinn, Maria Margaret. "William Henry Harrison Miller: Attorney General of the United States, 1889–1893." Ph.D. diss., Catholic University, Washington, D.C., 1965.

Richardson, James D., comp. *A Compilation of the Messages and Papers of the Presidents, 1789–1908*. 11 vols. N.p.: Bureau of National Literature and Art, 1909.

Rowland, Dunbar. *Courts, Judges, and Lawyers of Mississippi, 1798–1935*. Jackson: Mississippi Department of Archives and History, 1935.

———. *History of Mississippi: The Heart of the South*. Spartanburg, S.C.: Reprint, 1978.

Sefton, James E. *The United States Army and Reconstruction*. Westport, Conn.: Greenwood Press, 1980.

Sievers, Harry J. *Benjamin Harrison: Hoosier President*. Indianapolis, Ind.: Bobbs-Merrill, 1968.

Skowronek, Stephen. *Building a New American State: The Expansion of National Administrative Capacities, 1877–1920*. New York: Cambridge University Press, 1982.

Sloan, Richard E. *Memories of an Arizona Judge*. Stanford, Calif.: Stanford University Press, 1932.

Surrency, Erwin C. *History of the Federal Courts*. New York: Oceana Publications, 1987.

Swinney, Everette. "Supressing the Ku Klux Klan: The Enforcement of the Reconstruction Amendments, 1870–1874." Ph.D. diss., University of Texas, Austin, 1966.

Tilghman, Zoe A. *Spotlight: Bat Masterson and Wyatt Earp as U.S. Deputy Marshals*. San Antonio, Texas: Naylor, 1960.

Trelease, Allen W. *White Terror: The Ku Klux Conspiracy and Southern Reconstruction*. New York: Harper and Row, 1971.

Wagoner, Jay J. *Arizona Territory, 1863–1912: A Political History*. Tucson: University of Arizona Press, 1970.

Walker, Samuel E. *Popular Justice: A History of American Criminal Justice*. New York: Oxford University Press, 1980.

Webb, Ross A. *Benjamin Helm Bristow: Border State Politician*. Lexington: University of Kentucky Press, 1969.

Wharton, Vernon Lane. *The Negro in Mississippi, 1865–1890*. New York: Harper and Row, 1965.

White, Leonard Dupee, with the assistance of Jean Schneider. *The Republican Era, 1869–1901: A Study in Administrative History*. New York: Macmillan, 1958.

Whitely, H. C. *In It* [a history of the Secret Service]. Cambridge, Mass.: Riverside Press, 1894.

Whitney, Orson F. *History of Utah*. 4 vols. Salt Lake City: Cannon and Sons, 1892–1904.

———. *Popular History of Utah*. Salt Lake City: Deseret News, 1916.

Wiltse, Henry M. *The Moonshiners*. Chattanooga, Tenn.: Times Printing, 1895.

Woodward, C. Vann. *The Burden of Southern History*, rev. ed. Baton Rouge: Louisiana State University Press, 1968.

Younger, Richard D. *The People's Panel: The Grand Jury in the United States, 1634–1941*. Providence, R.I.: Brown University Press, 1963.

Contemporary Pamphlets

Akerman, Amos T. "Reconstruction: Extracts from the Speech Delivered at Atlanta, Georgia, September 1, 1870." Microcard reproduction of undated contemporary pamphlet. Louisville: Lost Cause Press, n.d. [1965?].

Andrews, George. "Instructions to United States Commissioners." Filed in Andrews to Edwards Pierrepont, August 5, 1875, SCF/ETN.

Anonymous. "The Mormon Endowment House! Graphic Exposure of the Treasonable Institution Where Polygamous Marriages are Solemnized, by an Eyewitness." Salt Lake City: Tribune Publishing, 1879. Copy inscribed by Philip Van Zile to President Hayes at Hayes Presidential Center, Fremont, Ohio.

Chandler, Greene C. "The Negro in Politics. The Paramount Political Question of the Day." Reprinted in Greene C. Chandler, *Journal and Speeches of Greene Callier Chandler*. N.p.: privately printed, 1953.

Dickson, William H. "Solid Facts From a Loyal Man: Speech of U.S. Attorney Wm. H. Dickson at G.A.R. Meeting, Tuesday Eve., July 27." Salt Lake City: Salt Lake Tribune, n.d. [1886]. Copy at State Historical Society of Wisconsin, Madison.

Minnis, John A. "Ku Klux in Alabama: Address of John A. Minnis, Charges of Hon. Richard Busteed." Montgomery: n.p., 1872. Copy in the Library of Congress main collection.

Pettibone, A. H. "Attention Republicans!" [prohibition broadside]. N.p.: n.p., n.d. Copy in McClung Collection, Lawson McGhee Public Library, Knoxville, Tenn.

Van Zile, Philip. "The Twin Relic," N.p.: n.p., n.d. [c. 1880]. Copy in Philip Van Zile Papers, Harold B. Lee Library, Brigham Young University, Provo, Utah.

Wheeler, Xenophon. "The Experiences of an Enlisted Man in the Hospital in the Early Part of the War." N.p.: n.p., n.d. [Cincinnati?, 1908?] Copy at U.S. Army Military History Institute, Carlisle Barracks, Pennsylvania.

Articles and Essays in Collections

Alexander, Thomas G. "Charles S. Zane, Apostle of the New Era." *Utah Historical Quarterly* 34 (1966): 290–314.

———. "Federal Authority Versus Polygamic Theocracy: James B. McKean and the Mormons." *Dialogue: A Journal of Mormon Thought* 1 (1966): 85–100.

Allen, James B. "The Unusual Jurisdiction of County Probate Courts in the Territory of Utah." *Utah Historical Quarterly* 36 (1968): 132–42.

Bashore, Melvin L. "Life Behind Bars: Mormon Cohabs of the 1880s." *Utah Historical Quarterly* 47 (1979): 22–41.

Cannon, Charles A. "The Awesome Power of Sex: The Polemical Campaign Against Mormon Polygamy." *Pacific Historical Review* 43 (1974): 61–82.

Cargill, Andrew Hays. "The Camp Grant Massacre: Reminiscences of Andrew Hays Cargill, 1907." *Arizona Historical Review* 7 (1936): 73–79.

Clayton, James L. "The Supreme Court, Polygamy, and the Enforcement of Morals in Nineteenth-Century America: An Analysis of *Reynold v. United States.*" *Dialogue: A Journal of Mormon Thought* 12, no. 4 (1979): 46–61.

Cobb, James C. "Beyond Planters and Industrialists: A New Perspective on the New South." *Journal of Southern History* 54 (1988): 45–68.

Coker, William L. "The United States Senate Investigation of the Mississippi Election of 1875." *Journal of Mississippi History* 37 (1975): 143–63.

Cresswell, Stephen. "The Attorney Generalship of Charles Devens." *Hayes Historical Journal* 3, no. 6 (1982): 32–45.

———. "The Case of Taylor Strauder." *West Virginia History* 44 (1983): 193–211.

———. "The Department of Justice in Utah Territory, 1870–1890." *Utah Historical Quarterly* 53 (1985): 204–22.

———. "Enforcing the Enforcement Acts: The Department of Justice in Northern Mississippi, 1870–1890." *Journal of Southern History* 53 (1987): 421–40.

Davis, Ray Jay. "Plural Marriage and Religious Freedom: The Impact of *Reynolds v. United States.*" *Arizona Law Review* 15 (1973): 287–306.

———. "The Polygamous Prelude." *American Journal of Legal History* 6 (1962): 1–27.

Donald, David H. "The Scalawag in Mississippi Reconstruction." *Journal of Southern History* 10 (1944): 447–60.

Dowd, Douglas F. "A Comparative Analysis of Economic Development in the American South and West." *Journal of Economic History* 16 (1956): 558–74.

Goldman, Robert M. "The 'Weakened Spring of Government' and the Executive Branch: The Department of Justice in the Late Nineteenth Century." *Congress and the Presidency* 11 (1984): 165–78.

Hall, Kermit L. "The Civil War Era as a Crucible for Nationalizing the Lower Federal Courts." *Prologue* 7 (Fall 1975): 177–86.

———. "Hacks and Derelicts Revisited: American Territorial Judiciary, 1789–1959." *Western Historical Quarterly* 12 (1981): 273–89.

———. "Political Power and Constitutional Legitimacy: The South Carolina Ku Klux Klan Trials, 1871–1872." *Emory Law Journal* 33 (1984): 936–51.

Halsell, Willie D. "James R. Chalmers and 'Mahoneism' in Mississippi." *Journal of Southern History* 10 (1944): 37–58.

———, ed. "Republican Factionalism in Mississippi." *Journal of Southern History* 7 (1941): 84–101.

Hastings, James R. "The Tragedy at Camp Grant in 1871." *Arizona and the West* 1 (1959): 146–60.

Hollingsworth, Harold M. "George Andrews, Carpetbagger." *Tennessee Historical Quarterly* 28 (1969): 310–23.

Holmes, William F. "Moonshining and Collective Violence: Georgia, 1889–1895." *Journal of American History* 67 (1980): 589–611.

———. "Whitecapping: Agrarian Violence in Mississippi, 1902–1906." *Journal of Southern History* 35 (1969): 165–85.

"The Inflation of the Attorney General." *Nation*, October 1, 1874, 214–15.

Kershen, Drew L. "The Jury Selection Act of 1879: Theory and Practice of Citizen Participation in the Judicial System." *University of Illinois Law Forum* (1980): 707–82.

Lamar, Howard R. "Carpetbaggers Full of Dreams: A Functional View of the Arizona Pioneer Politician." *Arizona and the West* 7 (1965): 187–206.

Larson, T. A. "Women's Role in the American West." *Montana: The Magazine of Western History* 24 (Summer 1974): 2–11.

Linford, Orma. "The Mormons, the Law, and the Territory of Utah." *American Journal of Legal History* 23 (1979): 213–35.

Mabry, William. "Disfranchisement of the Negro in Mississippi." *Journal of Southern History* 4 (1938): 318–33.

McFeely, William S. "Amos T. Akerman: The Lawyer and Racial Justice." In *Region, Race, and Reconstruction: Essays in Honor of C. Vann Woodward*, ed. J. Morgan Kousser and James M. McPherson. New York: Oxford University Press, 1982, pp. 395–415.

McNeilly, J. S. "The Enforcement Act of 1871 and the Ku Klux Klan in Mississippi." *Publications of the Mississippi Historical Society* 9 (1906): 109–71.

Magrath, C. Peter. "Chief Justice Waite and the 'Twin Relic': *Reynolds v. United States*." *Vanderbilt Law Review* 18 (1965): 507–43.

Miller, Wilbur. "The Revenue: Federal Law Enforcement in the Mountain South, 1870–1900." *Journal of Southern History* 55 (1989): 195–216.

Poll, Richard D. "The Political Reconstruction of Utah Territory, 1866–1890." *Pacific Historical Review* 27 (1958): 111–26.

Pomeroy, Earl S. "Carpet-baggers in the Territories: 1861 to 1890." *The Historian* 2 (1939): 53–64.

Schlup, Leonard, ed. "Augustus Hill Garland: Gilded Age Democrat" [letters]. *Arkansas Historical Quarterly* 40 (1981): 338–46.

Seligman, G. L. "Crawley P. Dake, U.S. Marshal." *Arizoniana* 2 (1961): 13–14.

Swenson, Raymond T. "Resolution of Civil Disputes by Mormon Ecclesiastical Courts." *Utah Law Review* (1978): 573–95.

Swinney, Everette. "Enforcing the Fifteenth Amendment, 1870–1877." *Journal of Southern History* 27 (1962): 202–18.

Teiser, Sidney. "Life of George H. Williams: Almost Chief Justice." *Oregon Historical Quarterly* 47 (1946): 255–80, 417–40.

Walker, Henry P. "Retire Peaceably to Your Homes: Arizona Faces Martial Law, 1882." *Journal of Arizona History* 10 (1969): 1–18.

Wunder, John R. "Freedom from Government. Case Study: The Mormon Frontier Experience." In Carl Ubbelohde and Jack R. Fraenkel, eds., *Values of the American Heritage: Challenges, Case Studies, and Teaching Strategies*, 46th yearbook of the National Council for the Social Studies. N.p.: National Council for the Social Studies, 1976.

———. "Law and the Chinese on the Southwest Frontier, 1850s–1902." *Western Legal History* 2 (1989): 139–58.

Documents and Archives

The most important executive source materials used were the Records of the Department of Justice, Record Group 60, at the National Archives in Washington. The Source-Chronological File (SCF) for each judicial district contains the letters written by U.S. attorneys, marshals, judges, and private citizens to the attorney general up to 1884. After 1884 the incoming letters are arranged by case or topic in a cumbersome Year File (YF). The letters sent by the Washington office to the field employees are contained in letterbooks optimistically labeled the "Instruction Books" (INST). Letters from the attorney general to members of Congress and the cabinet are in the Executive and Congressional Letterbooks (E&C), while letters to judges are in books called Letters to Judges and Clerks (J&C). Letters containing background information on the attorneys and marshals are in the Appointment Files (AF), arranged by district and then by name of the applicant.

Also useful for many cases that made it to the U.S. Supreme Court are the records of that Court in the National Archives, Record Group 267. These records were particularly useful for the Utah chapter. Many of the records of the U.S. district courts are no longer extant. Those that remain are in Record Group 21 and are housed in the various Federal Records centers. Very useful were the records of the District Court for Northern Mississippi housed at the Federal Records Center at East Point, Georgia. Among these records were docket books and minute books. One docket book, dating from G. Wiley Wells's tenure of office, is still in the possession of the clerk of the district court at Oxford and was examined there. The "Territorial Case Files of the U.S. District Courts of Utah" are available as National Archives Micropublication M1401. These records commonly include complaints, subpoenas, appearance bonds, and indictments. Trial records are occasionally included; judgment and sentencing are only rarely given.

Among published records, most useful were the annual reports of the attorney general, the commissioners of internal revenue, the commissioners of pensions, and the Utah commissioners. Published annually by the Government Printing Office, these reports are also in the Congressional Serial Set, often with different pagination. For basic information on individual marshals, attorneys, judges, and clerks, see the irregular *Register of the Department of Justice*. The register also lists the counties contained in each judicial district and the times and places for holding court.

Congressional Documents

U.S. Congress. House. "Correspondence Between the War Department and Colonel Emory." H. Ex. Doc. 209, 42d Cong., 2d sess. (1872).

———. "Views of the Commissioner of Pensions Upon the Adjudication of Pension Cases." H. Misc. Doc. 29, 45th Cong., 2d sess. (1878).

———. "Jurors and Witnesses in the Territories." H. Rep. 1288, 46th Cong., 2d sess. (1880).

———. "Lawlessness in Arizona." H. Ex. Doc. 188, 47th Cong., 1st sess. (1882).

———. "Lawlessness in Parts of Arizona." H. Ex. Doc. 58, 47th Cong., 1st sess. (1882).

———. "*Chalmers v. Manning:* Papers and Testimony." H. Misc. Doc. 15, 48th Cong., 1st sess. (1884).
———. "Expenditures in the Department of Justice." H. Misc. Doc. 38, 48th Cong., 1st sess. (1884).
———. "Suppression of Polygamy in Utah." H. Rep. 2735, 49th Cong., 1st sess. (1886).
———. "Convictions for Polygamy in Utah and Idaho." H. Ex. Doc. 447, 50th Cong., 1st sess. (1888).
———. "George T. Larkin." H. Ex. Doc. 402, 51st Cong., 1st sess. (1890).
U.S. Congress. Joint Select Committee to Inquire into the Condition of Affairs in the Late Insurrectionary States. "Report of the Joint Select Committee . . . ," vols. 11 and 12 (Mississippi). Washington: GPO, 1872.
U.S. Congress. Senate. "Mississippi Election of 1875" [Boutwell Report.] S. Rep. 327, 44th Cong., 1st sess. (1876).
———. "Denial of the Elective Franchise in Mississippi in 1875 and 1876." S. Misc. Doc. 45, 44th Cong., 2d sess. (1877).
———. "Mississippi in 1878." S. Rep. 855, 45th Cong., 3d sess. (1879).
———. "Salaries of Revenue Officers." S. Ex. Doc. 23, 46th Cong., 1st sess. (1879).
———. "Mississippi in 1883." S. Rep. 512, 48th Cong., 1st sess. (1884).
———. "Methods of Transacting the Public Business." S. Rep. 507, 50th Cong., 1st sess. (1888).
———. "Letter from the Attorney General Transmitting a Statement Relative to the Execution of the Law Against Bigamy." S. Ex. Doc. 21, 50th Cong., 2d sess. (1888).

Manuscripts

Akerman, Amos T. Letterbooks. Special collections, Alderman Library, University of Virginia, Charlottesville.
Arthur, Chester A. Papers. Manuscripts Division, Library of Congress.
Bristow, Benjamin H. Papers. Manuscripts Division, Library of Congress.
Camp, Eldad Cicero. Personal Docket. McClung Collection, Lawson McGhee Public Library, Knoxville, Tenn.
Devens, Charles. Papers. Hayes Presidential Center, Fremont, Ohio.
Harrison, Benjamin. Papers. Manuscripts Division, Library of Congress.
Hayes, Rutherford B. Papers. Hayes Presidential Center, Fremont, Ohio.
Houk, L. C. Papers. McClung Collection, Lawson McGhee Public Library, Knoxville, Tenn.
Howry, C. B. Papers. Manuscripts Division, Library of Congress.

United States Marshals [Arizona]. Papers. Arizona State Historical Society, Tucson.

Van Zile, Philip. Scrapbook. Special collections, Harold B. Lee Library, Brigham Young University, Provo, Utah.

Index

Numbers in **boldface** indicate illustrations.

About the Author

Stephen Cresswell is Assistant Professor of History, West Virginia Wesleyan College. He received his bachelor's and doctoral degrees from the University of Virginia and his master's degree from Catholic University.